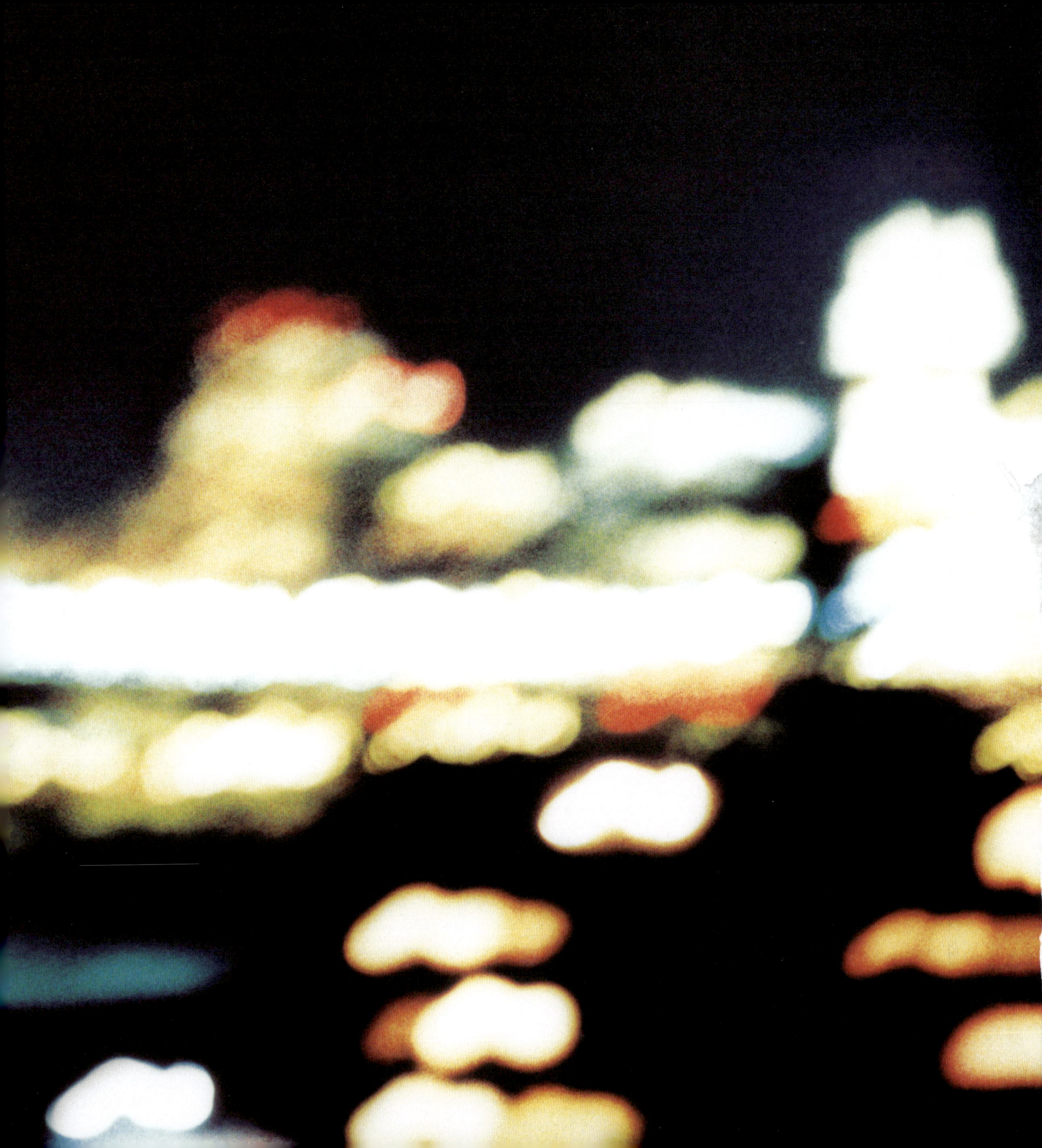

BROOKLYN

PHOTOGRAPHS NOW

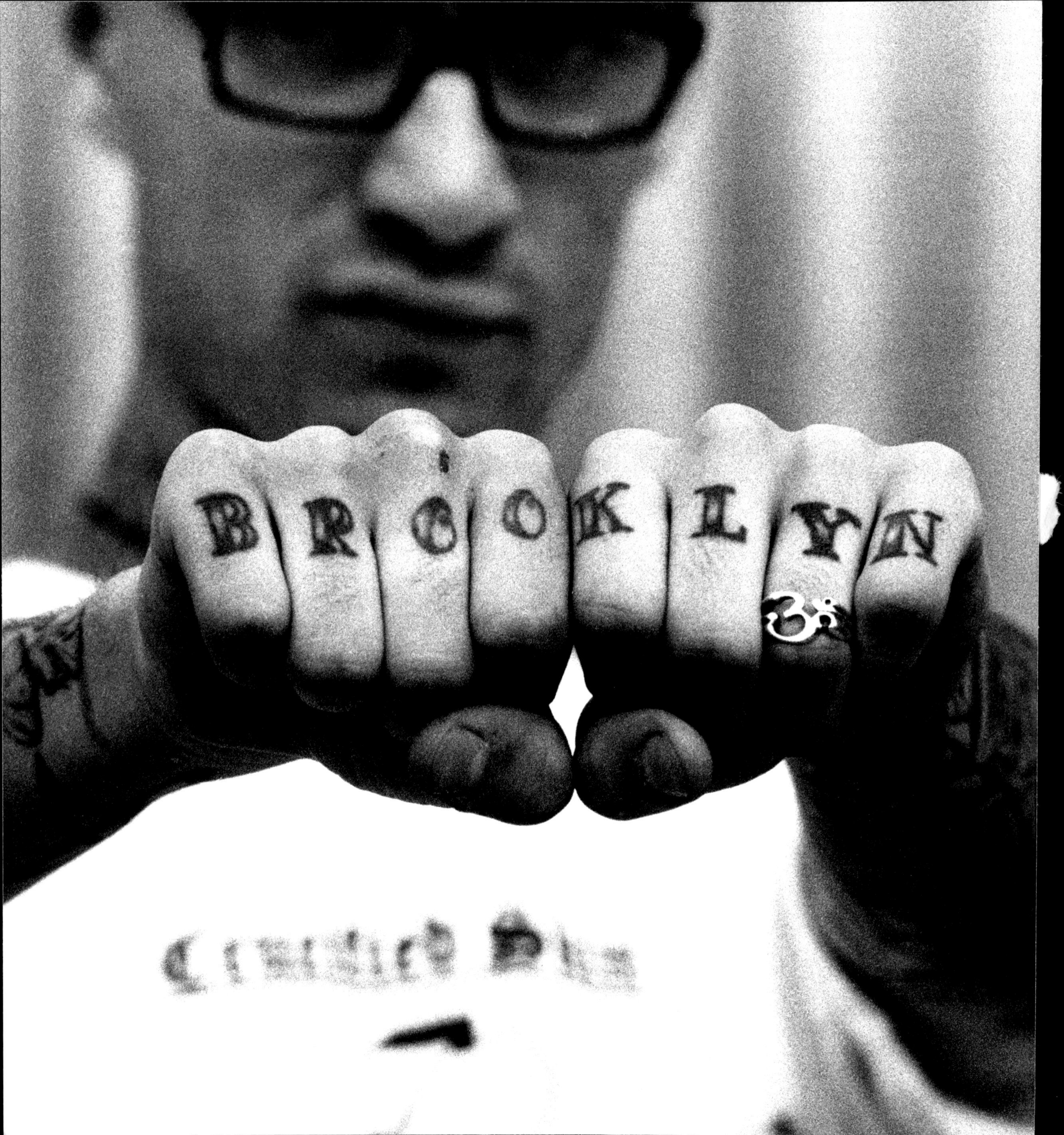
BROOKLYN

Marla Hamburg Kennedy

with contributions by Anne Pasternak and Phillip Lopate
co-edited by John Patrick Fitzgerald

BROOKLYN

PHOTOGRAPHS NOW

RIZZOLI
NEW YORK
New York · Paris · London · Milan

BROOKLYN IS . . .

Anne Pasternak

Shelby White and Leon Levy Director, Brooklyn Museum

Brooklyn is a place of deep pride. The Brooklyn Dodgers, Nathan's Famous Hot Dogs, the Coney Island Cyclone, and, of course, the world's most famous bridge, the Brooklyn Bridge, are just a few of the urban icons that contribute to a strong sense of self and honor. Mostly it is the romance for Brooklyn and all its contradictions that have been chronicled in countless novels, poems, songs, films, and photographs that have made it the legend it is today.

Brooklyn also is the hottest urban brand on the planet, though not because of nostalgia. Rather, Brooklyn has become the preeminent cultural capital. There must be more artists, designers, architects, filmmakers, dancers, writers, and musicians living here than anywhere else. Jean-Michel Basquiat was born here; enough said.

Brooklyn is an attitude. It's got more grit, chutzpah, and moxie than anyplace else. And unlike its neighbor across the river, Manhattan, it has a great sense of humor about itself. It is this quality that helped create the distinctive and beloved characters of Brooklyn's famed prodigy. Rosie Perez, Larry David, John Turturro, Eddie Murphy, Joan Rivers, and the Three Stooges are just a few of the great comedic actors who have hailed from Brooklyn. So too have more than a few trailblazing filmmakers, from Woody Allen and Mel Brooks to Spike Lee. Singers from Barbra Streisand and Neil Diamond to Lil' Kim, Jay-Z, and the Notorious B.I.G. found their musical chops in Brooklyn. Even the national political figures we've produced have big personalities: U.S. Senator Bernie Sanders and Supreme Court Justice Ruth Bader Ginsburg developed more than their sense of civics in Brooklyn: they developed personalities worthy of satire on *Saturday Night Live*.

Brooklyn is home. Whether on treelined streets with gorgeous brownstones and nineteenth-century carriage houses or dense enclaves of public housing alongside new high-rise apartment buildings, more than 2.5 million people live here in relative harmony. If it had not been for what Brooklynites call "The Great Mistake"—when, in 1898, the independent City of Brooklyn was unified with Manhattan, along with the other boroughs—Brooklyn would be the fourth-largest city in the United States. And it contains multitudes; within its roughly 69.5 square miles, you can visit cultures from around the globe. The culinary delights of Russia and Ukraine fill the air along the Brighton Beach boardwalk and extend to Sheepshead Bay, while the pierogi of Poland can still be found in Greenpoint. The aromas of Italy are everywhere, but especially in Bensonhurst and Carroll Gardens. Ireland can be found in Marine Park, China in Sunset Park, and the Caribbean pulses along Eastern Parkway and Flatbush. The young titans of finance have taken over Williamsburg, so emerging artists can now be found in the raw spaces industry left vacant in Bushwick. And it was on the streets of Fort Greene, East New York, Bed-Stuy, and Crown Heights that the titans of hip-hop created a powerful African American art form that shook the world.

Brooklyn is a bridge, but to what? For some, it is a bridge to Manhattan and the cosmopolitan upward mobility it represents. Yet more and more people are going the other way—leaving Manhattan's suffocating privilege in favor of the diversity, vibrancy, and cool of Brooklyn. Brooklyn is the place to be. And yet with this pull to the borough comes gentrification and all the problems it creates. Where do the displaced residents go? And what are the effects of rising prices on the quality of life for the many different populations that call the borough home? When inequity abounds, Brooklyn's great cultural diversity and its source of greatness are put in jeopardy. Maybe Brooklyn will use some of its fabled ingenuity to solve the problems of gentrification. I hope so, and please let it happen quickly because Brooklyn is changing. In the meantime—as the photographers in this volume have done—take your pictures because Brooklyn is still like no place else on earth.

INTRODUCTION

Phillip Lopate

The other day I was walking home in my Carroll Gardens neighborhood when I passed a young couple. The man was trying to stoke up an amorous flame with his hesitant date, saying to her: "Come on, here we are in Brooklyn! It's so romantic, it's like we're in a movie!" I looked around at my street's familiar moldy brownstones, trying to see it as they might, through a rom-com's cinematic lens. I had the same dislocating sensation as when I encountered Italians in Rome who waxed ecstatic about their brief stays in Brooklyn, or when I saw someone in Shanghai wearing a T-shirt emblazoned with my zip code. How had Brooklyn become an international brand? It seemed like only yesterday that taxi drivers in Manhattan would refuse to cross the Brooklyn Bridge, and before that was a dark era when banks redlined the borough, denying mortgages to prospective homeowners. As a native son I am dubious of this Brooklyn craze. It seemed to me it was never so bad in the old days, nor so incredible now. Perhaps I suffer from that typical phlegmatic unenthusiasm of the old-school Brooklynite, the classic "Forgetaboutit" reflex.

Yes, of course, Brooklyn is amazing, wonderful, unique—I don't deny it. But as a native I would like to assert a modicum of proprietary caution about falling for all the hype. It may well be that I'm just afraid of being psychologically elbowed out of the new Brooklyn, of no longer feeling I belong. Though that could never happen: I grew up here, it shaped my whole mentality at a time when all the little geniuses in our high schools who would become Nobel scientists and Pulitzer Prize authors were plotting their escapes to Manhattan and the larger world; having returned, I hope to be buried here someday in one of the vast cemeteries that line the Brooklyn-Queens border, by one of the many funeral parlors that happen to be a Carroll Gardens specialty.

I left Brooklyn to go to college, and did not return for another thirty years, when my wife and I, soon to have a baby, needed more space and were outpriced from Manhattan. Fortunately it was still possible in those days for people of modest means to buy a house in Brooklyn, but the initial transformation had already begun. To borrow the words of James Agee: "Everywhere the returning traveler saw signs of change, signs of no change at all, signs of change but too fast, signs of change but not fast enough, signs by the millions."

Historically, Brooklyn as a cultural sign tended to be read down-to-earth white working class: in every 1940s war movie there was a no-bullshit soldier from Brooklyn (usually played by William Bendix), and the loyal, goodhearted girlfriend in *Anchors Aweigh* was actually named "Brooklyn." When I returned to the borough, there were still plentiful remnants around of that hardy white ethnic class of Brooklynites that might be called urban peasants, like the Italian American family that ran the No Baloney Café around the corner from us, with the TV on constantly to soap operas and the mother nursing her baby while the grandmother made grilled cheese sandwiches on request. In short order, the café closed and was replaced by an ambitious haute cuisine restaurant called The Grocery that even managed to earn several stars in the Michelin Guide.

There now occurred a constant upgrading in sophistication: chic boutiques and trendy coffee houses and interior design specialty shops and restaurants that required reservations replaced grungy semi-amateur retail, and frankly I was happy for the improvement. It was part of the larger process of gentrification happening all over Brooklyn. Younger people with money were pouring in: the unspeakable downside was that they were displacing older working poor or lower-middle-class tenants, yet the upside was that they were restoring old residential and commercial buildings that desperately needed renovation. I had seen neighborhoods untouched by gentrification, going to seed, and it is not a pretty sight. In any case, like it or not, Brooklyn had become hip. Even Williamsburg, that slum of my youth where any kid with the slightest ambition itched to escape, suddenly became a magnet for the young. Brooklyn, formerly an industrial giant and the City of Churches, which had lost hundreds of thousands of blue-collar factory jobs from the 1950s on and whose parishes had dramatically shrunk from suburban flight, was now finding that its factories and houses of worship could be repackaged as pricey condos.

It was as though everyone had awakened to an understanding that what was thirty minutes by subway from downtown Manhattan *was* Manhattan, in effect. And in line with that realization came an explosion of high-rise construction. The Manhattanization of Brooklyn had arrived. I remember an activist neighbor urging me to participate in a campaign to prevent the building of a tall structure on Court Street that would be out of scale with the surrounding blocks. He assumed I would agree, but I didn't. Beyond the fact that I welcomed the multiplex and bookstore that would be housed in that structure, it seemed to me Brooklyn was too important to put a lid over it, especially just in order to keep it homey and quaint. When every metropolitan area on the planet was subject to skyscrapers, why should Brooklyn alone be exempt from this late modern form?

Nevertheless, I sensed a panic in my neighbors as they/we saw one high-rise apartment house after another sprouting up. Some of it was a reaction against ghastly design, but some of the new architecture was not bad at all, and still one was aware of an anxious revulsion on the part of old-timers as at an unwanted barbarian invasion. Was it a reasonable or unreasonable fear that Brooklyn's uniqueness or its spiritual essence would be compromised? Brooklyn had long been a largely horizontal environment with two- or three-story homes, six-floor apartment walkups, car repair shops, low-slung factories, and only one skyscraper, the Williamsburg Savings Bank Building. It had more sky than Manhattan, and the clouds seemed fluffier, more dramatic, more Dutch-landscape serene: would all that be lost?

Another change, less visible in terms of the built environment, has been demographic: dense pockets of immigrants from the West Indies, Bangladesh, Haiti, Vietnam, the Ivory Coast, South Korea, etc. Brooklyn has long been home to a diversity from every corner of the globe. Even when the newcomers move off to other parts of the country, it is estimated that one out of seven American families have had ties to Brooklyn at some point or other. There are stretches of blocks today in the Sunset Park district almost entirely Chinese; others where Belorussian Jews hold sway. These new strivers bring with them a dynamism that replenishes the borough's soulfulness and makes nostalgia for a grittier, earthier Brooklyn of old seem uninformed, if not racist.

The remarkable collection of images in this volume is not just a testimony to the vibrancy of the art of photography but a record of Brooklyn's unquenchable dynamism: its refusal to stop changing, as well as an unwillingness to shed its more traditional aspects. So we get shots of Brooklyn's new high-rise verticality, either in celebration or dismay, but also an array of aluminum-sided bungalows and two- or three-story brick houses. There are the backyards and alleys and delicatessen or pizza parlor storefronts that contribute to Brooklyn's popular image as a homey, unpretentious, defiantly unglamorous cluster of residential neighborhoods. But there are also dignified portraits of some of the borough's more famous monuments and landmarks, like the Brooklyn Museum or Coney Island's Wonder Wheel. Some architecture is framed for maximum hieratic grandeur, while other structures are shot in a throwaway, casual manner, surrounded by the messy detritus and routine of everyday life. There are pictures of passersby that seize on droll "decisive moments" or ironic juxtapositions, while others eschew the anecdotal Cartier-Bresson approach and instead dote on a more uninflected or deadpan style such as one associates with Stephen Shore.

It is interesting to note that while Manhattan has had a rich overt tradition of street photography (Helen Levitt, Robert Frank, Garry Winogrand, Louis Faurer, Joel Meyerowitz and so on), Brooklyn's is relatively more undercover. The typical Manhattan sidewalk is densely packed with foot traffic, offering multiple foreground-to-background layers of complex simultaneity, whereas public space in Brooklyn tends to come across as more open, airy, sparsely populated and leisurely. It almost looks as though the streets were wider in Brooklyn, but that impression may issue from the lower, less-impinging scale of most buildings and the sky's greater presence.

The fact that some of the photographers are well-established veterans and others are younger, more up-and-coming practitioners helps to account for the full range of aesthetic choices on display. There are many examples of the latest fast-speed digital technology as well as more traditional long-exposure shots. Color photography, no longer looked down upon as less artistic than black and white, predominates, sometimes with breathtaking palettes, but there are also some gorgeous black-and-white images. Nighttime in Brooklyn seems to be an irresistible temptation for contemporary photographers, capturing the vaguely menacing, noir undercurrents that have historically attached to the borough, in contrast to its ultra-normal daytime face.

"Only the dead know Brooklyn" was the famous title of Thomas Wolfe's story. That may well be, since Brooklyn is vast and various, but the photographers in these pages have made a splendid effort to snatch its profile as accurately as can be achieved. If you want to know what is going on in Brooklyn these days, a good place to start would be right here.

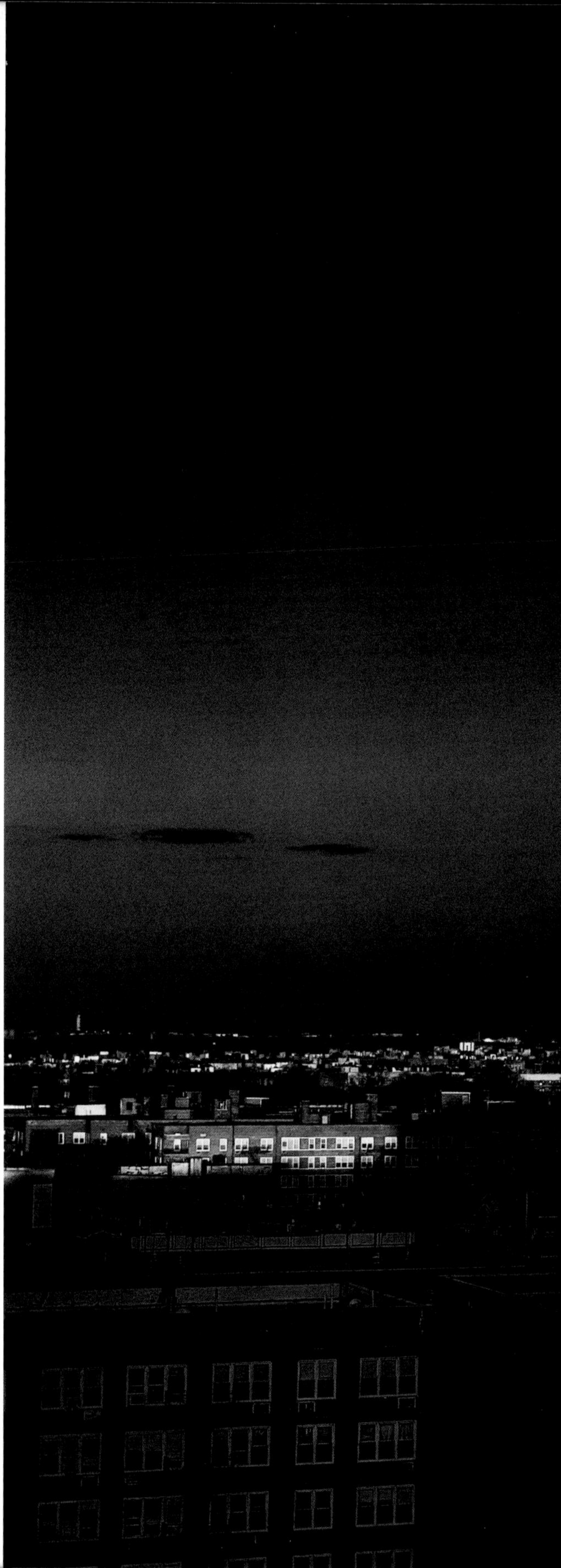

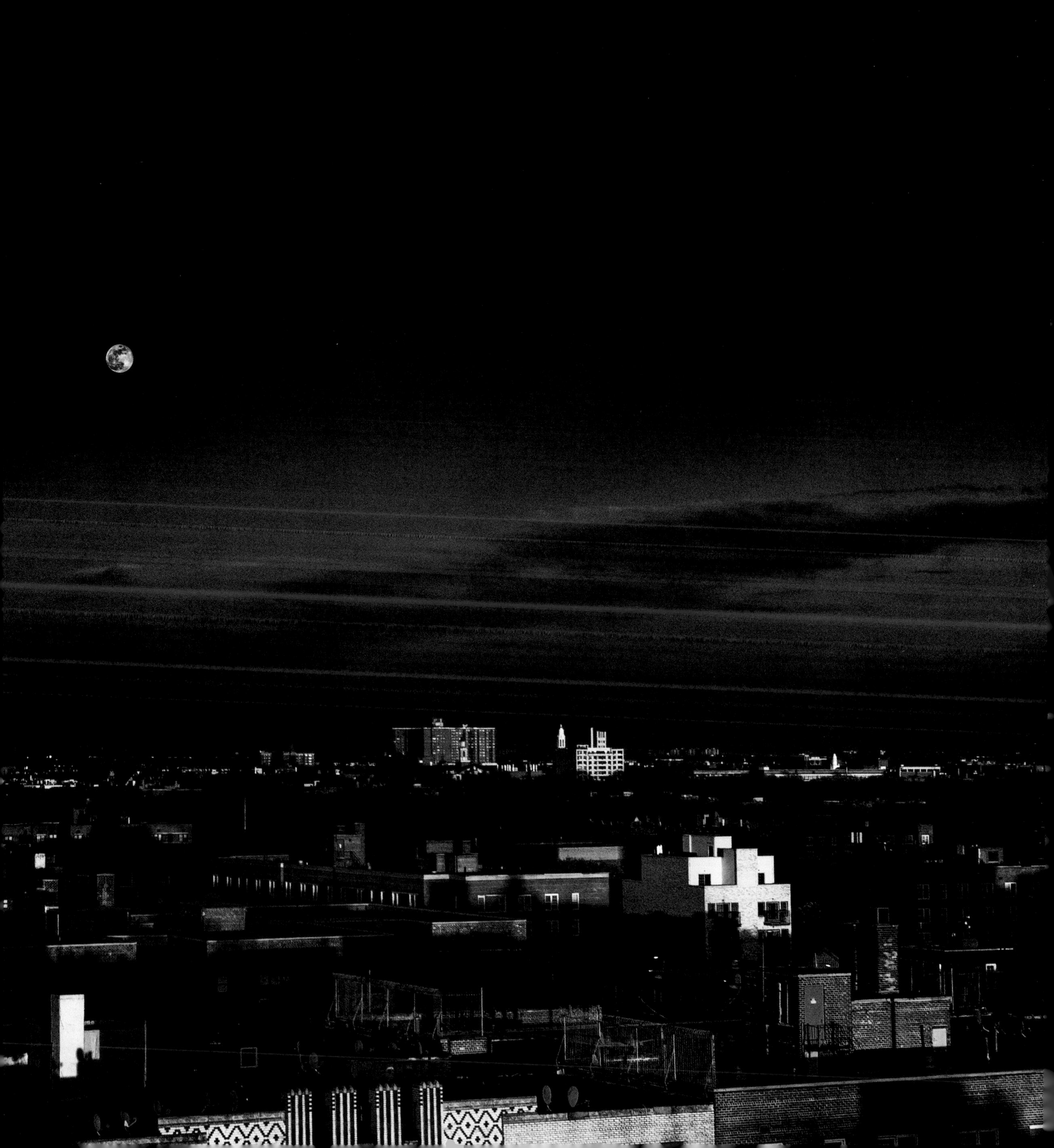

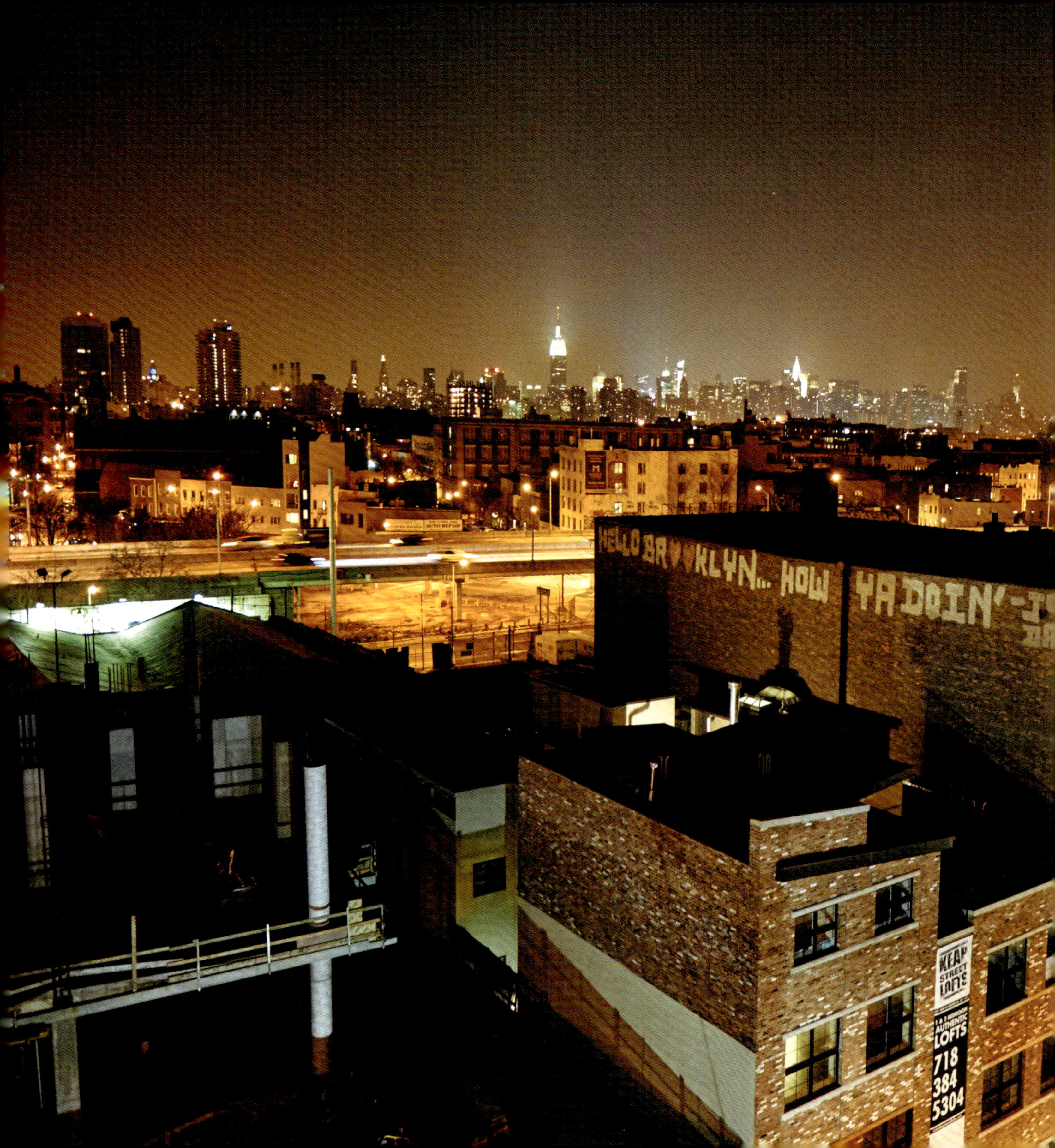
HELLO BR♥KLYN.. HOW YA DOIN'
AUTO REPAIR
KEAP STREET LOFTS
AUTHENTIC LOFTS
718 384 5304

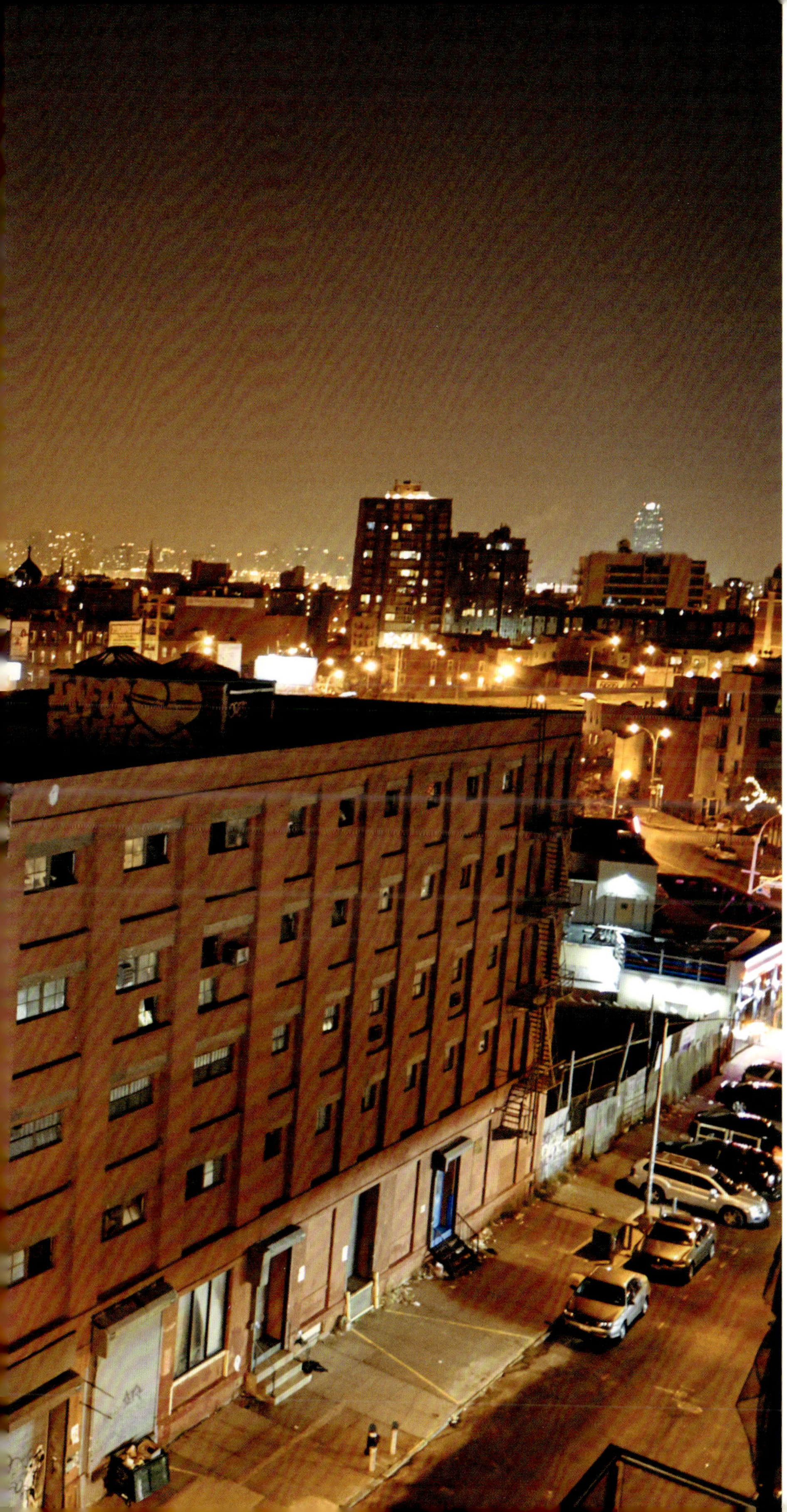

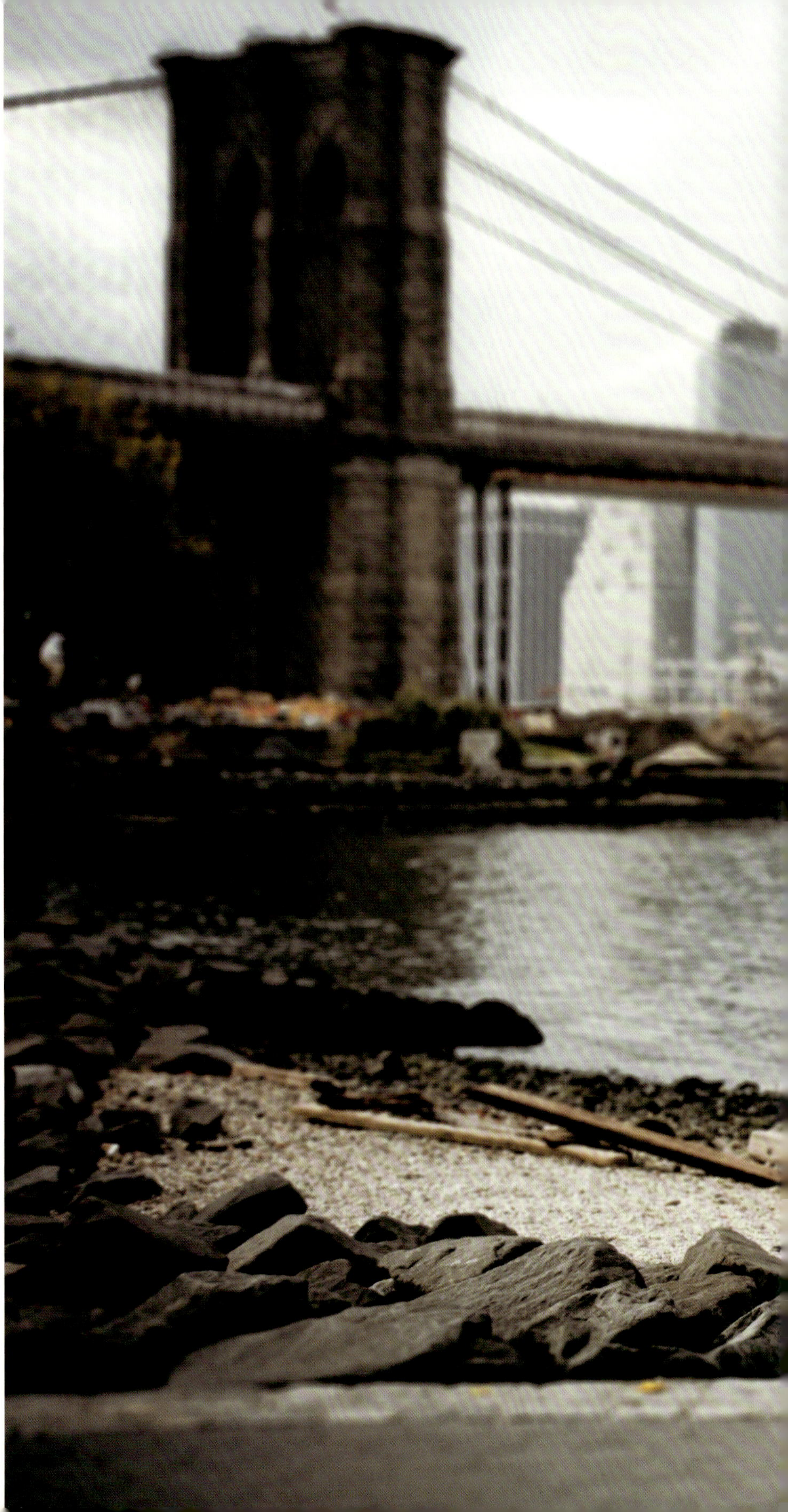

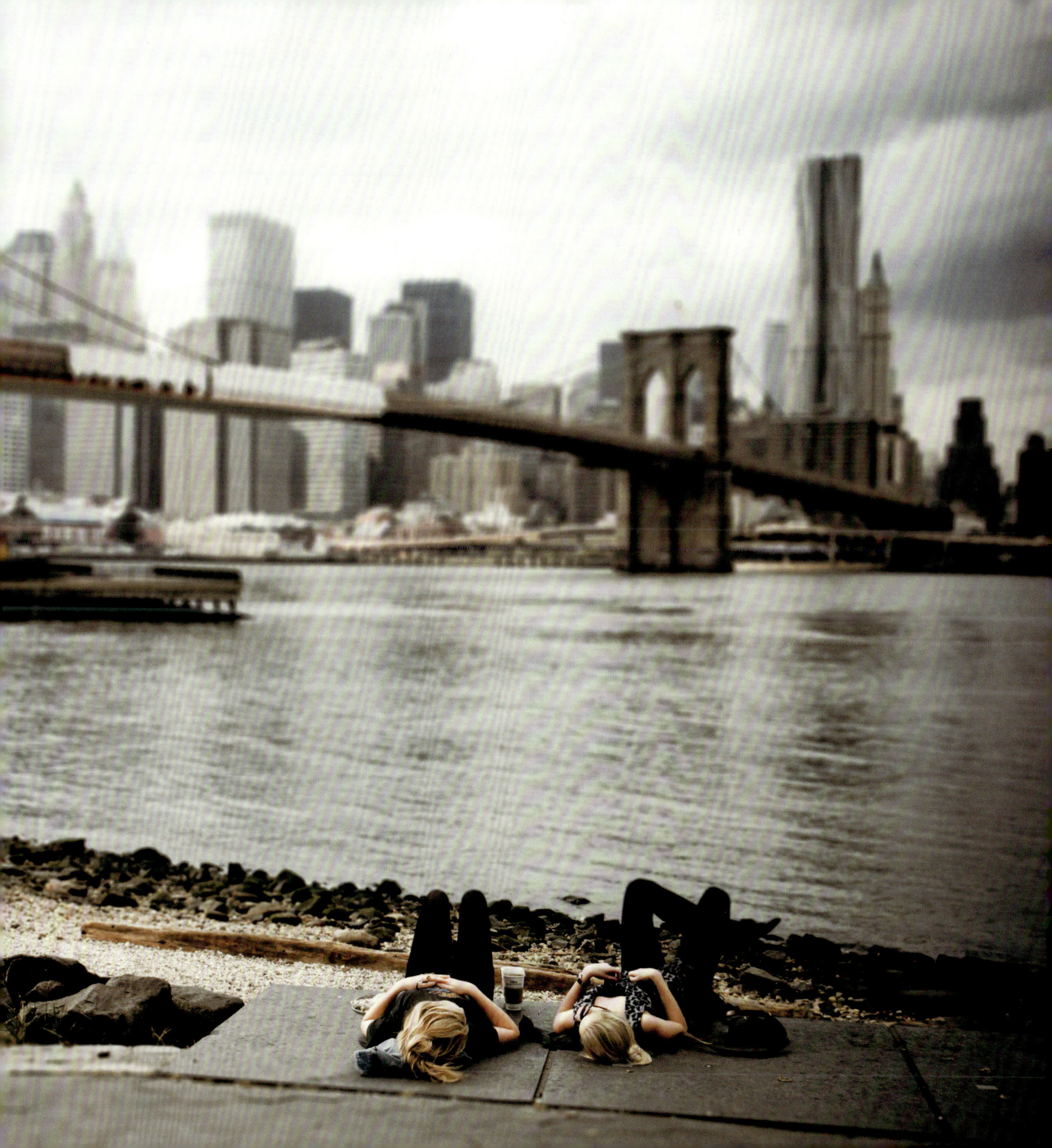

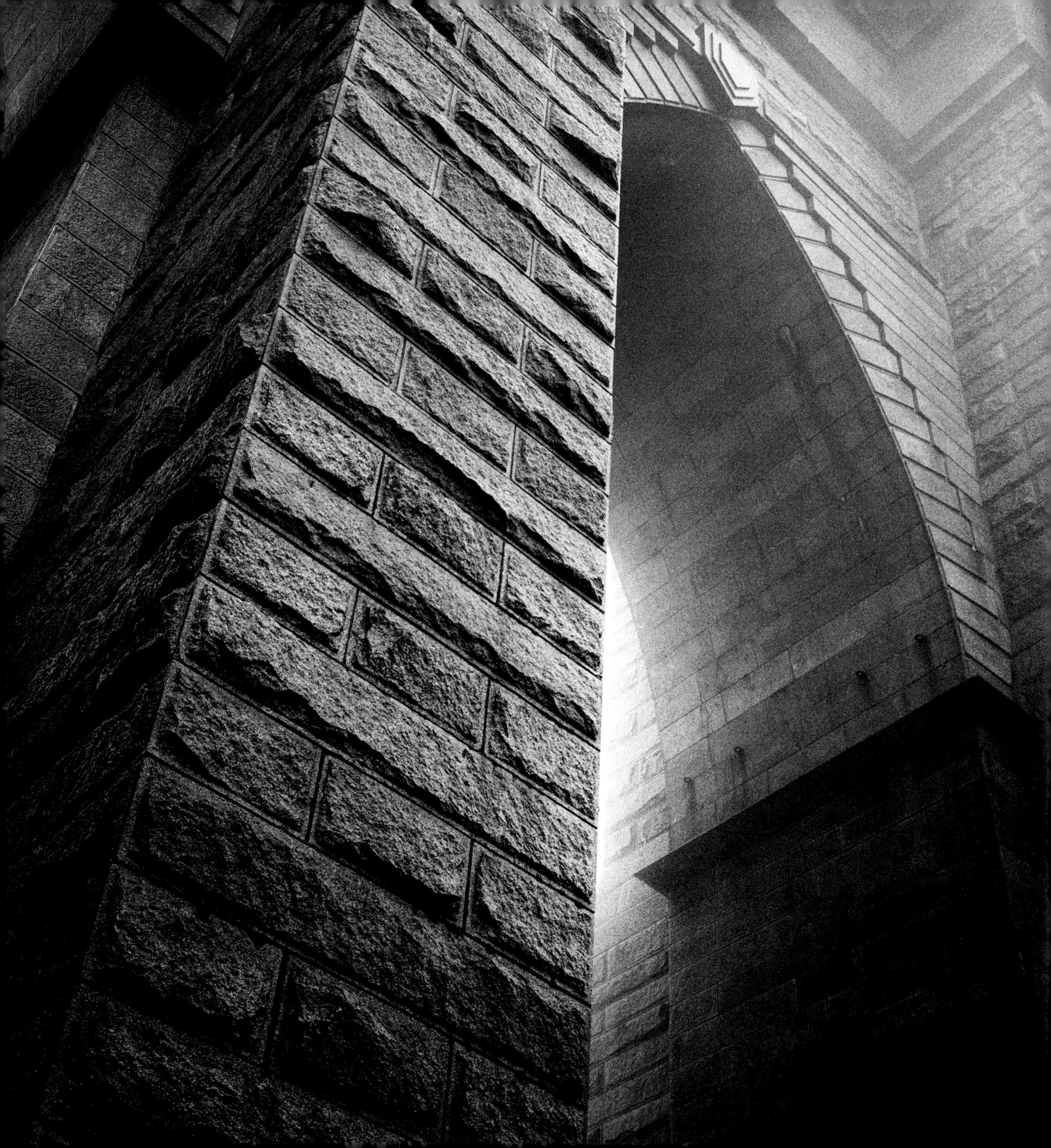

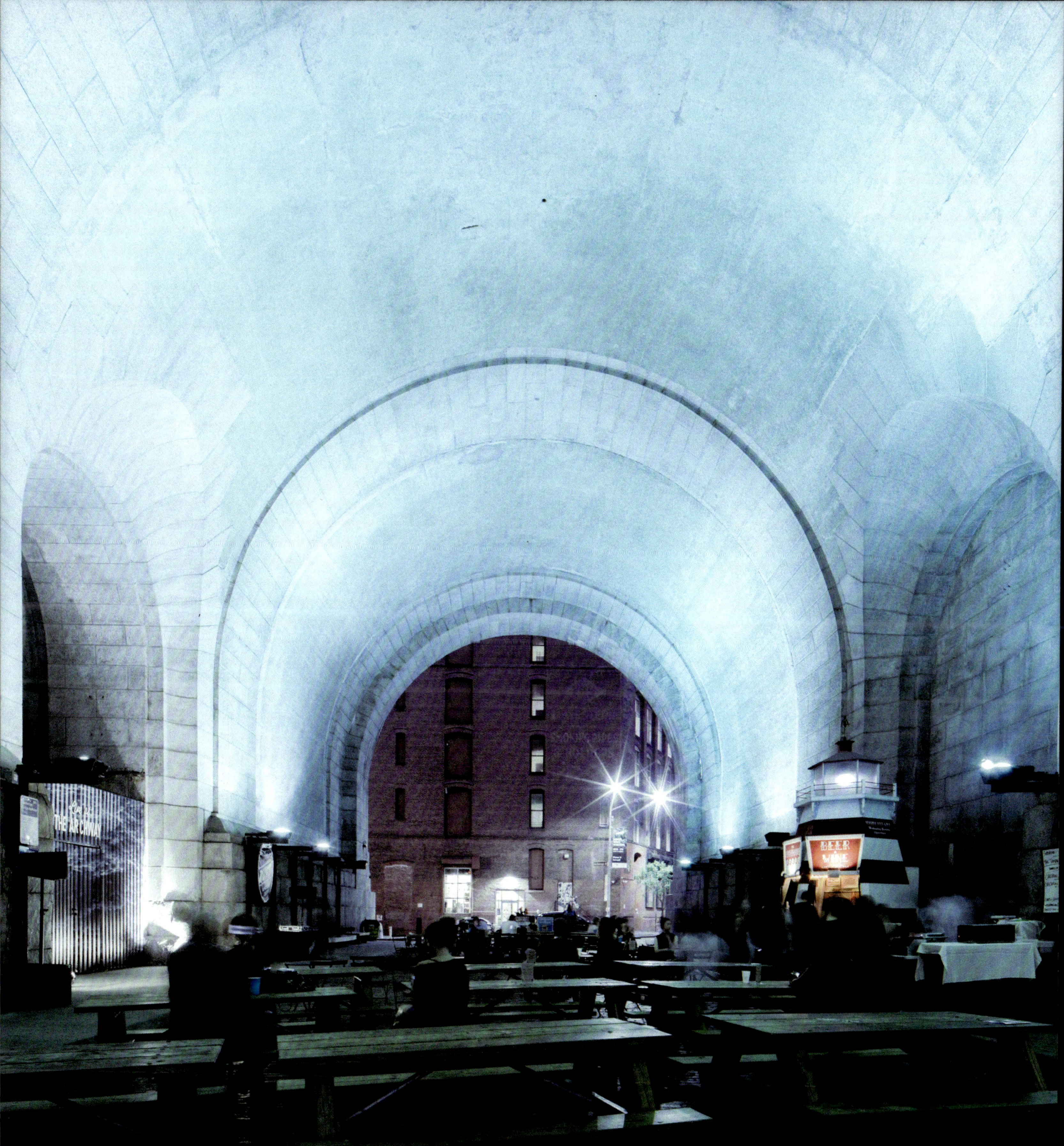
THE ARCHWAY
BEER
WINE

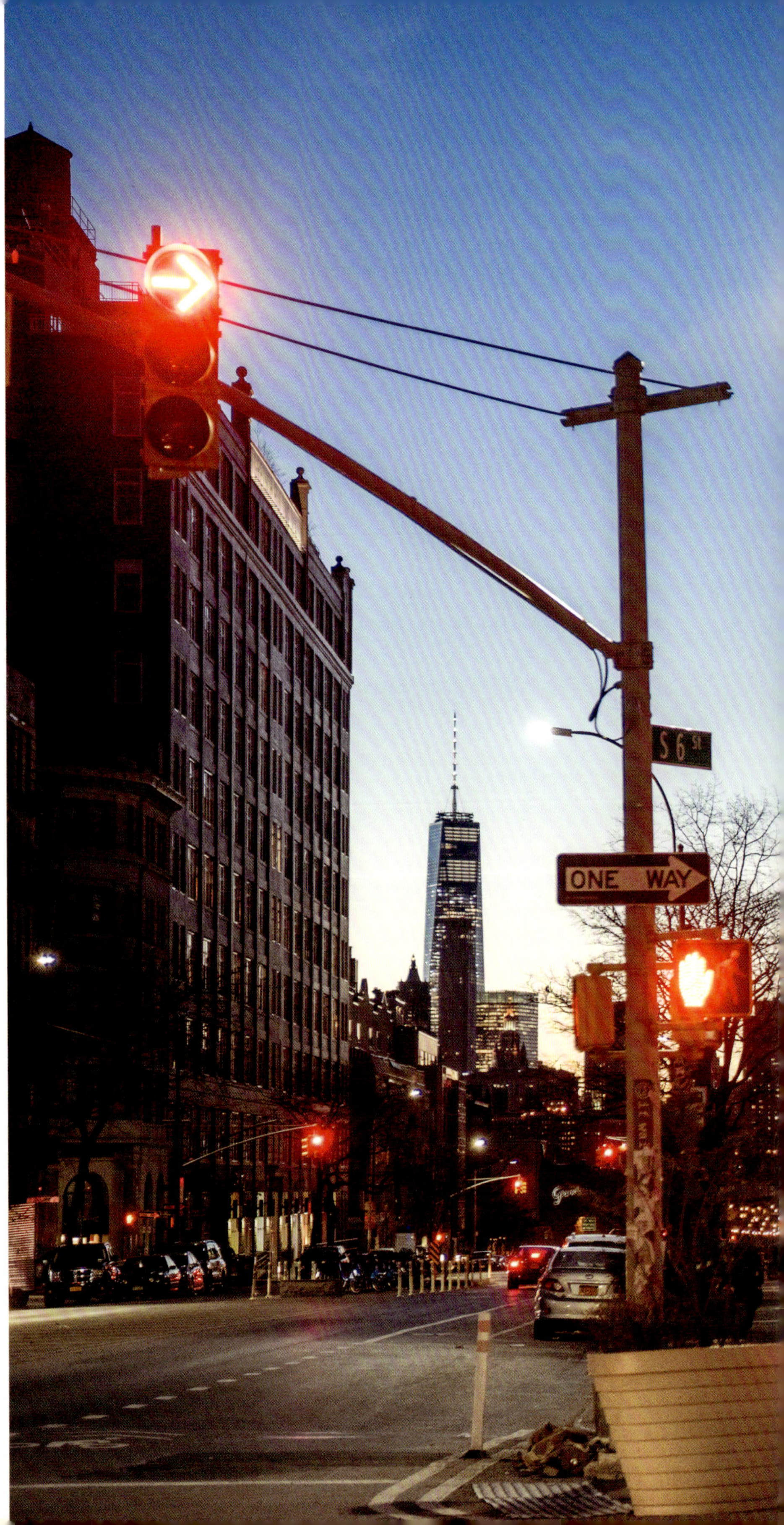
S 6 St
ONE WAY

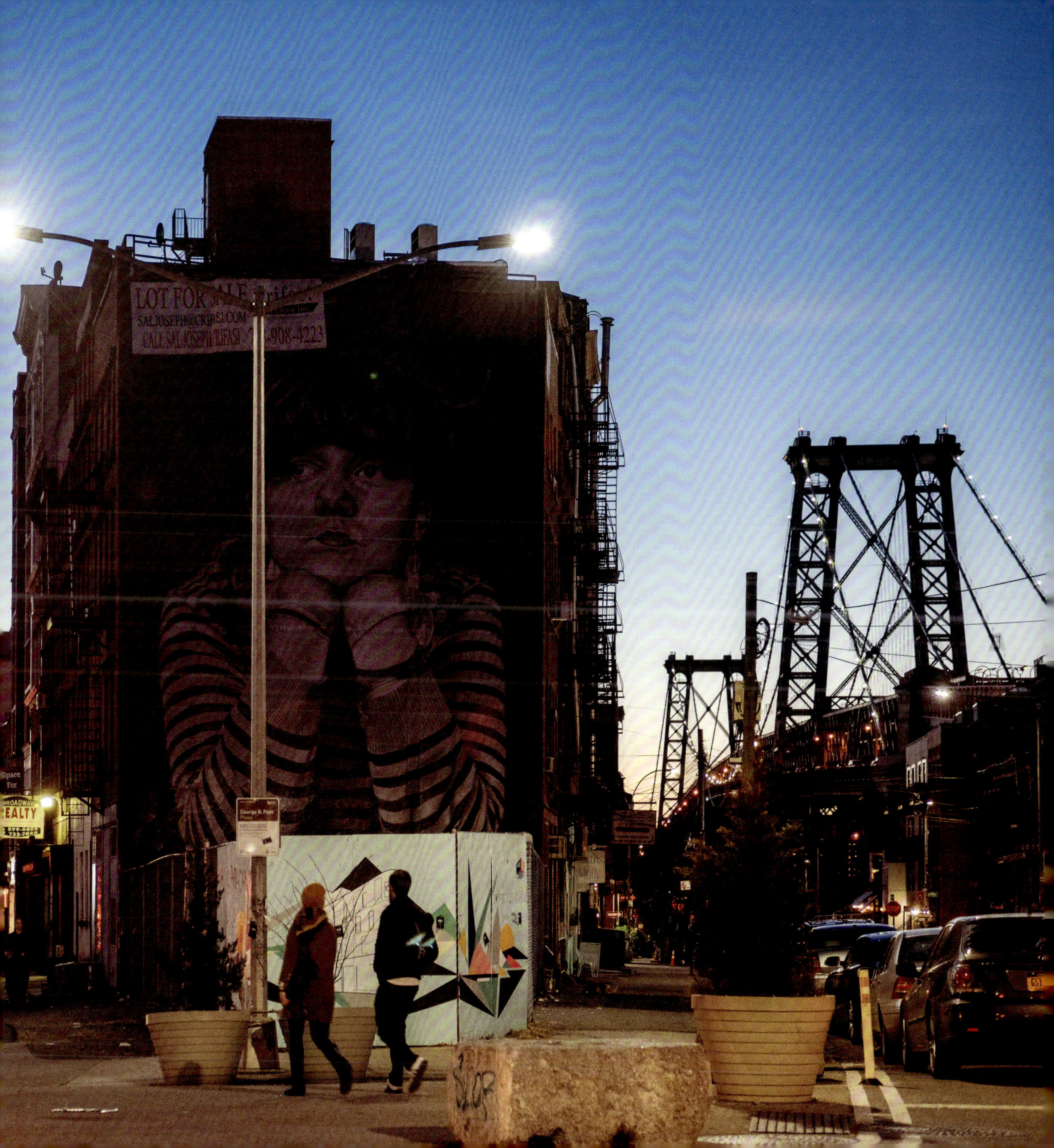
LOT FOR
908-4223

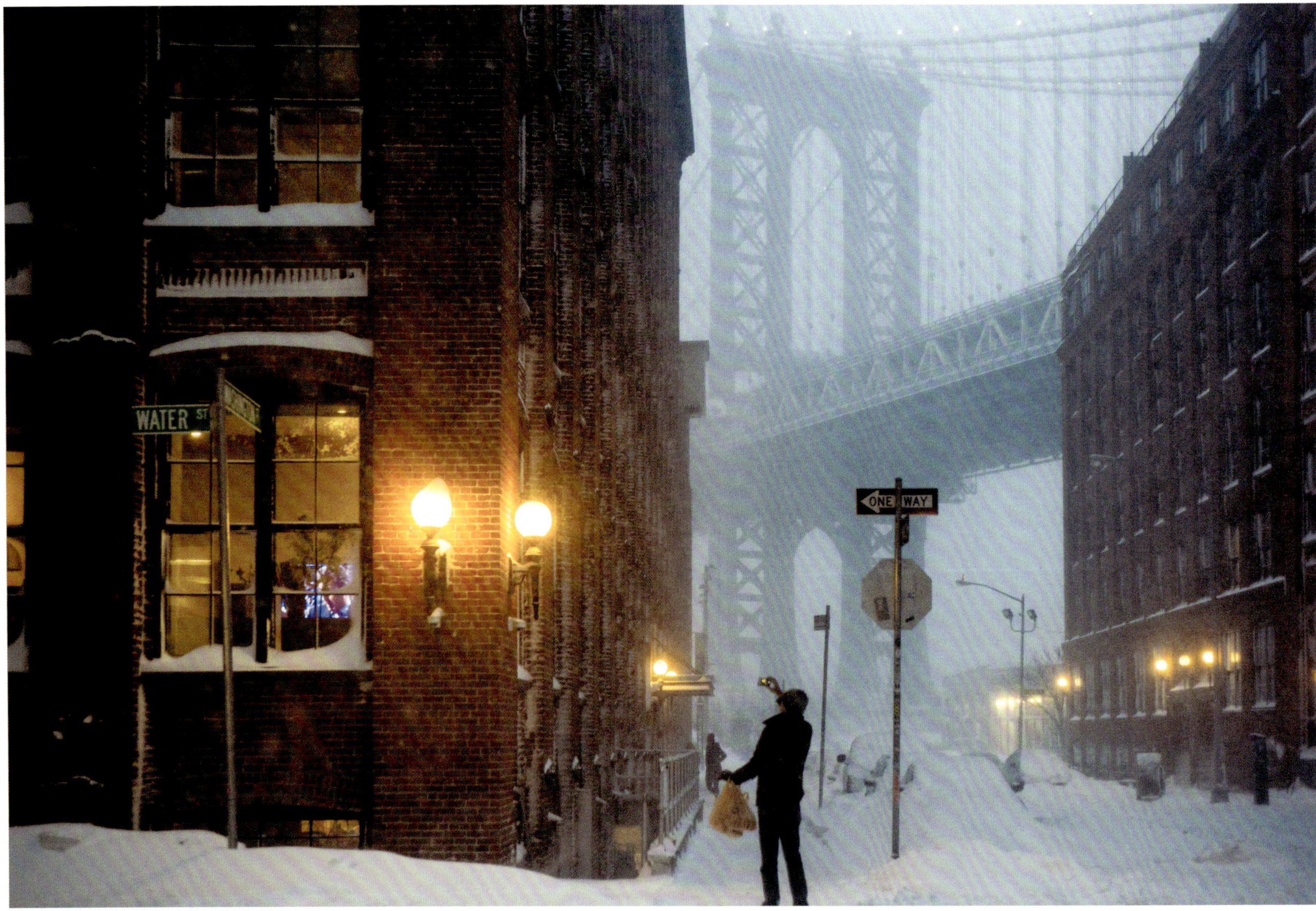
WATER ST
ONE WAY

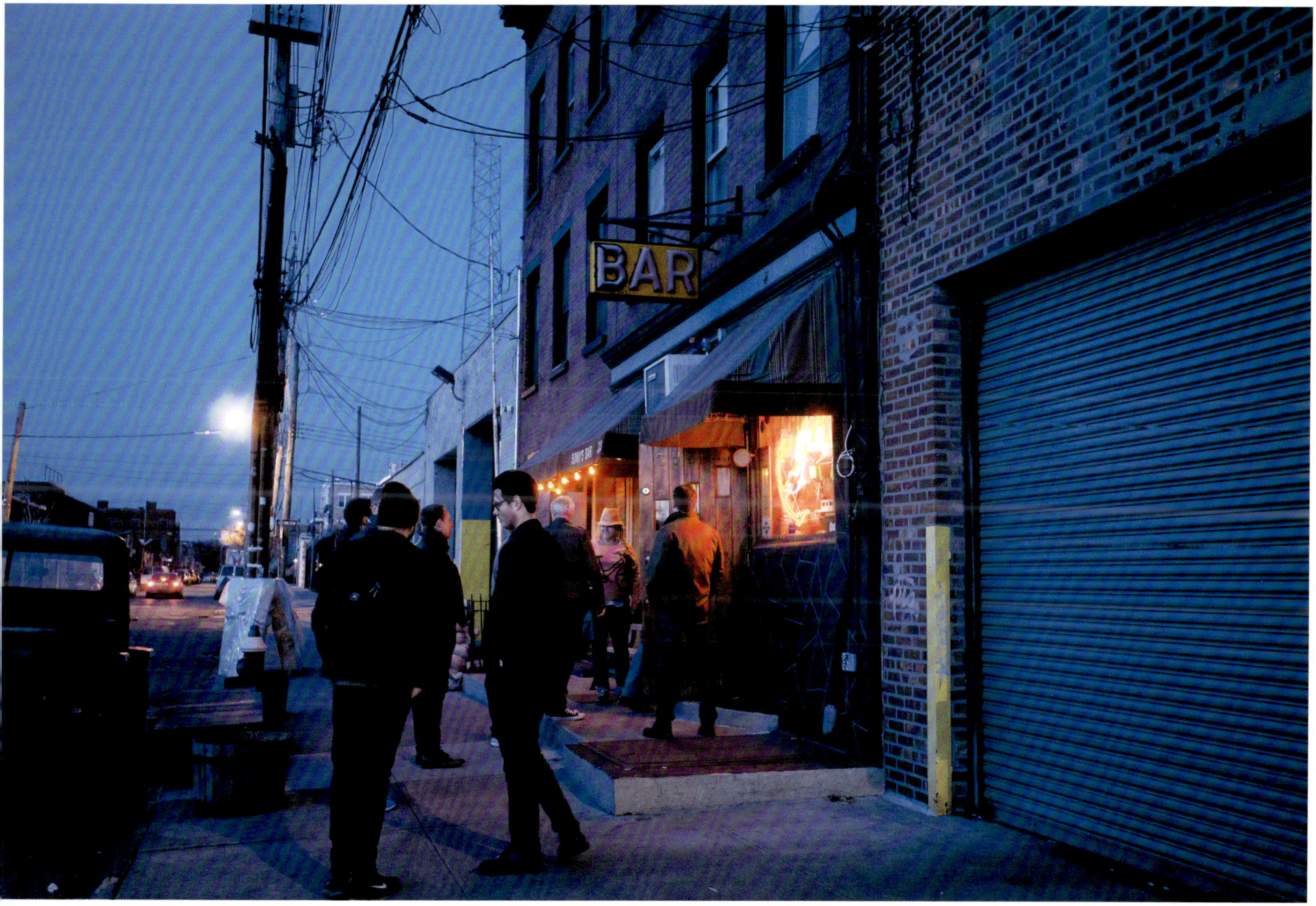
BAR

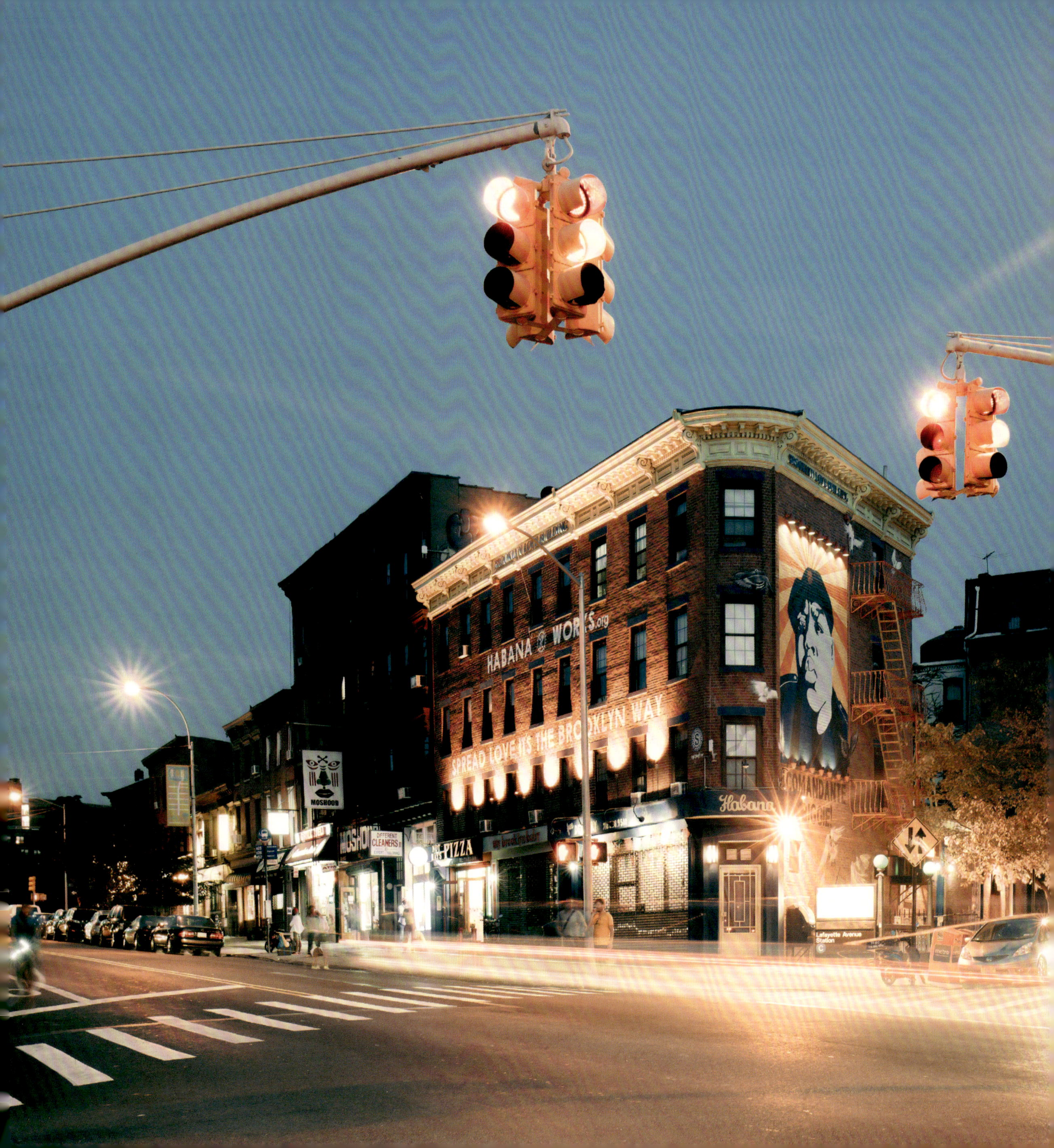
HABANA WORKS.org
SPREAD LOVE IT'S THE BROOKLYN WAY
MOSHOOD
DIFFERENT CLEANERS
PIZZA
Habana

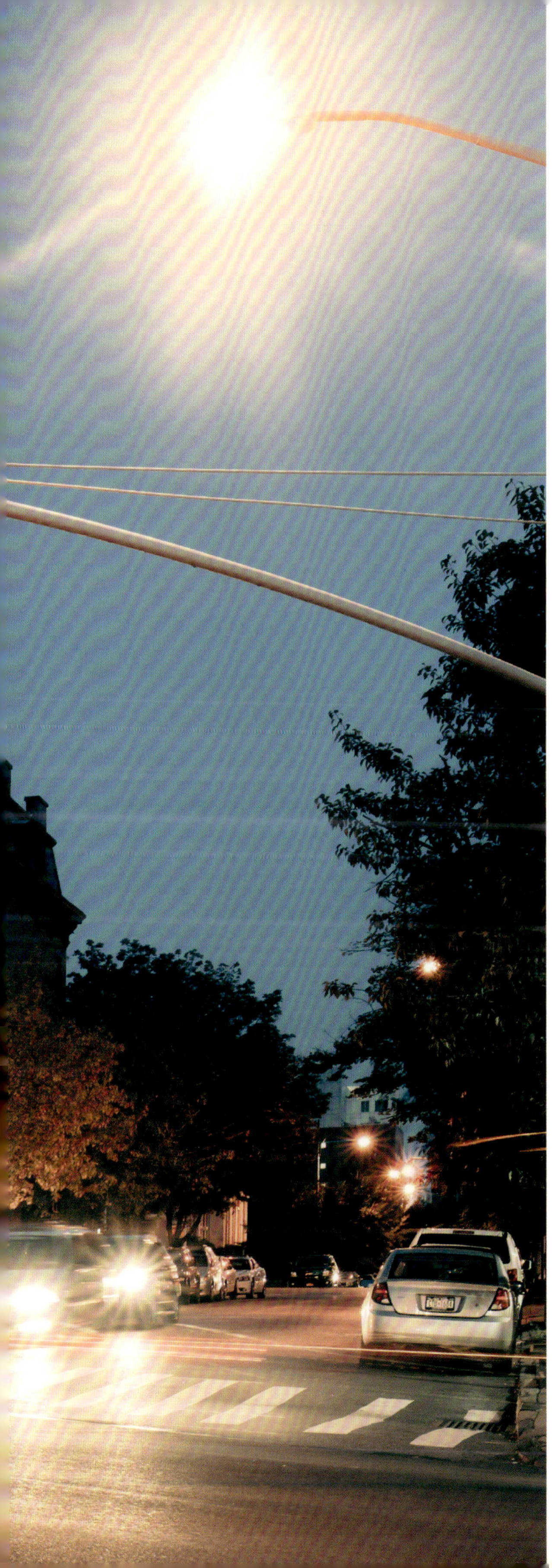

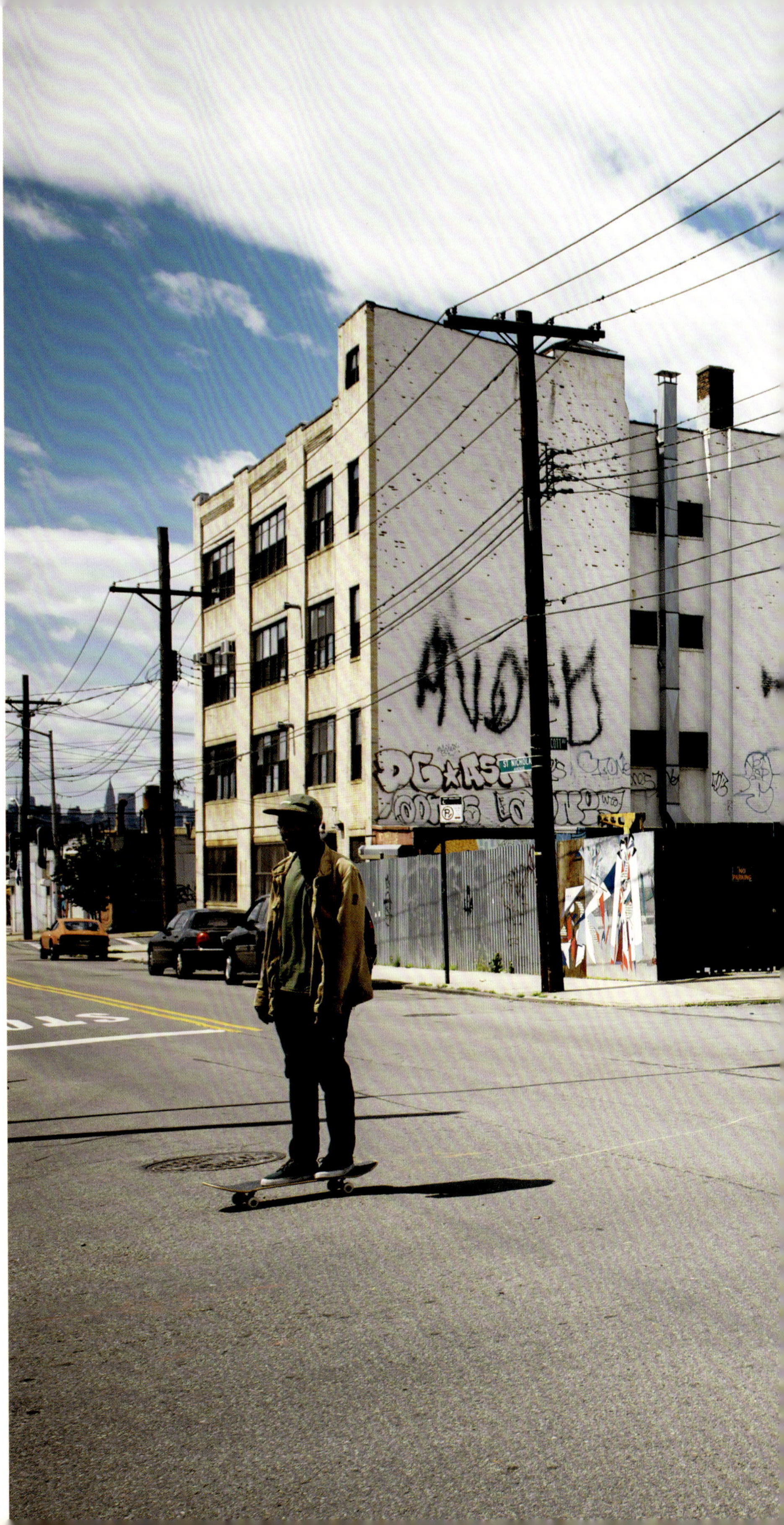

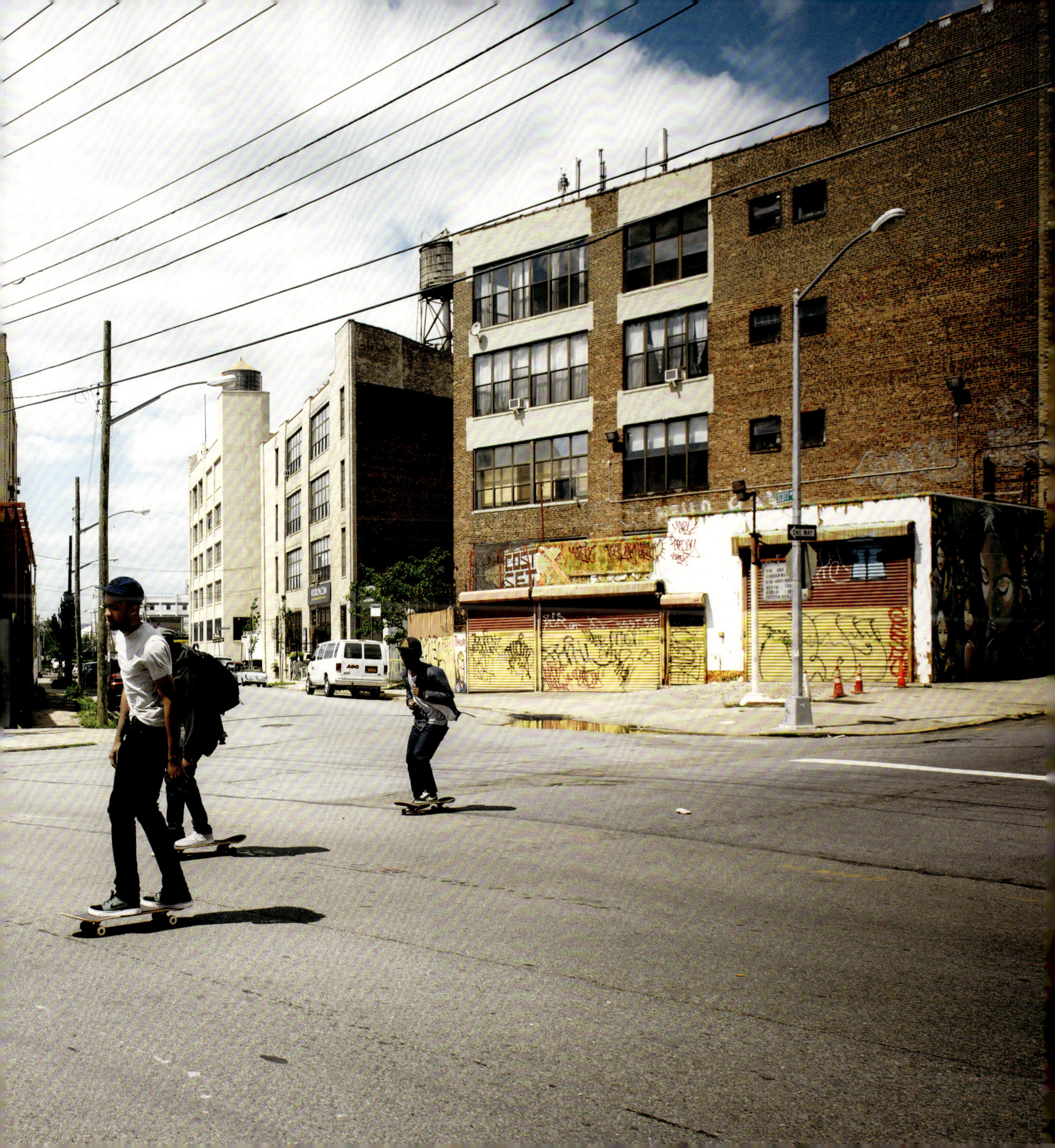
ONE WAY

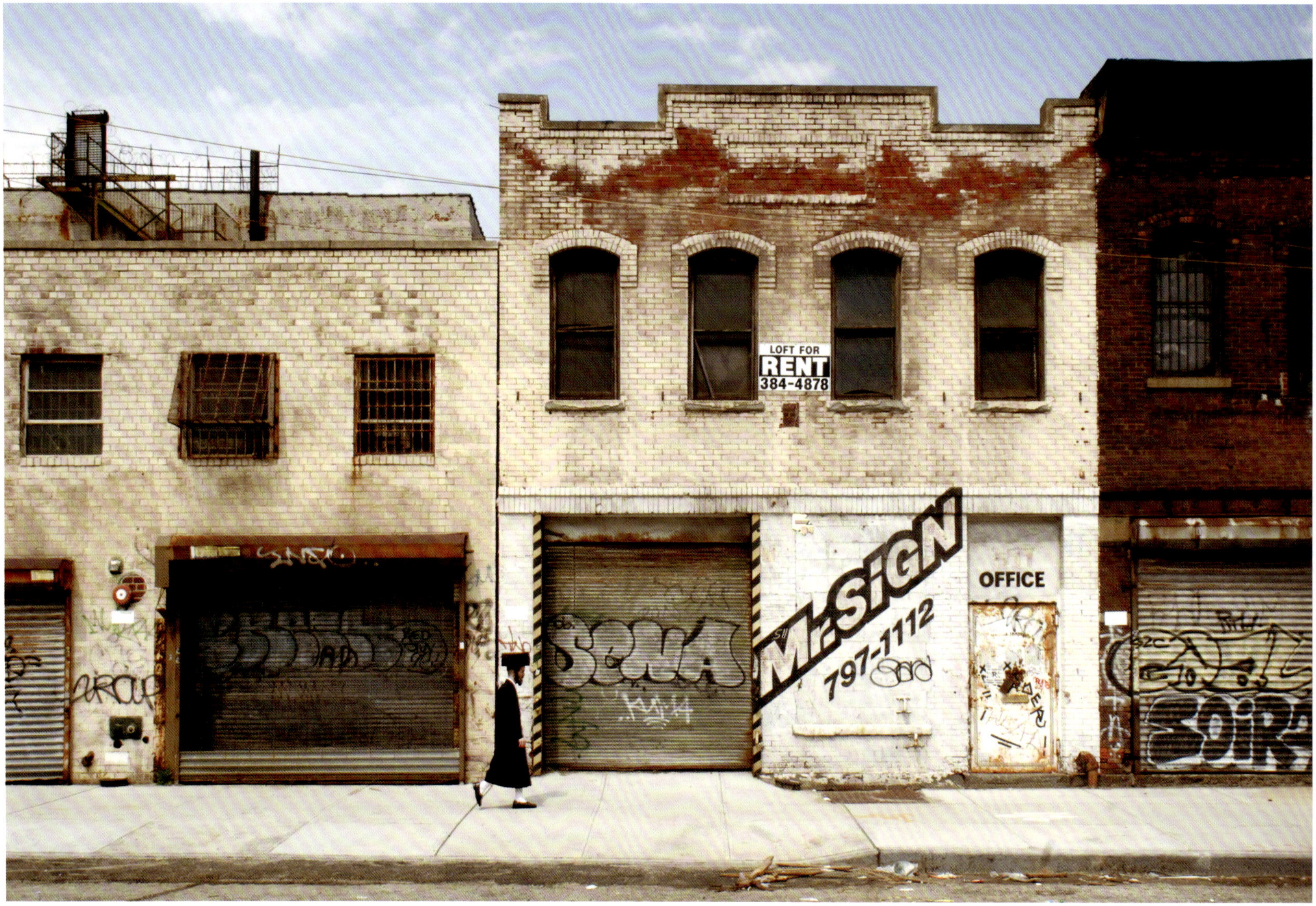
LOFT FOR
RENT
384-4878
OFFICE
Mr. SIGN
797-1112

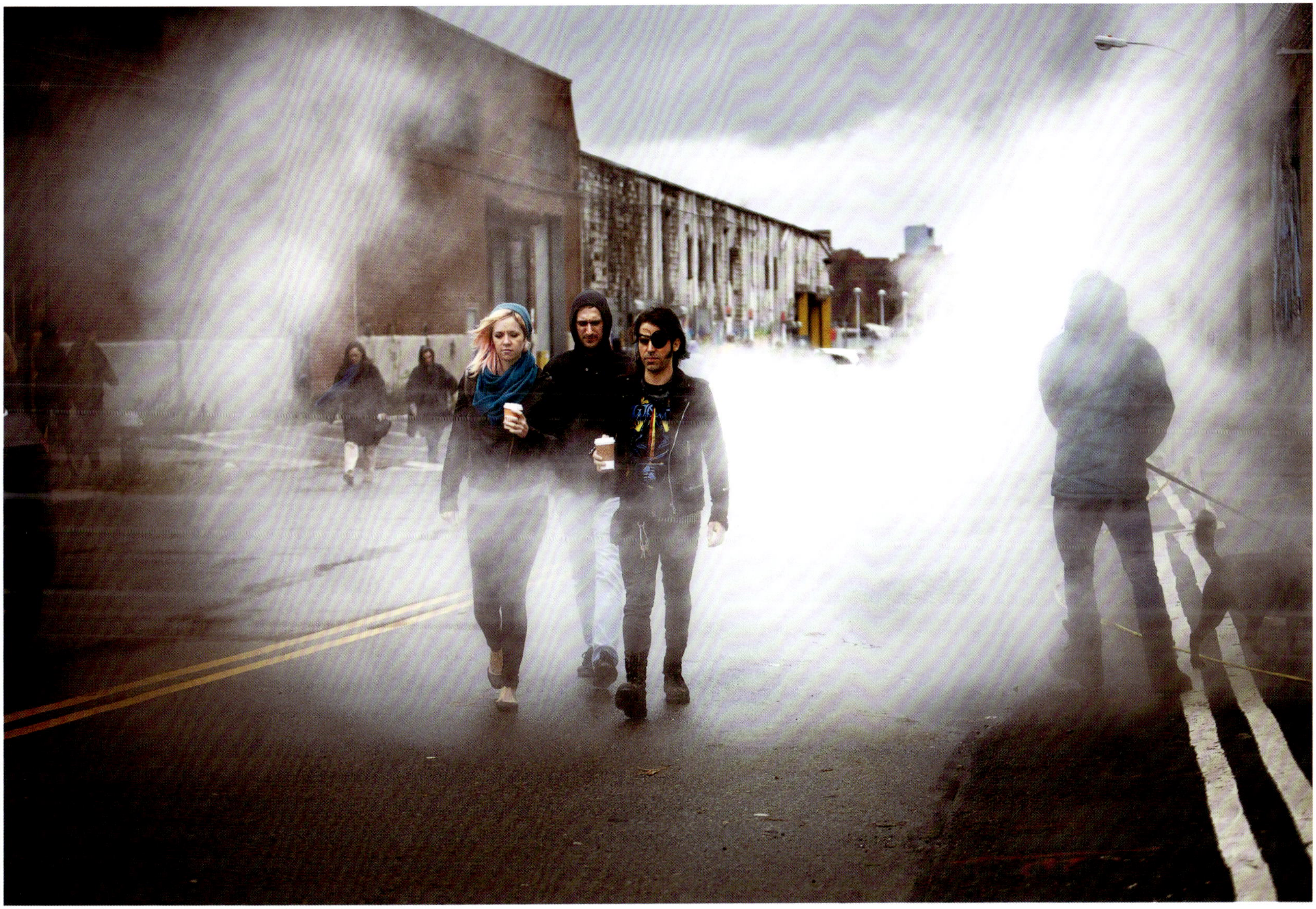

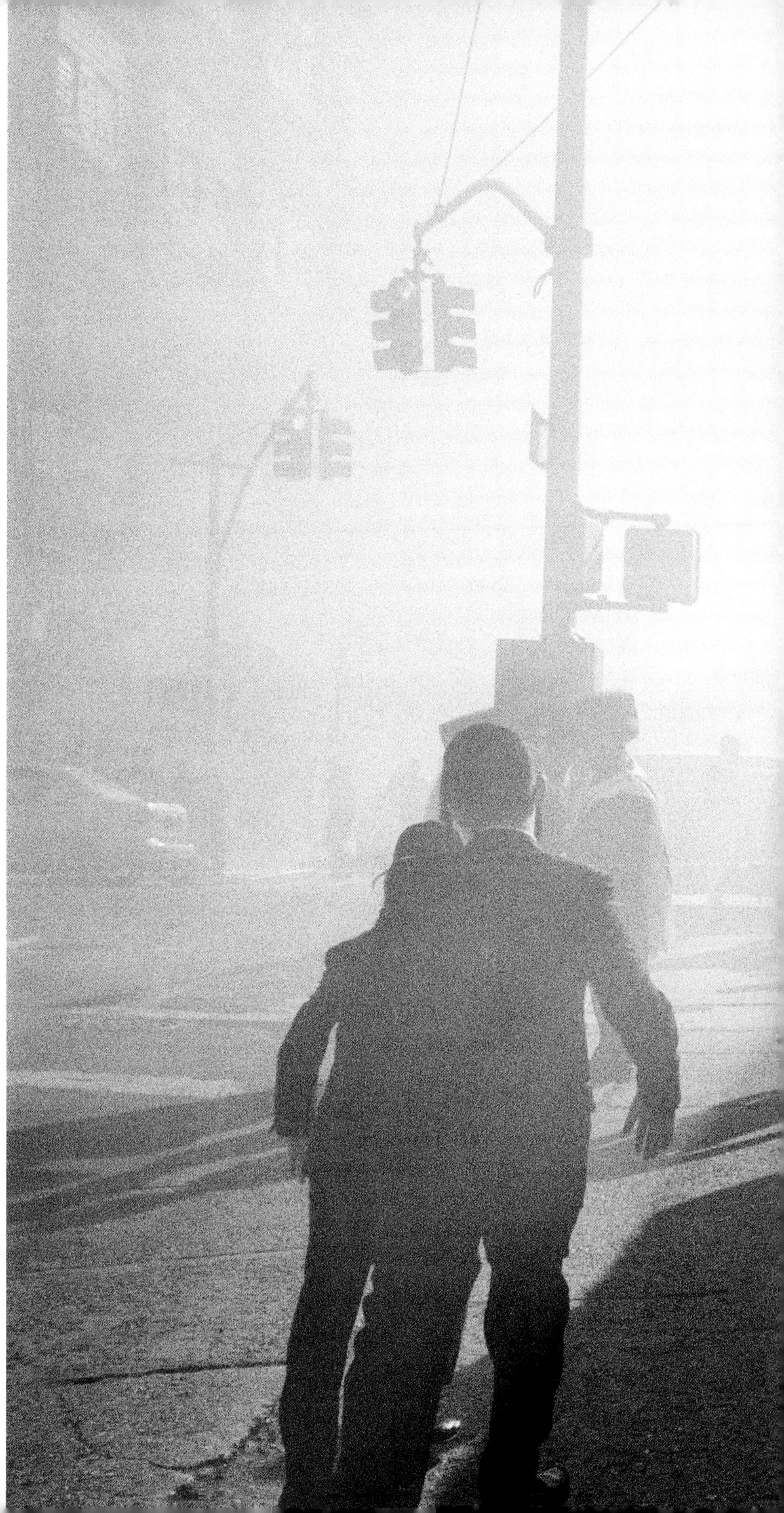

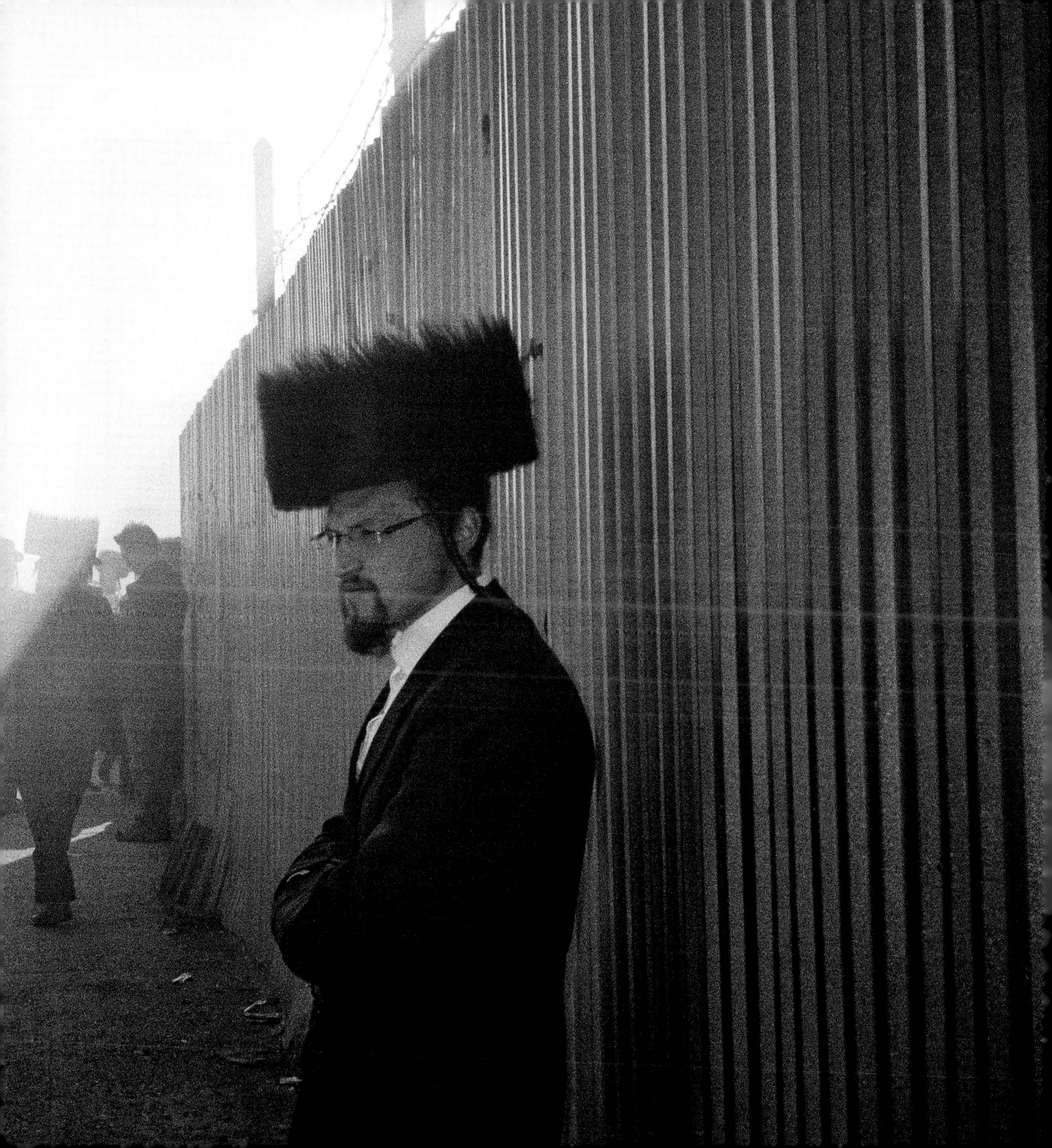

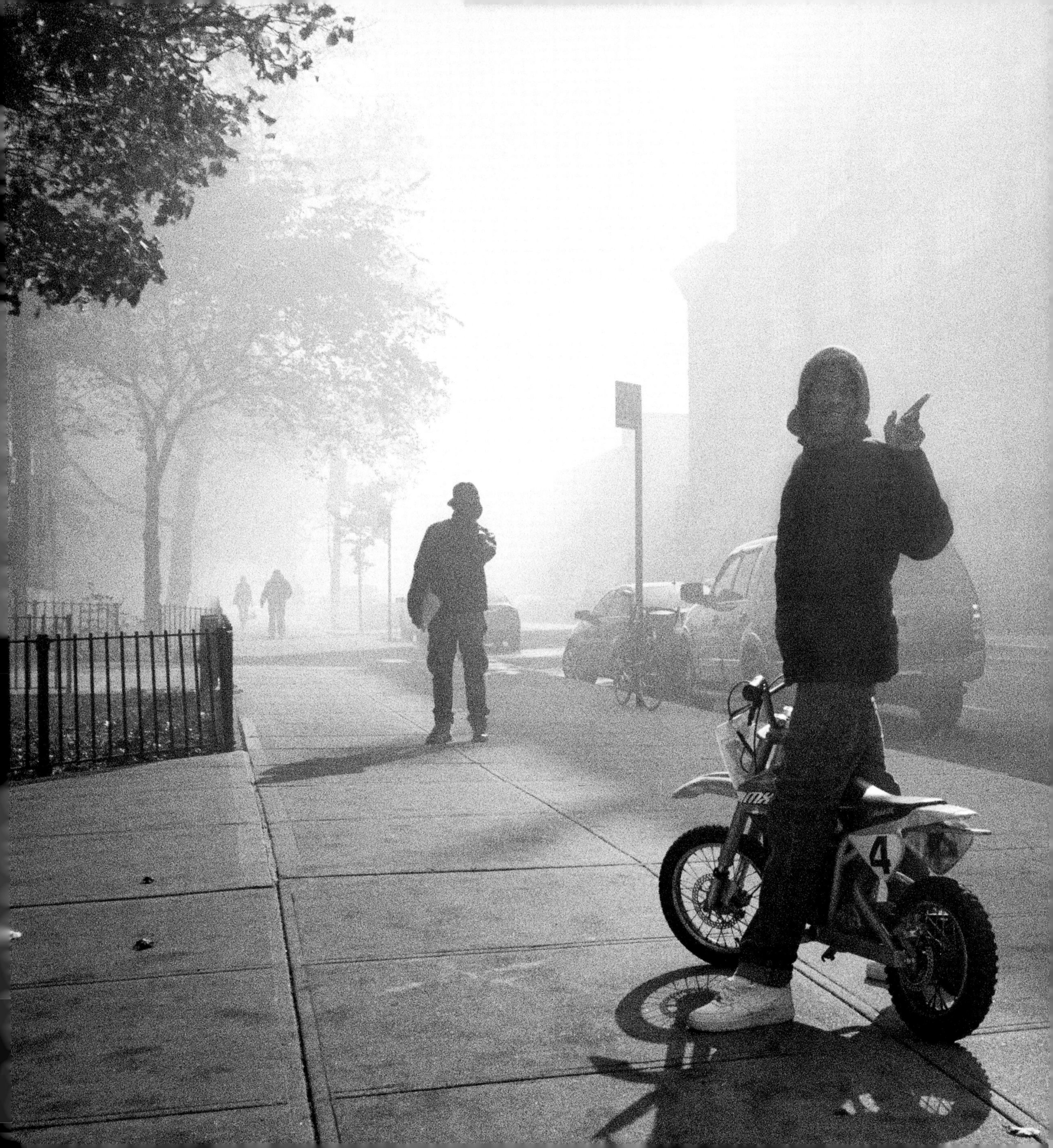
4

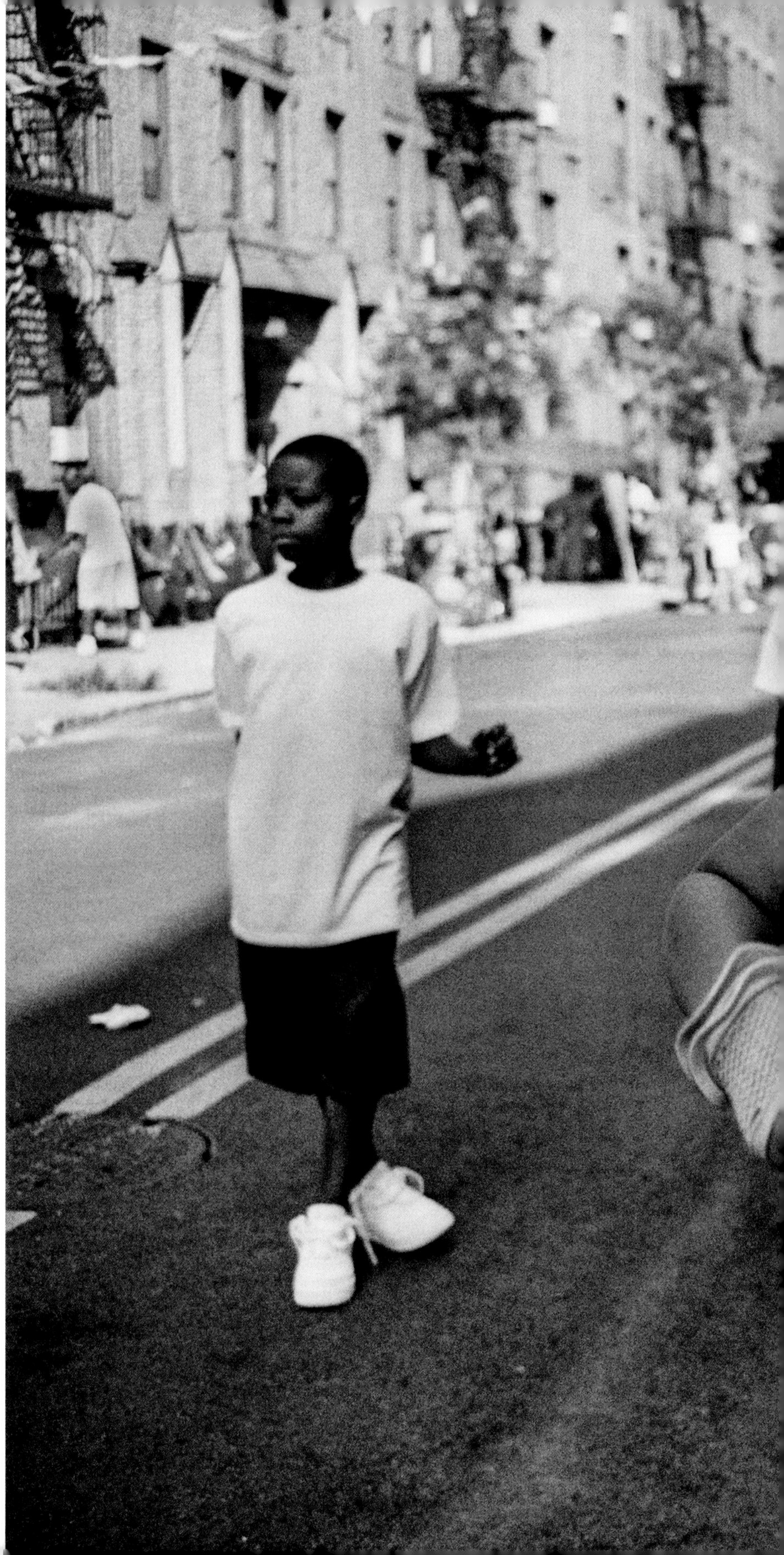

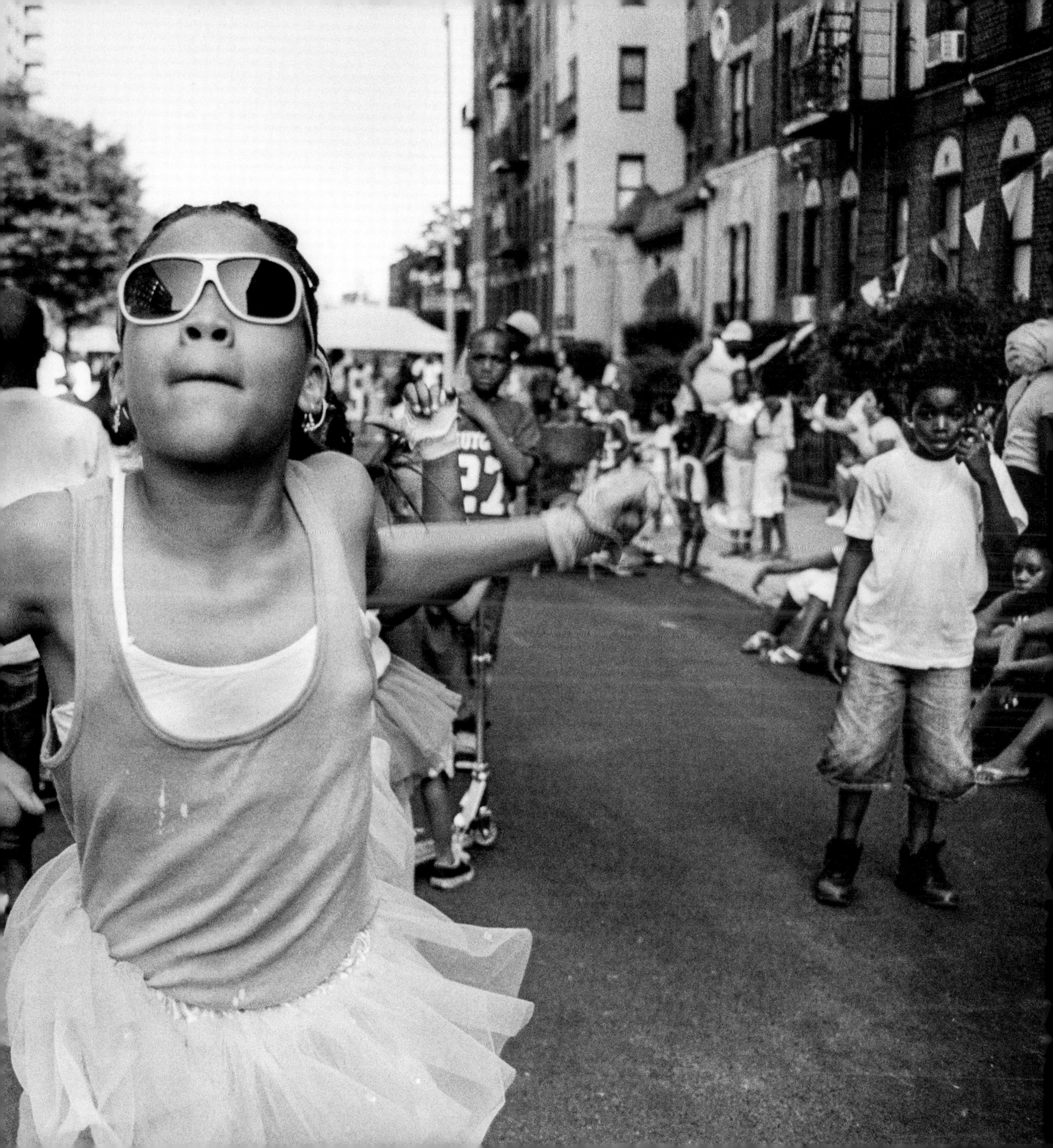

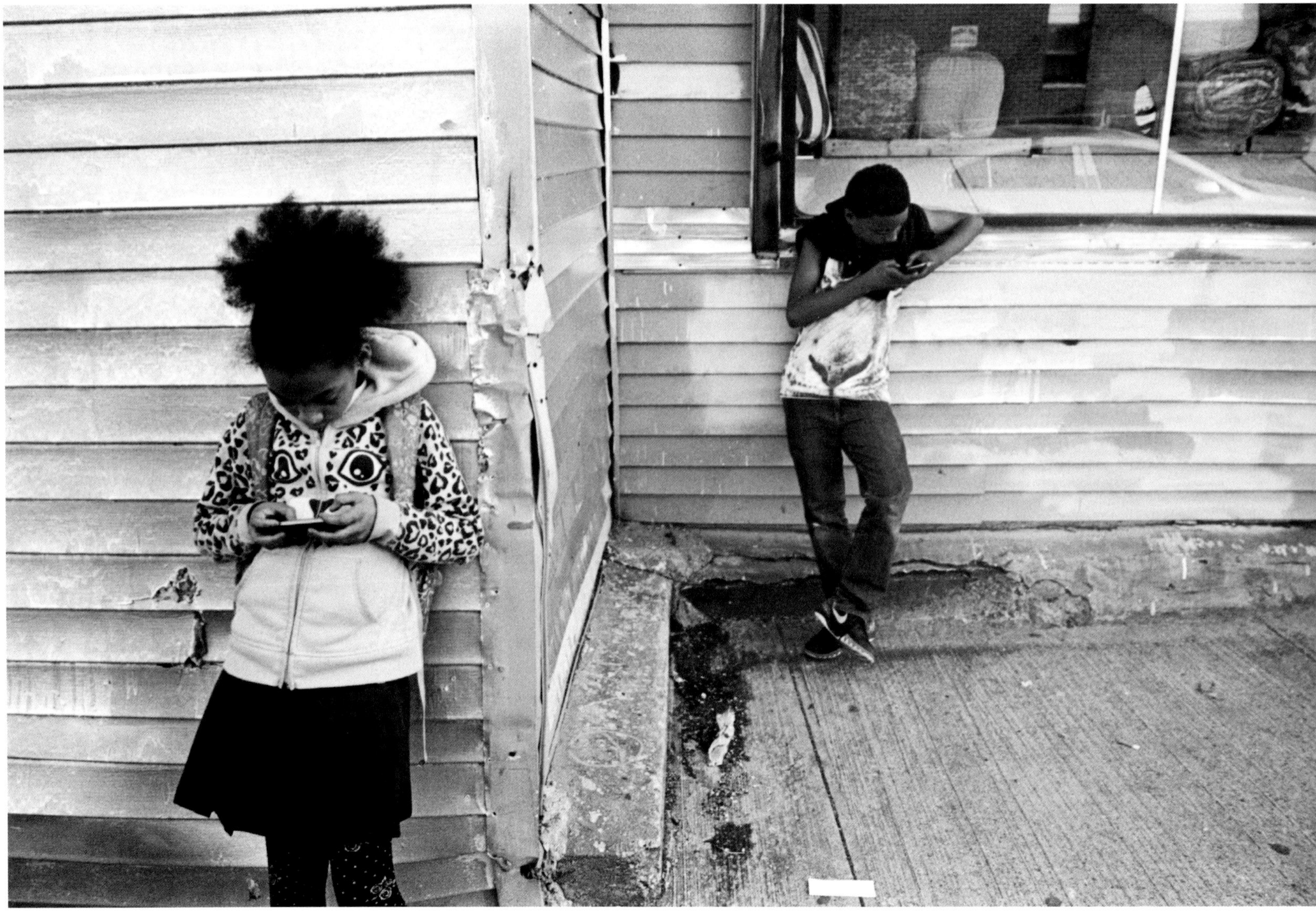

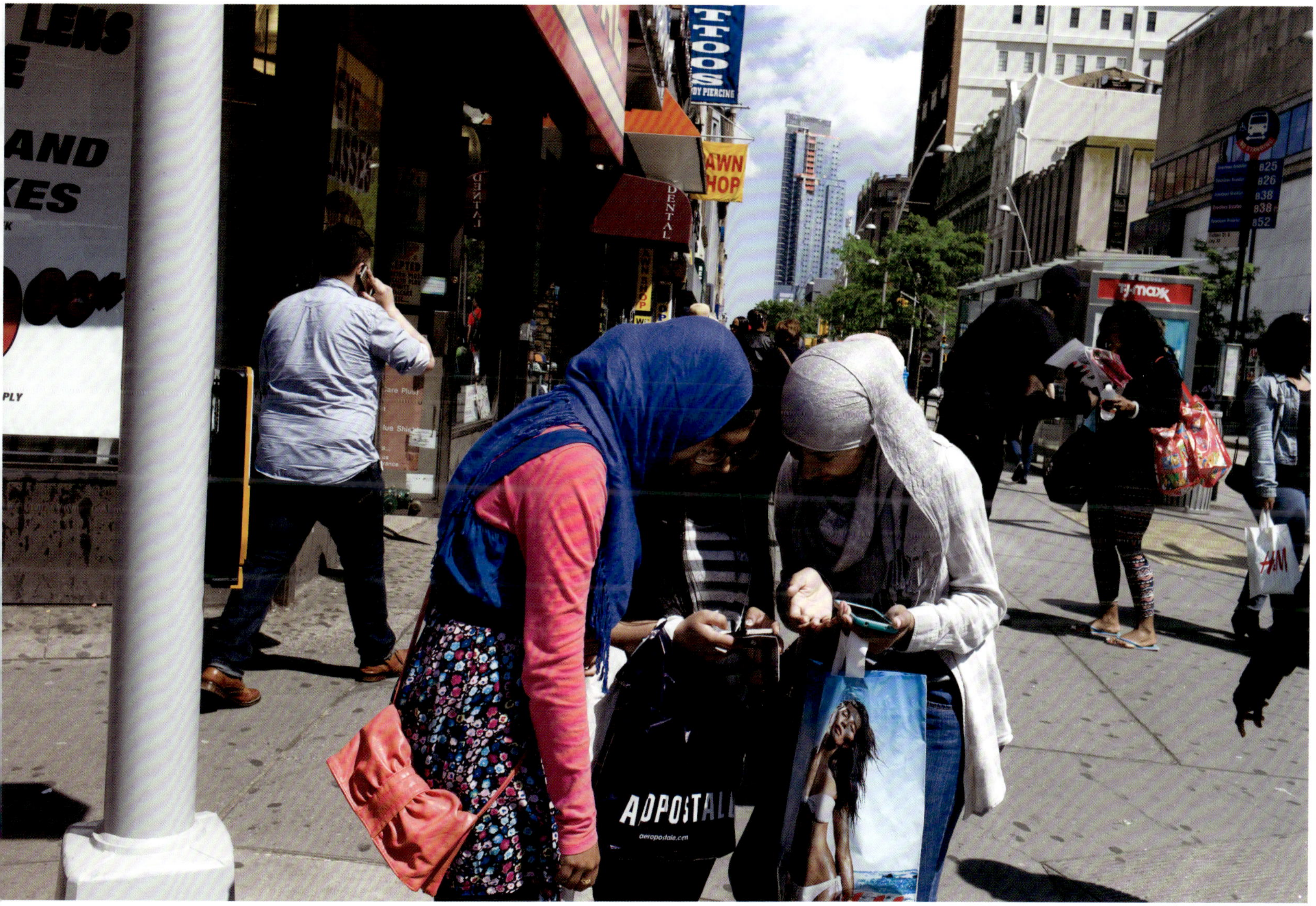
LENS
AND
KES
TTOOS
DY PIERCING
AWN
HOP
DENTAL
B25
B26
B38
B38
B52
ADPOSTALE
H&M

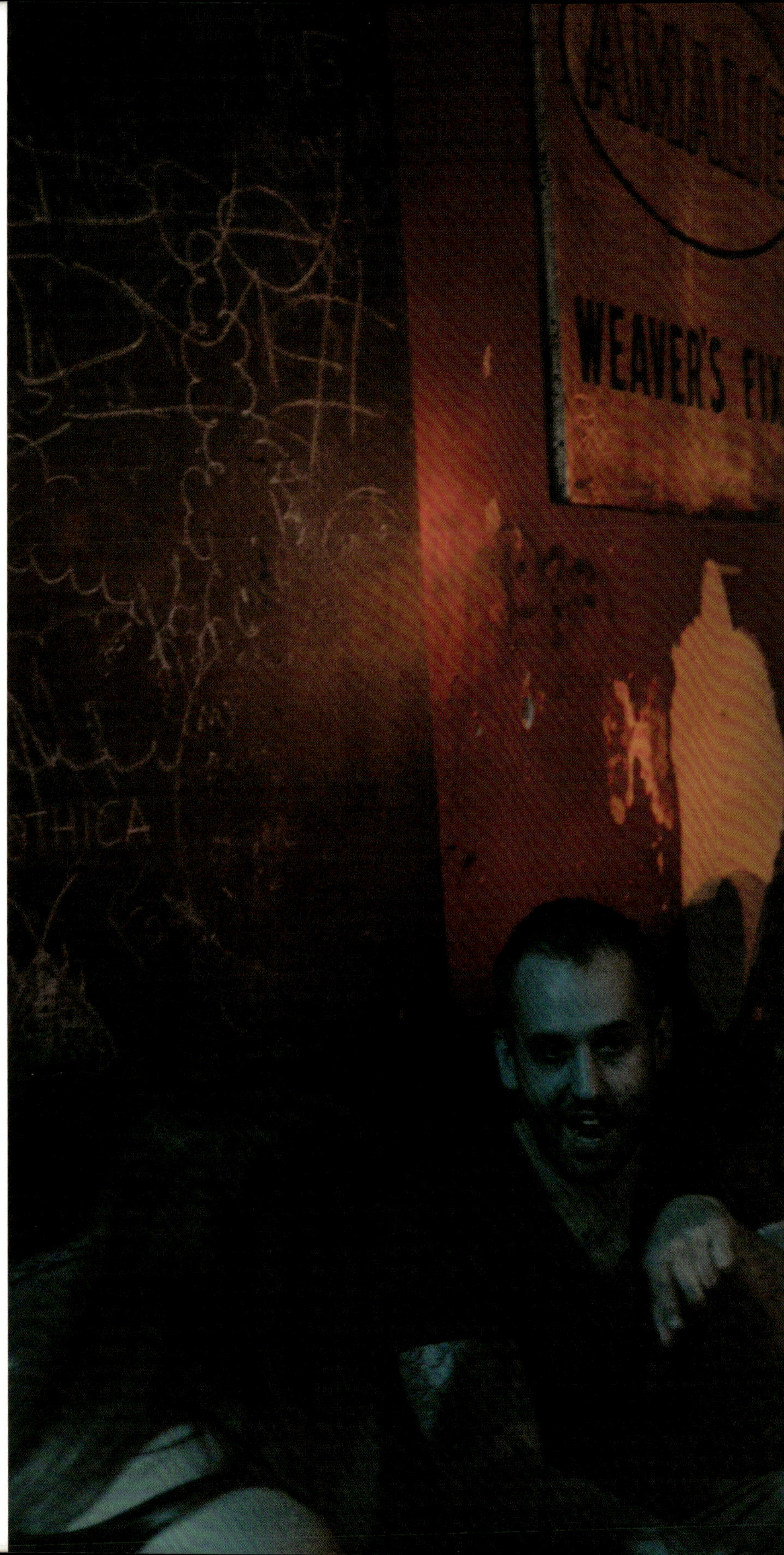
WEAVER'S

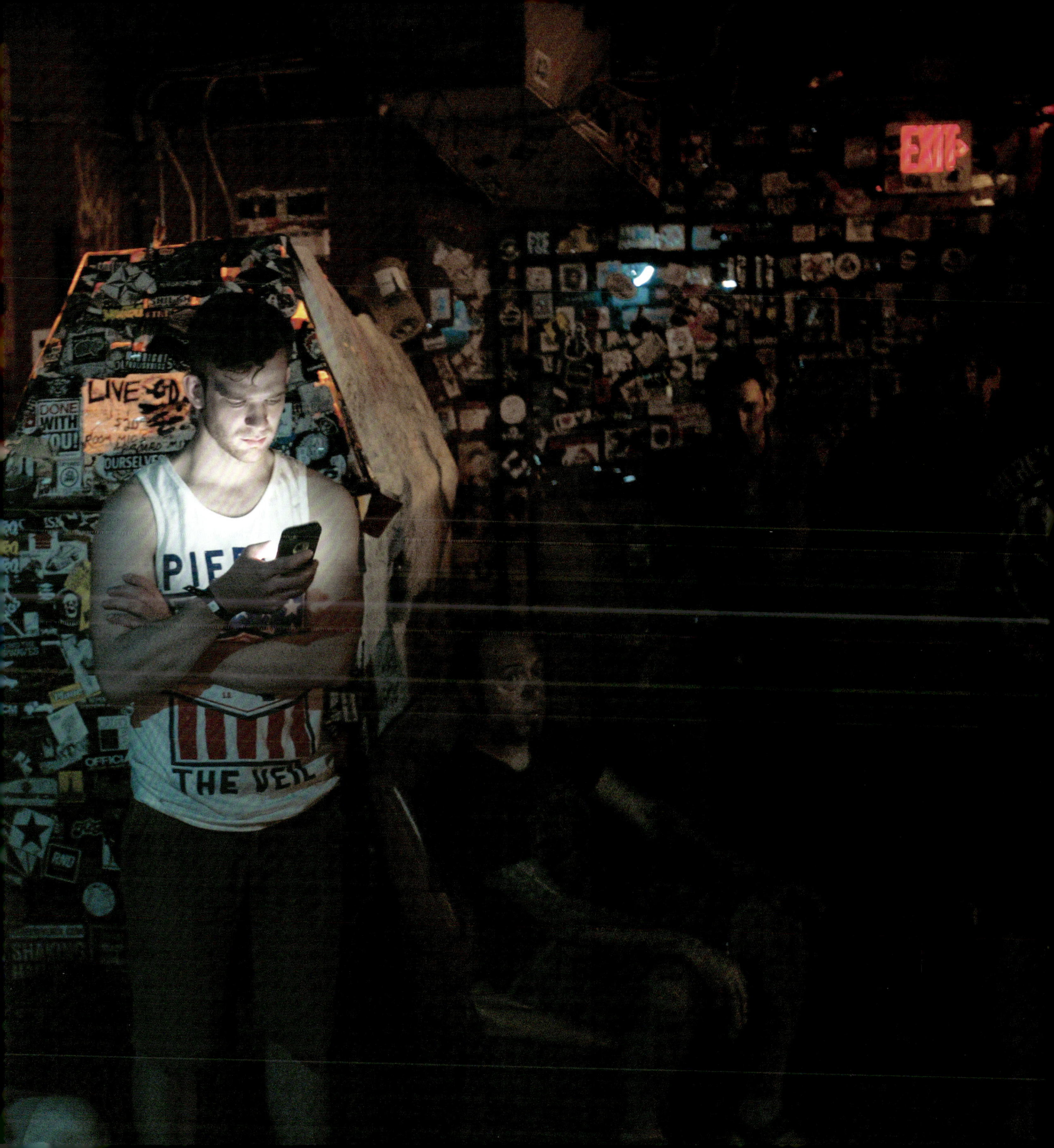
EXIT
LIVE
DONE WITH YOU!
THE VEIL

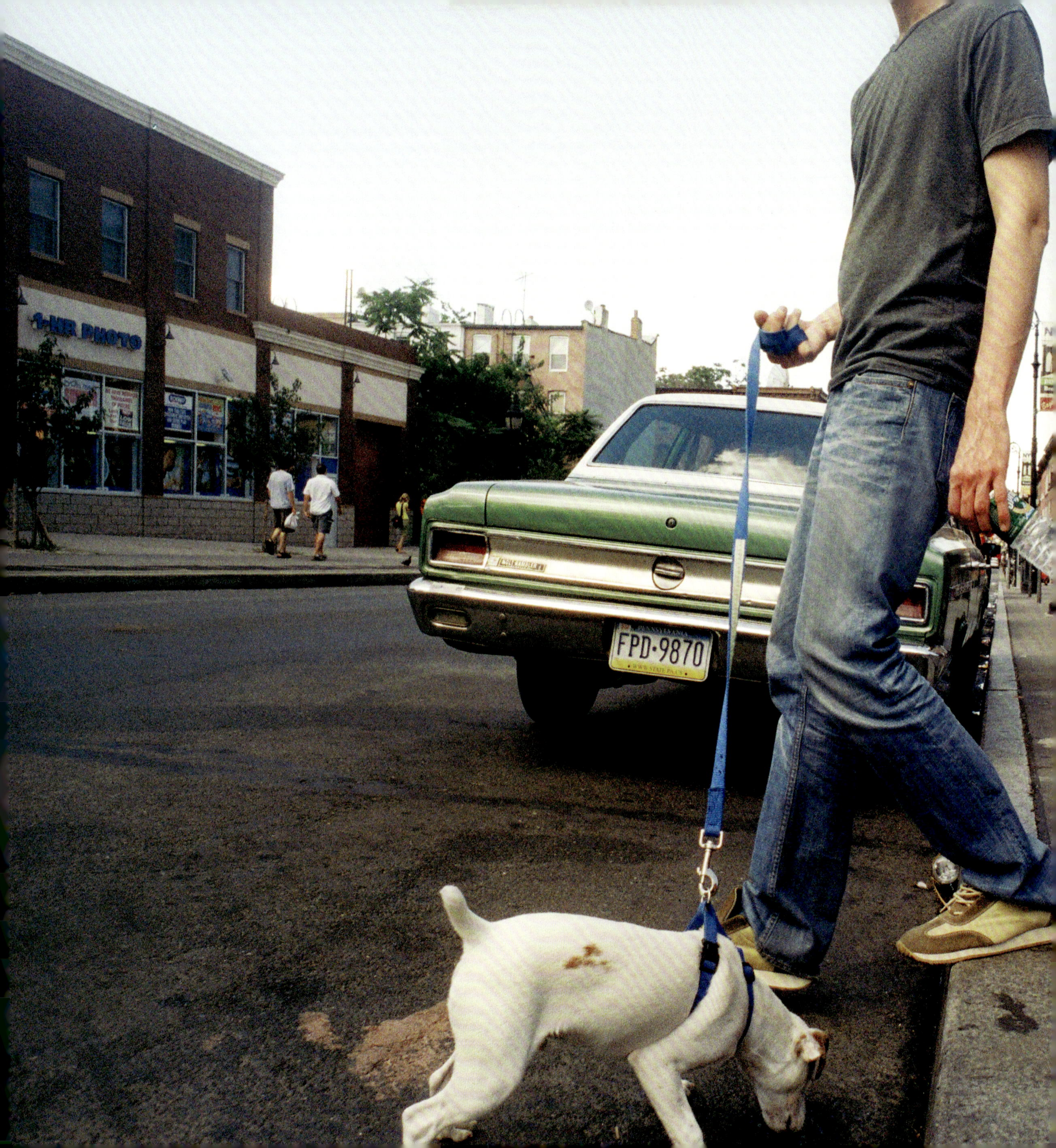
1-HR PHOTO
FPD·9870

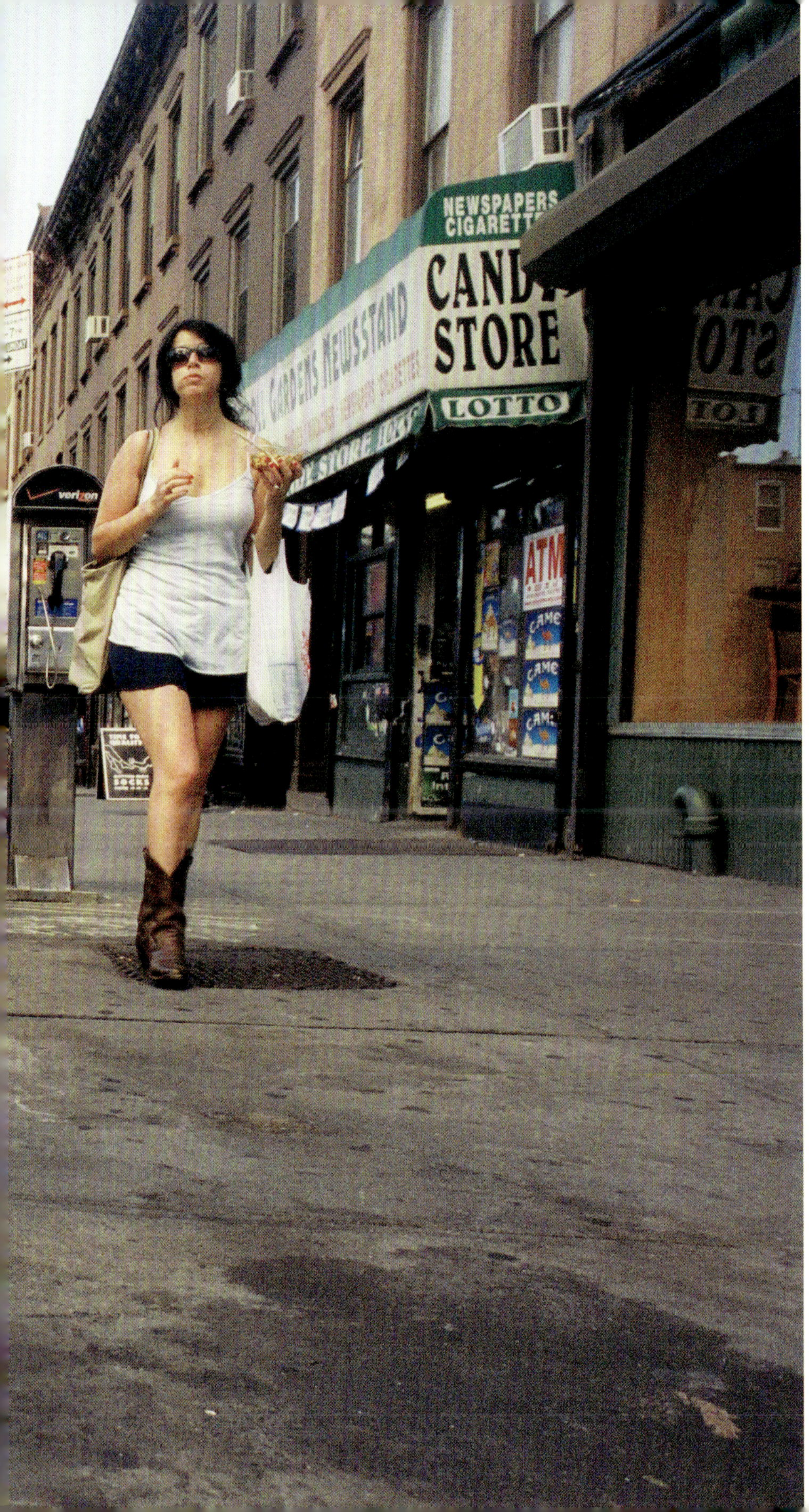
NEWSPAPERS
STORE
GARDENS NEWSSTAND
LOTTO
verizon
ATM

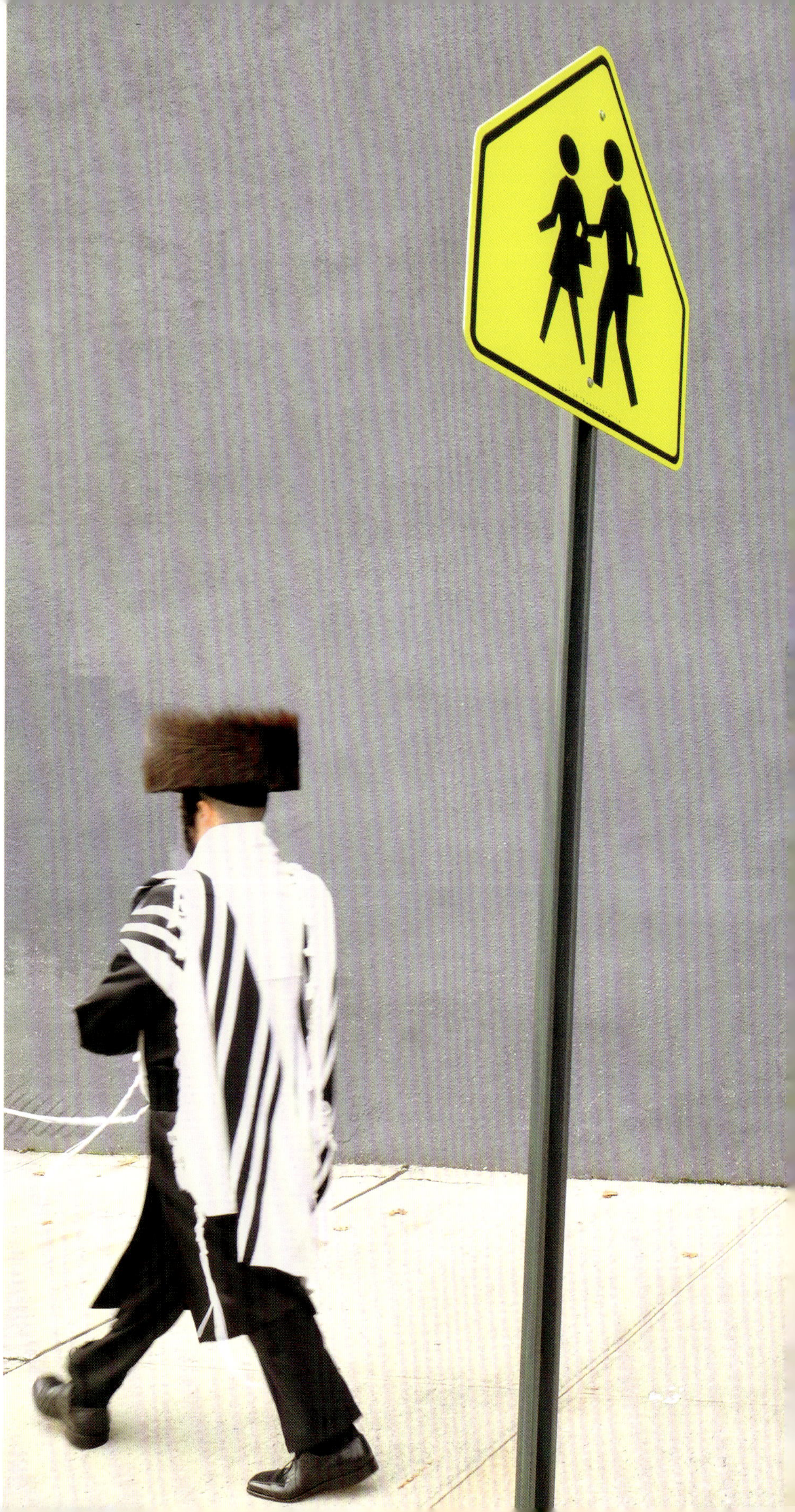

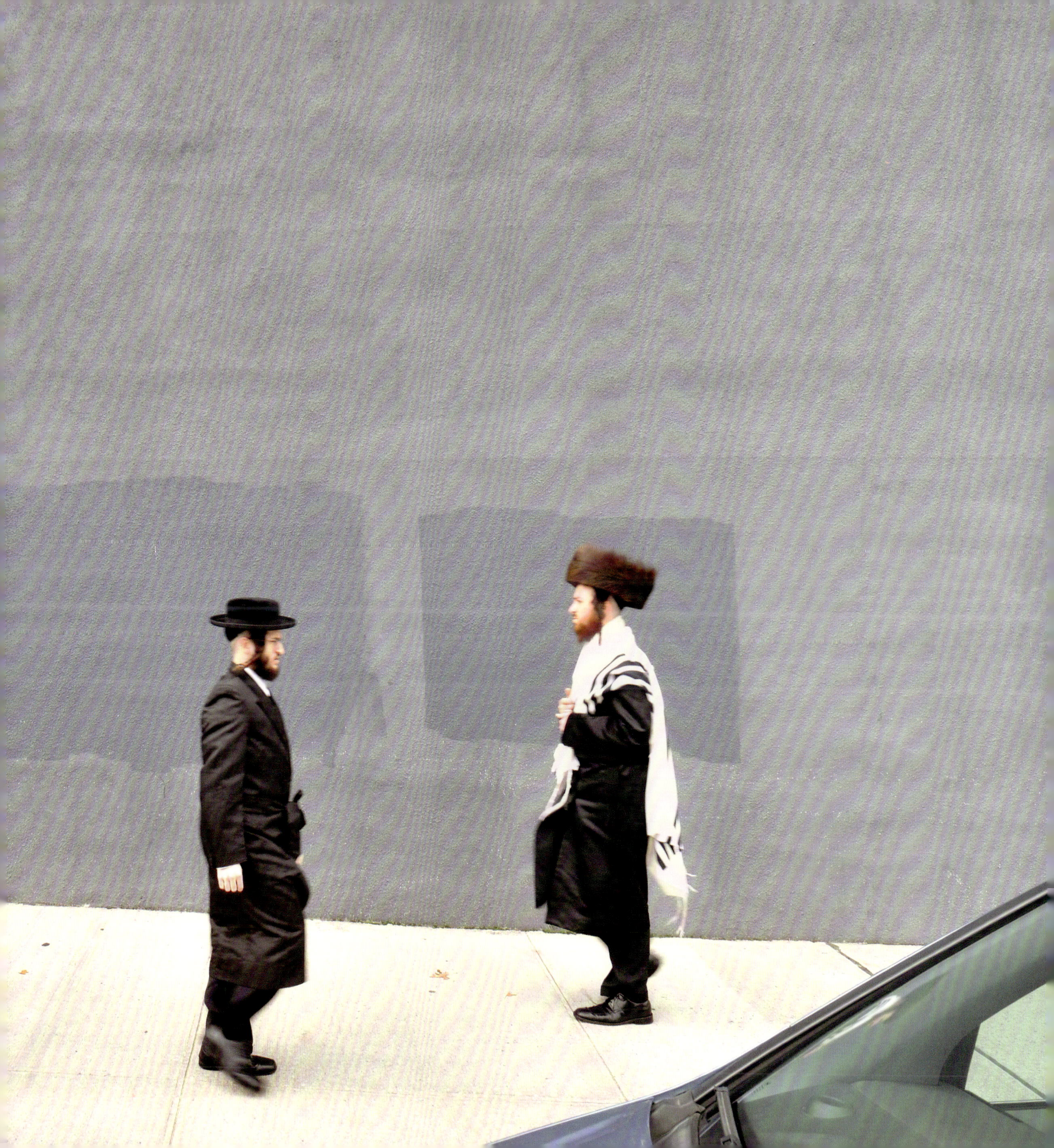

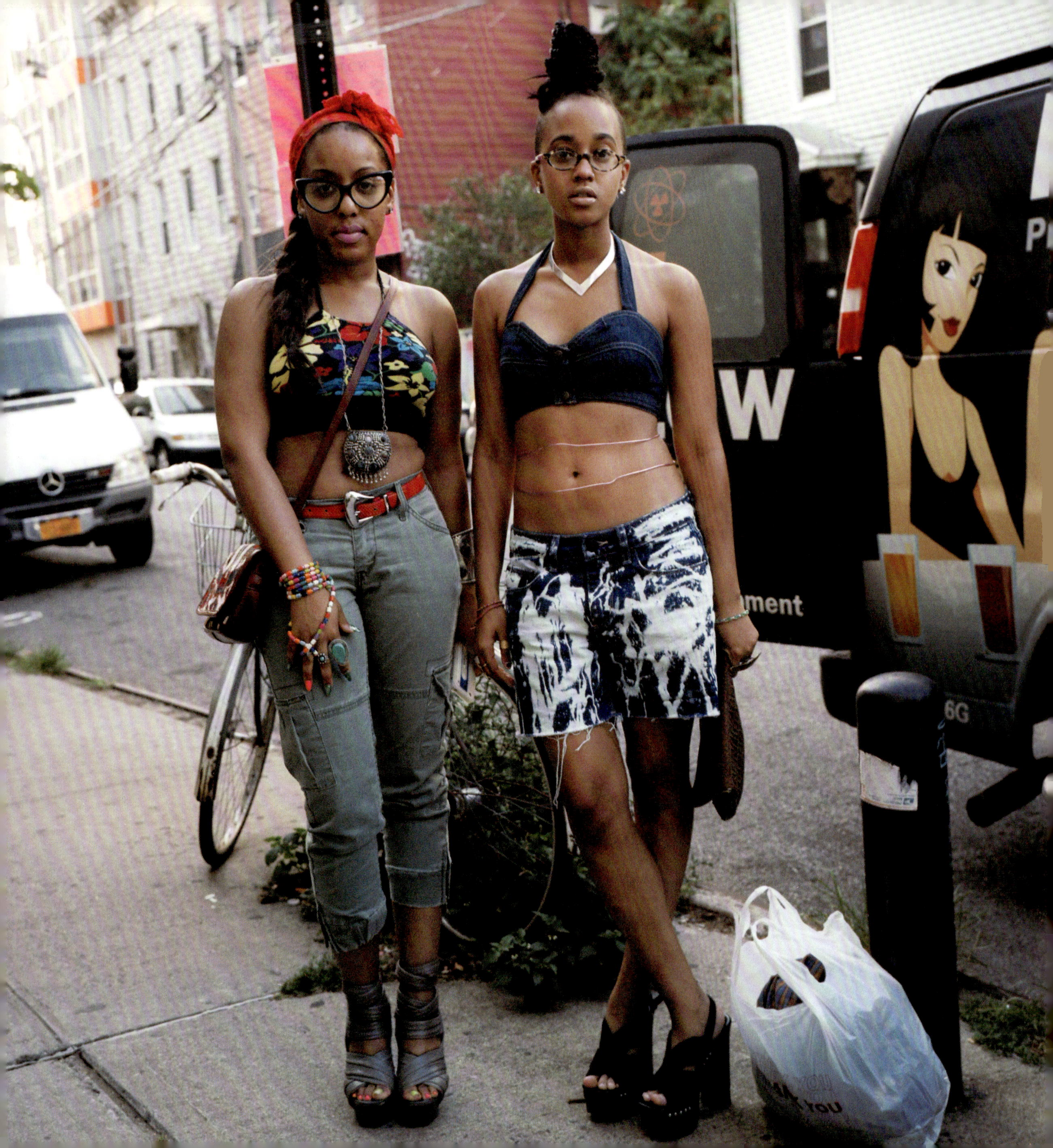

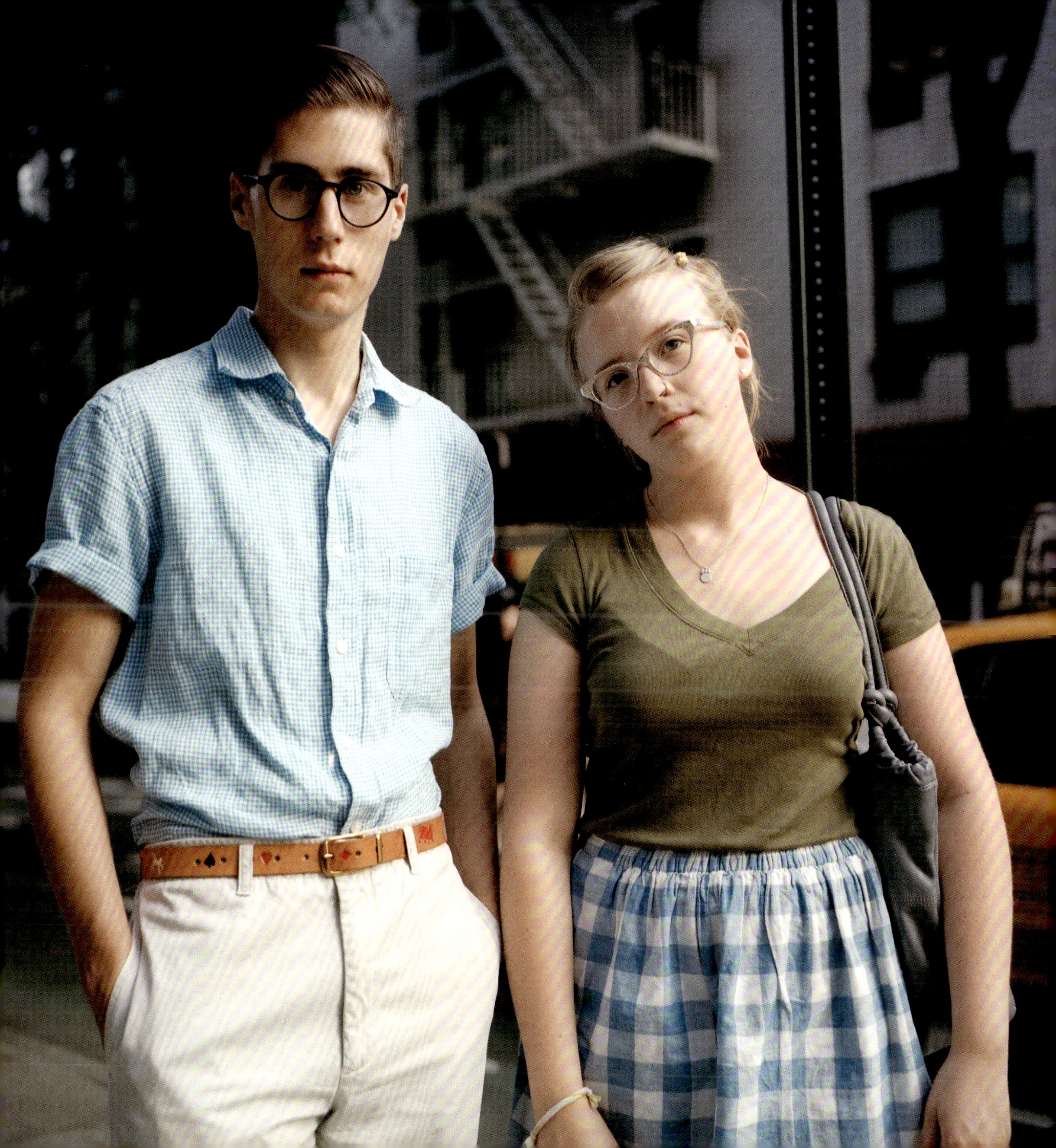

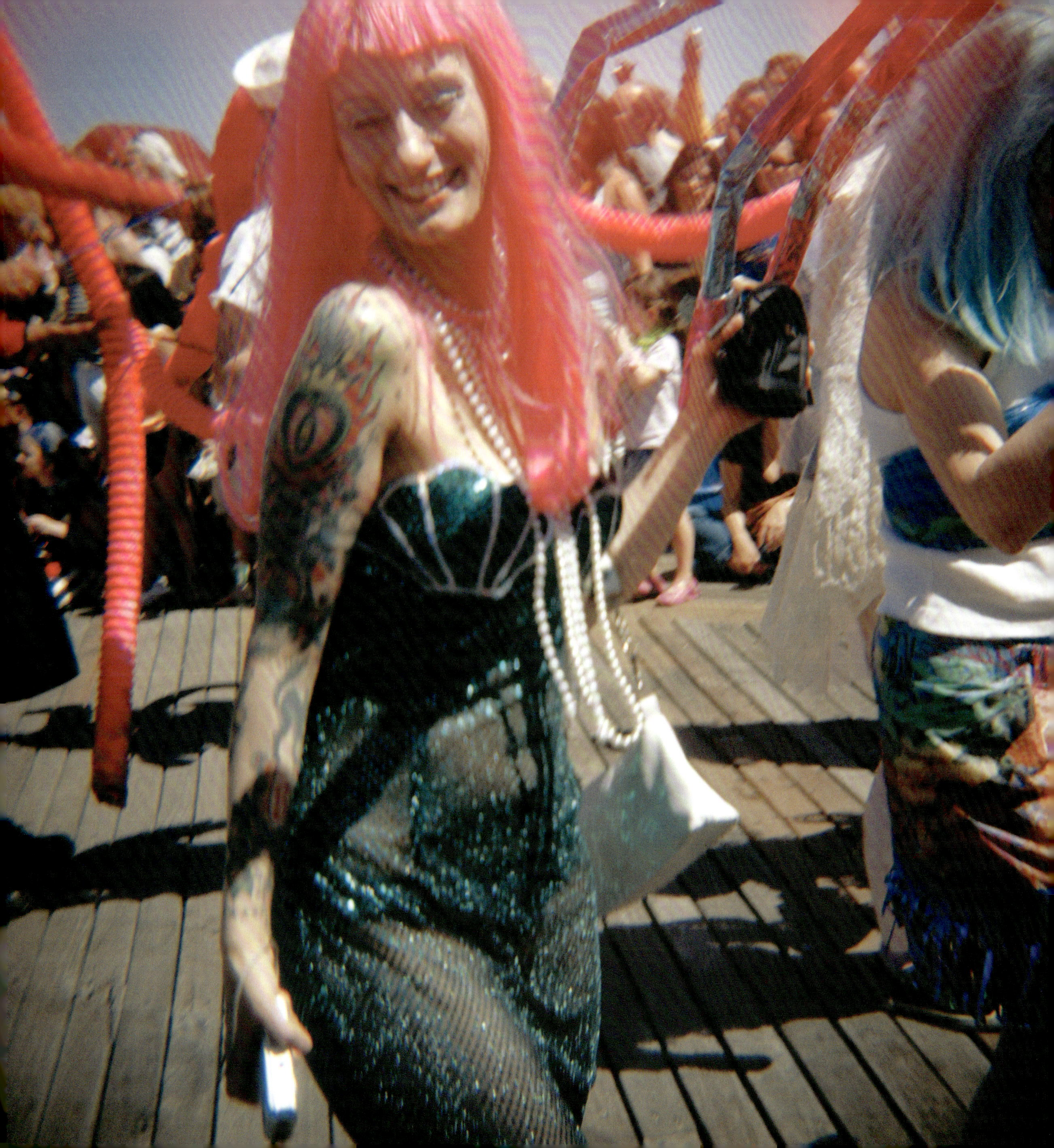

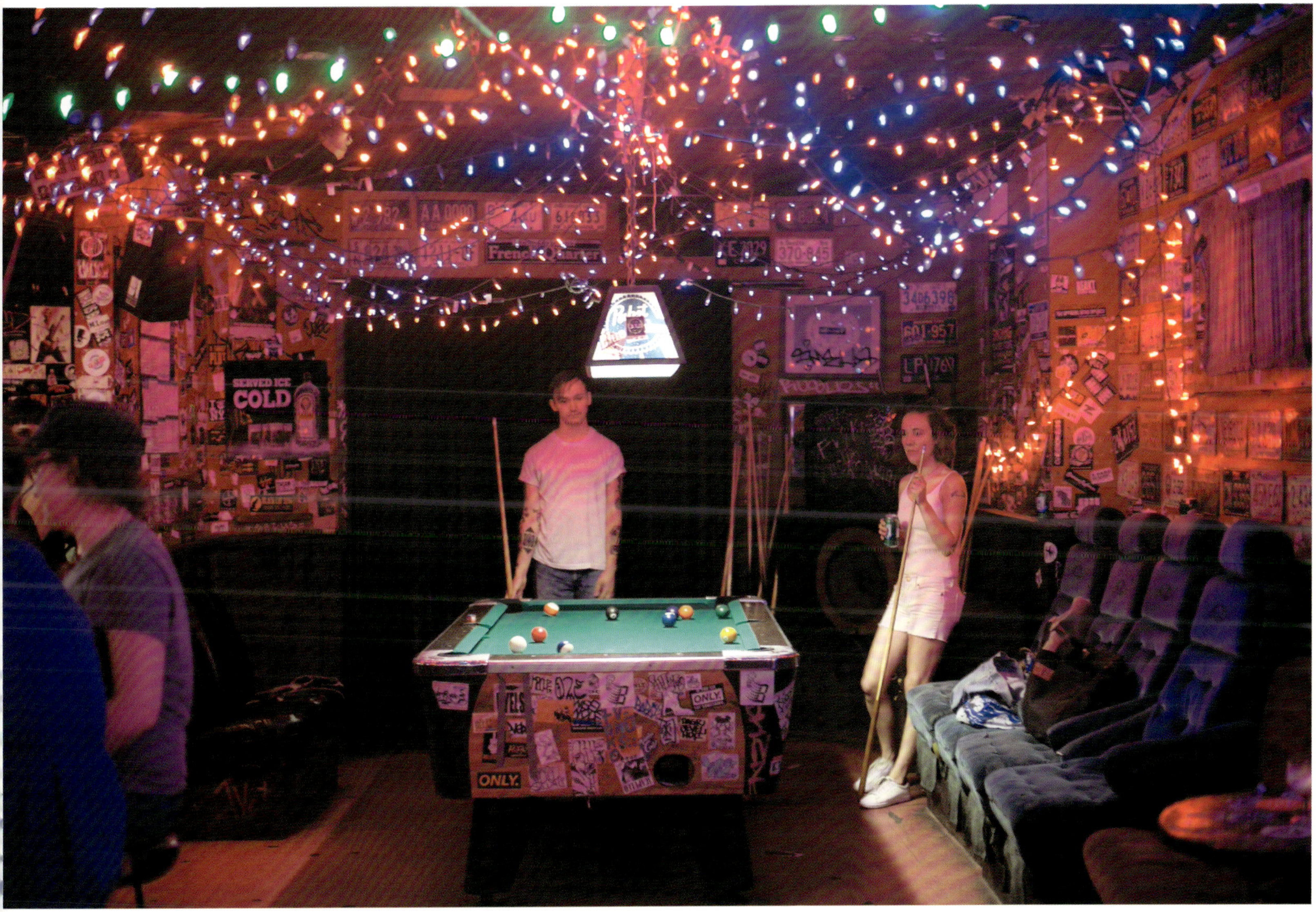
SERVED ICE
COLD
ONLY.

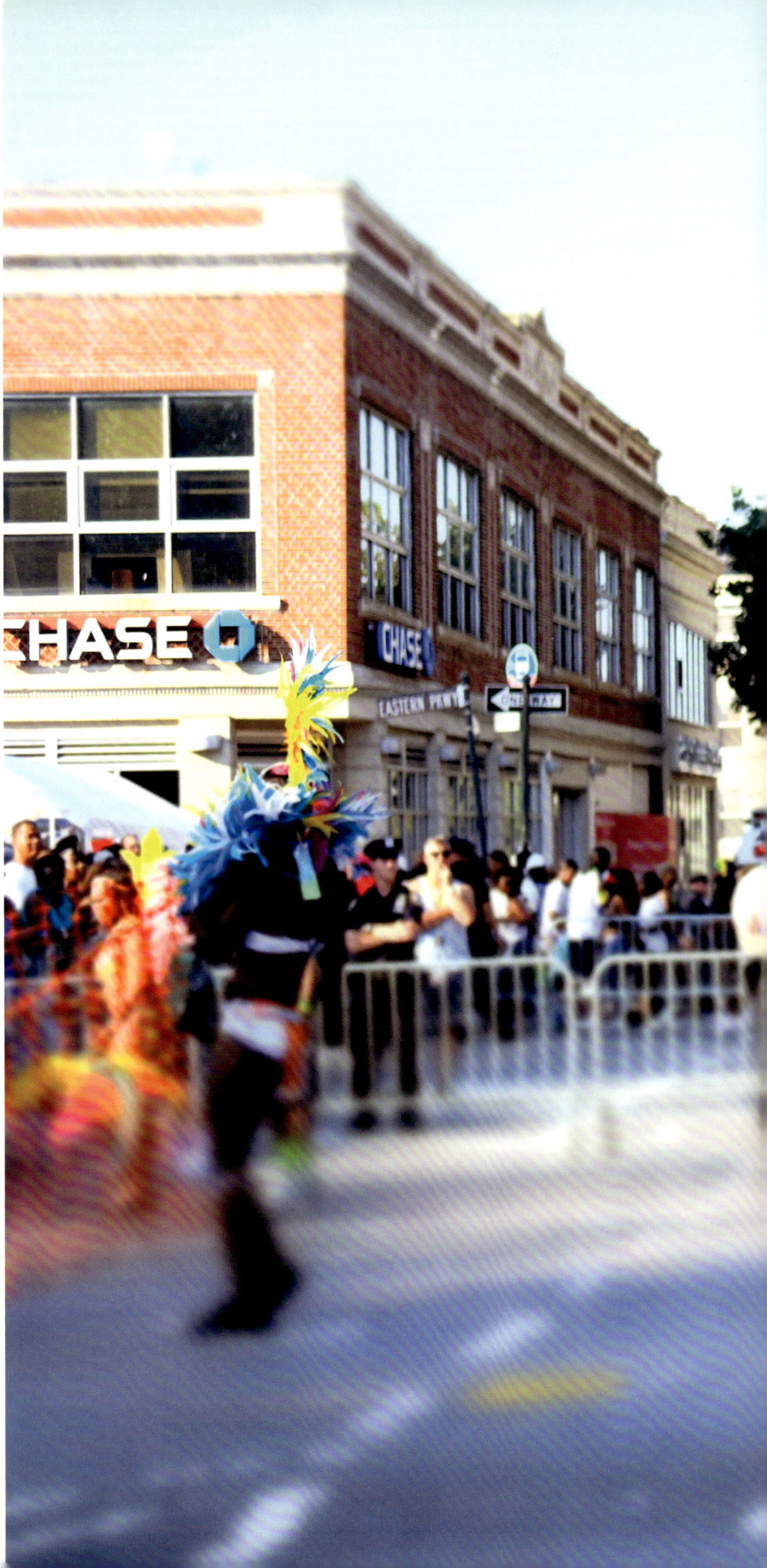
CHASE
EASTERN PKWY

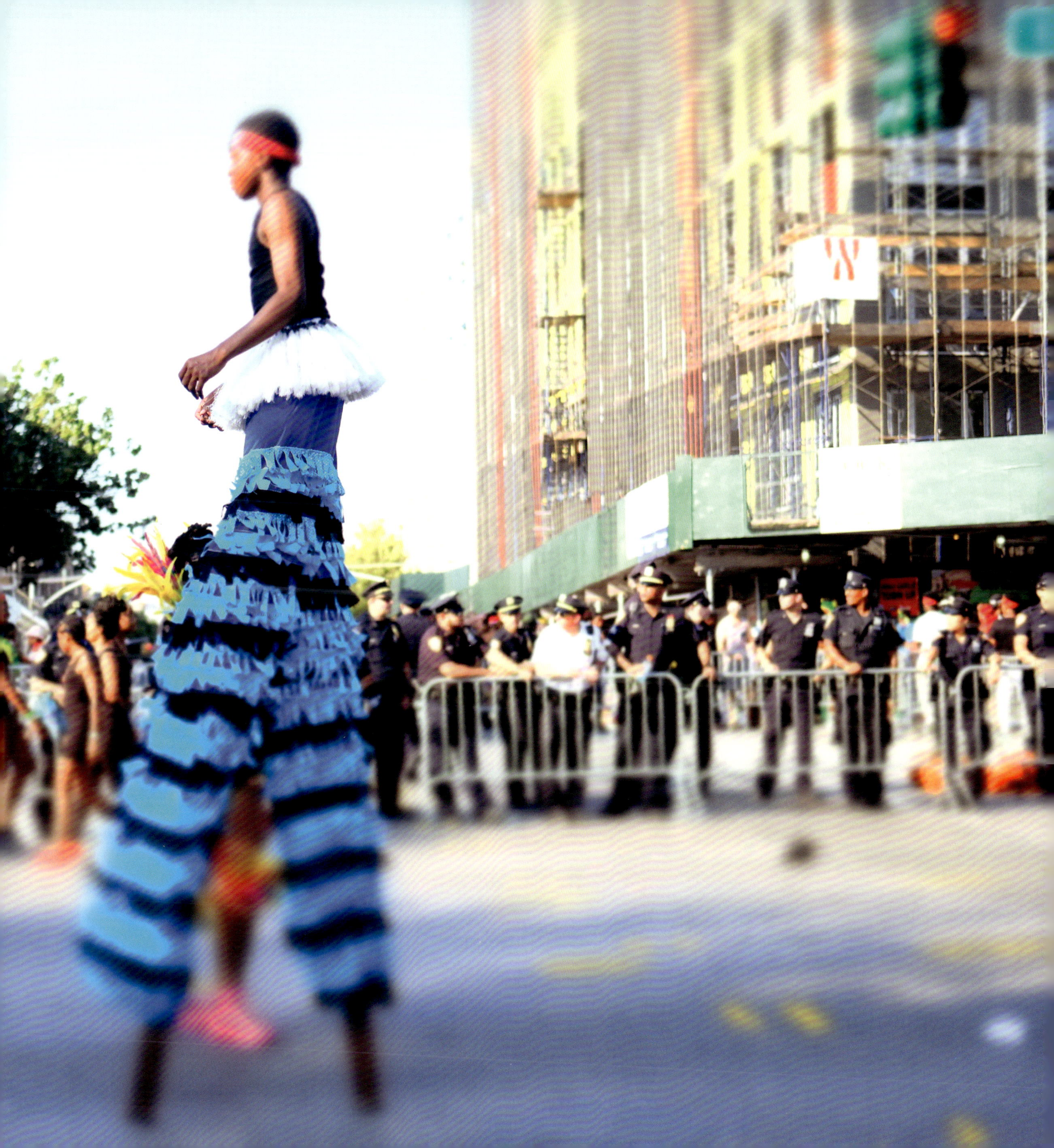

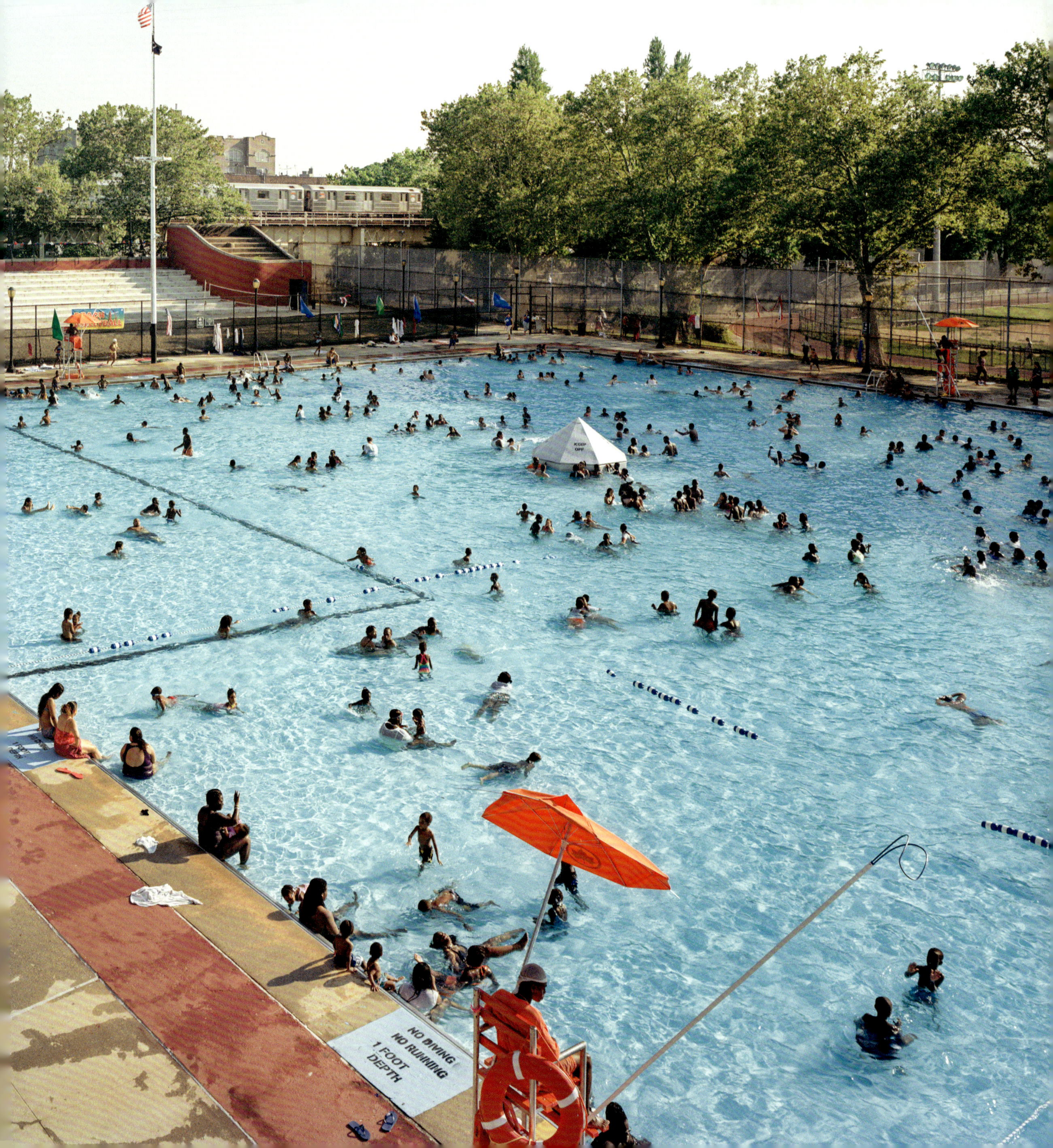
NO DIVING
NO RUNNING
1 FOOT
DEPTH

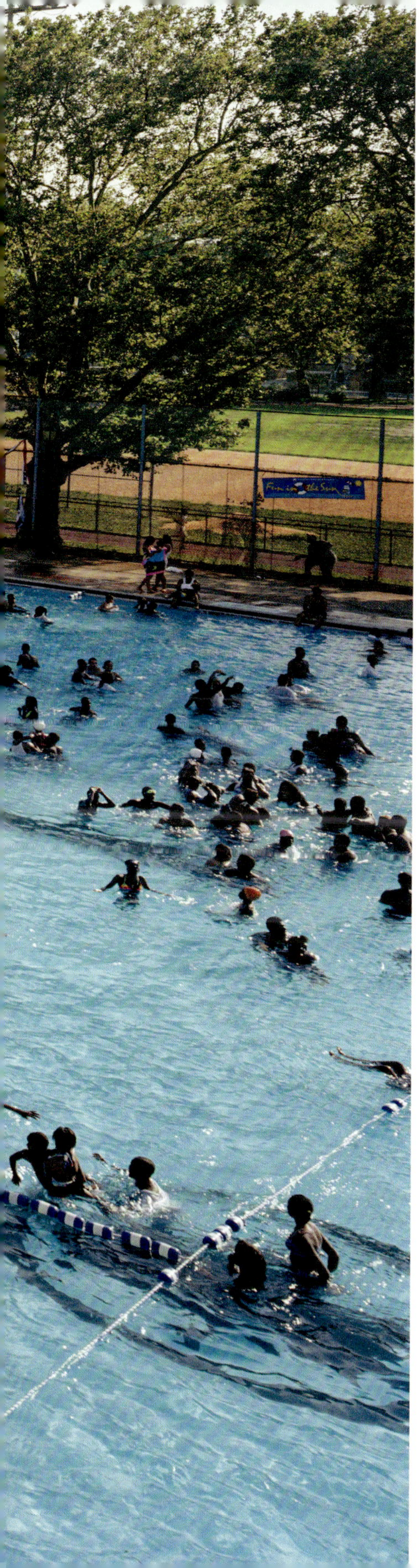

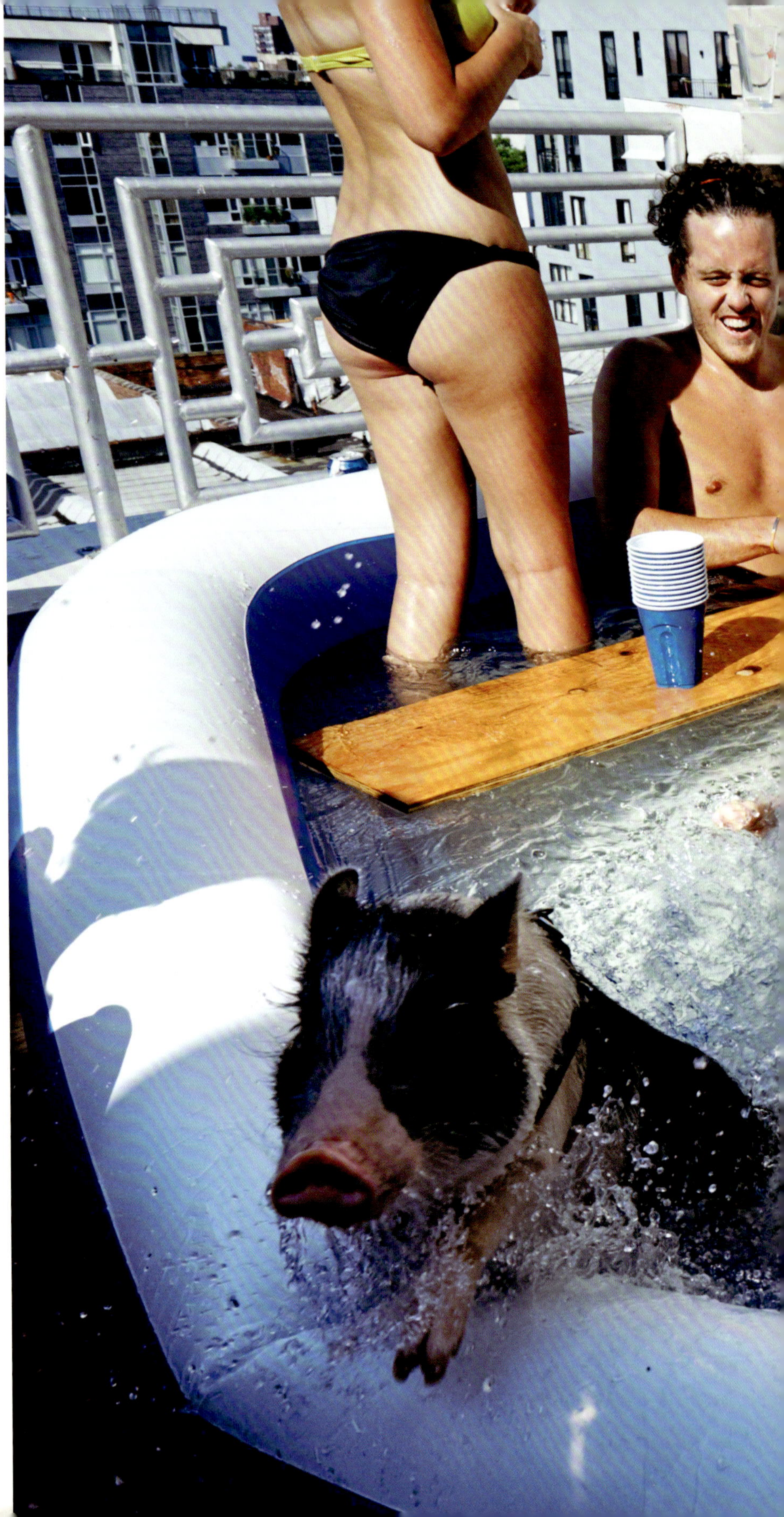

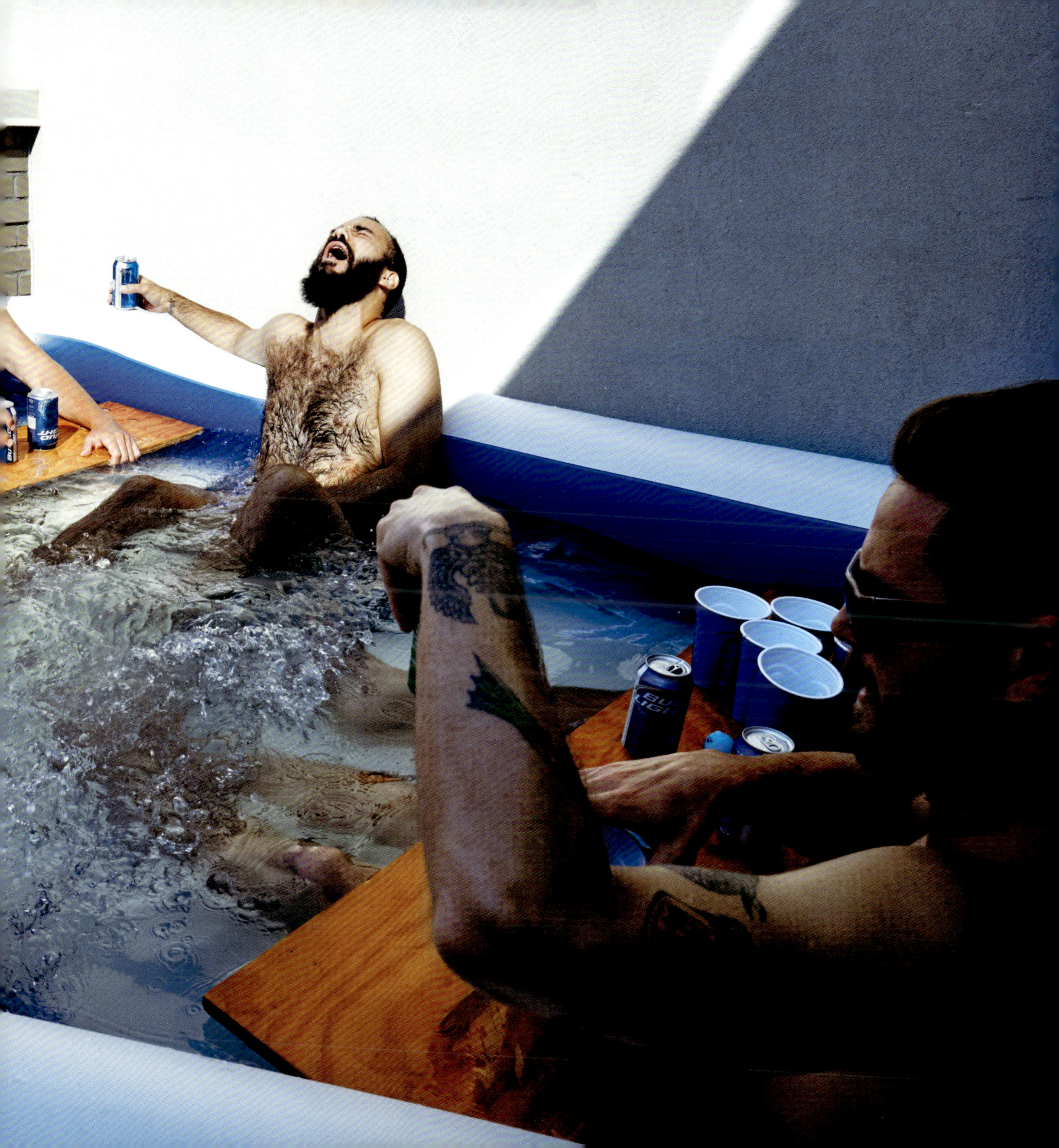

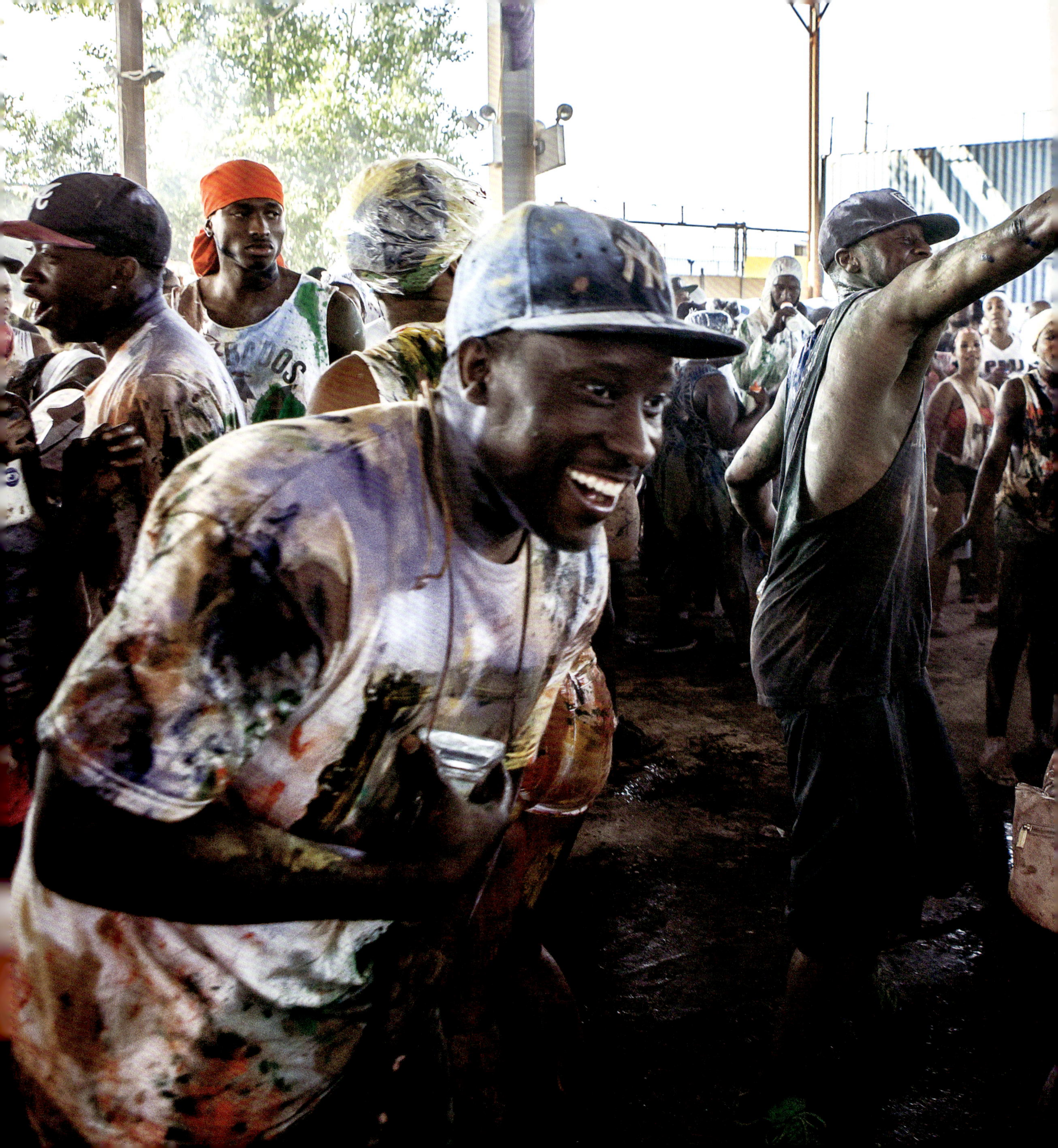

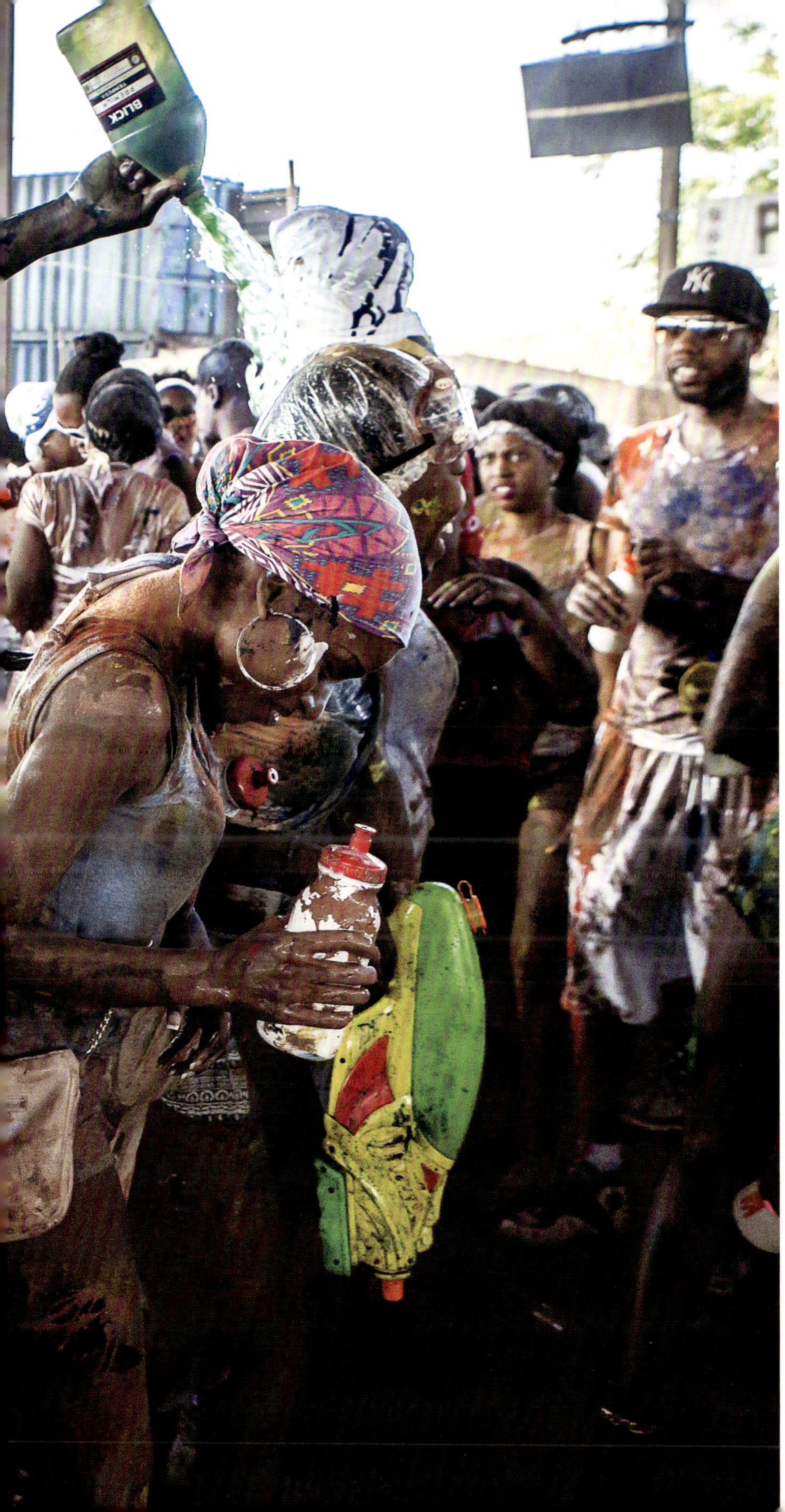
BLICK

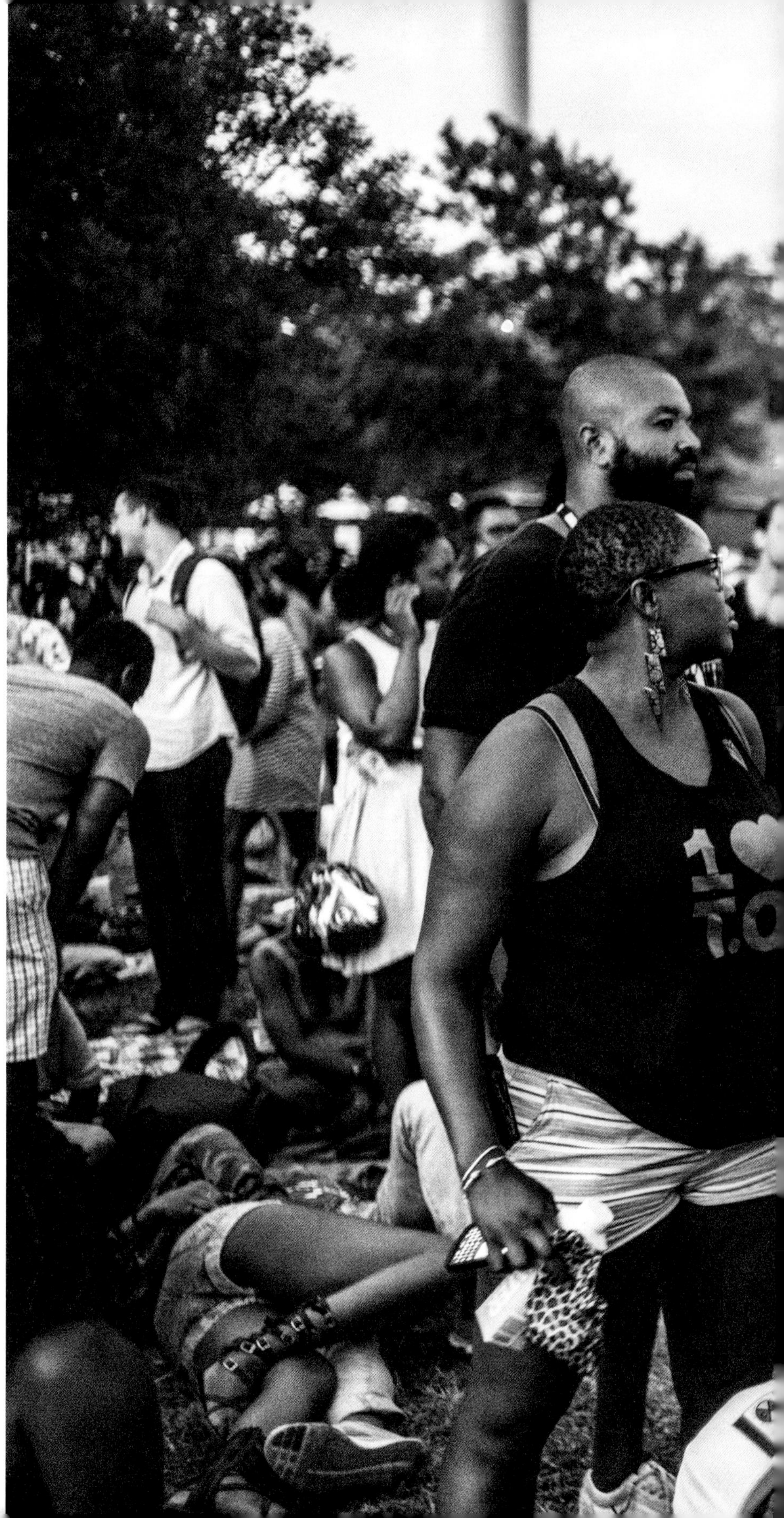

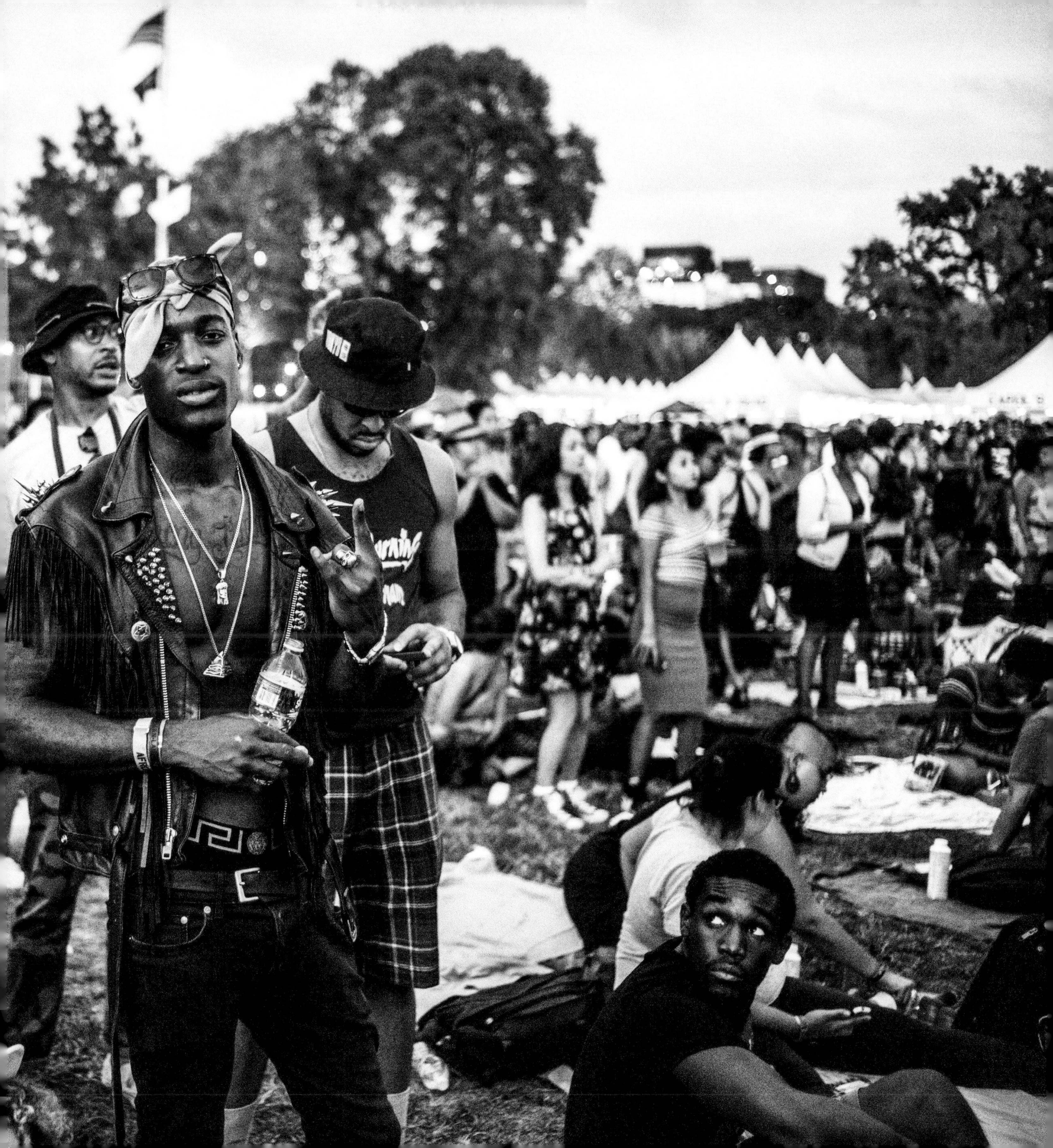

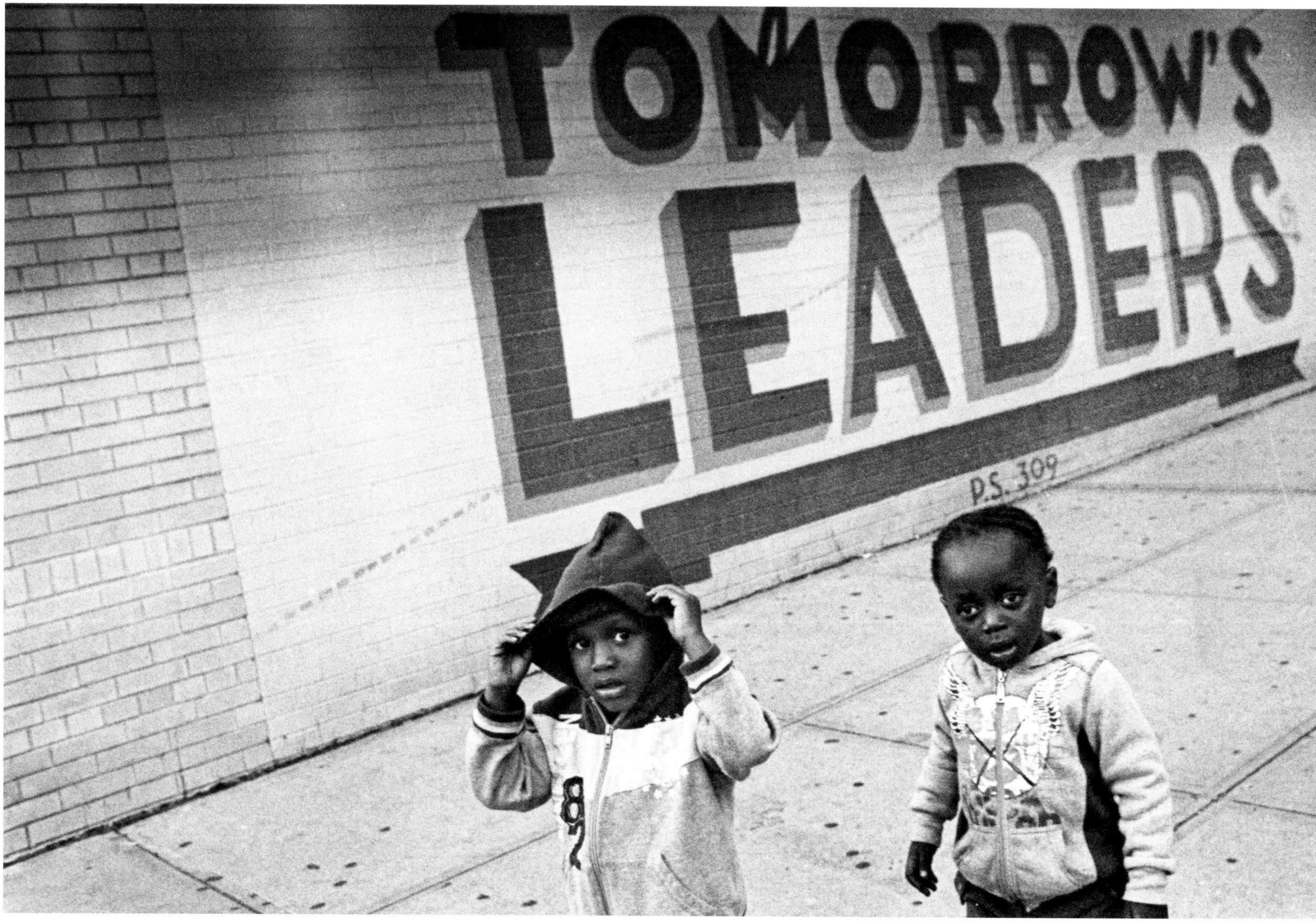
TOMORROW'S
LEADERS
P.S. 309

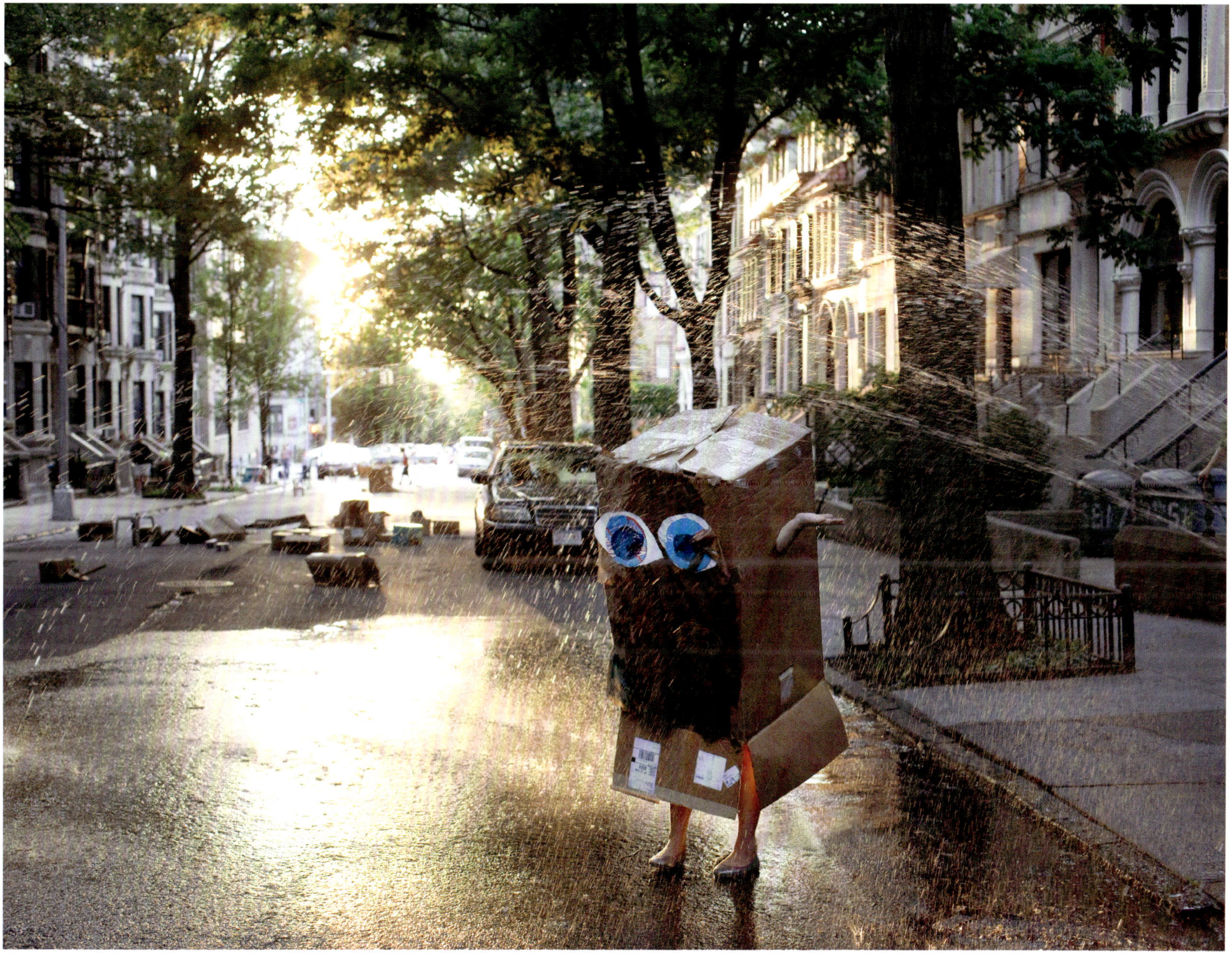

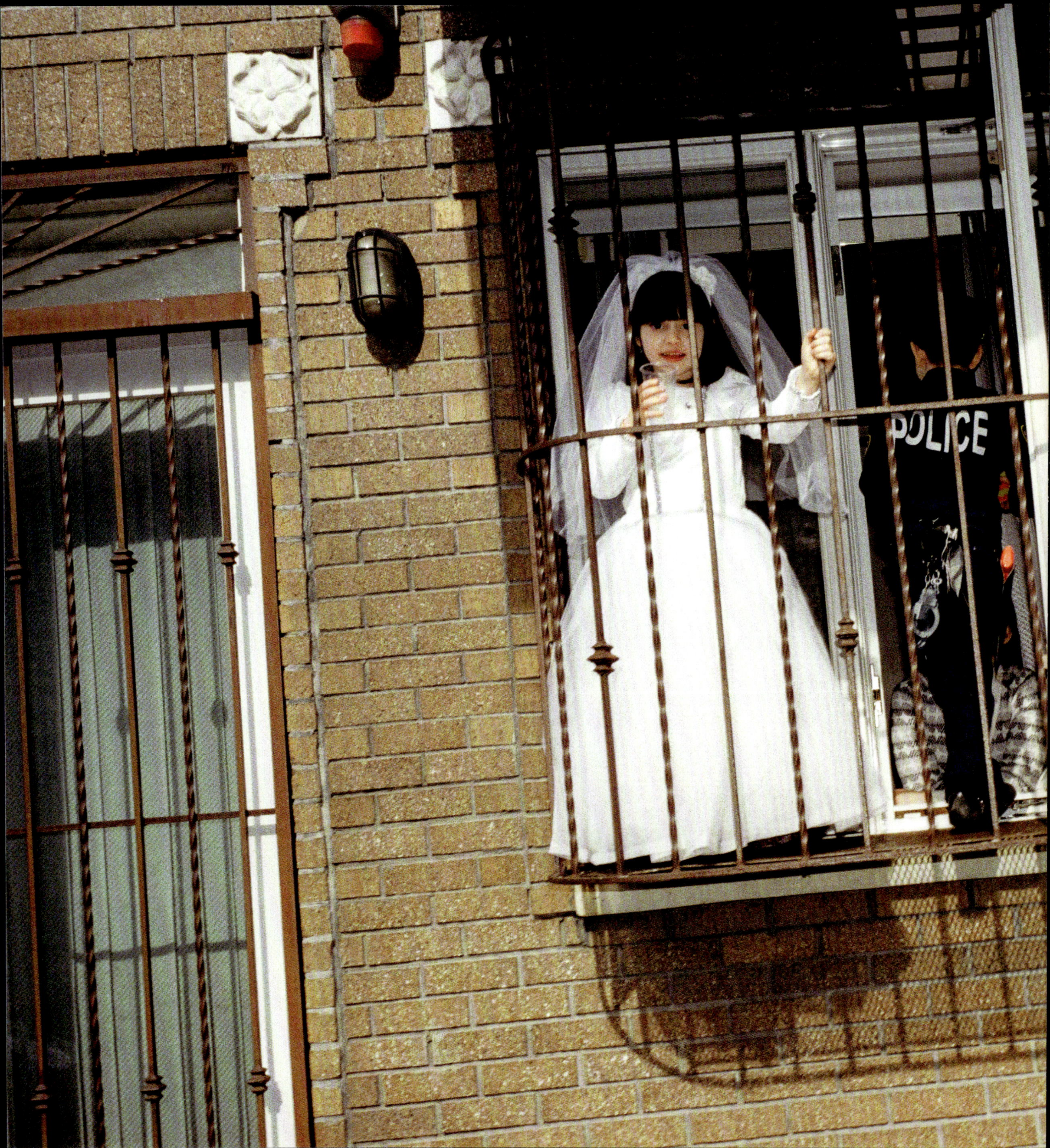
POLICE

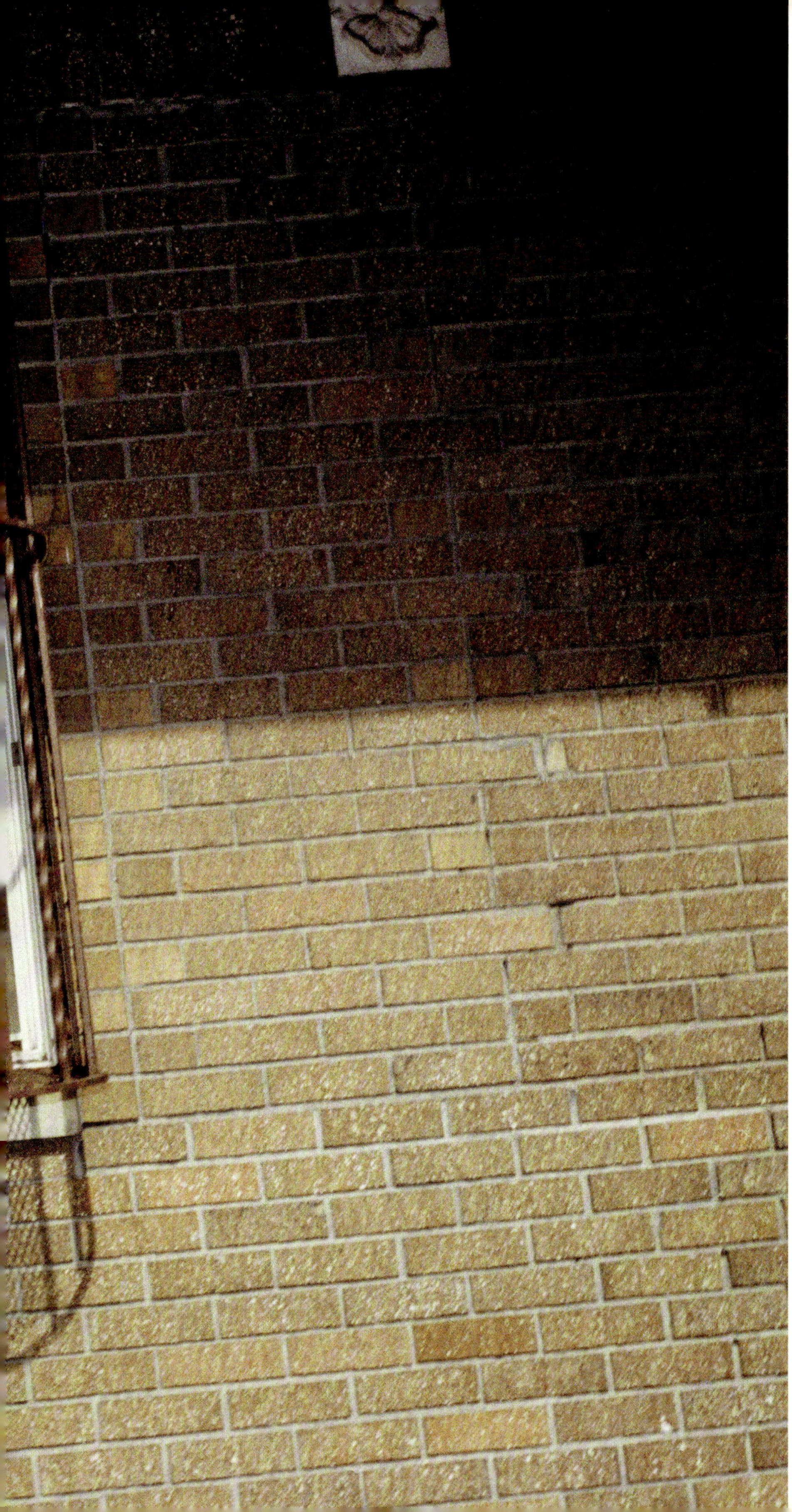

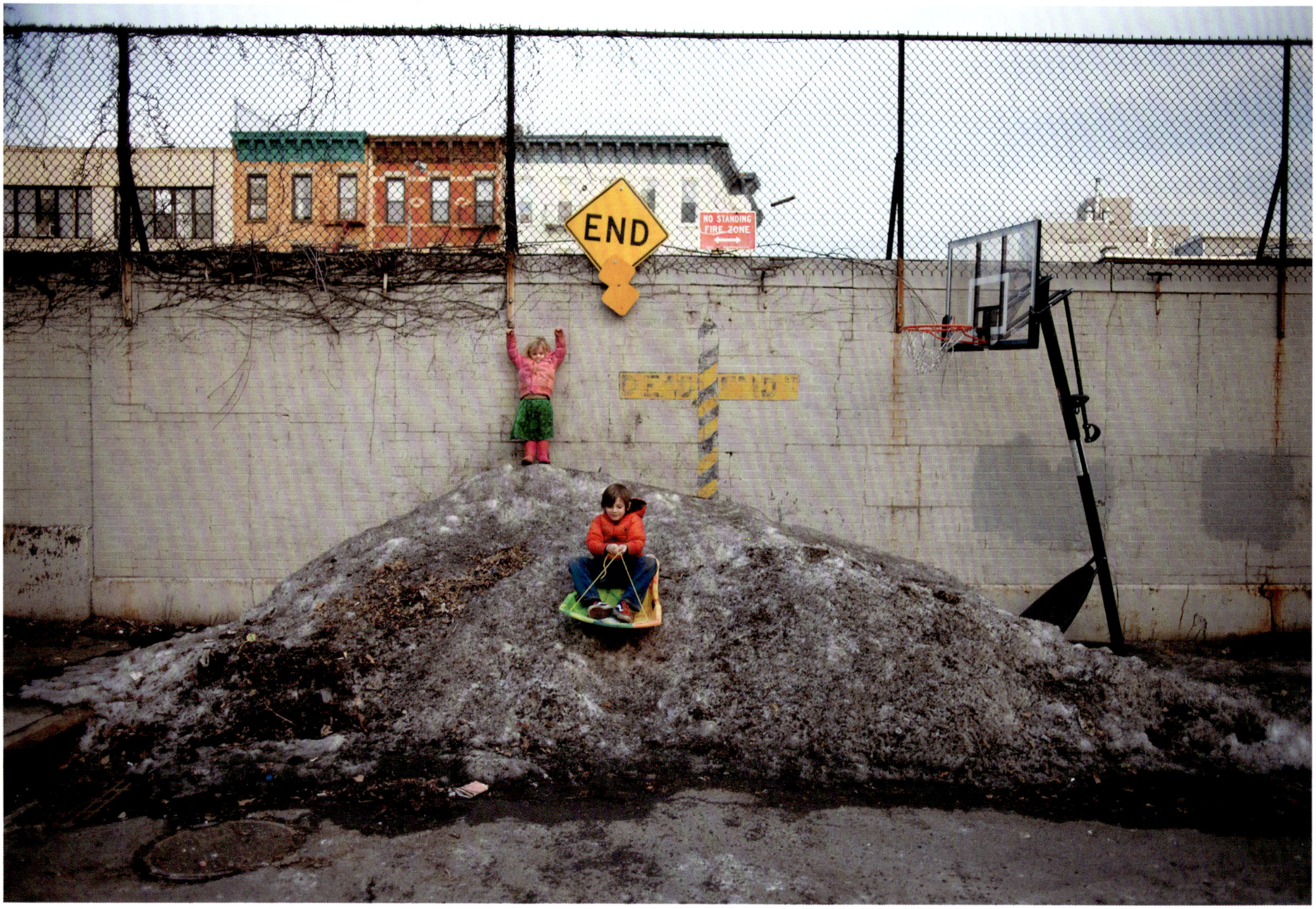
END
NO STANDING
FIRE ZONE

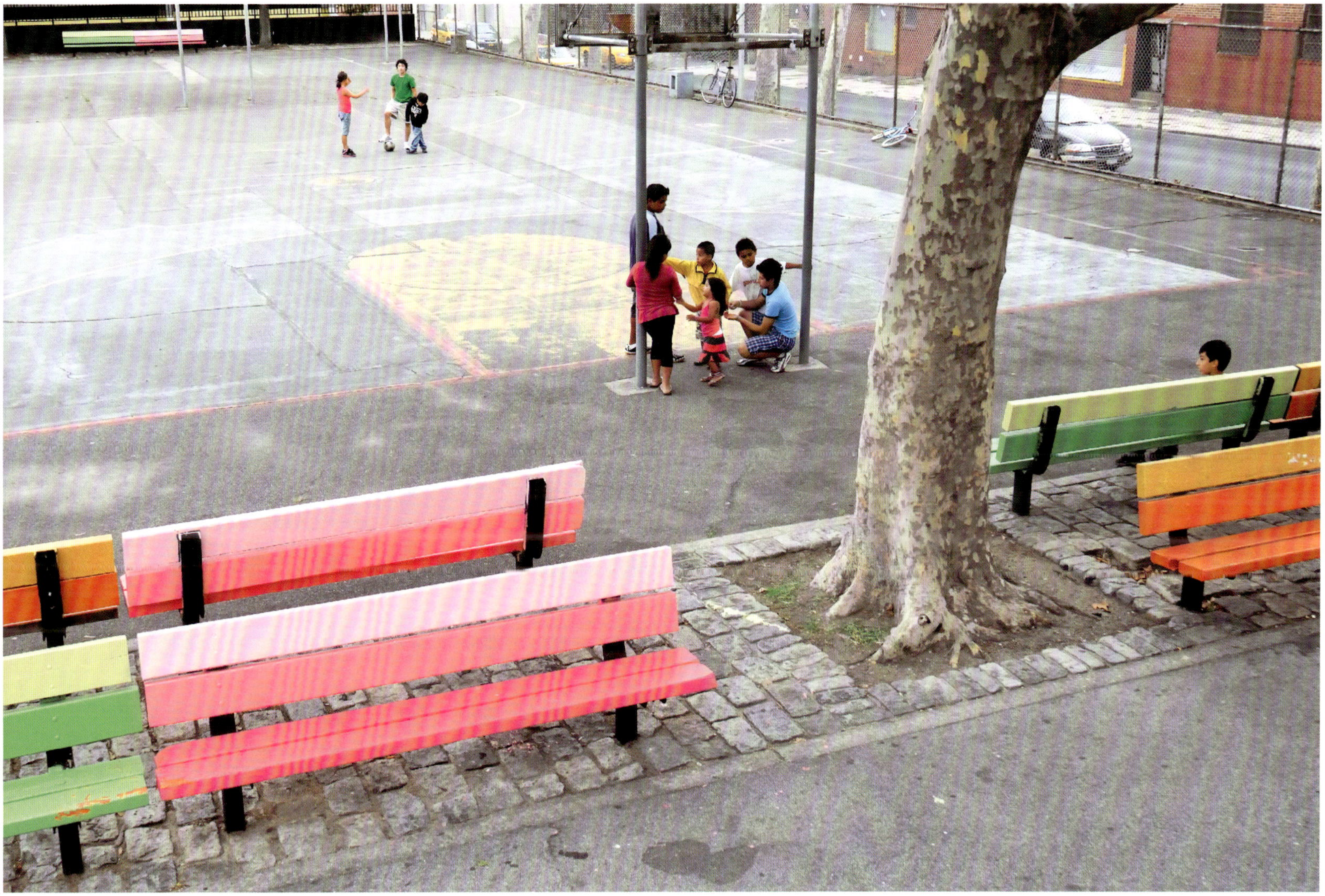

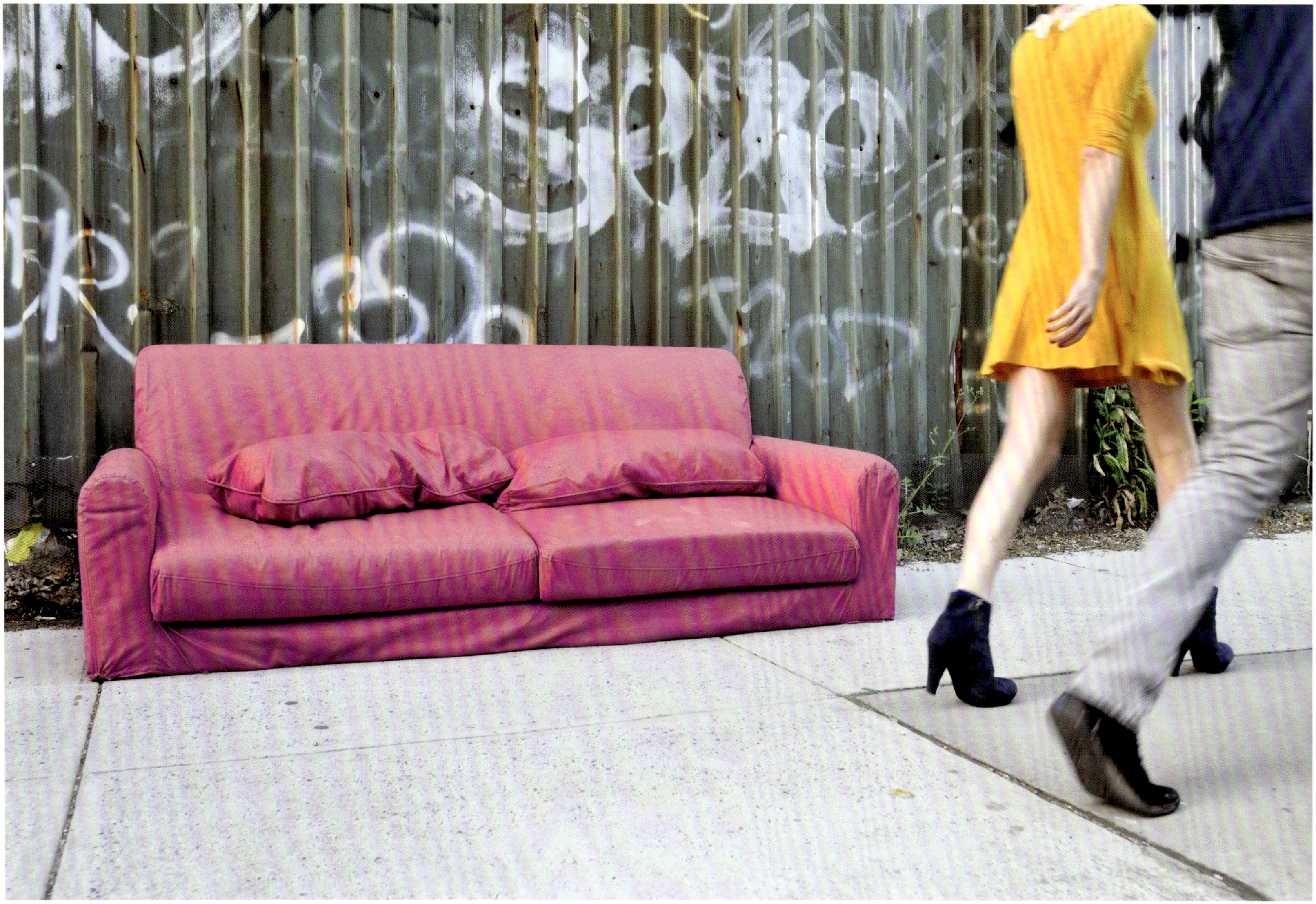

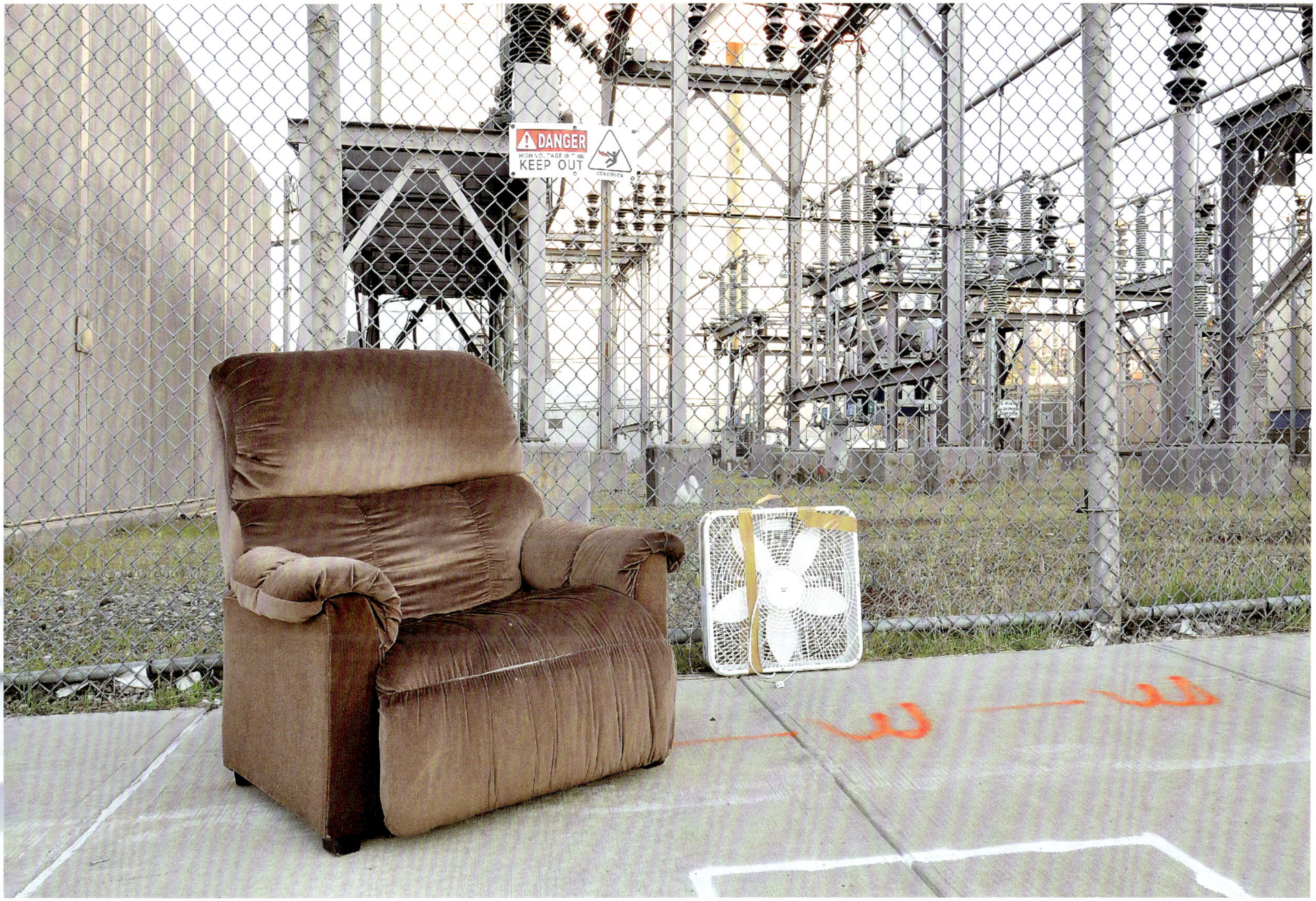
DANGER
KEEP OUT

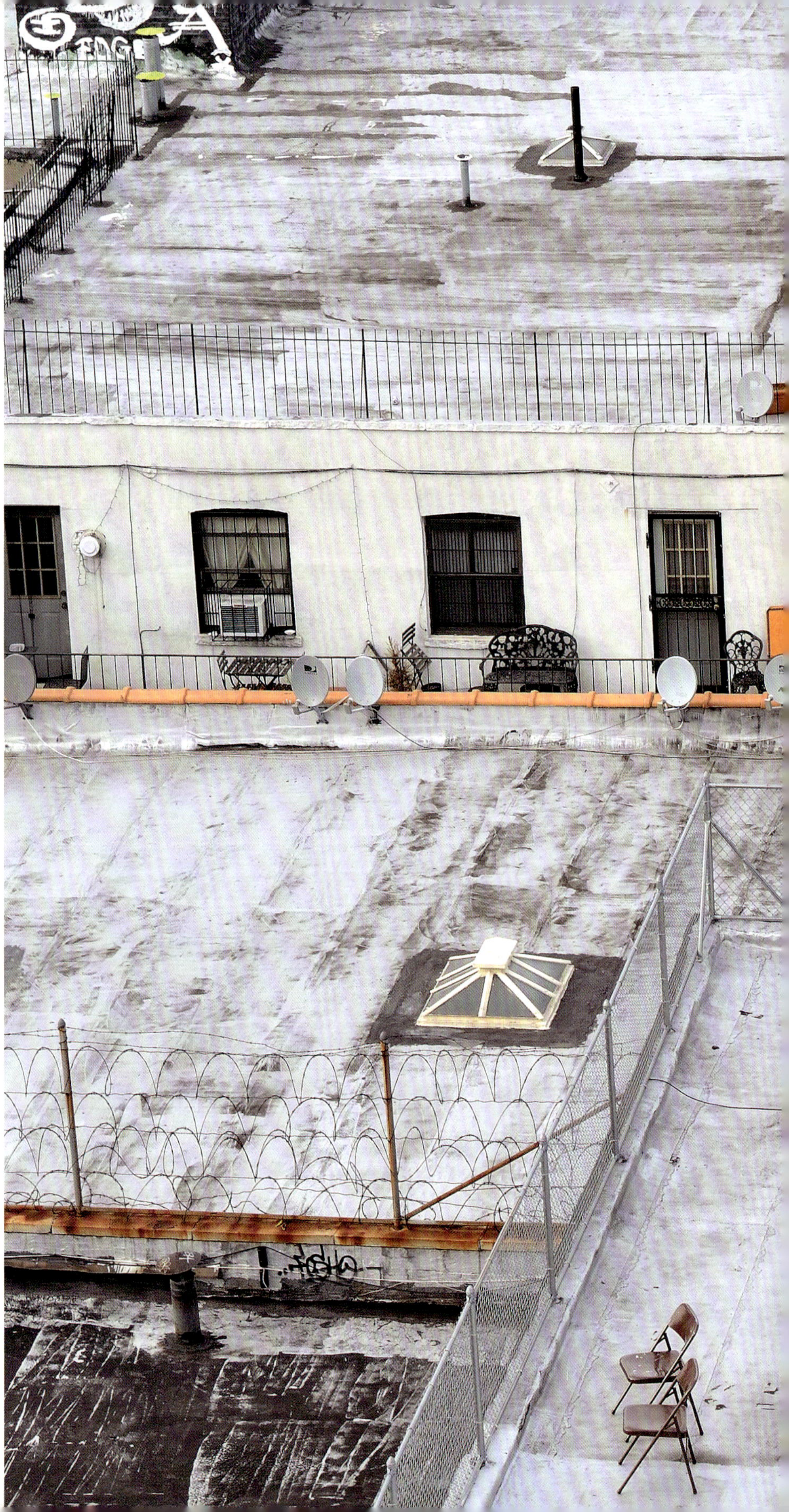

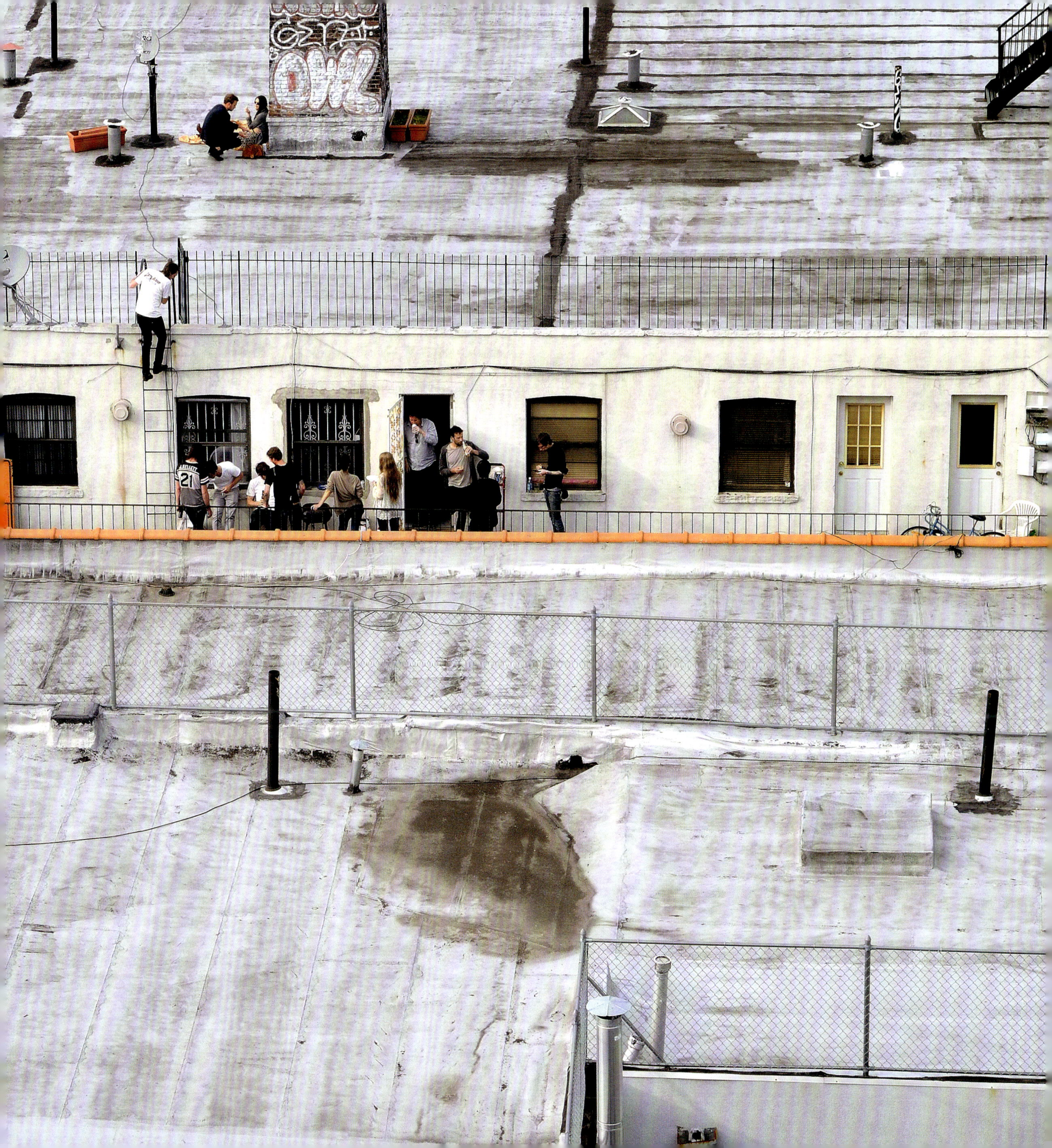

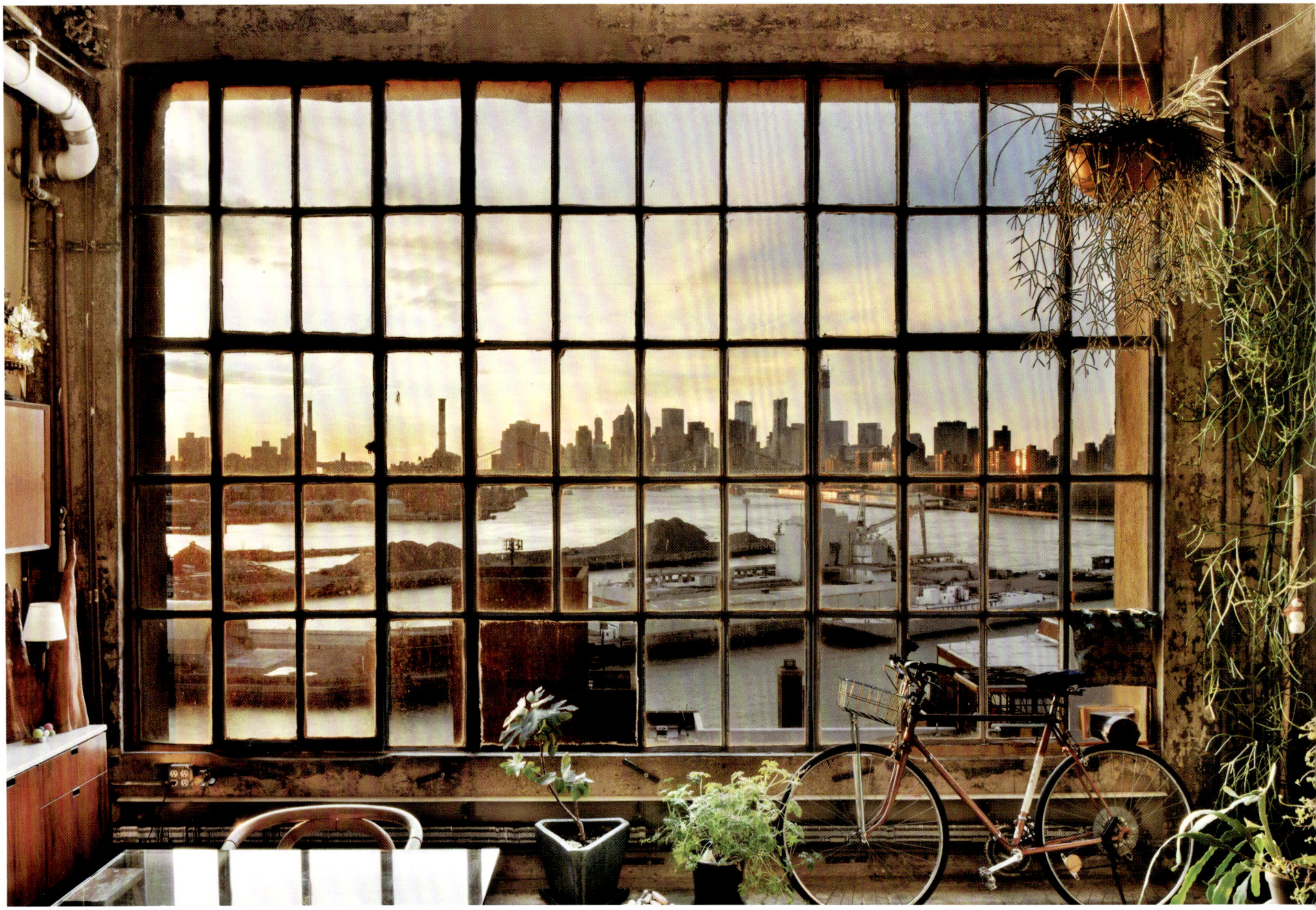

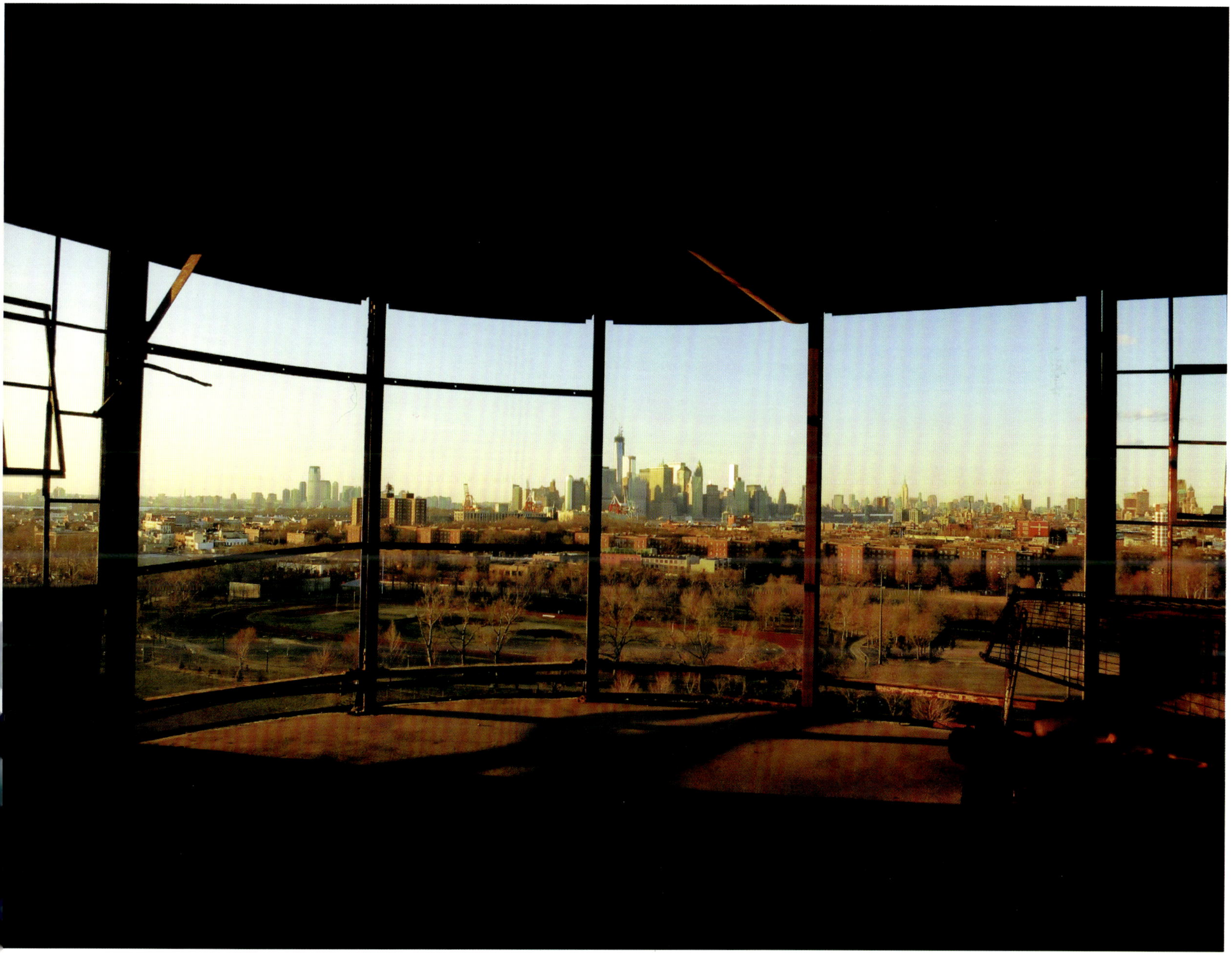

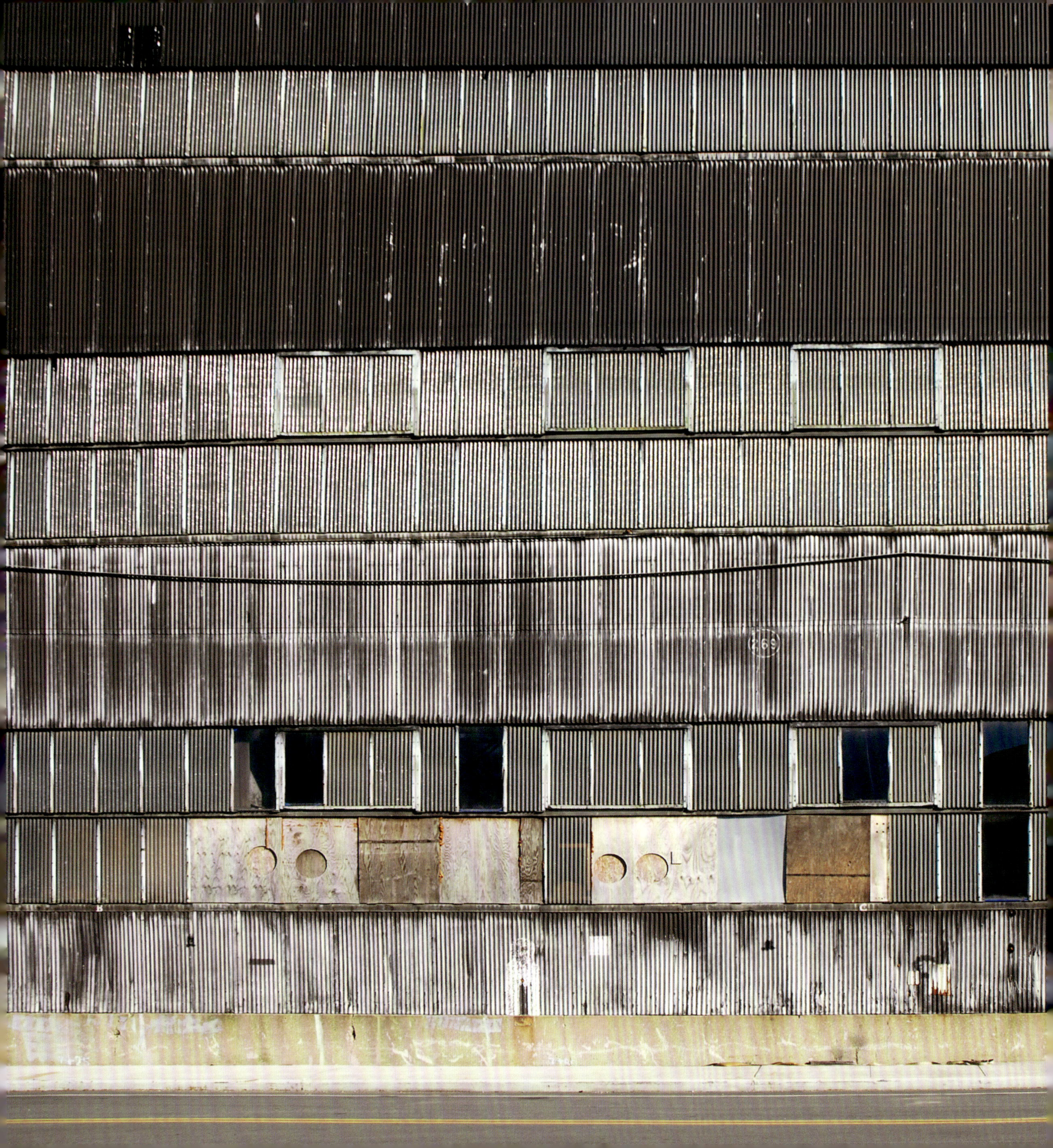
269

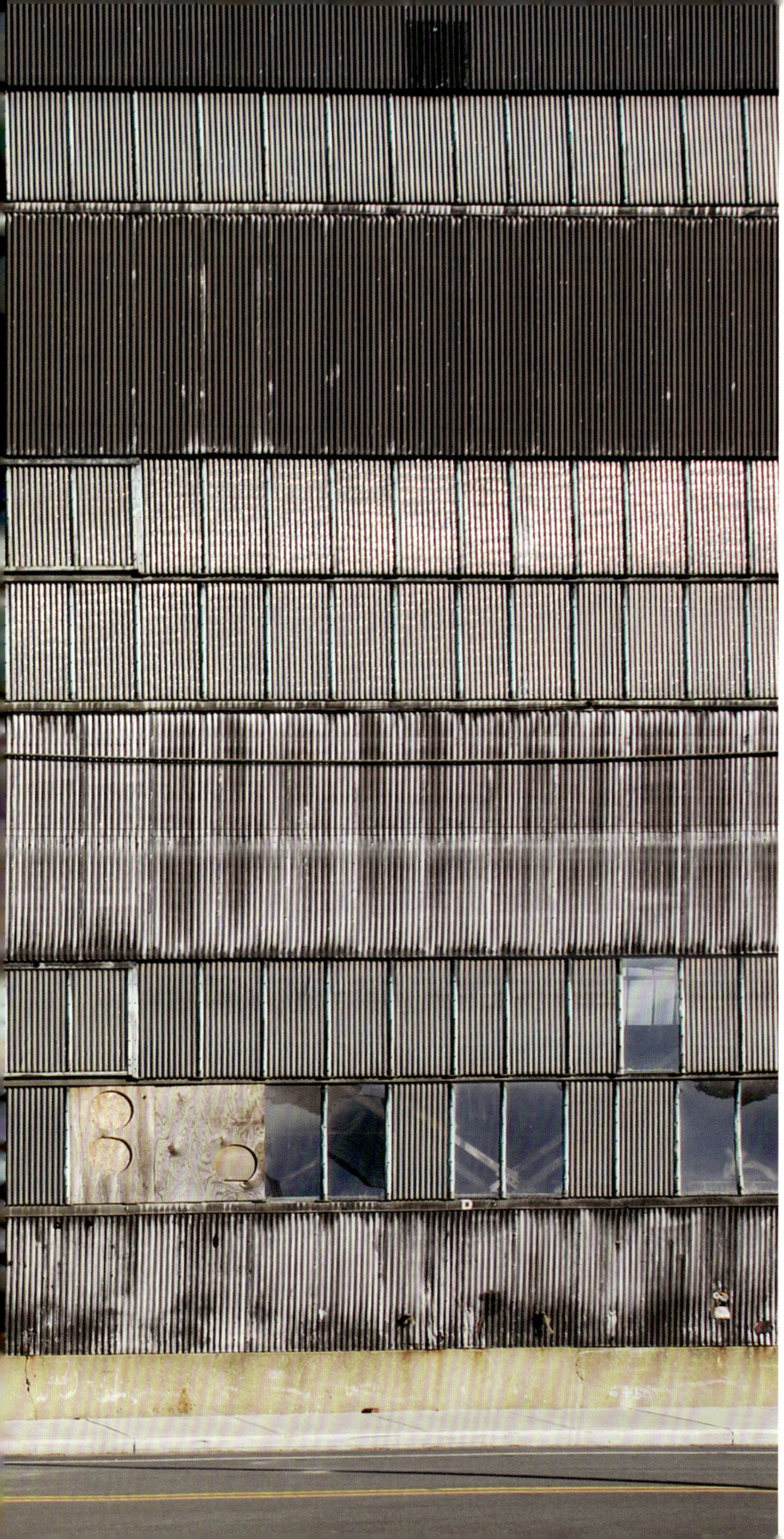

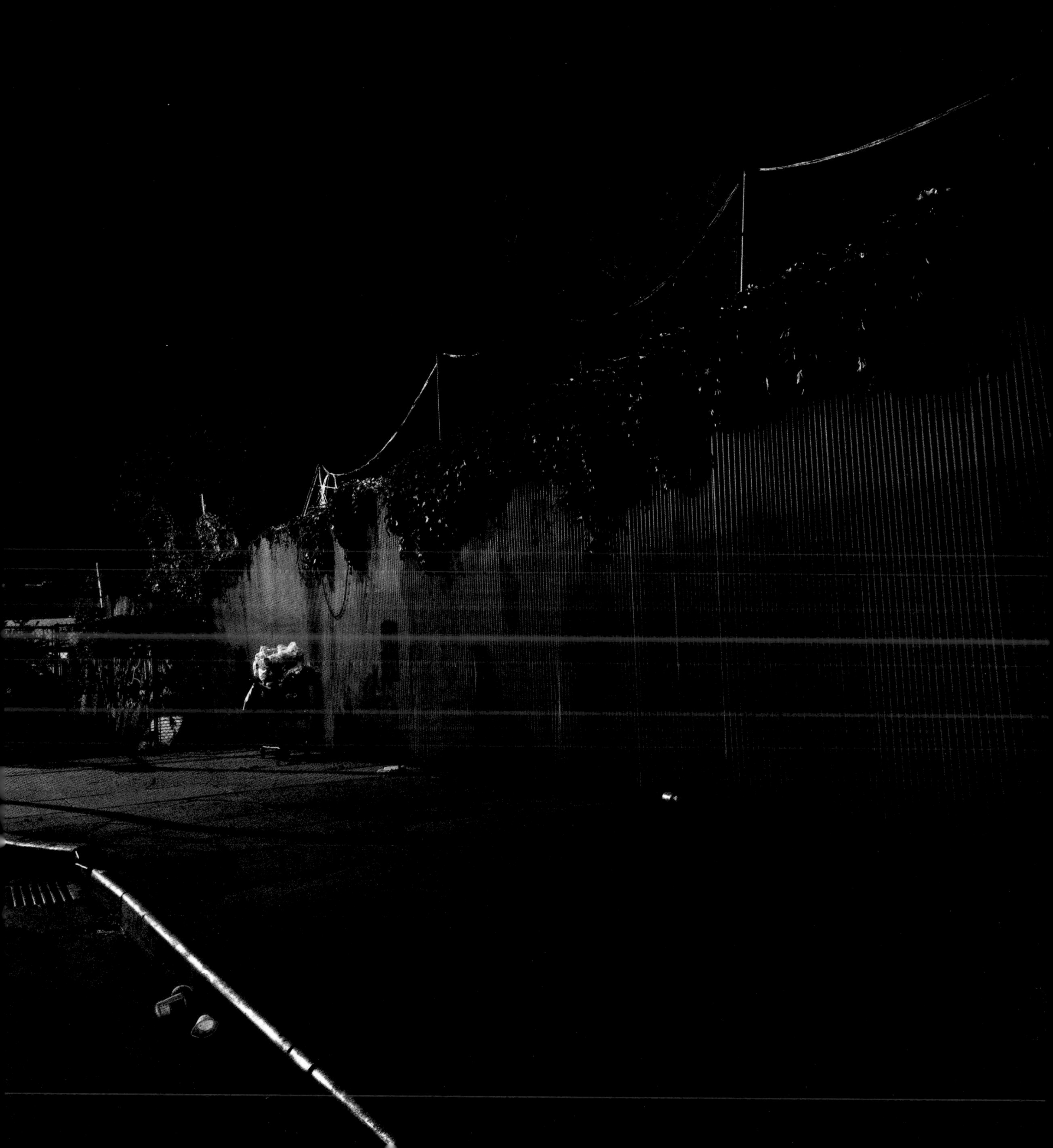

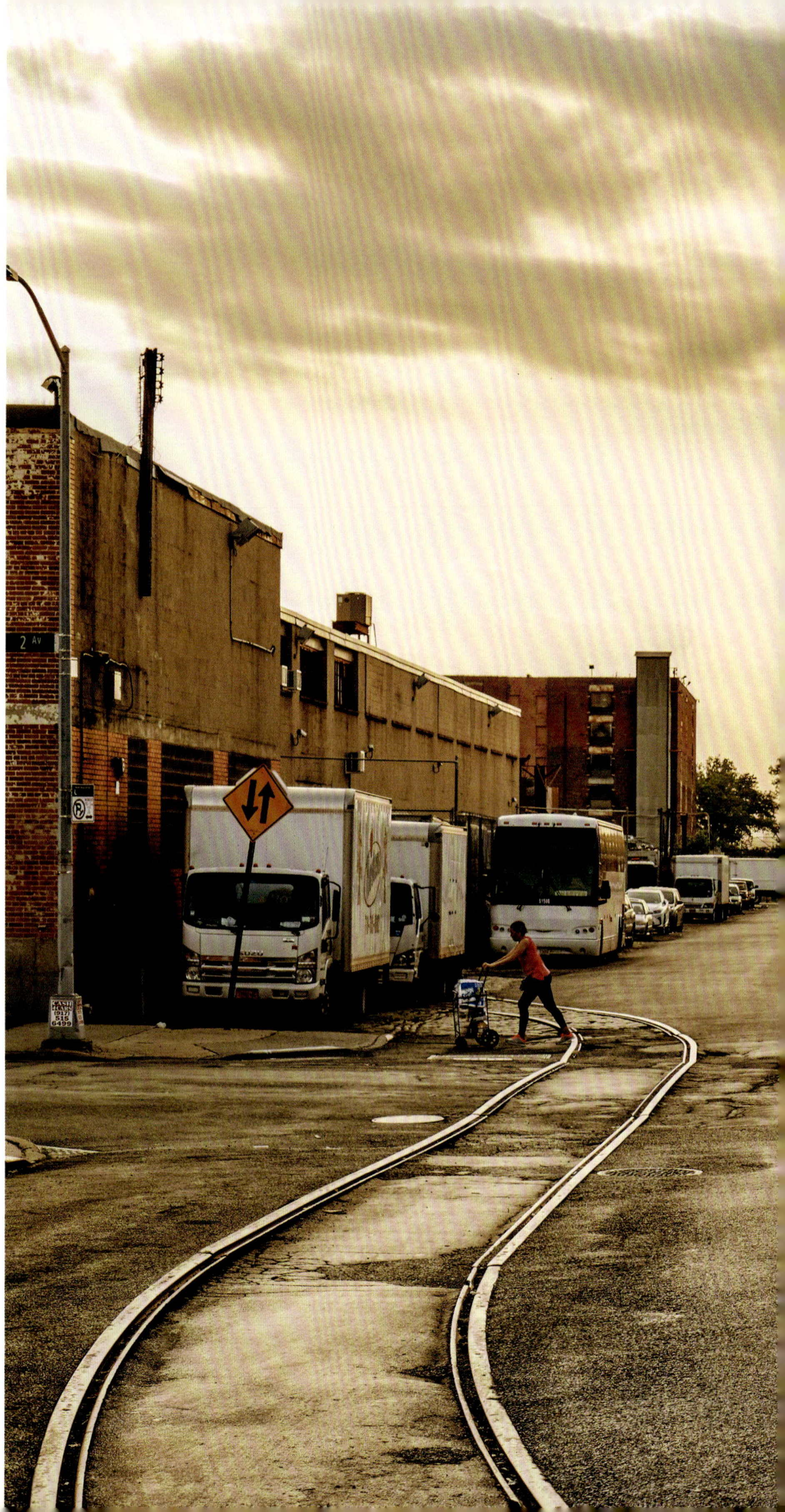
2 Av
CASH
CARS
(917)
515
6499

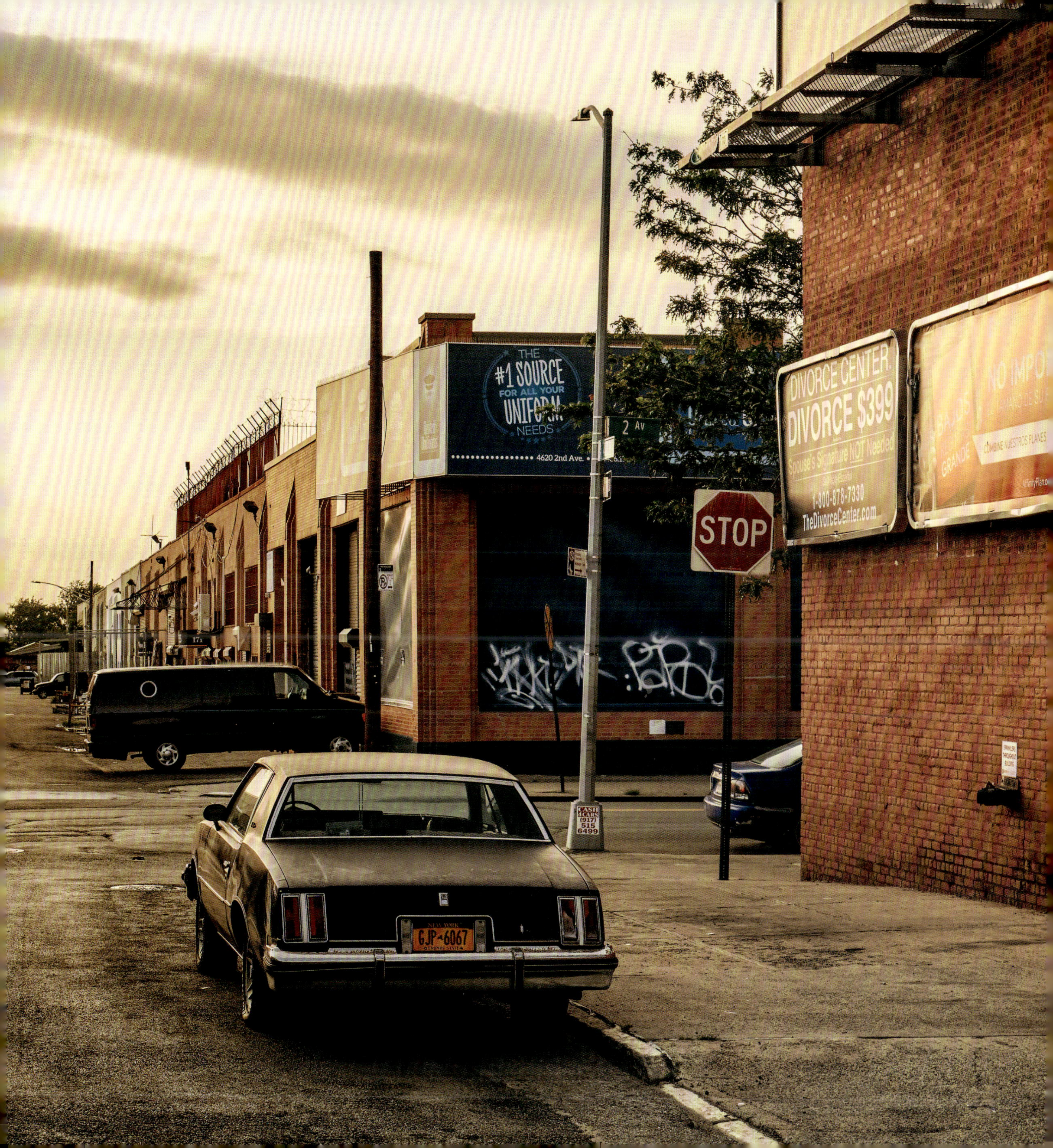

THE
#1 SOURCE
FOR ALL YOUR
NEEDS
4620 2nd Ave.
2 Av
STOP
DIVORCE CENTER
DIVORCE $399
Spouse's Signature NOT Needed
1-800-878-7330
TheDivorceCenter.com
CASH 4 CARS
(917) 515 6499
NEW YORK
GJP 6067
EMPIRE STATE
COMBINE NUESTROS PLANES

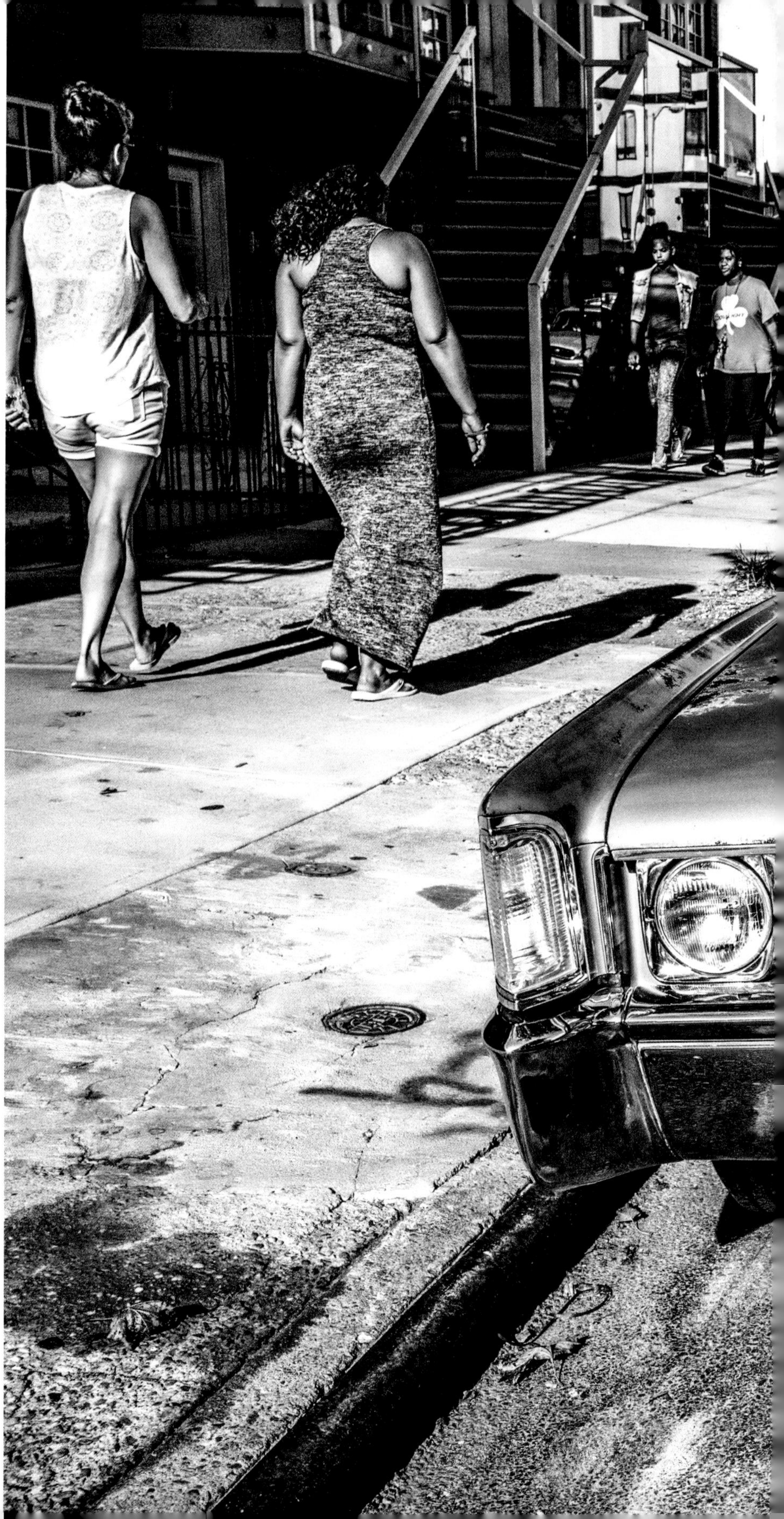

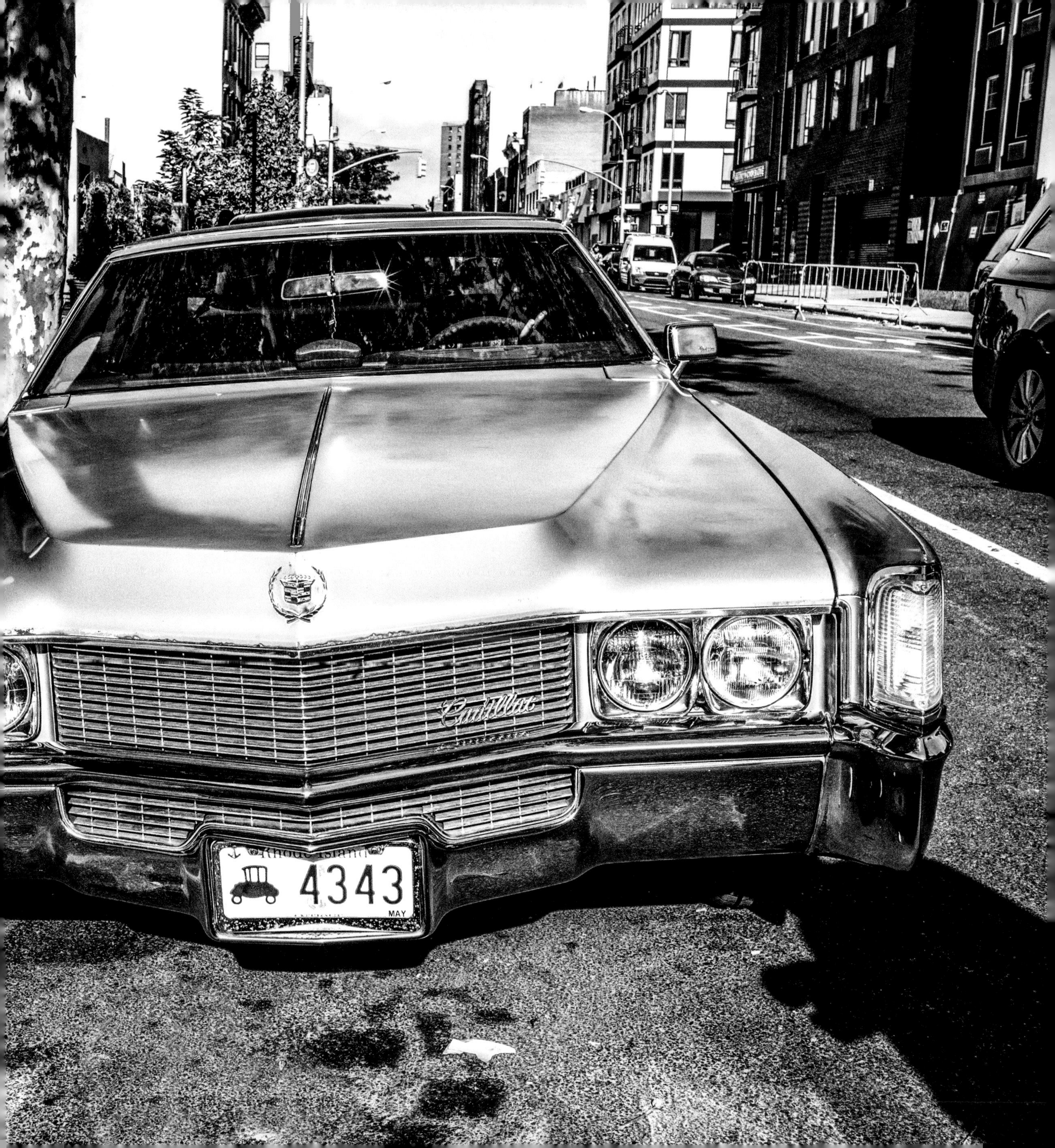
Cadillac
Rhode Island
4343
MAY

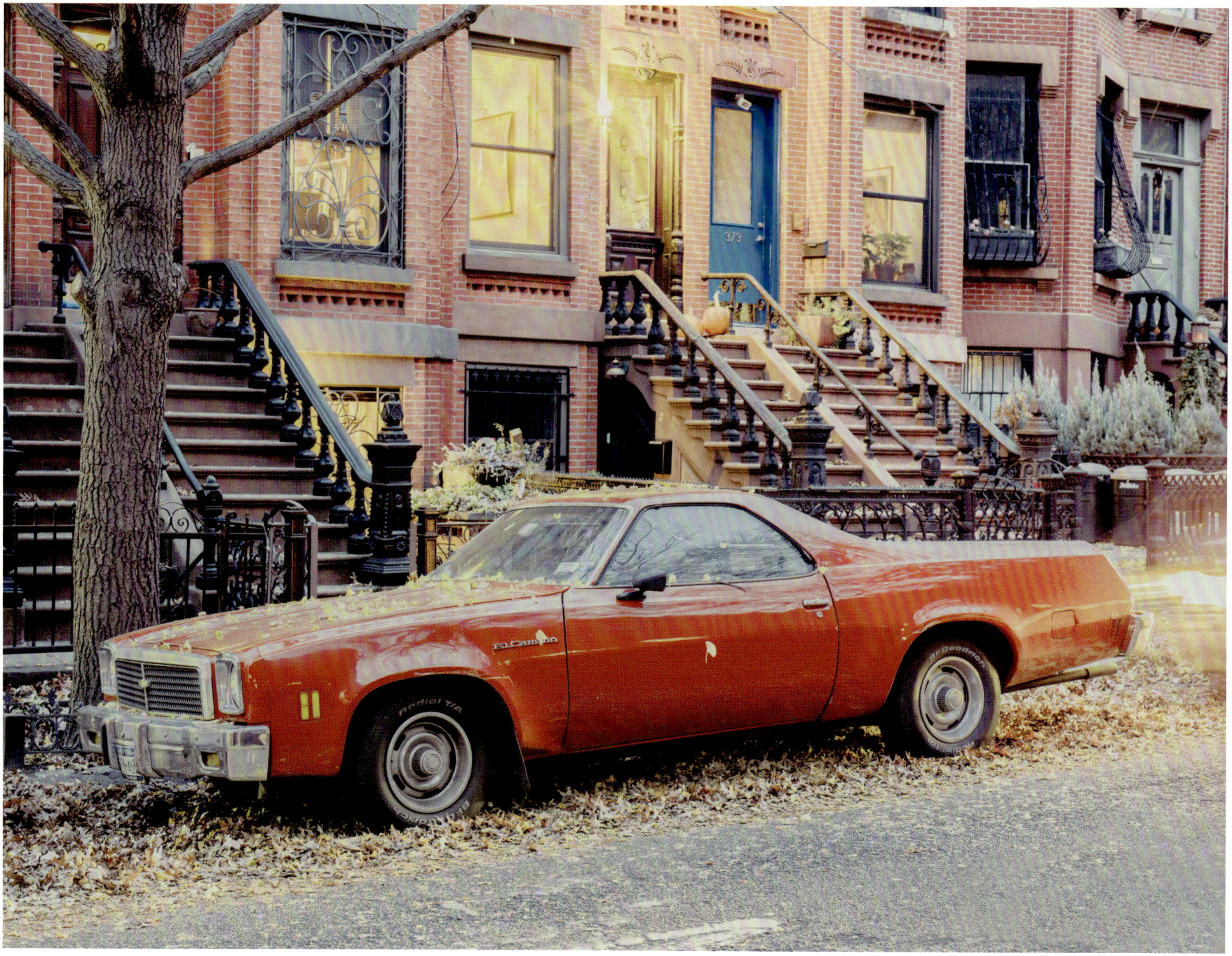
373
El Camino

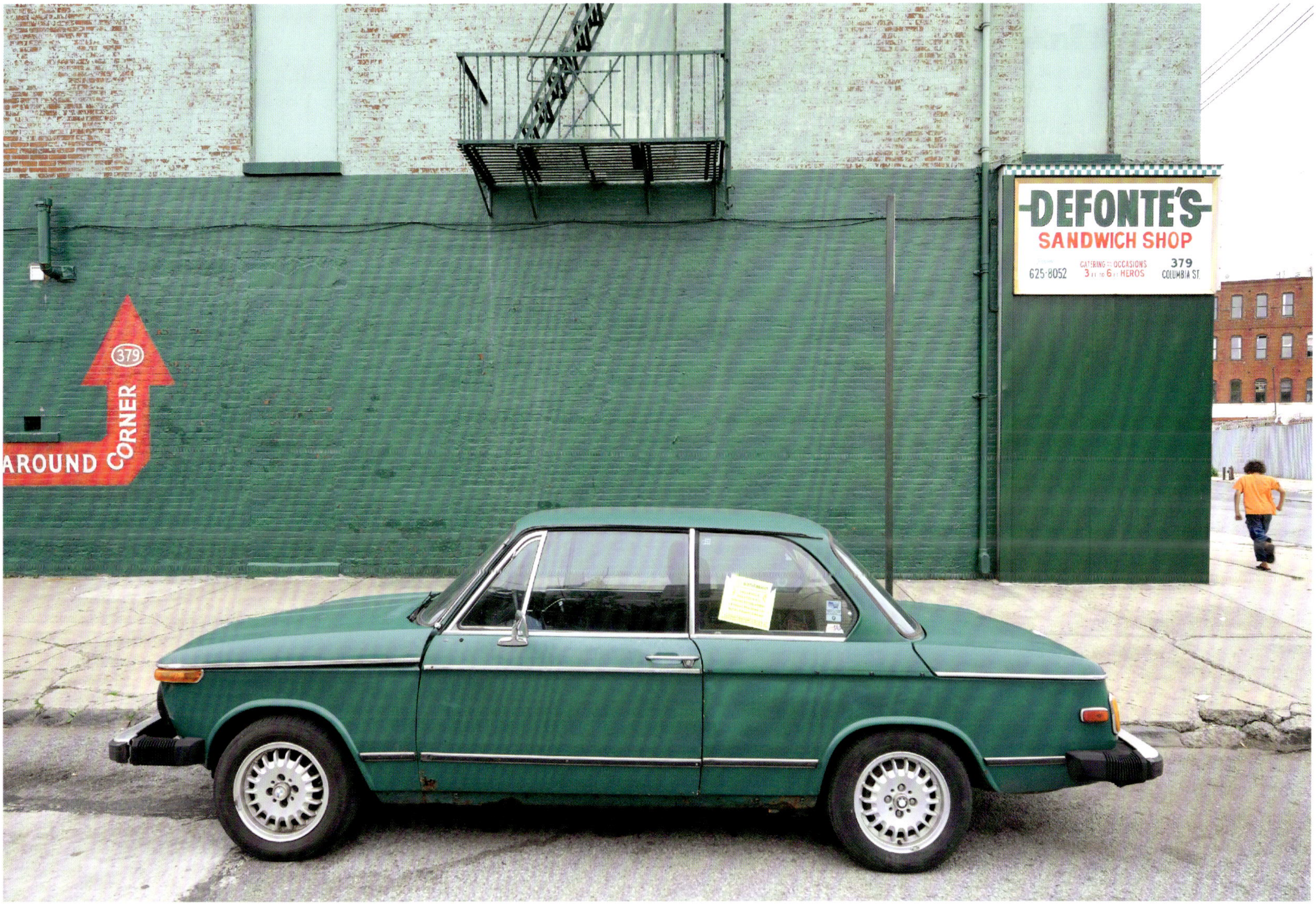
379
AROUND CORNER
DEFONTE'S
SANDWICH SHOP
625-8052
379
COLUMBIA ST.

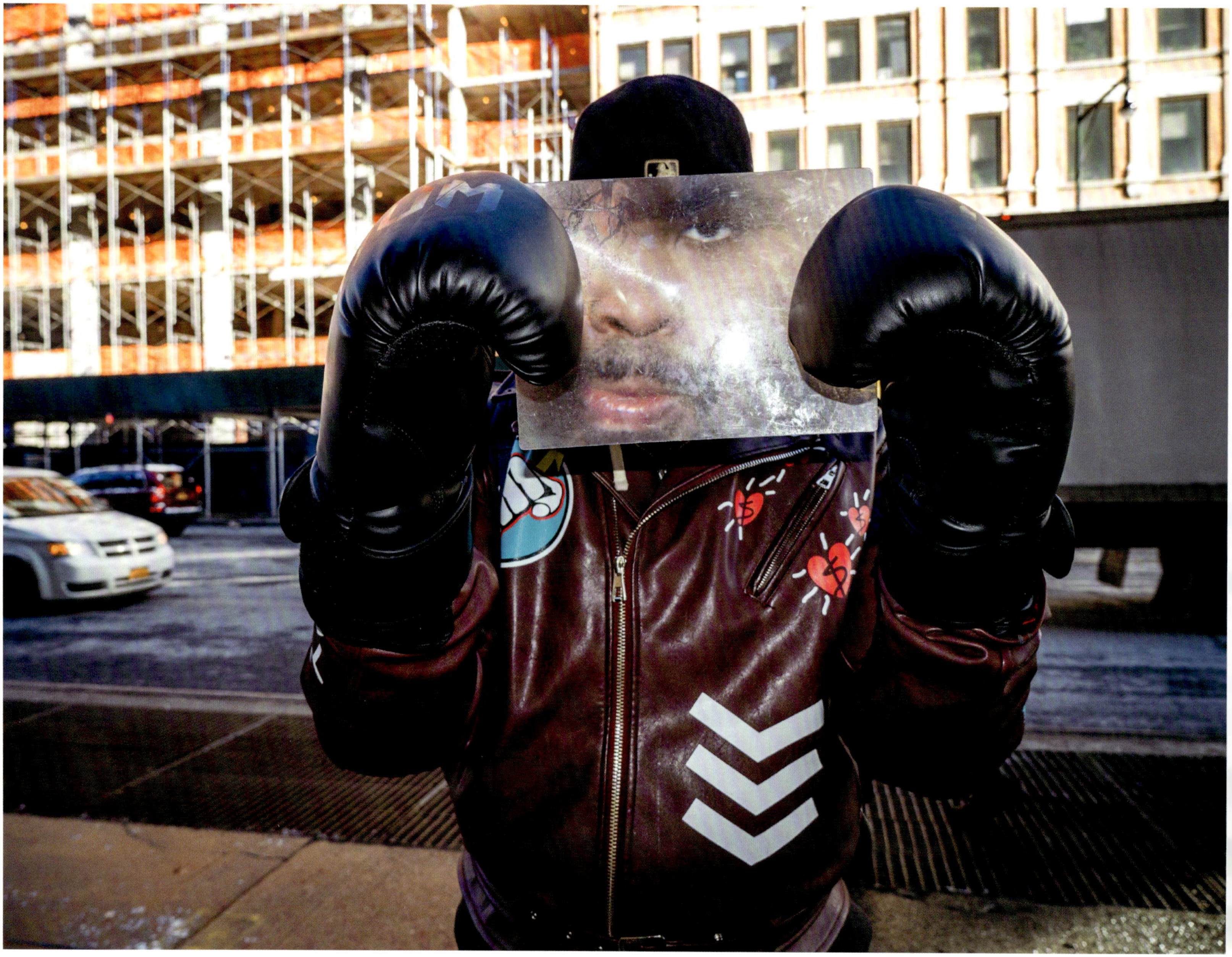

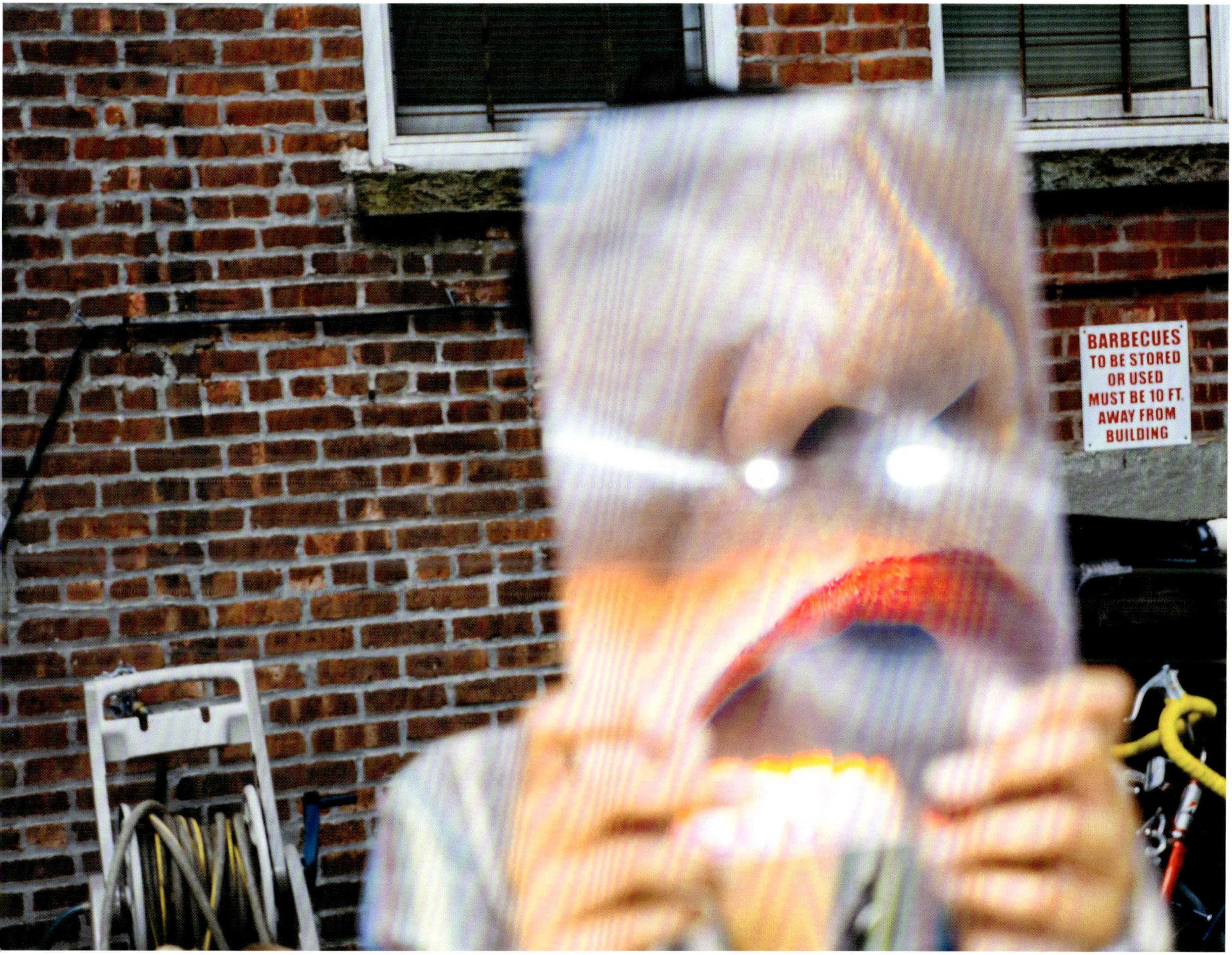
BARBECUES
TO BE STORED
OR USED
MUST BE 10 FT.
AWAY FROM
BUILDING

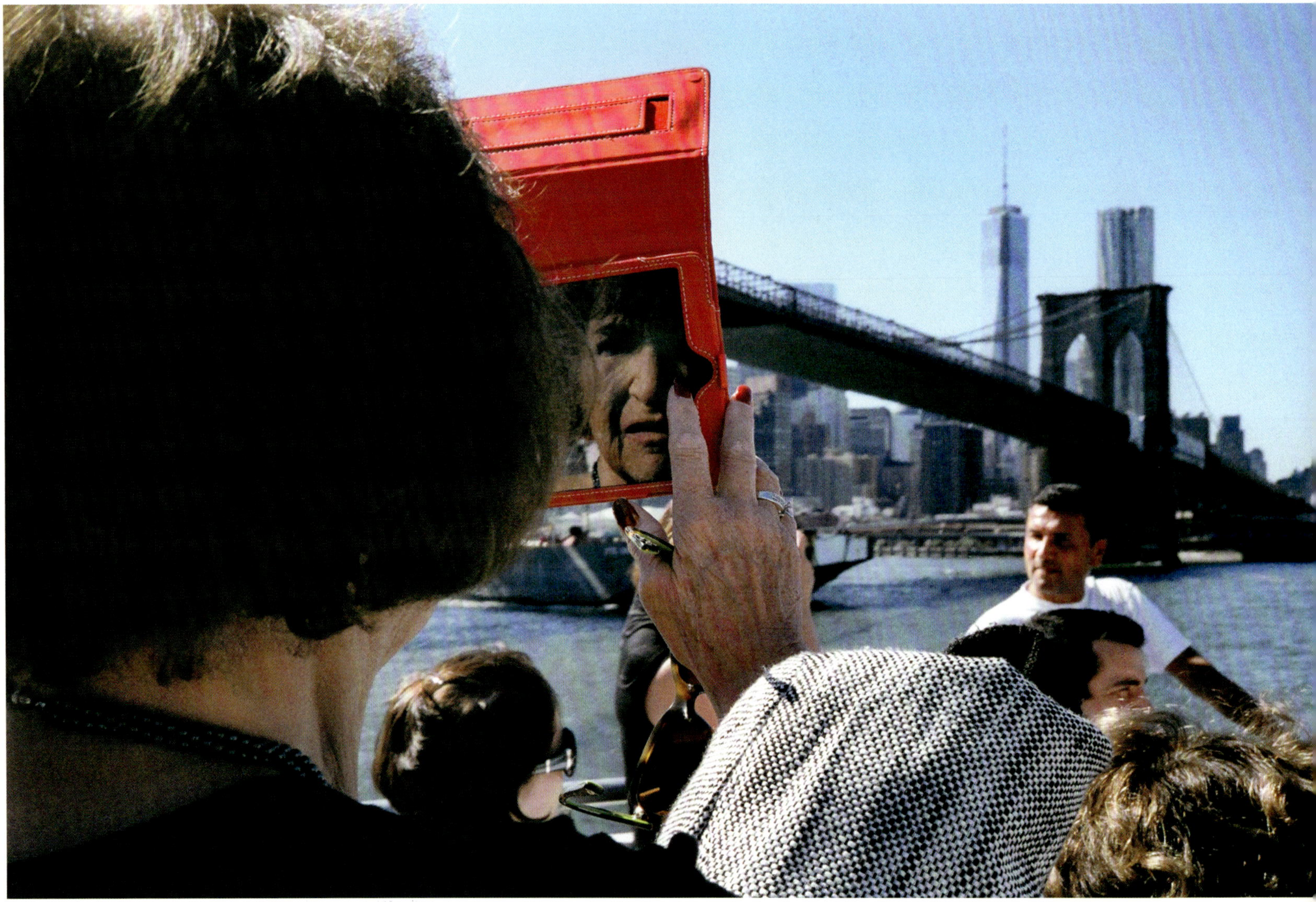

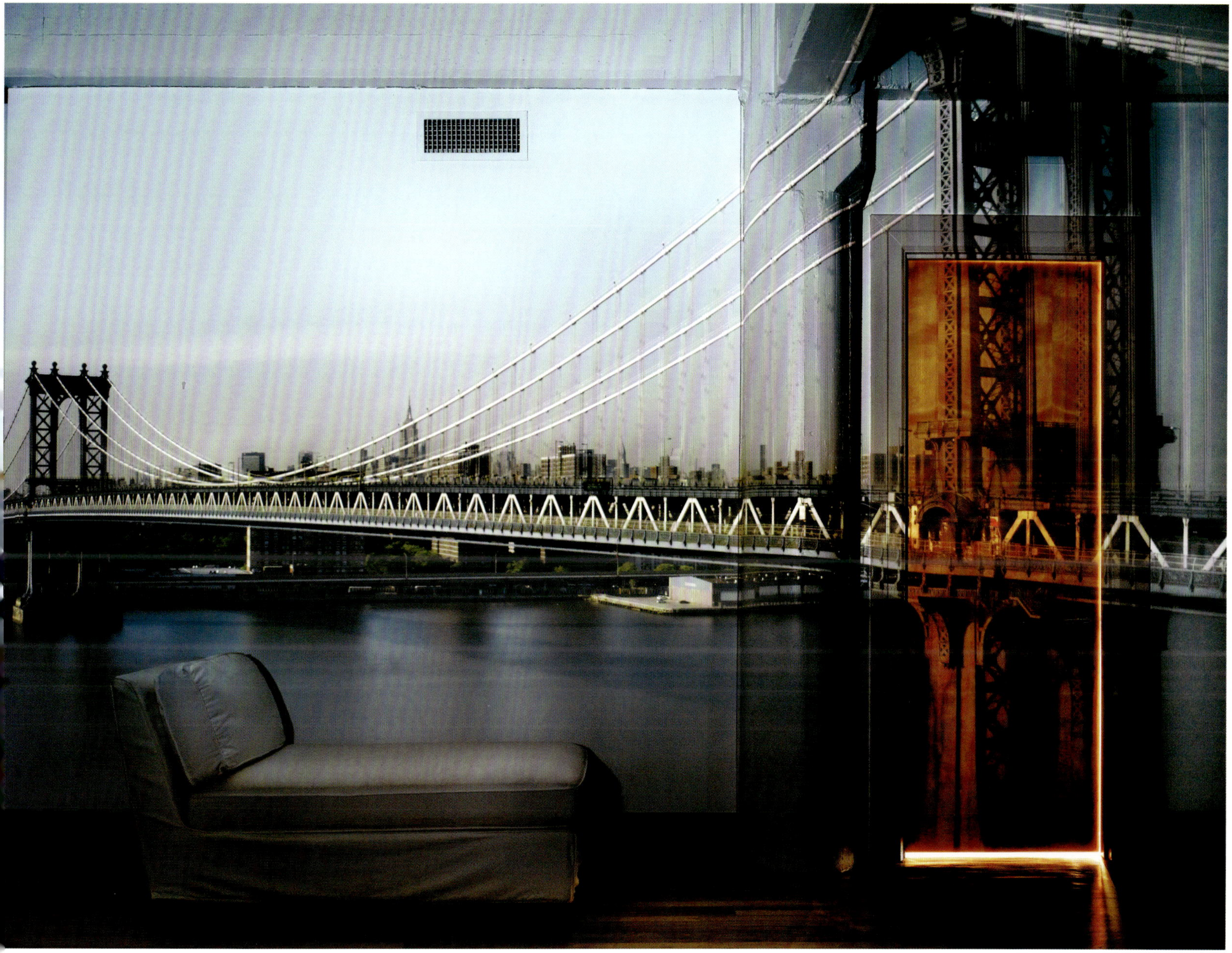

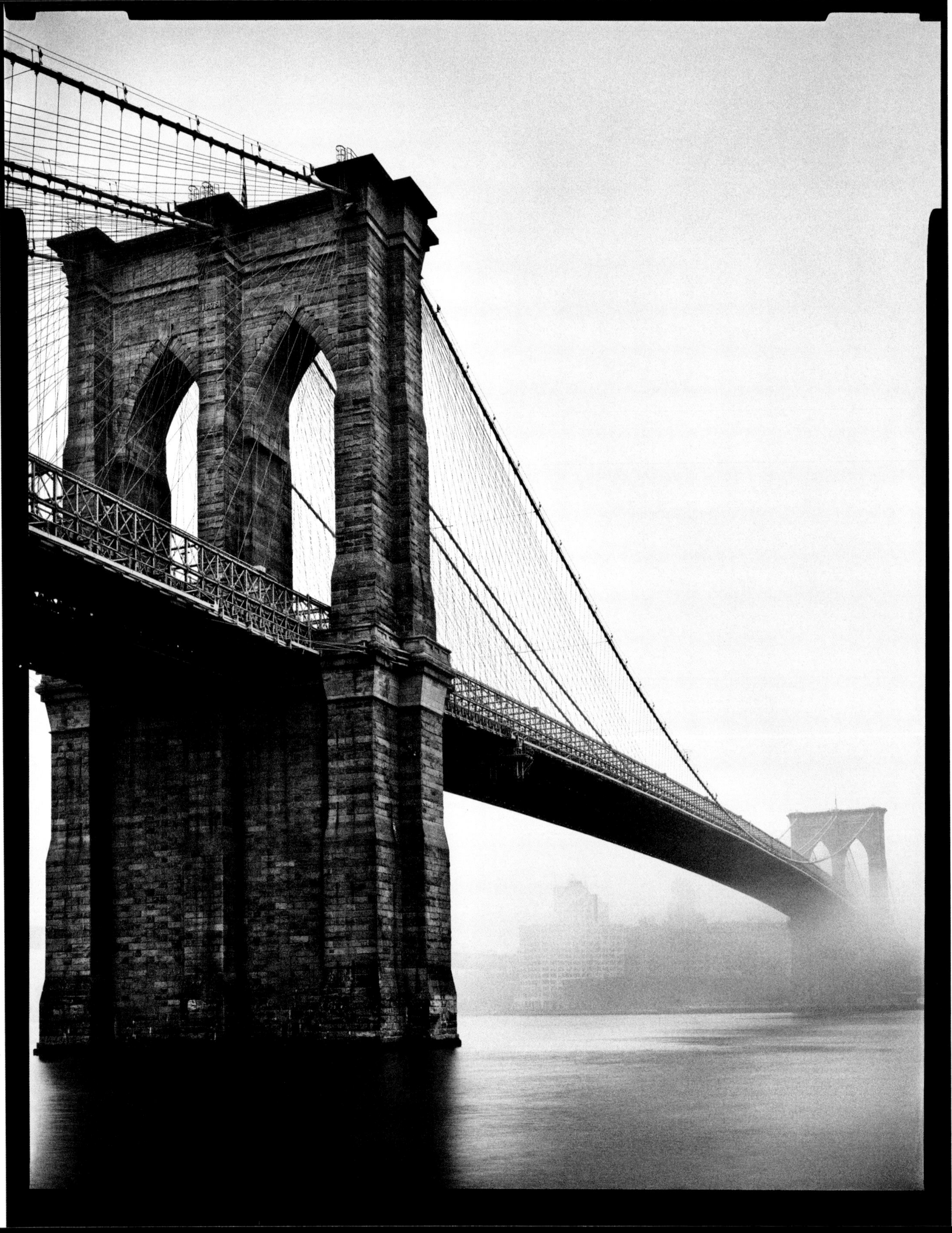

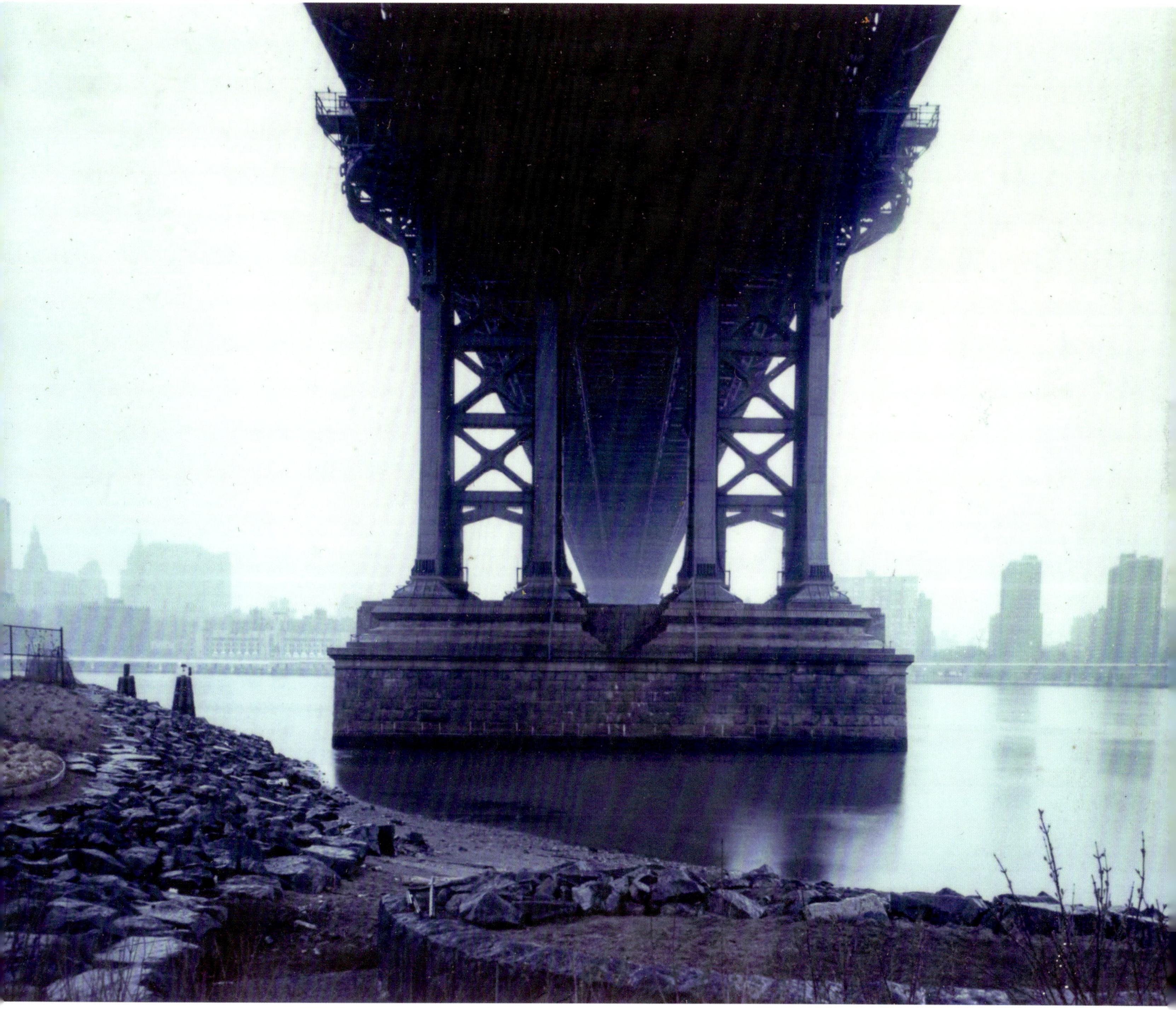

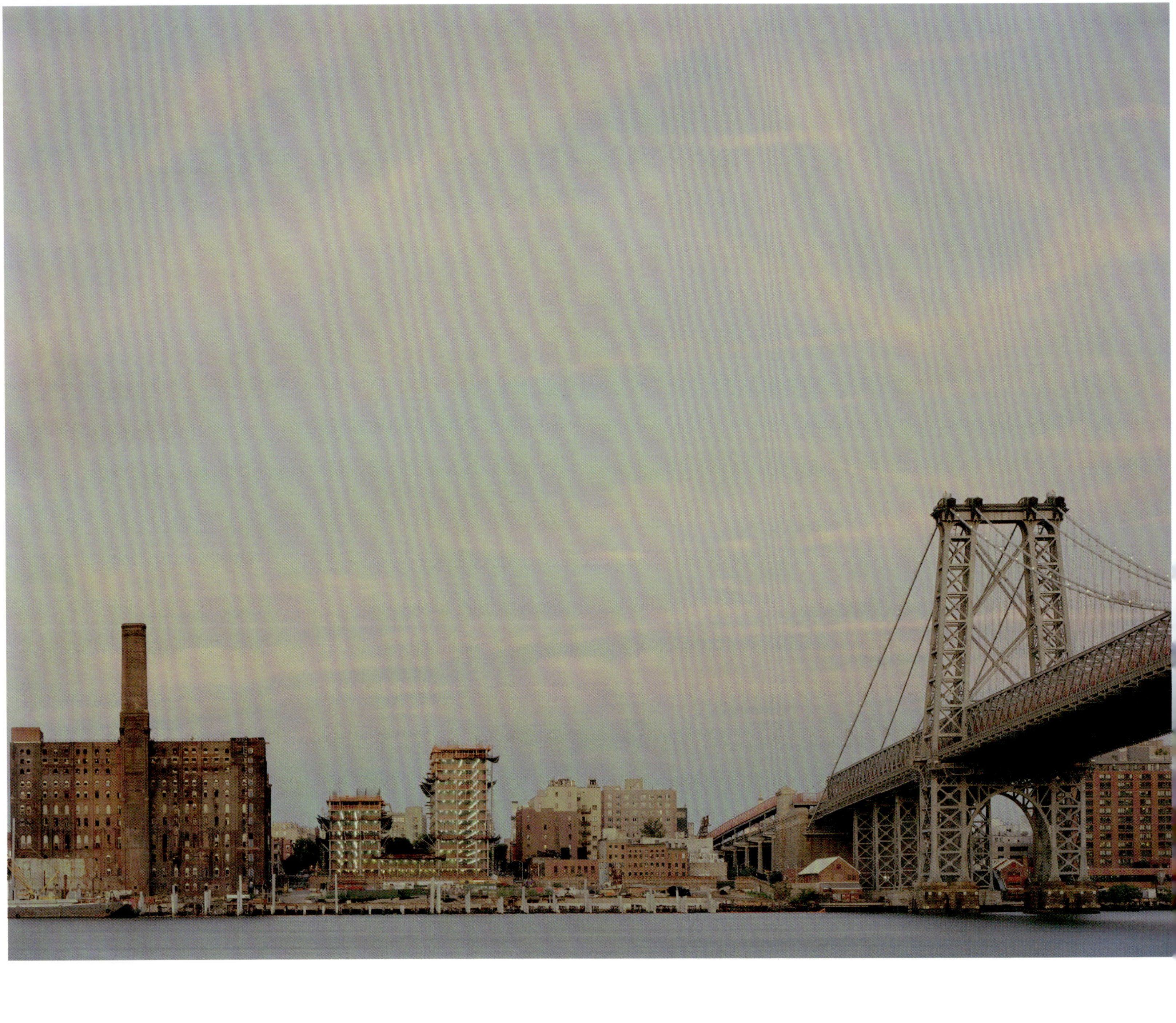

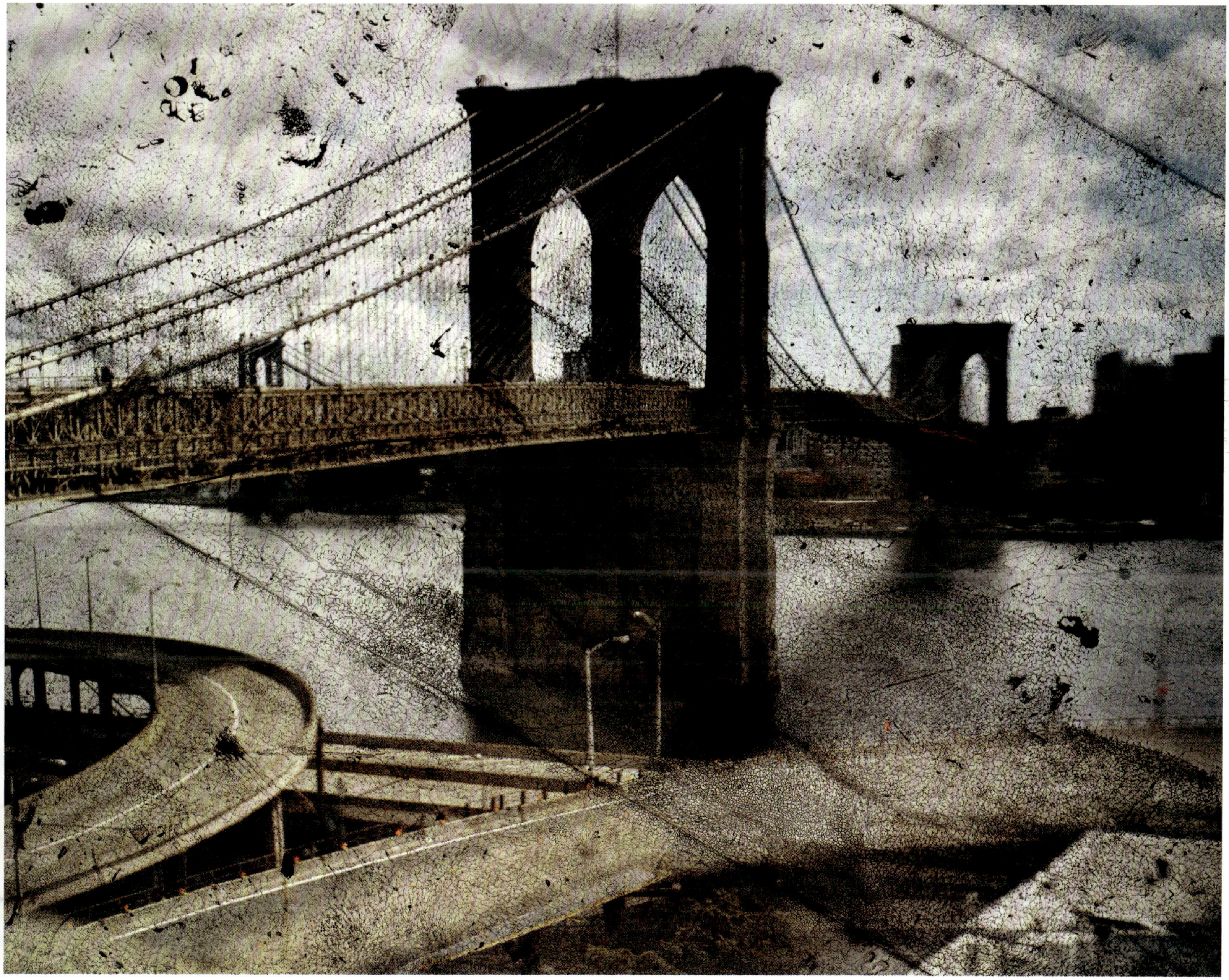

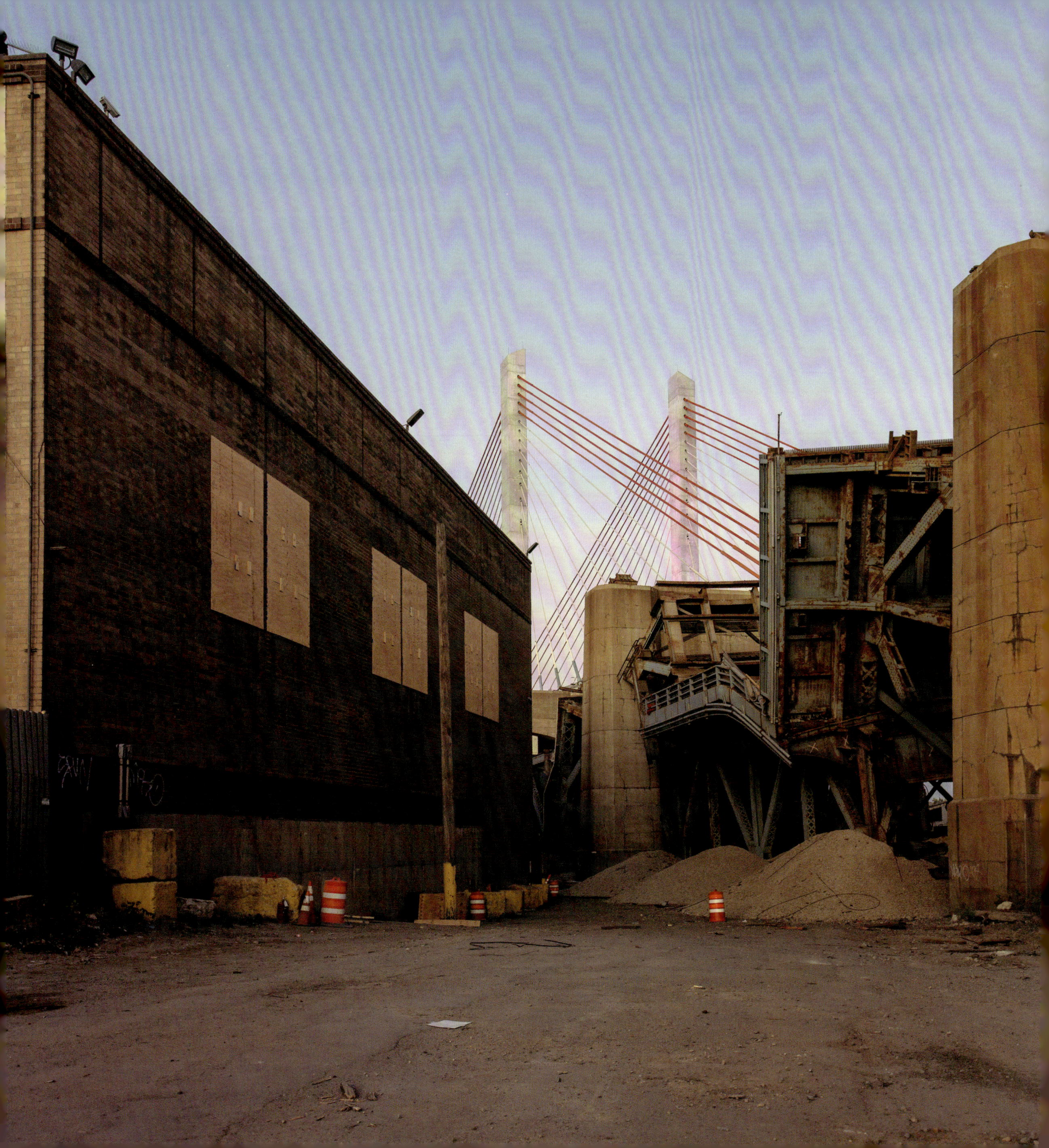

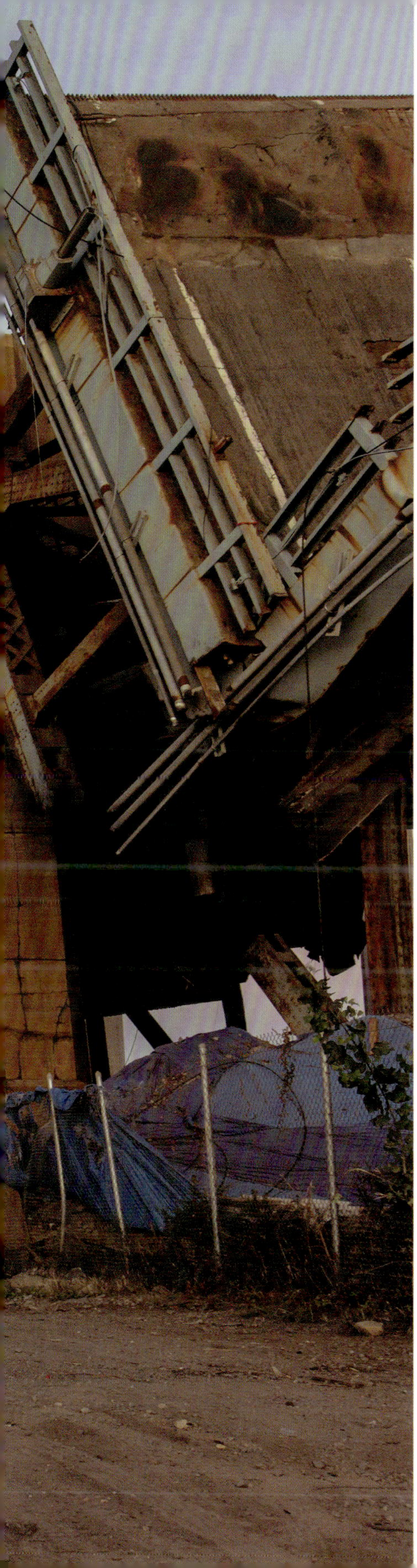

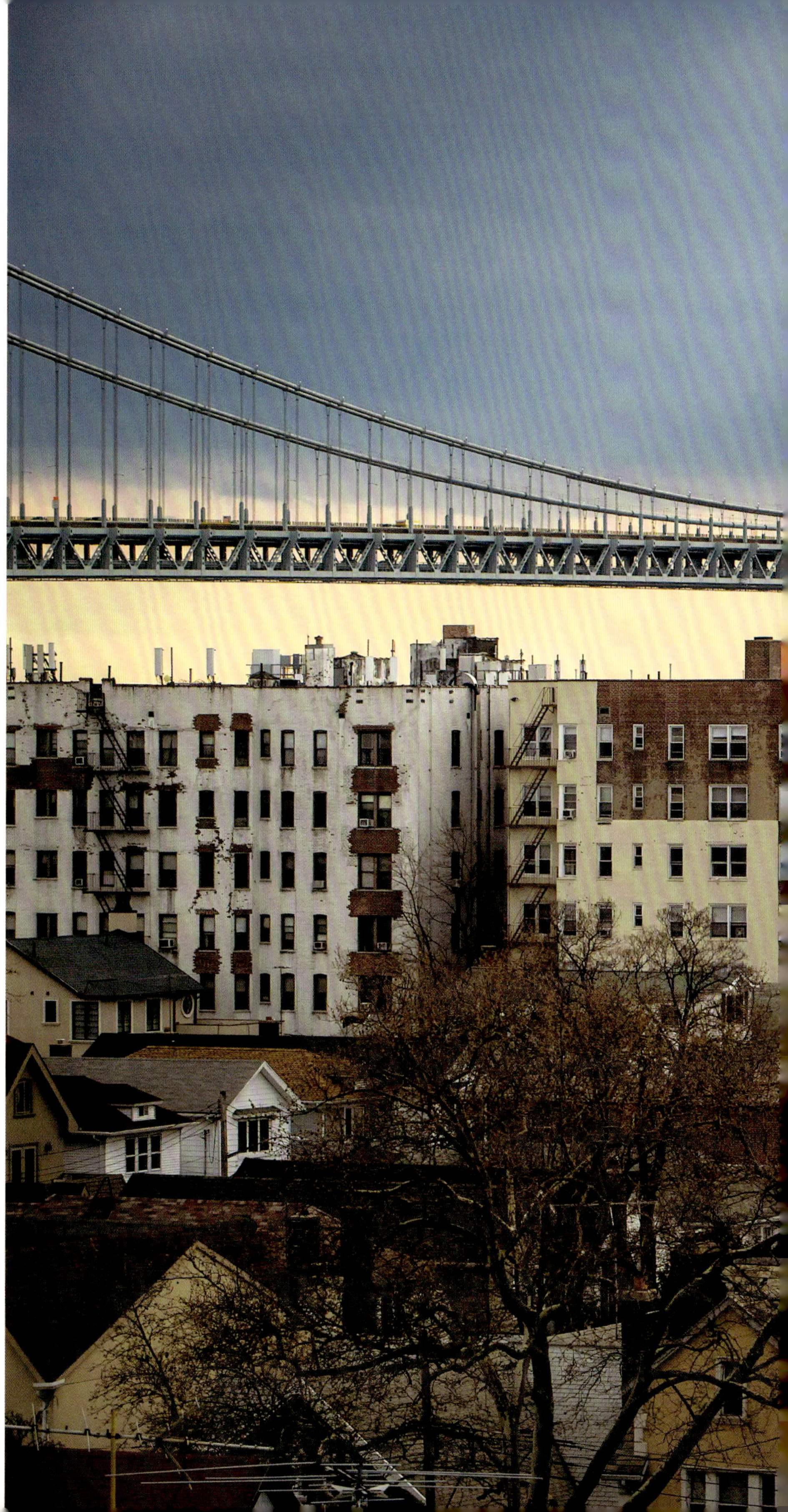

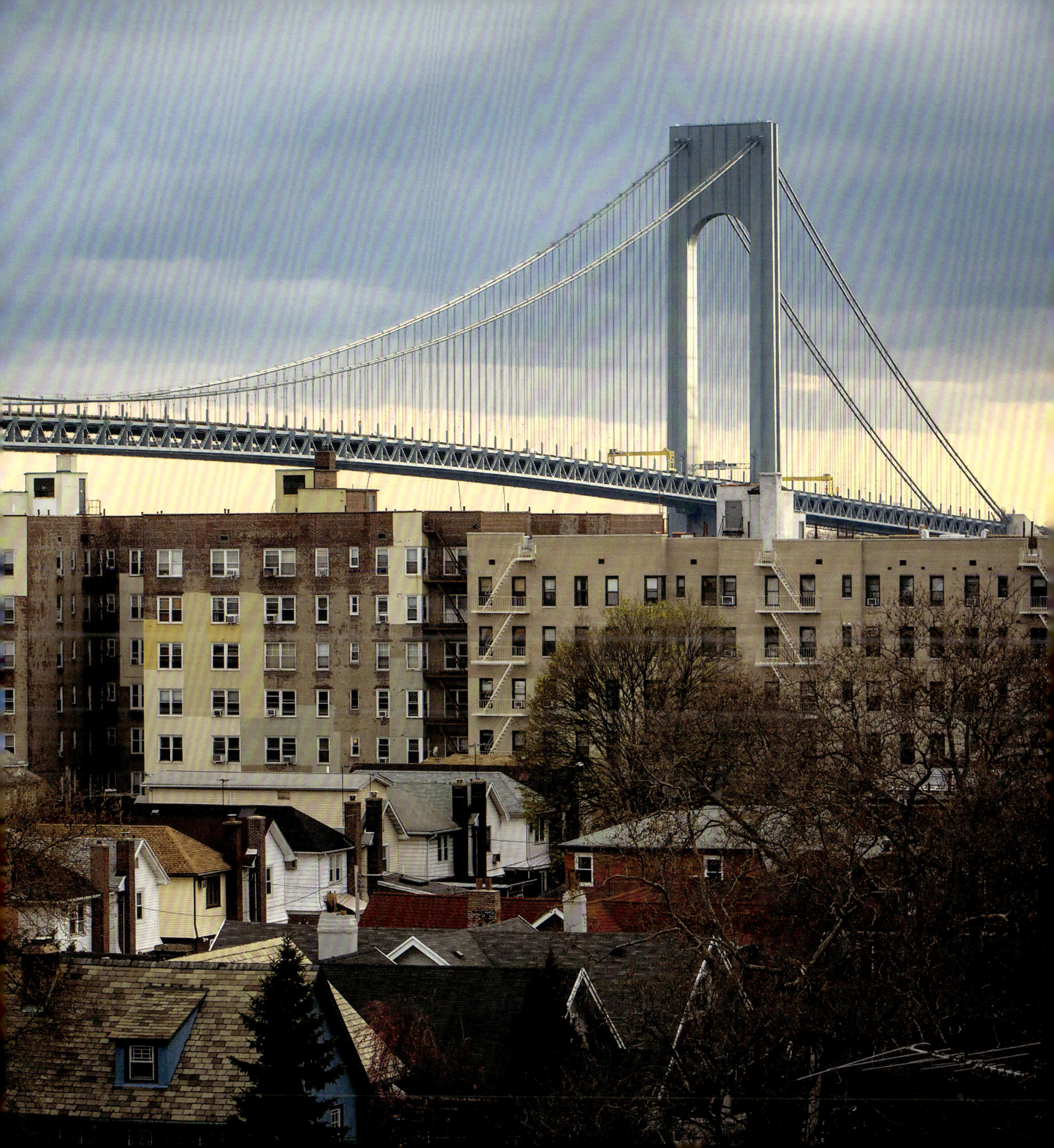

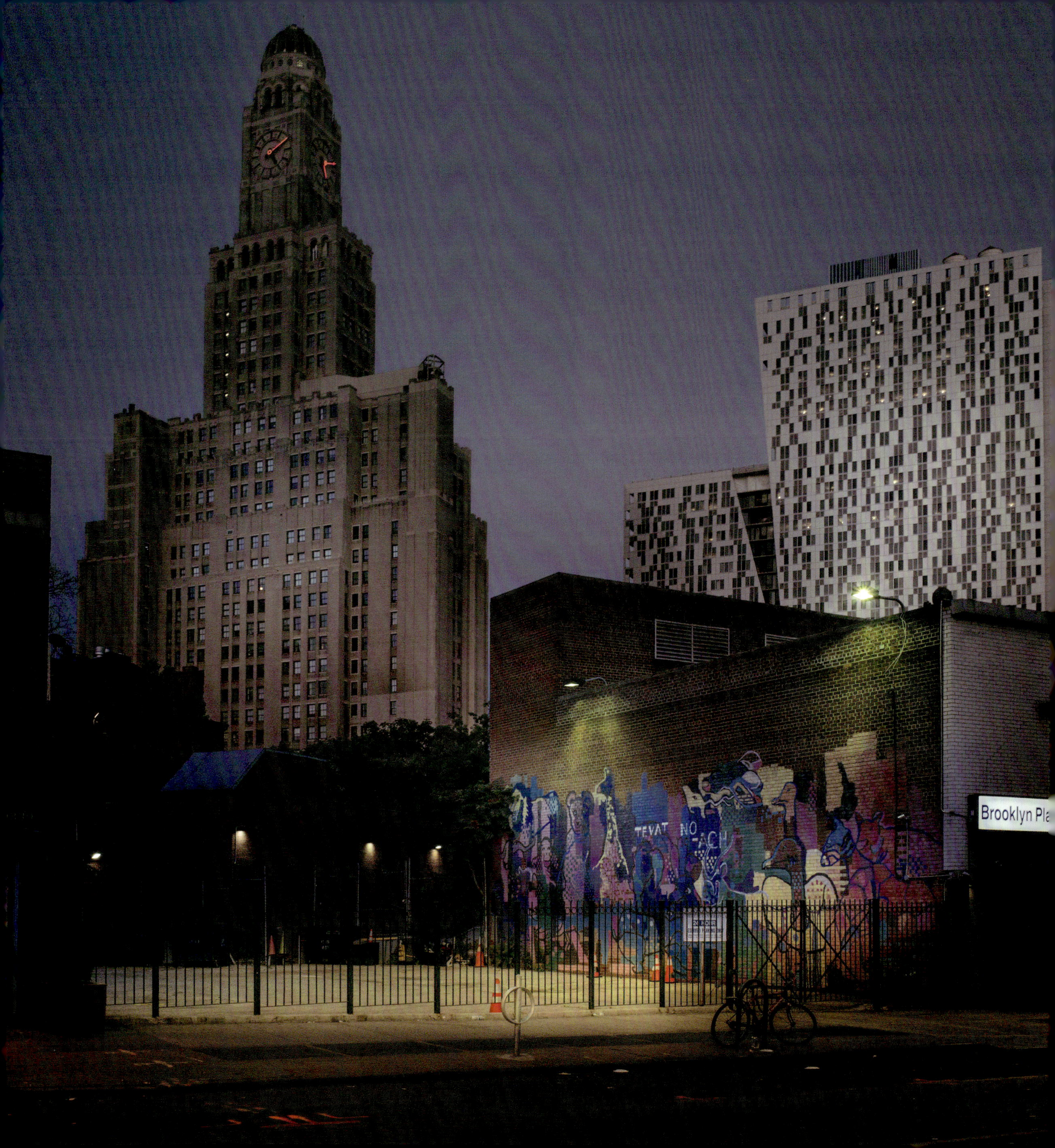
Brooklyn Pla

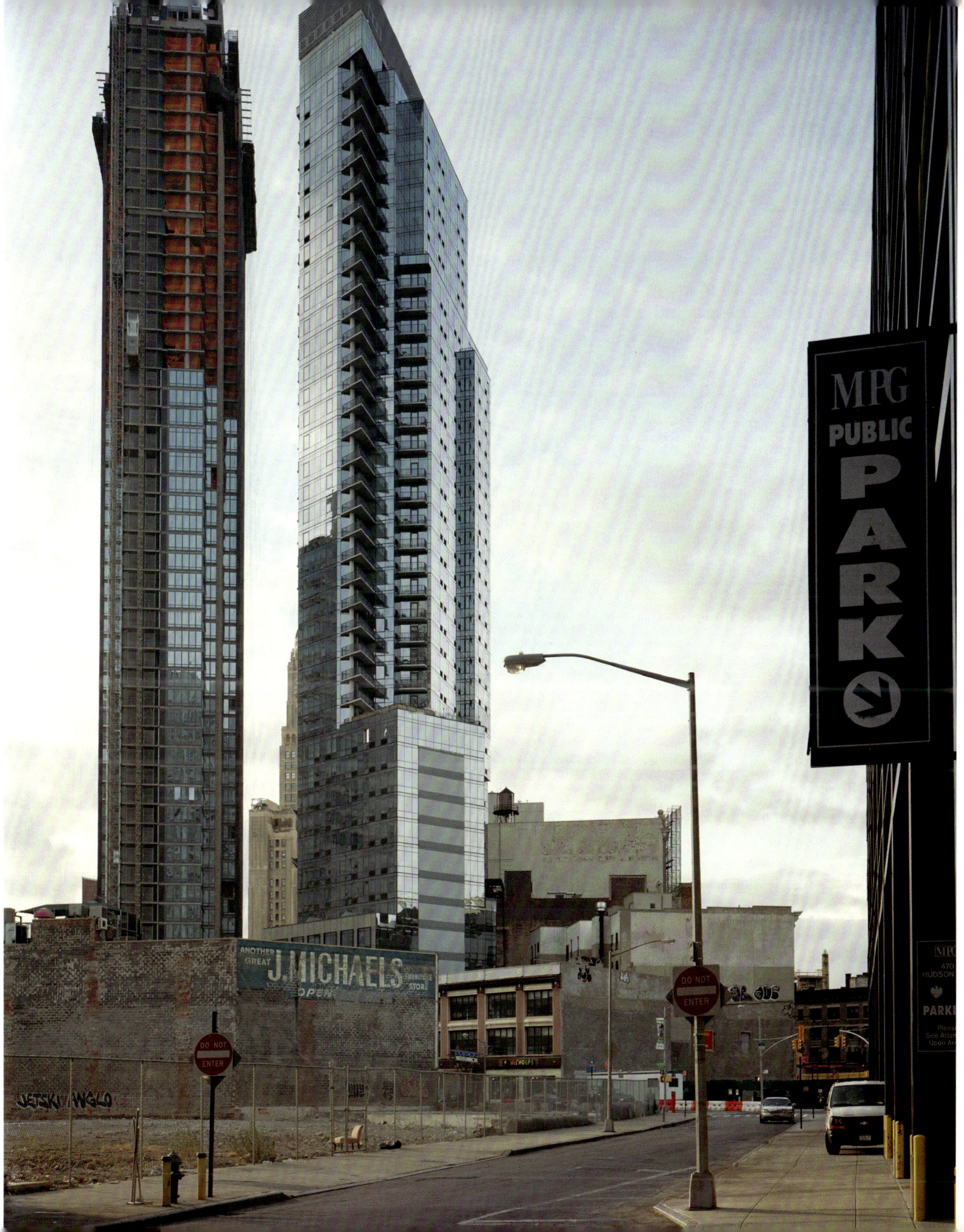
MPG
PUBLIC
PARK
ANOTHER GREAT
J.MICHAELS
OPEN
DO NOT ENTER

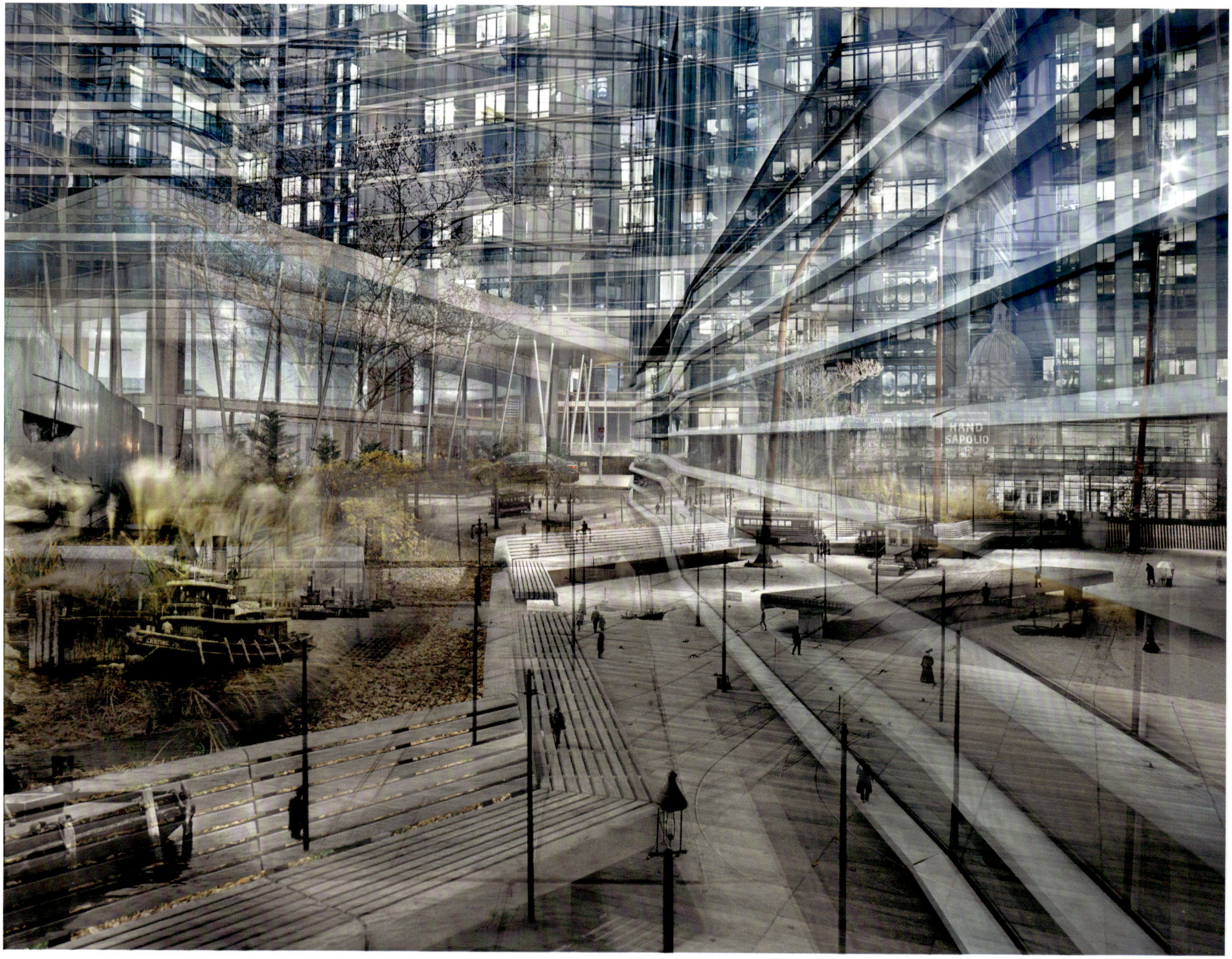
HAND
SAPOLIO

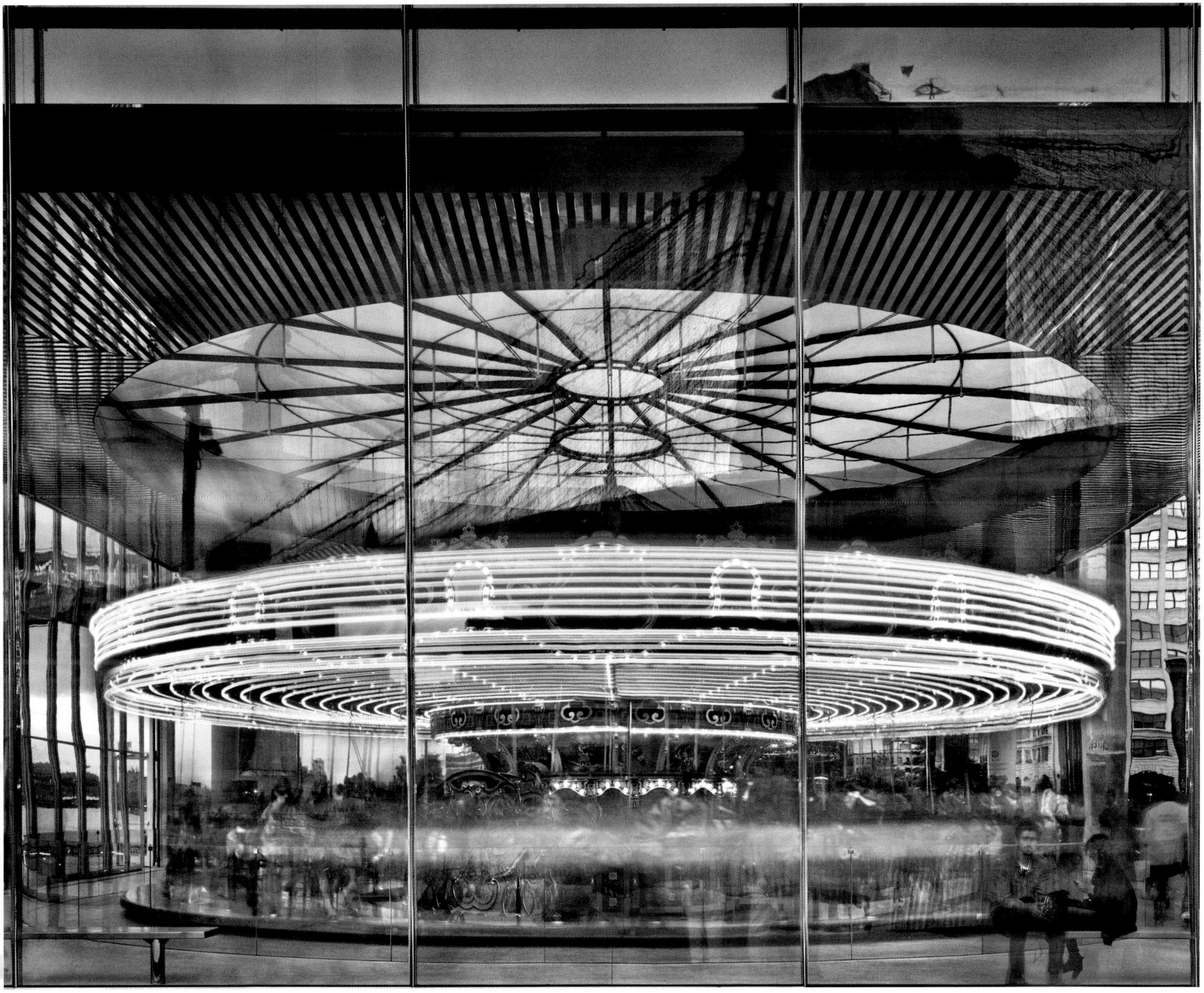

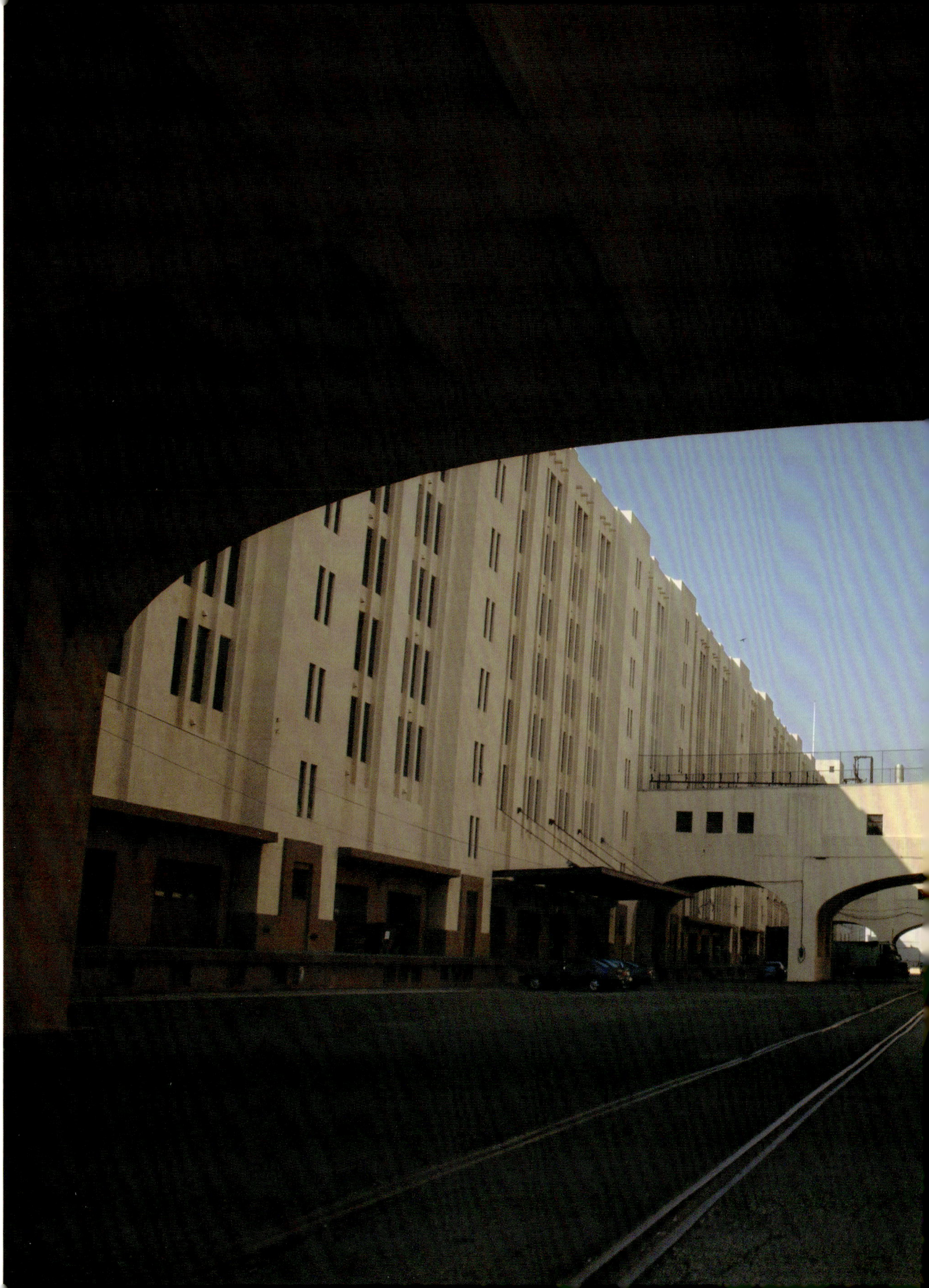

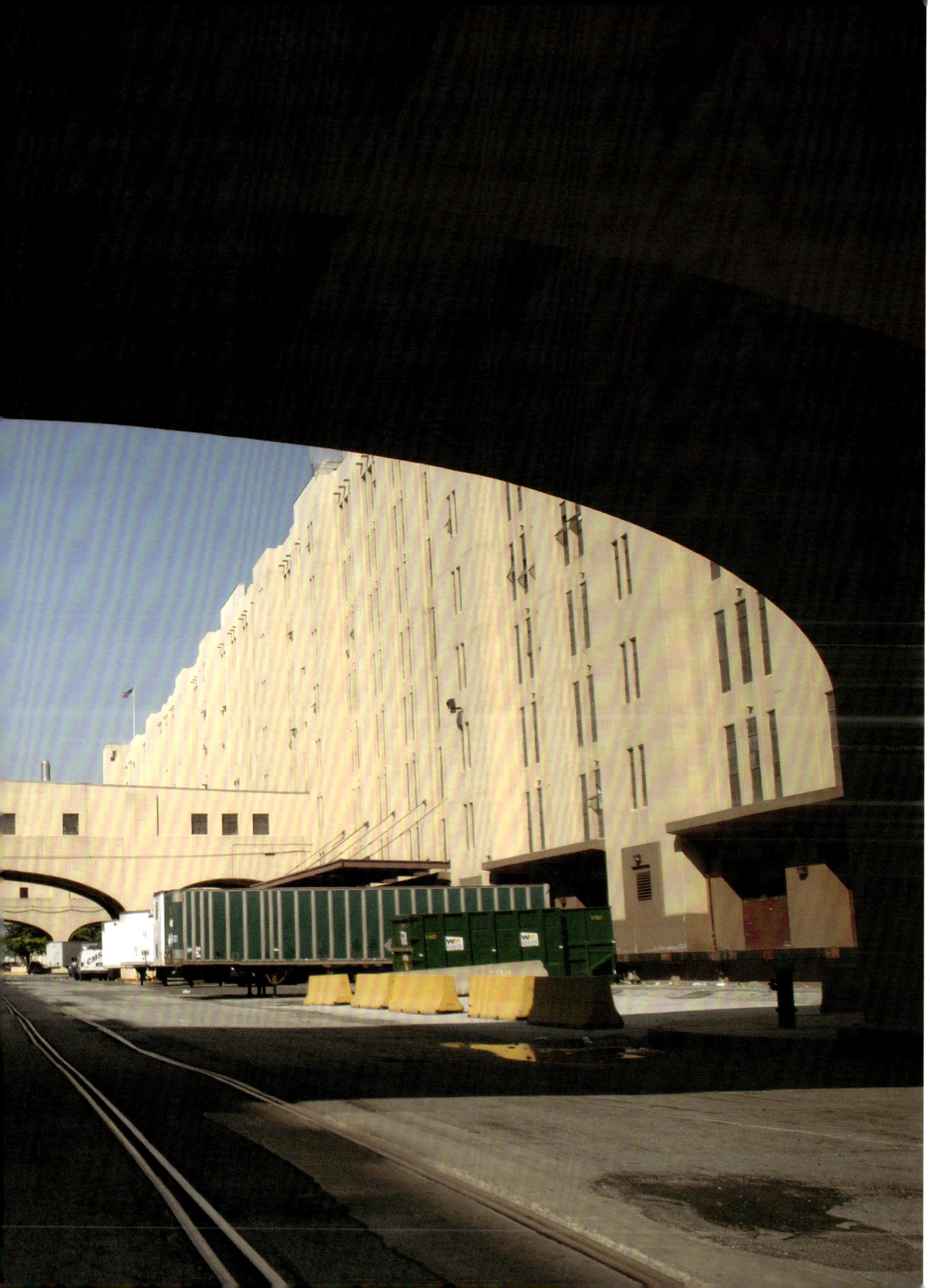

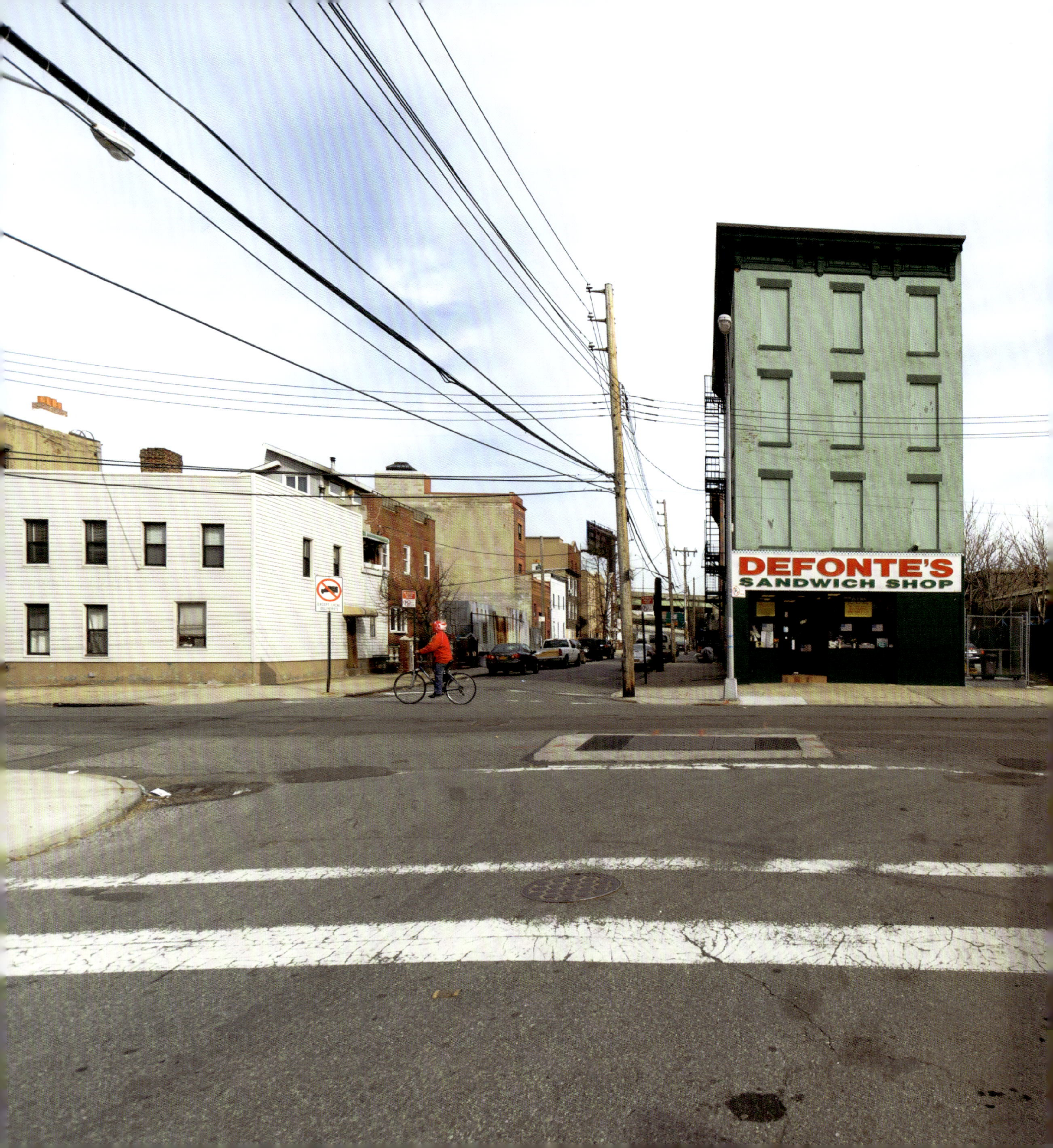
DEFONTE'S
SANDWICH SHOP

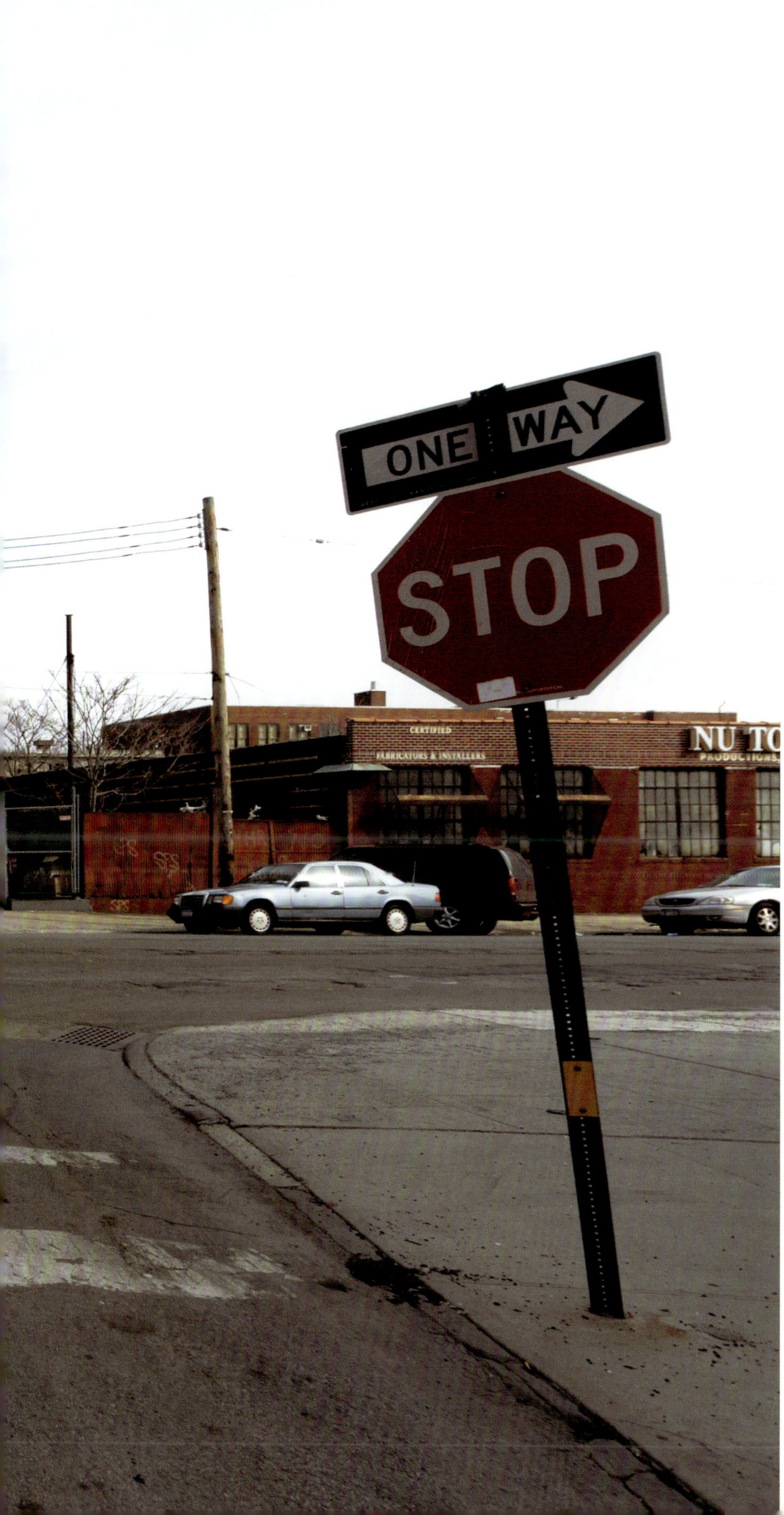
ONE WAY
STOP
CERTIFIED
FABRICATORS & INSTALLERS

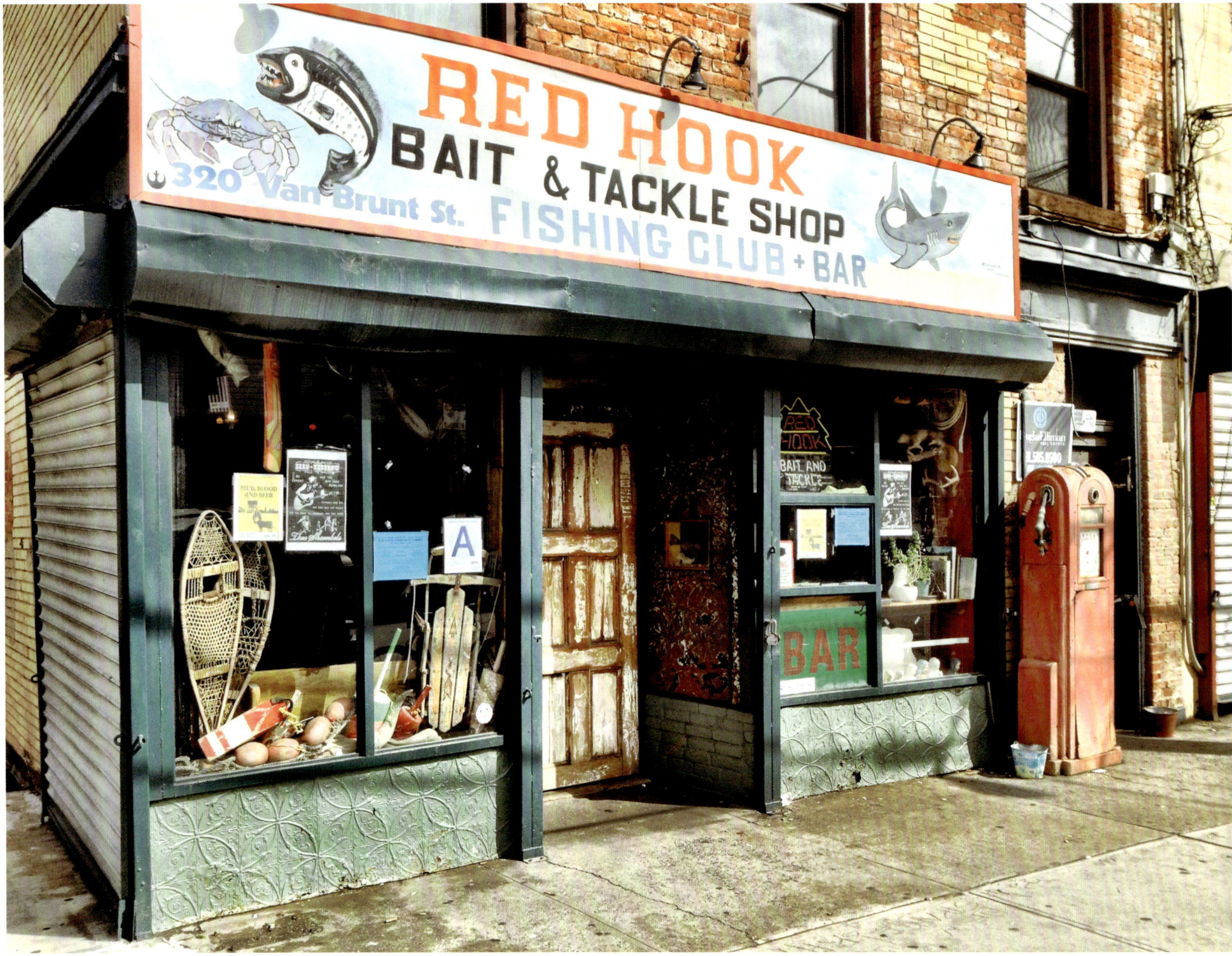
RED HOOK
BAIT & TACKLE SHOP
320 Van Brunt St.
FISHING CLUB + BAR
RED HOOK
BAIT AND TACKLE
A
BAR

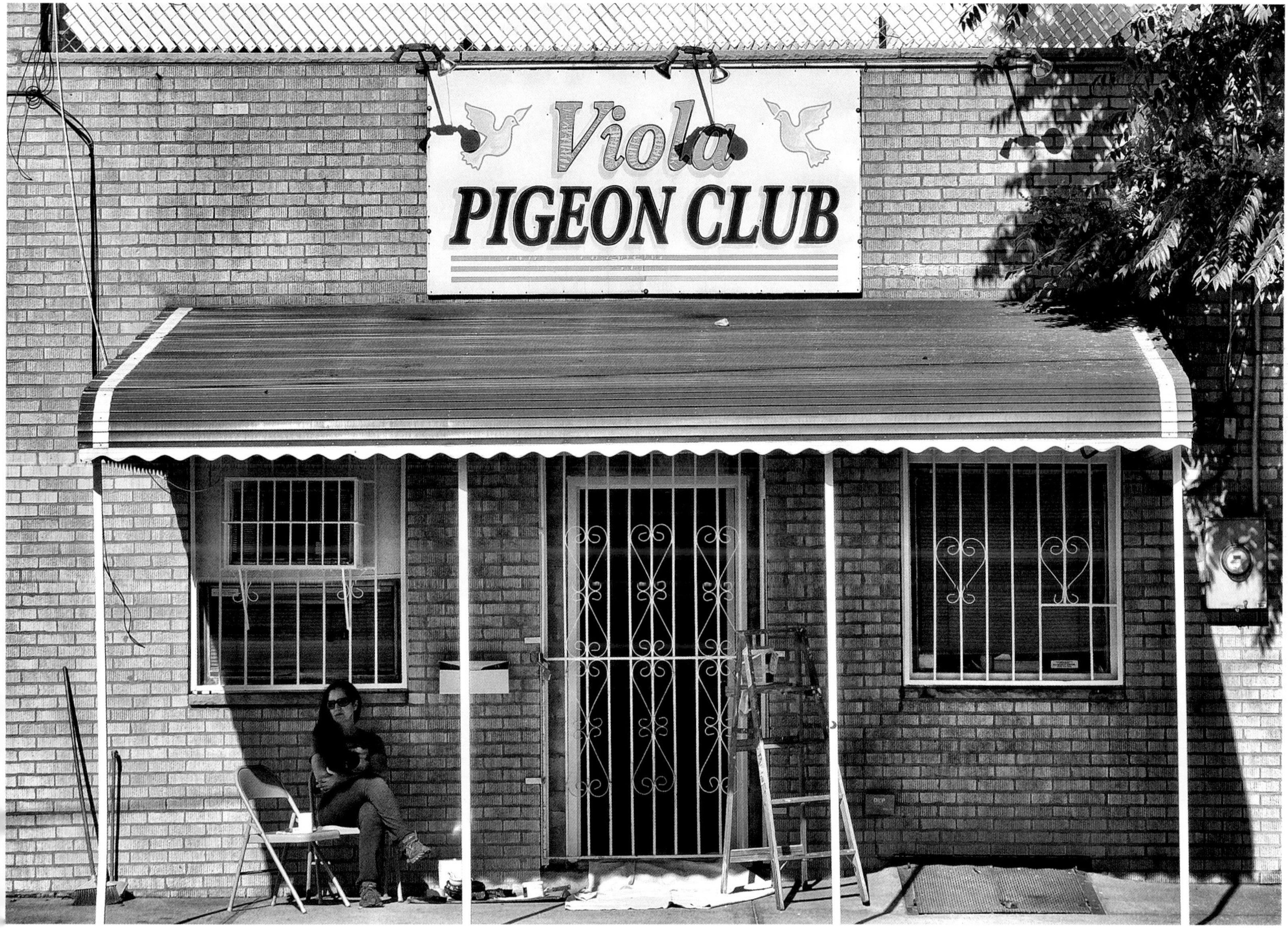
Viola
PIGEON CLUB

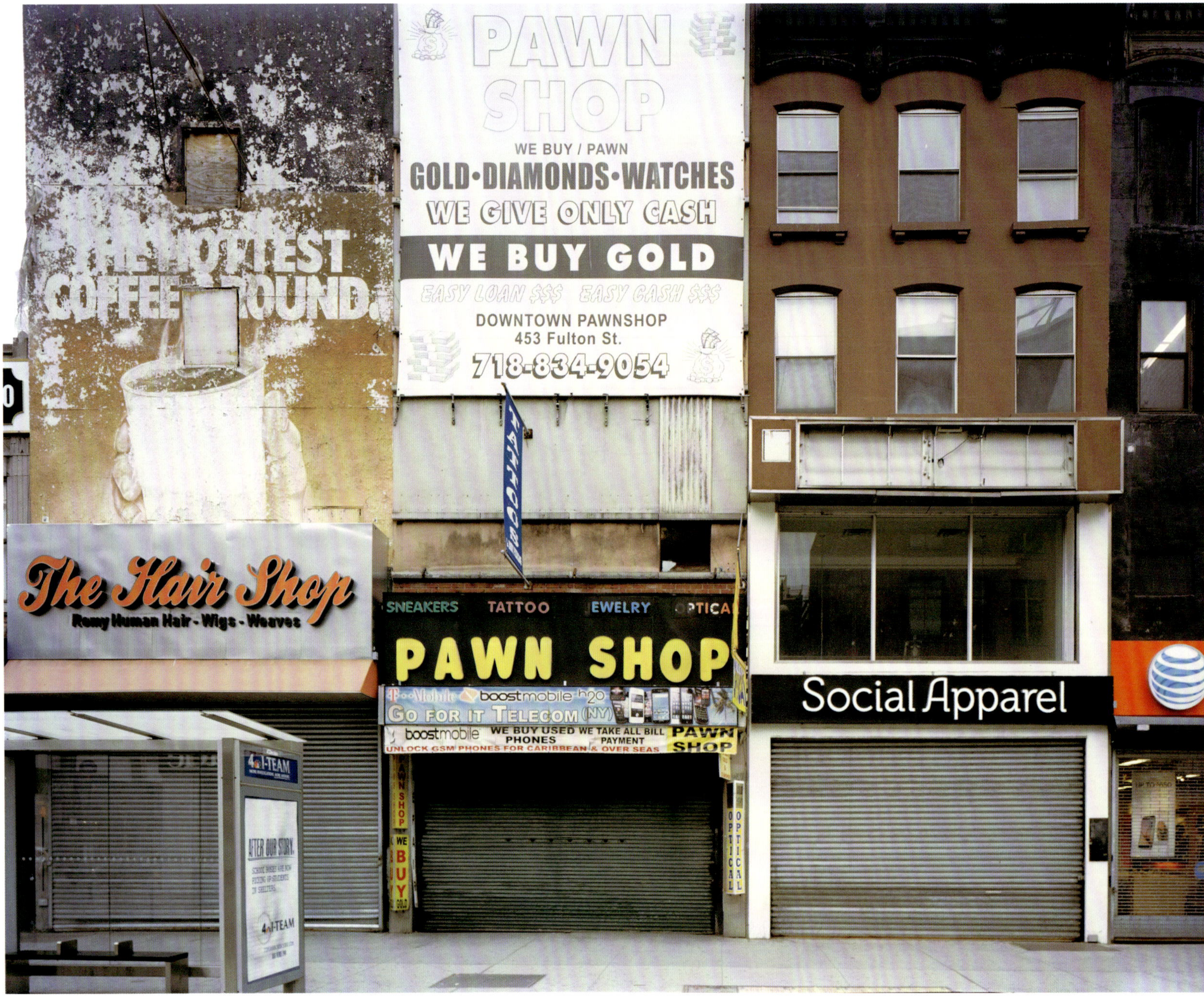
THE HOTTEST
COFFEE AROUND.
PAWN
SHOP
WE BUY / PAWN
GOLD•DIAMONDS•WATCHES
WE GIVE ONLY CASH
WE BUY GOLD
EASY LOAN $$$ EASY CASH $$$
DOWNTOWN PAWNSHOP
453 Fulton St.
718-834-9054
The Hair Shop
Remy Human Hair - Wigs - Weaves
SNEAKERS TATTOO JEWELRY OPTICAL
PAWN SHOP
boostmobile
GO FOR IT TELECOM (NY)
WE BUY USED PHONES
WE TAKE ALL BILL PAYMENT
PAWN SHOP
UNLOCK GSM PHONES FOR CARIBBEAN & OVER SEAS
Social Apparel
OPTICAL
WE BUY
AFTER OUR STORY,

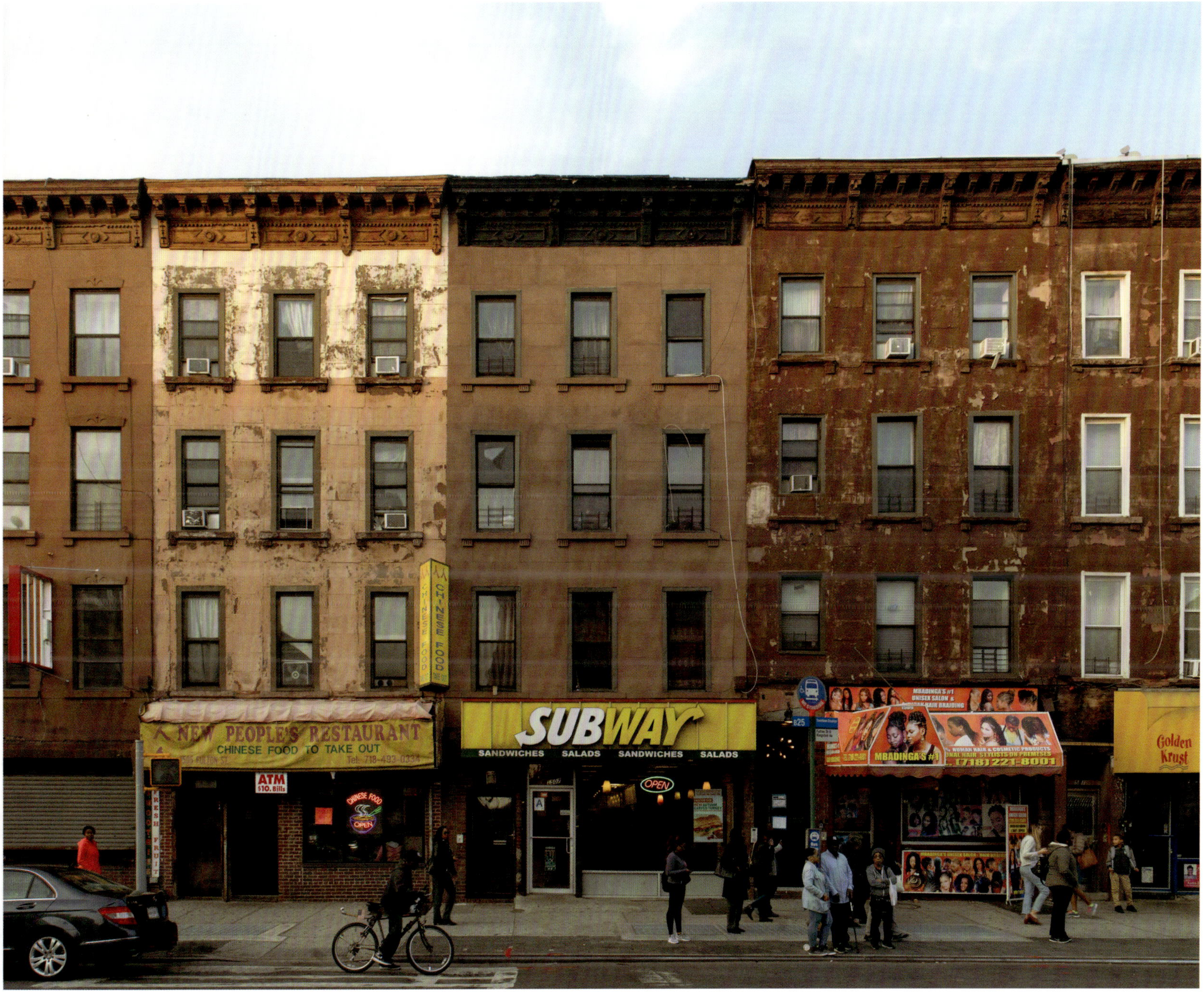
CHINESE FOOD
NEW PEOPLE'S RESTAURANT
CHINESE FOOD TO TAKE OUT
ATM
$10. Bills
SUBWAY
SANDWICHES SALADS SANDWICHES SALADS
OPEN
MBADINGA'S #1
(718)221-8001
Golden Krust

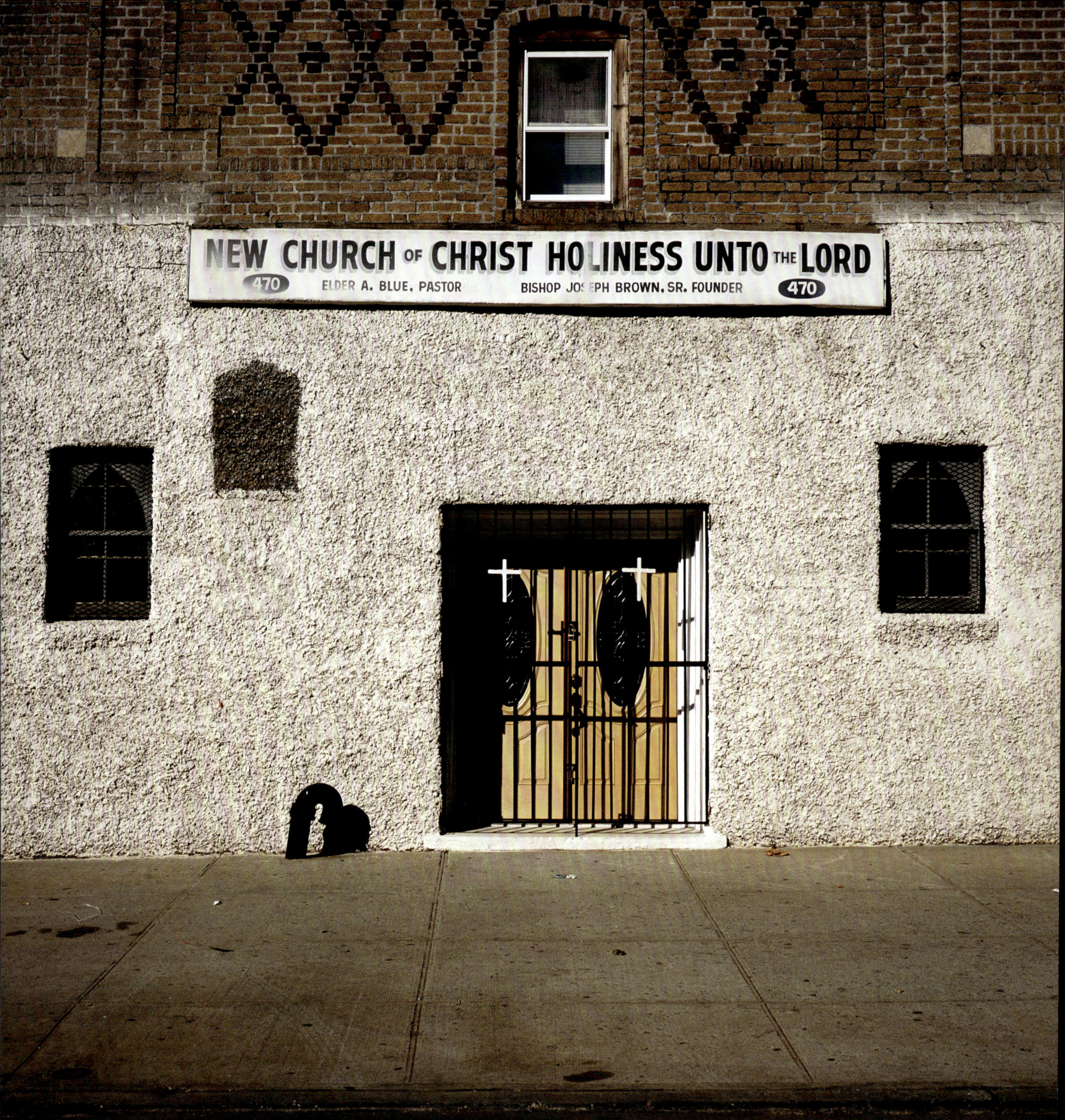
NEW CHURCH OF CHRIST HOLINESS UNTO THE LORD
470
ELDER A. BLUE, PASTOR
BISHOP JOSEPH BROWN, SR. FOUNDER
470

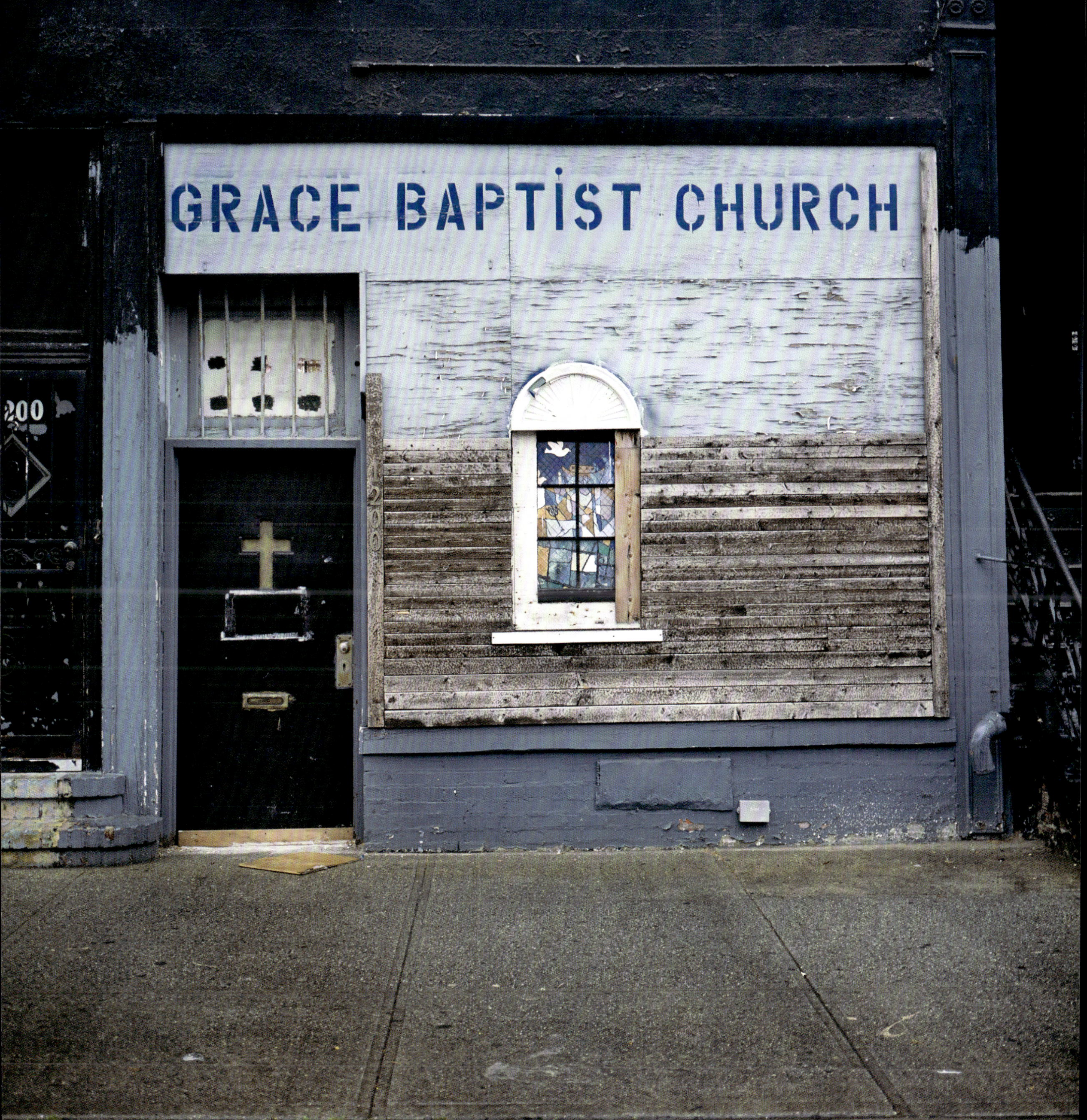
GRACE BAPTIST CHURCH
200
1200

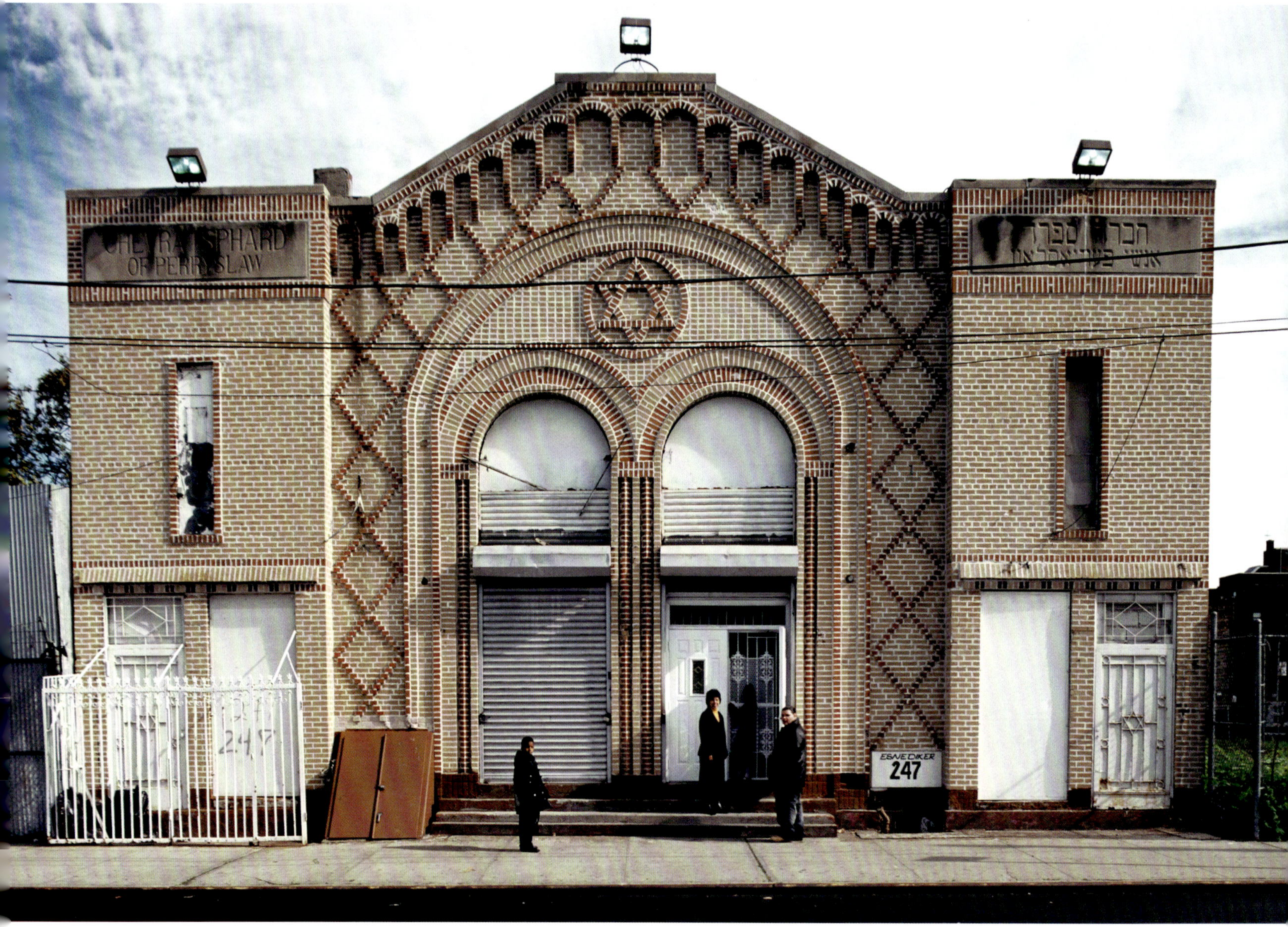
SPHARD
247

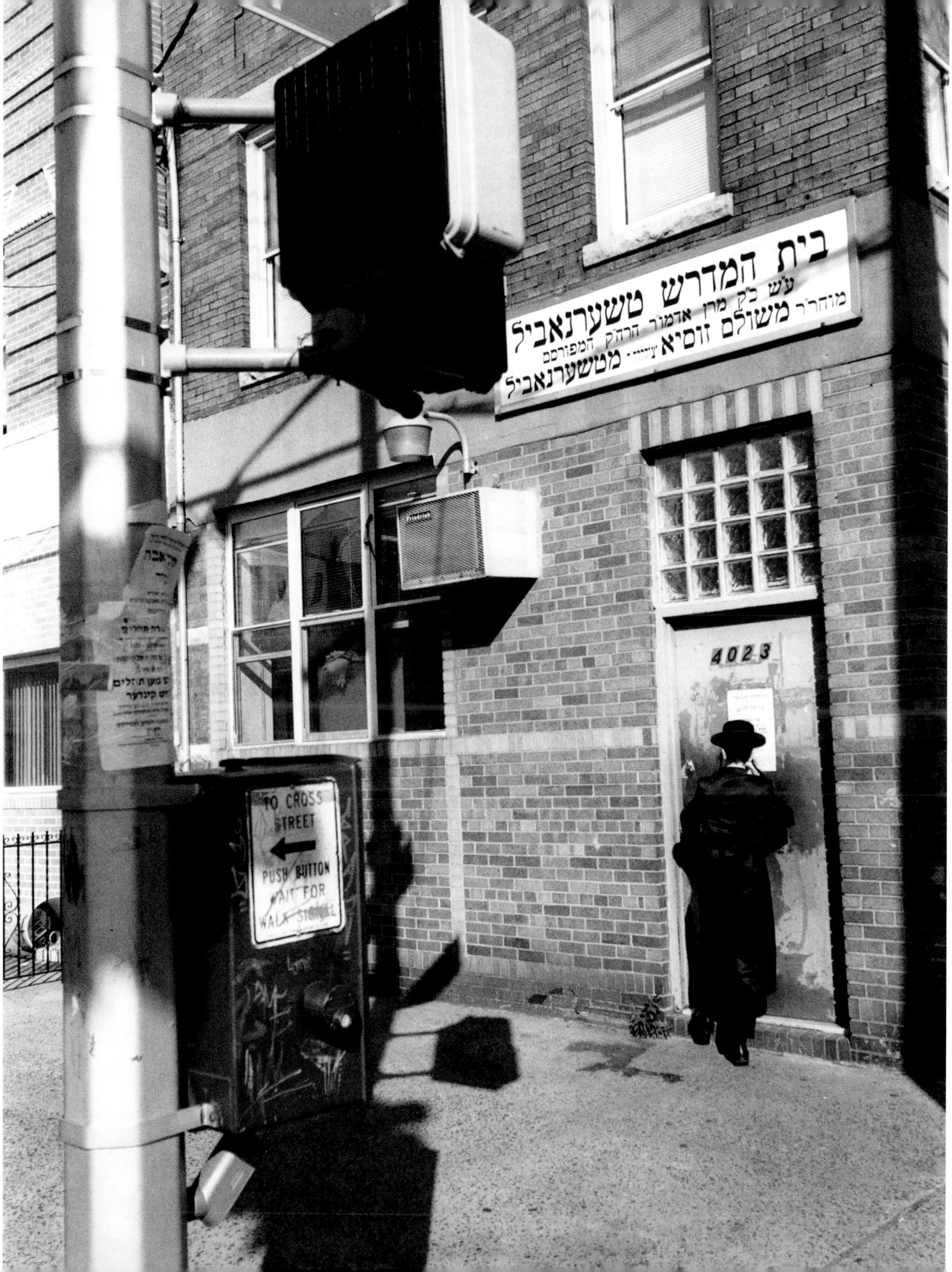
בית המדרש טשערנאביל
ע"ש כ"ק מרן אדמו"ר הרה"ק המפורסם
מוהר"ר משולם זוסיא מטשערנאביל
4023
TO CROSS STREET
PUSH BUTTON
WAIT FOR

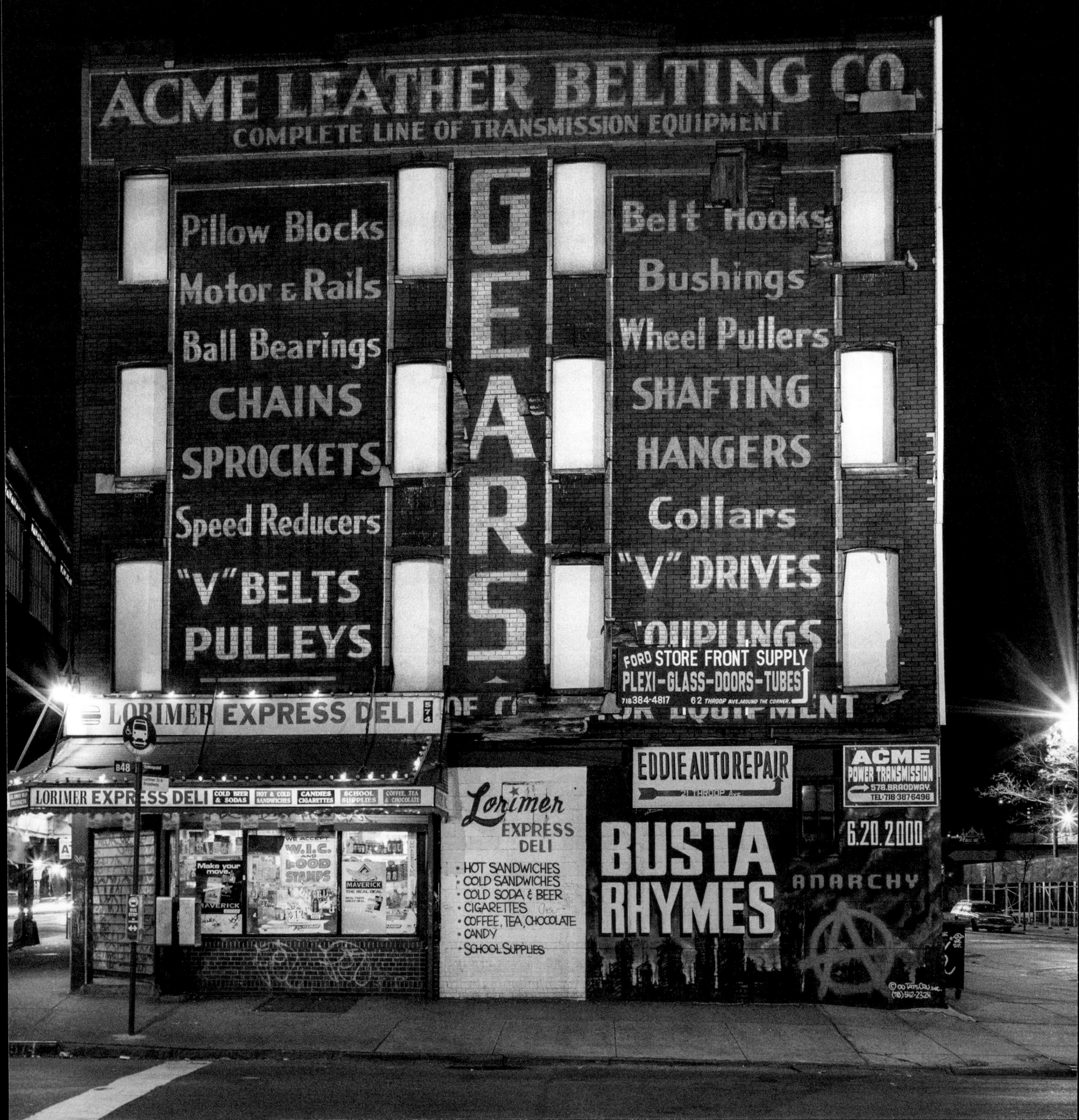
ACME LEATHER BELTING CO.
COMPLETE LINE OF TRANSMISSION EQUIPMENT
Pillow Blocks
Motor & Rails
Ball Bearings
CHAINS
SPROCKETS
Speed Reducers
"V" BELTS
PULLEYS
GEARS
Belt Hooks
Bushings
Wheel Pullers
SHAFTING
HANGERS
Collars
"V" DRIVES
FORD STORE FRONT SUPPLY
PLEXI-GLASS-DOORS-TUBES
718 384-4817
62 THROOP AVE. AROUND THE CORNER.
LORIMER EXPRESS DELI
LORIMER EXPRESS DELI
COLD BEER & SODAS
HOT & COLD SANDWICHES
CANDIES CIGARETTES
SCHOOL SUPPLIES
COFFEE, TEA & CHOCOLATE
WE ACCEPT W.I.C. AND FOOD STAMPS
Lorimer
EXPRESS DELI
HOT SANDWICHES
COLD SANDWICHES
COLD SODA & BEER
CIGARETTES
COFFEE, TEA, CHOCOLATE
CANDY
SCHOOL SUPPLIES
EDDIE AUTO REPAIR
21 THROOP Ave.
ACME
POWER TRANSMISSION
578 BROADWAY.
TEL: 718 3876496
BUSTA
RHYMES
6.20.2000
ANARCHY

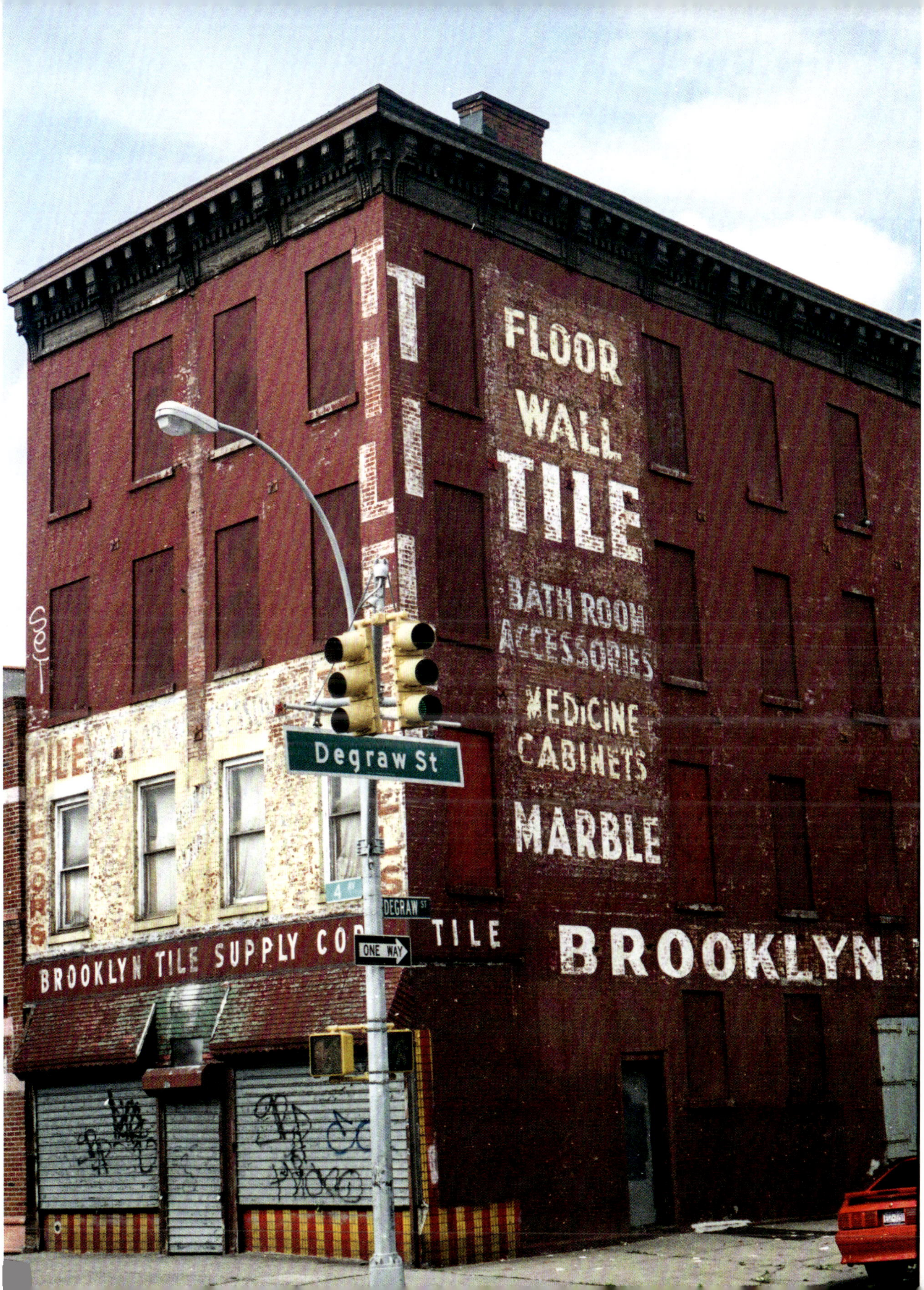
FLOOR
WALL
TILE
BATH ROOM
ACCESSORIES
MEDICINE
CABINETS
MARBLE
TILE
BROOKLYN
BROOKLYN TILE SUPPLY CO
Degraw St
DEGRAW ST
ONE WAY

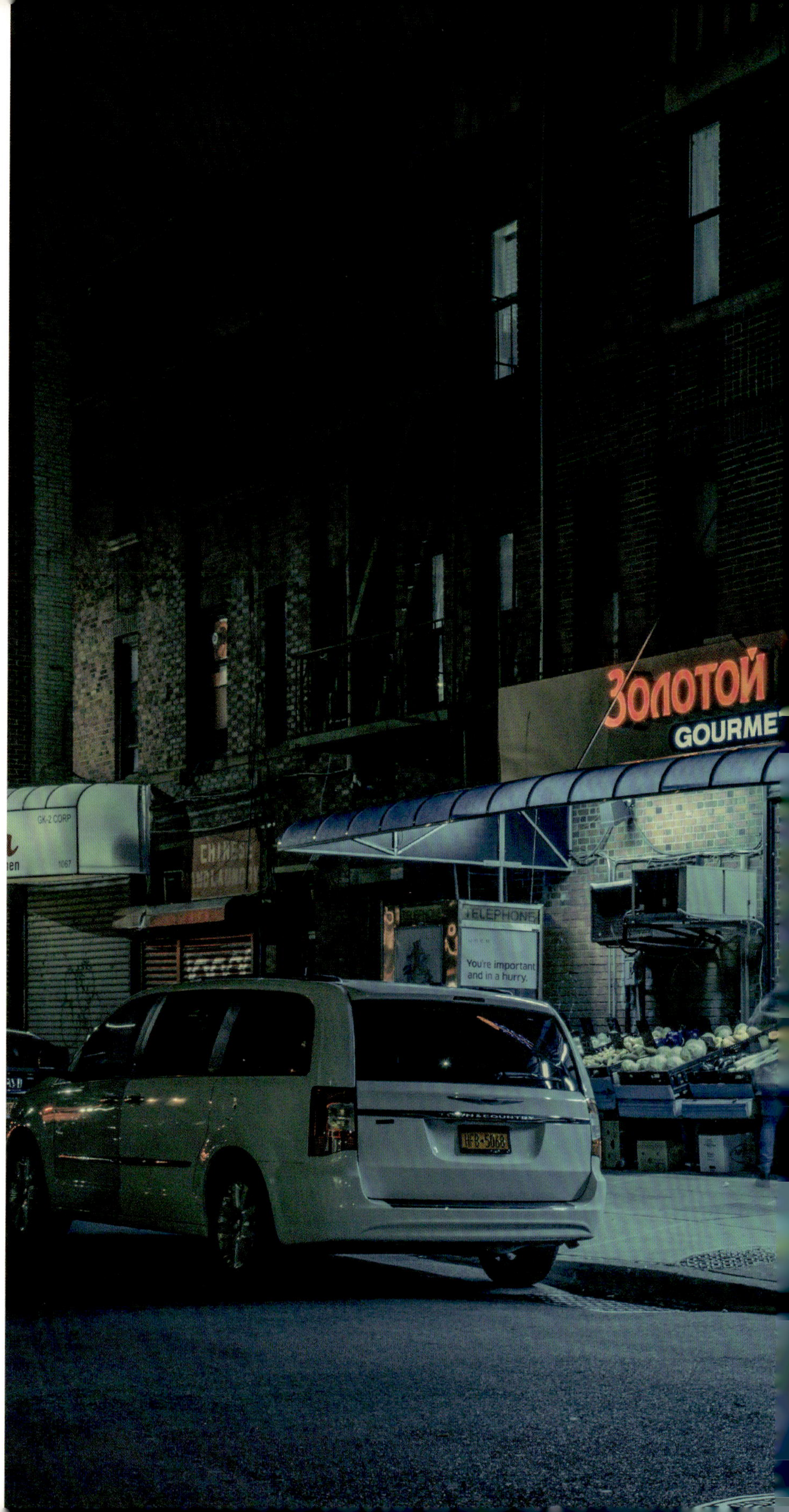
Золотой
GOURME
GK-2 CORP
1067
TELEPHONE
You're important
and in a hurry.

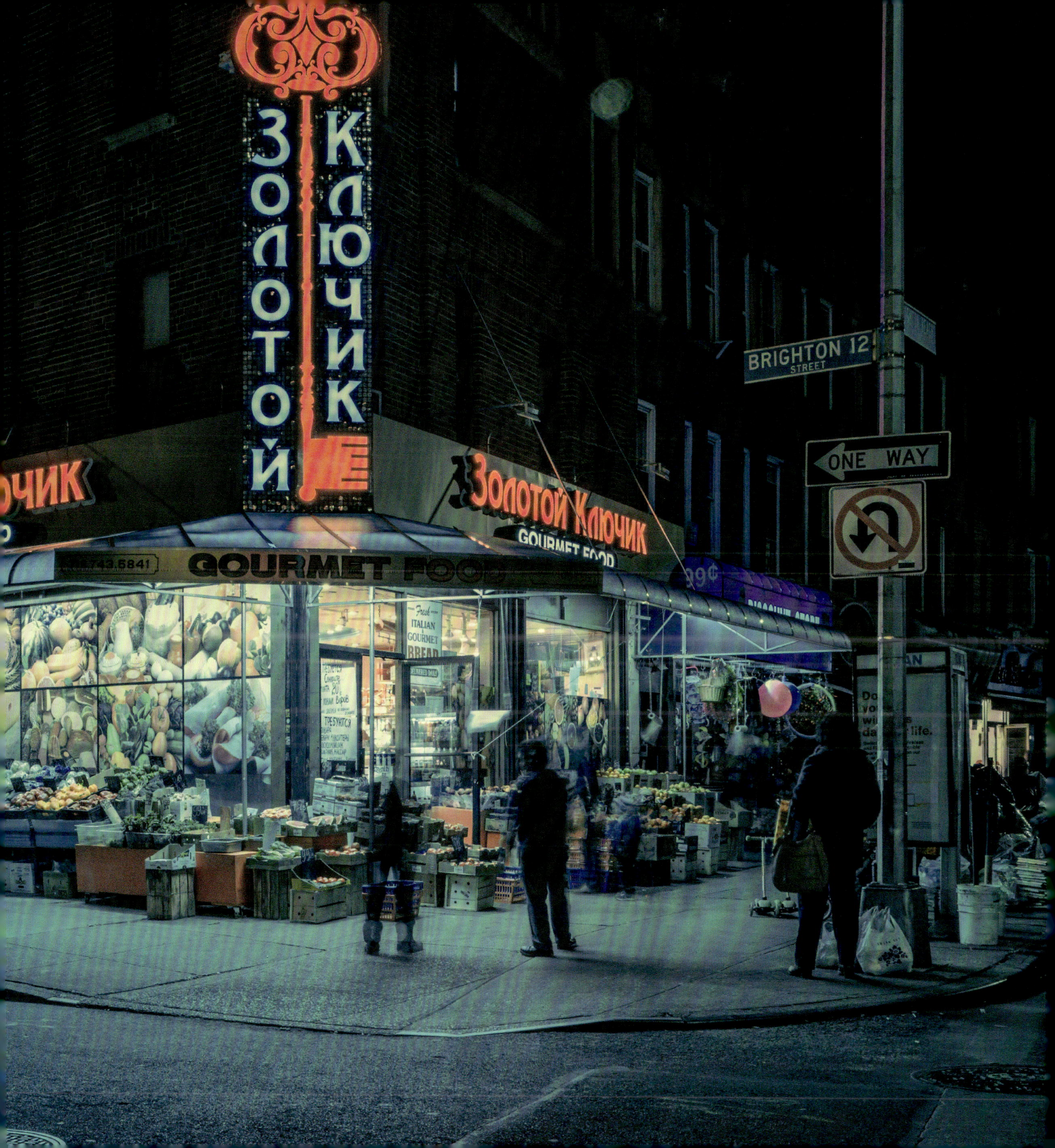
ЗОЛОТОЙ КЛЮЧИК
Золотой Ключик
GOURMET FOOD
GOURMET FOOD
BRIGHTON 12
STREET
ONE WAY
99¢
Fresh
ITALIAN
GOURMET
BREAD

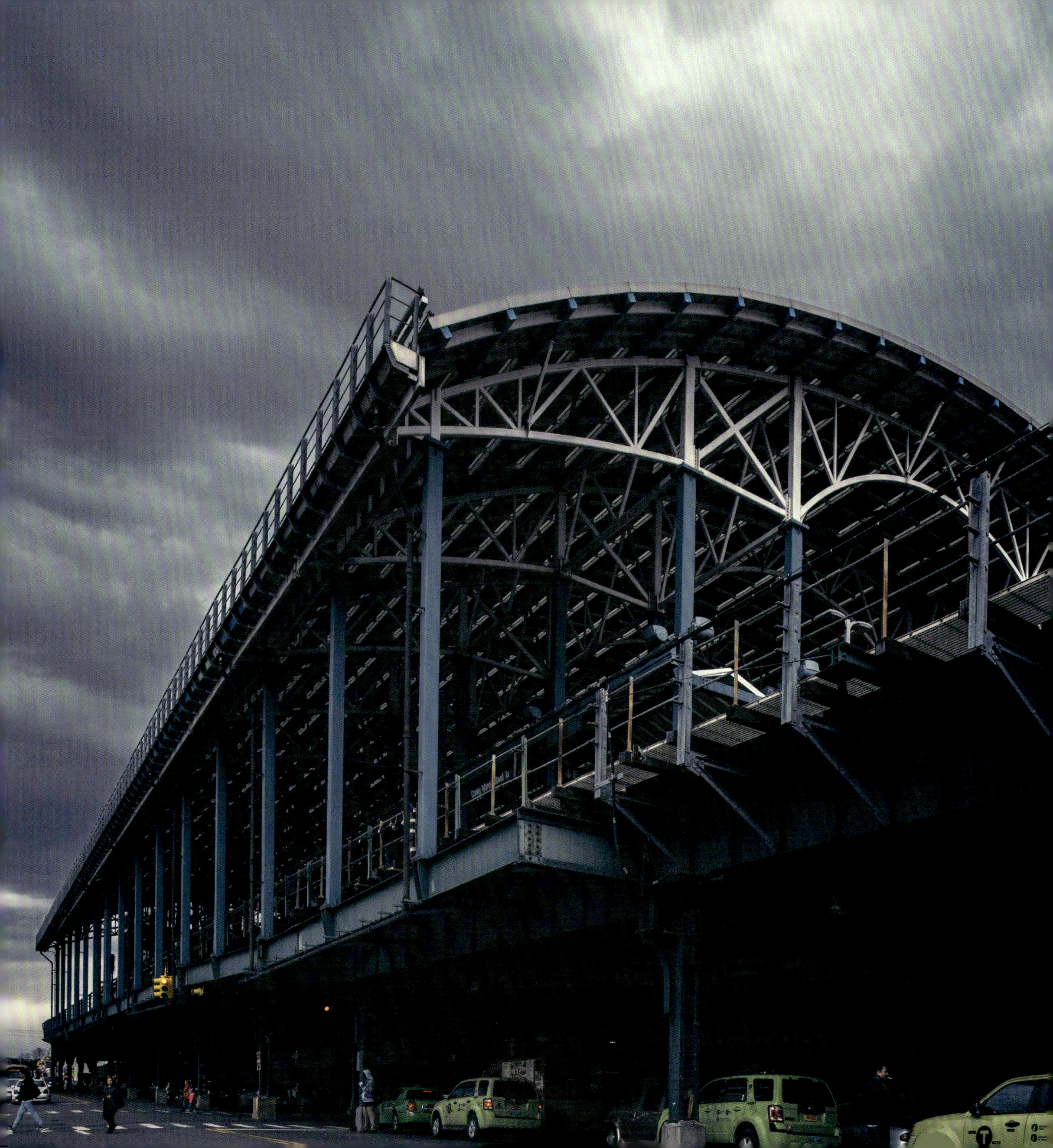

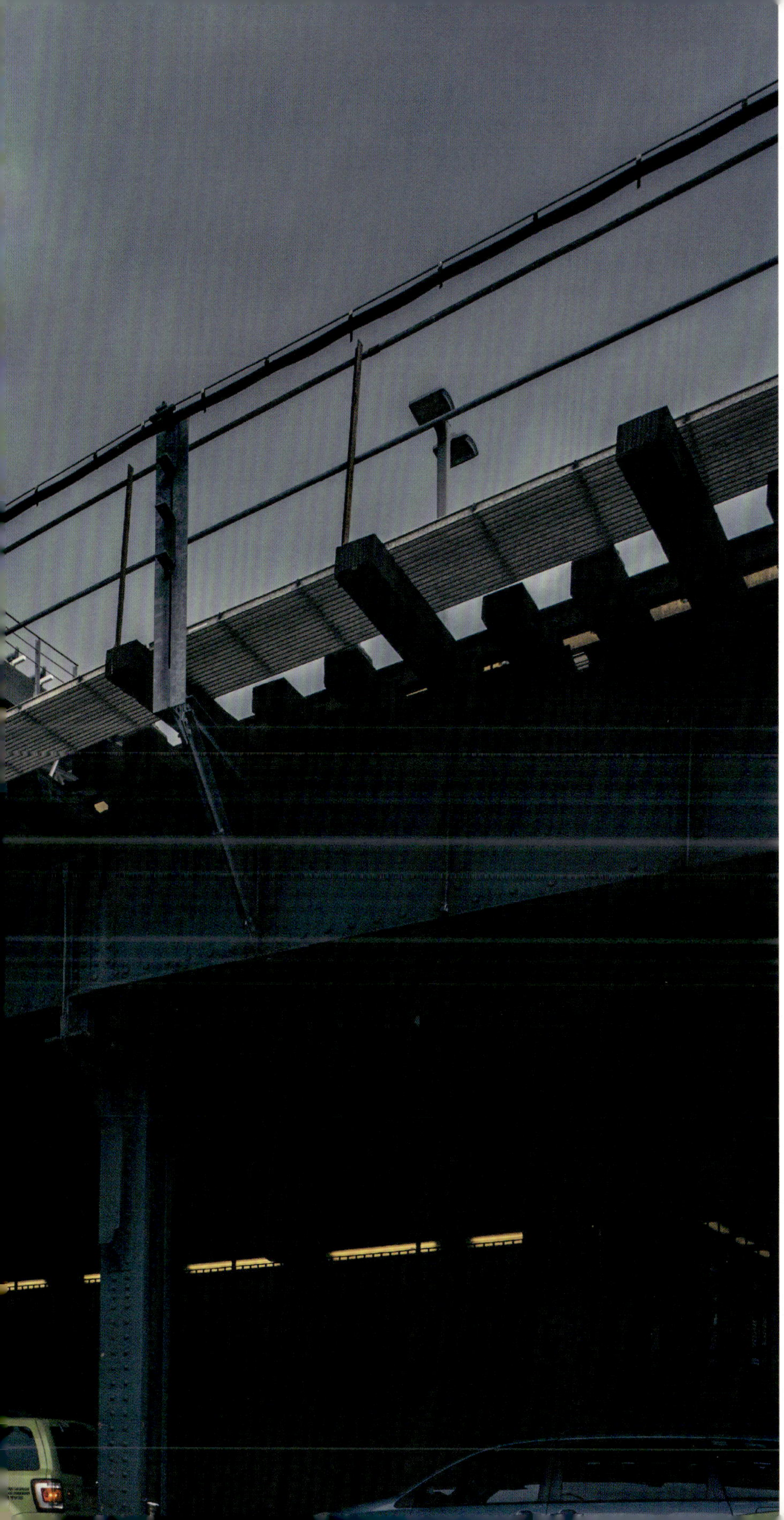

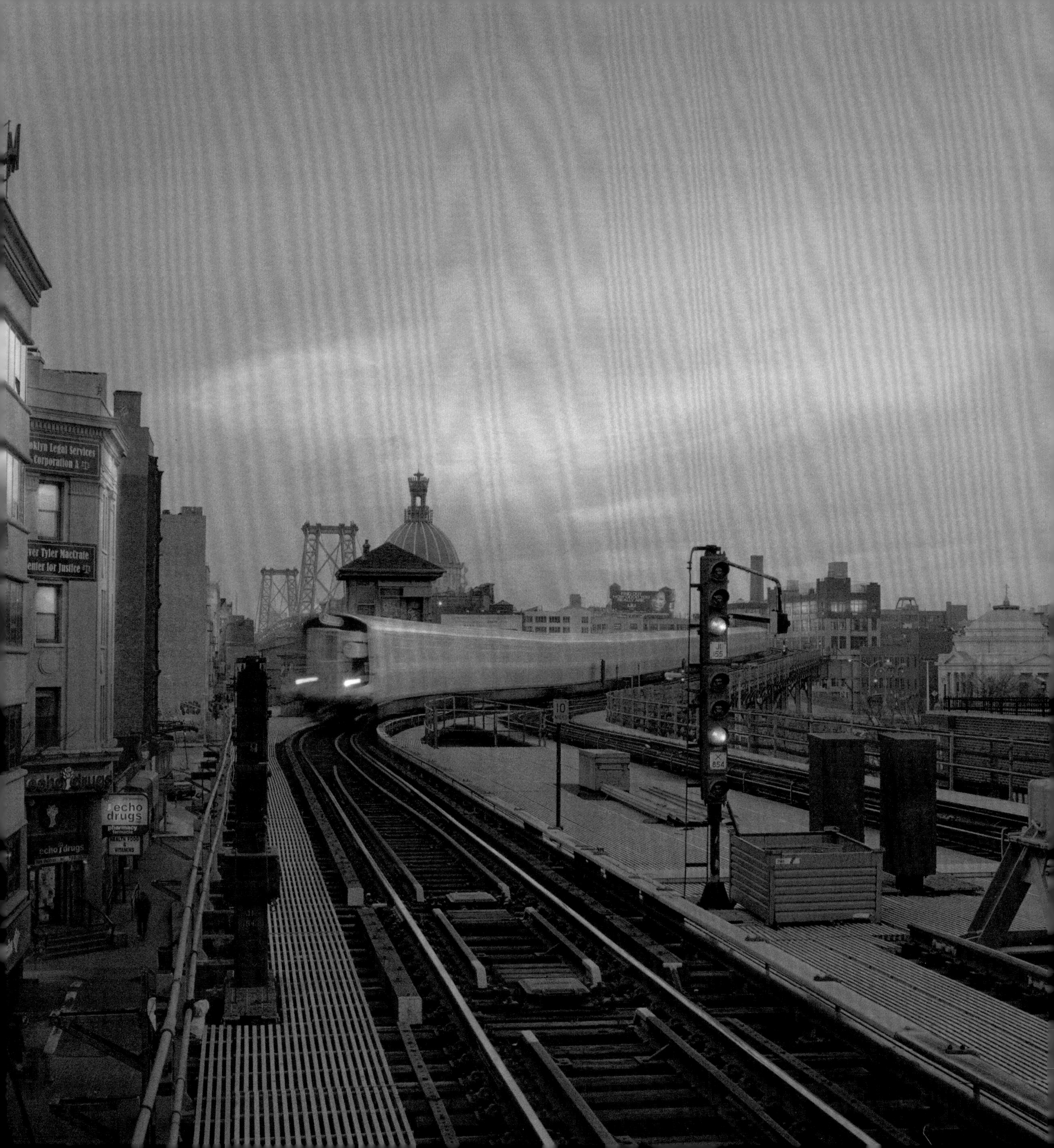
Legal Services
Corporation A
Tyler Macrate
for Justice
echo drugs
echo
drugs
pharmacy
VITAMINS
echo drugs
10

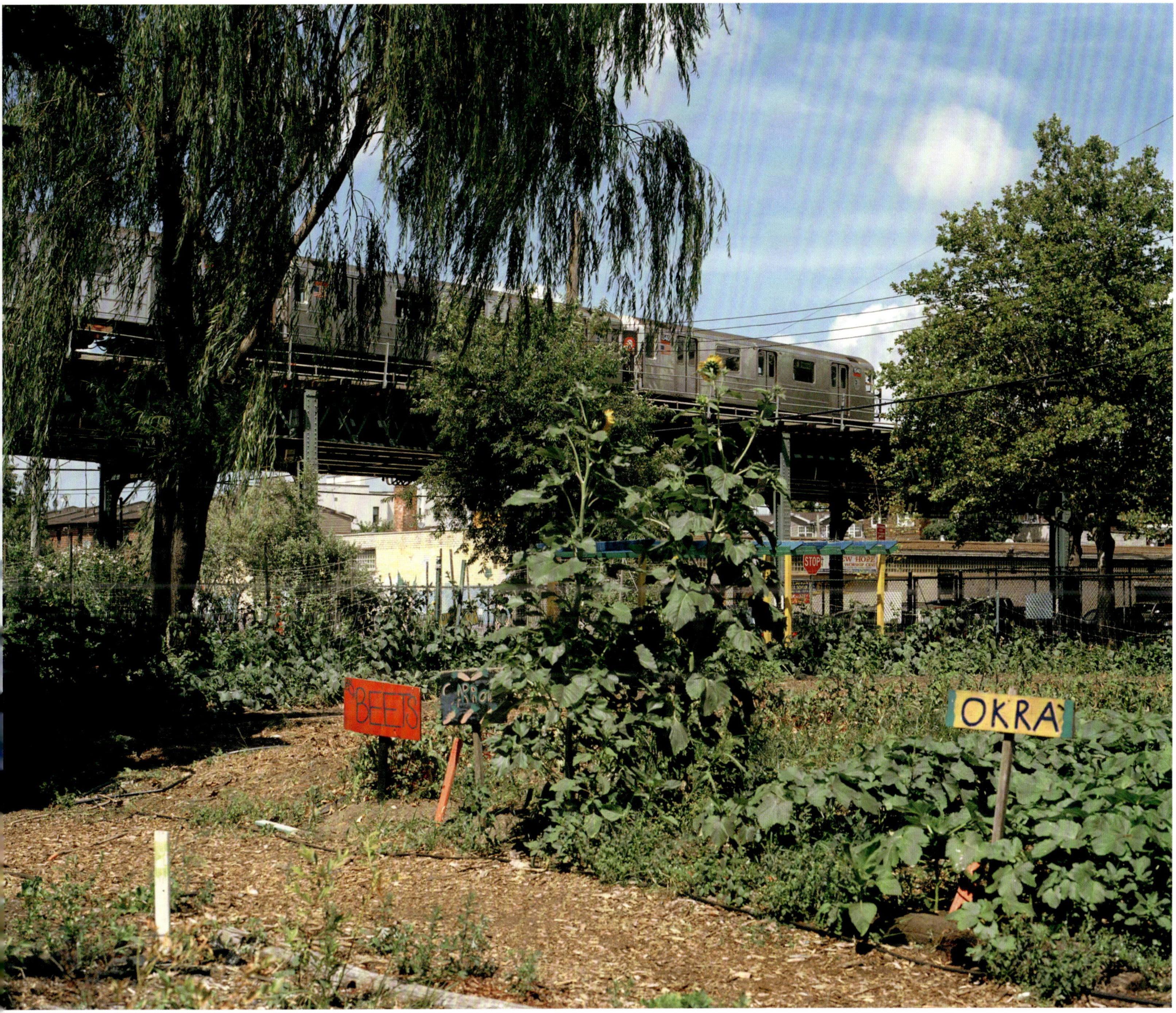
BEETS
OKRA
STOP

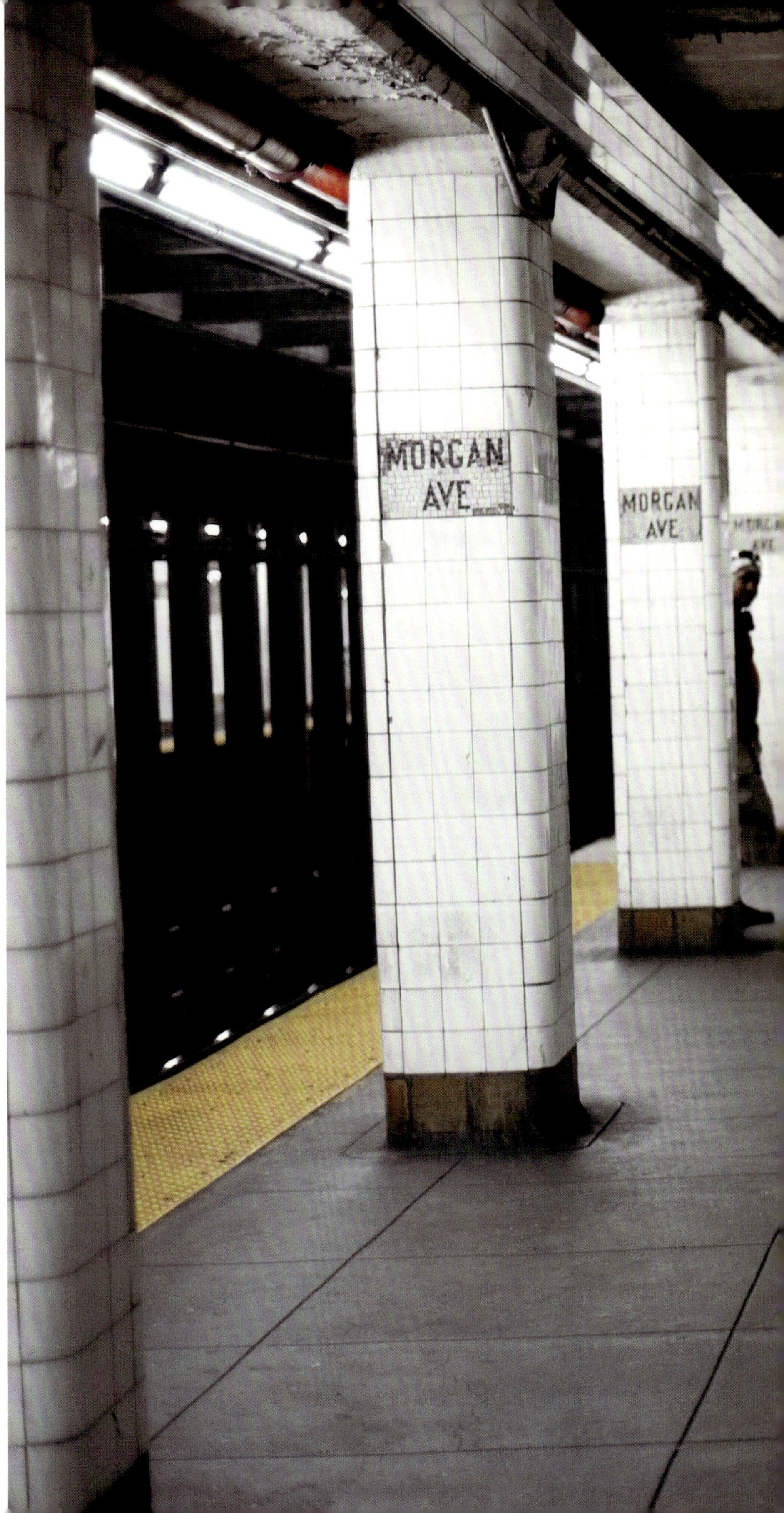
MORGAN
AVE
MORGAN
AVE

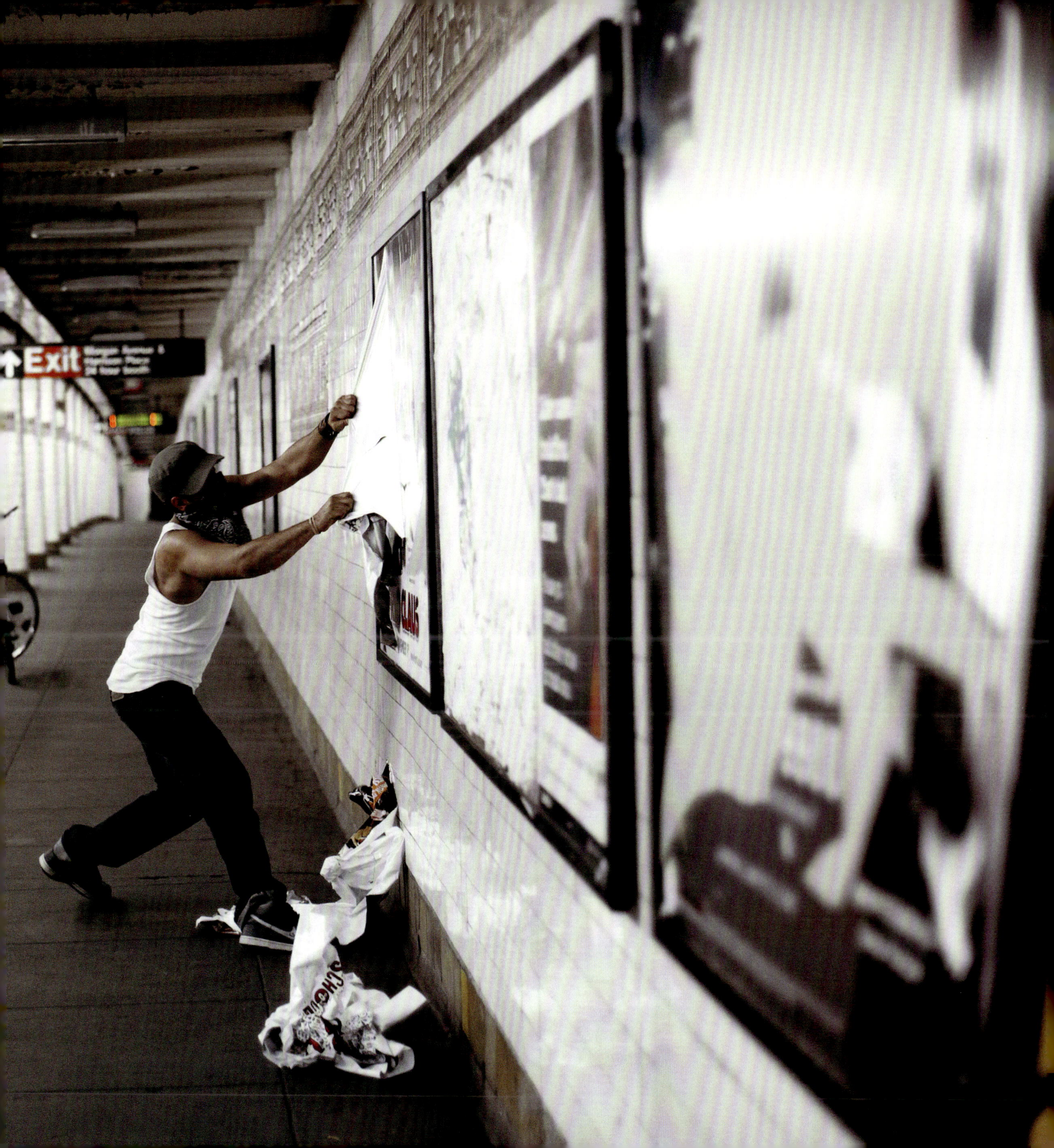
Exit

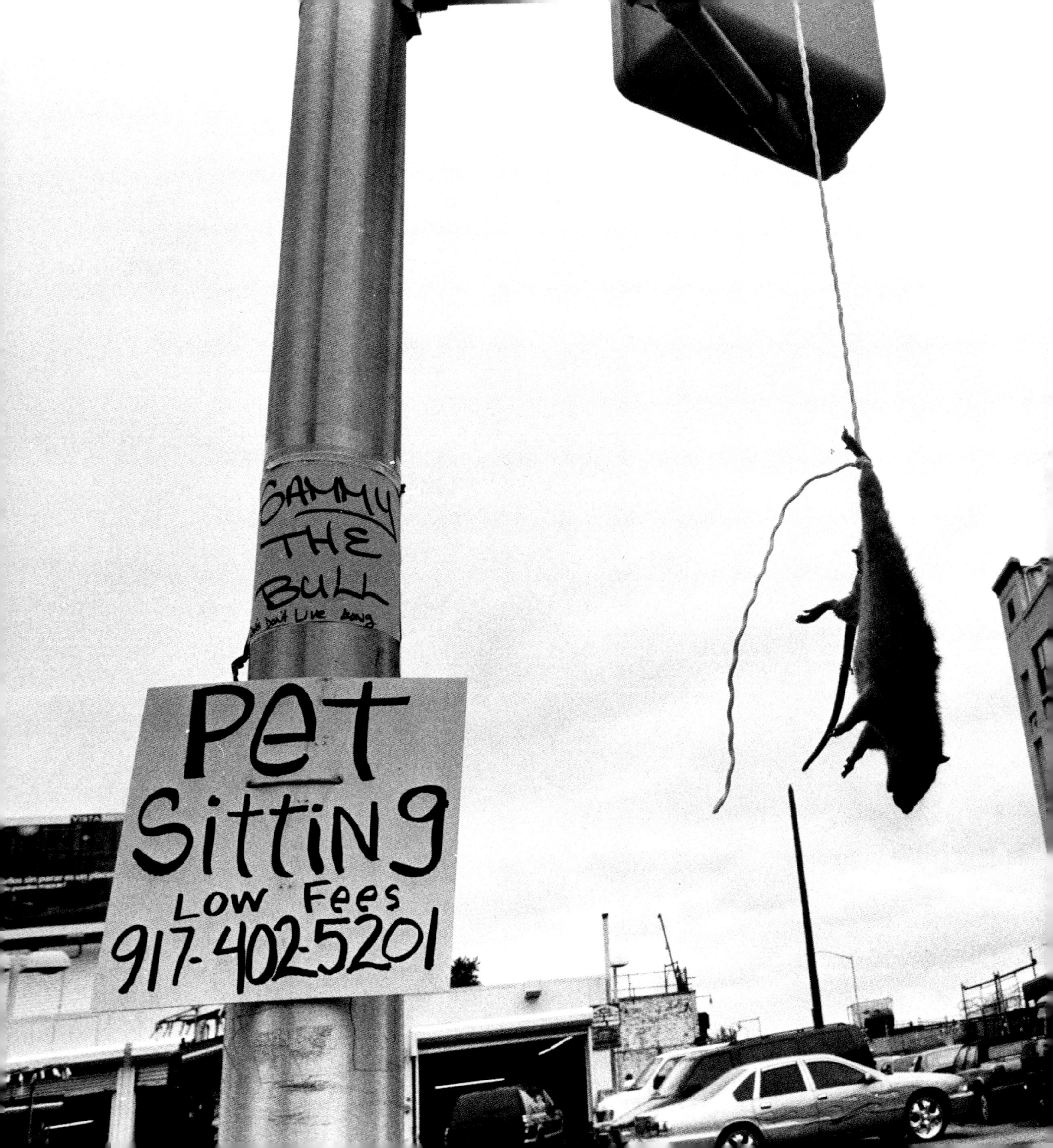
SAMMY
THE
BULL
Pet
Sitting
Low Fees
917-402-5201

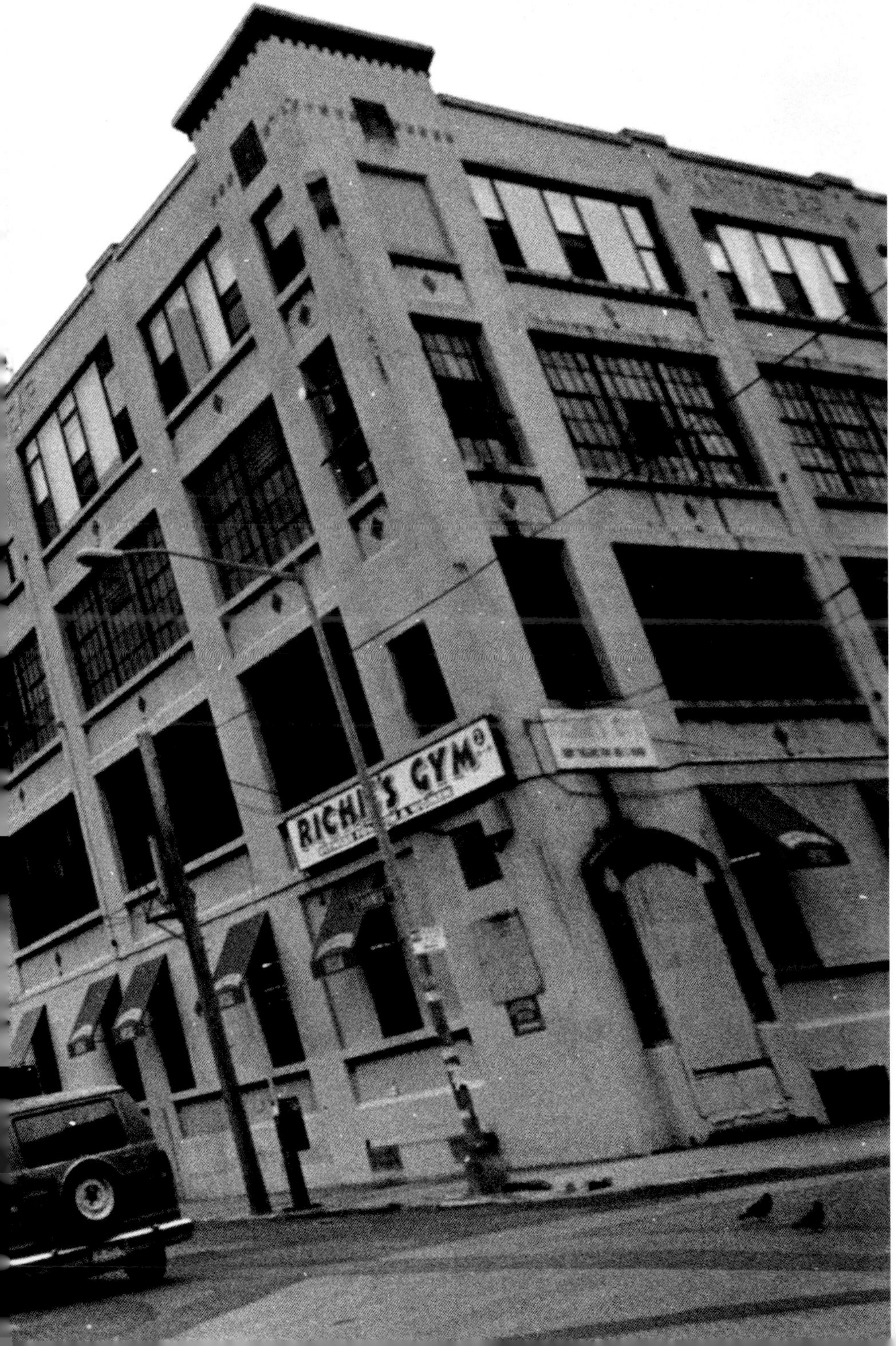
RICHI S GYM

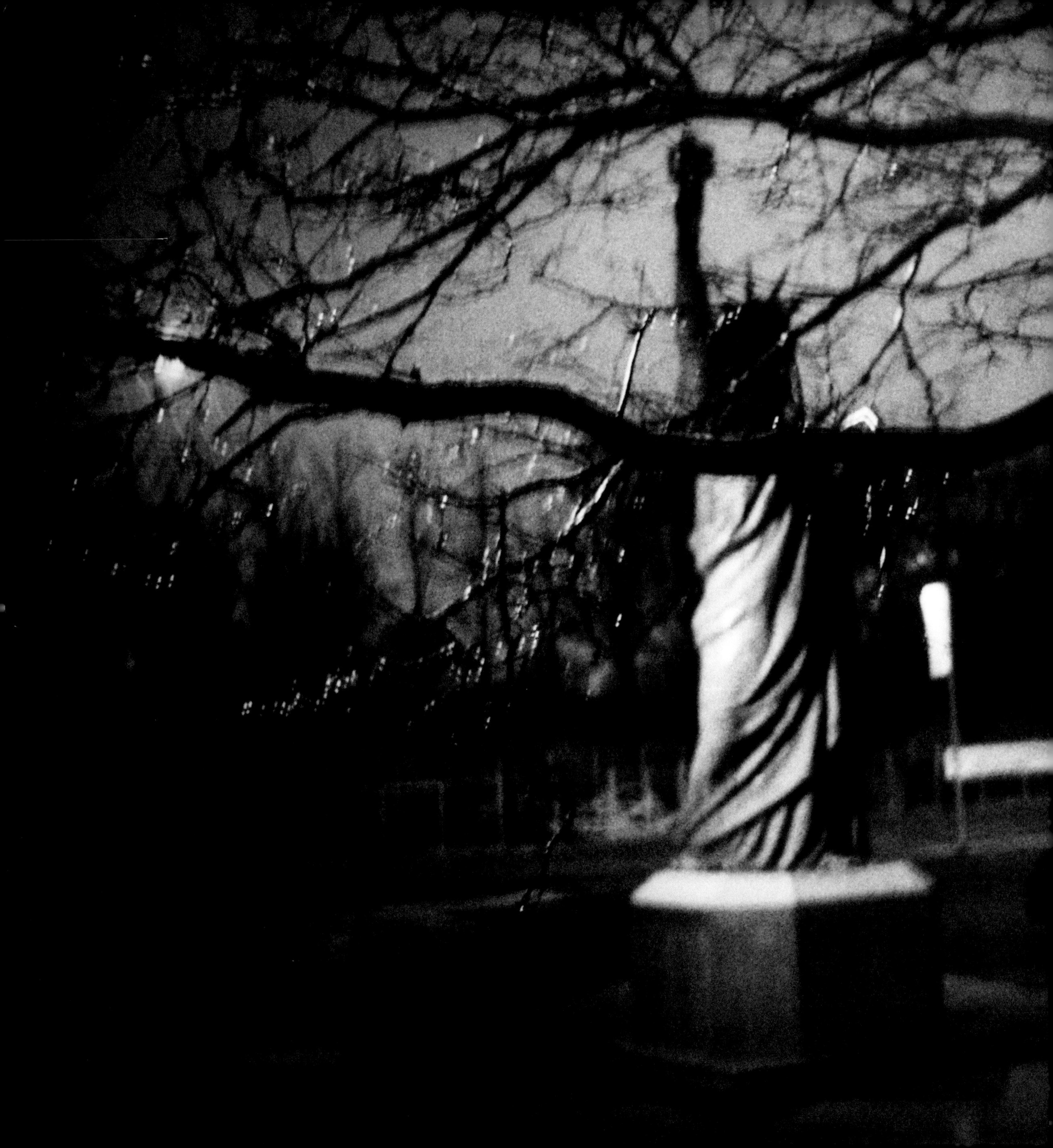

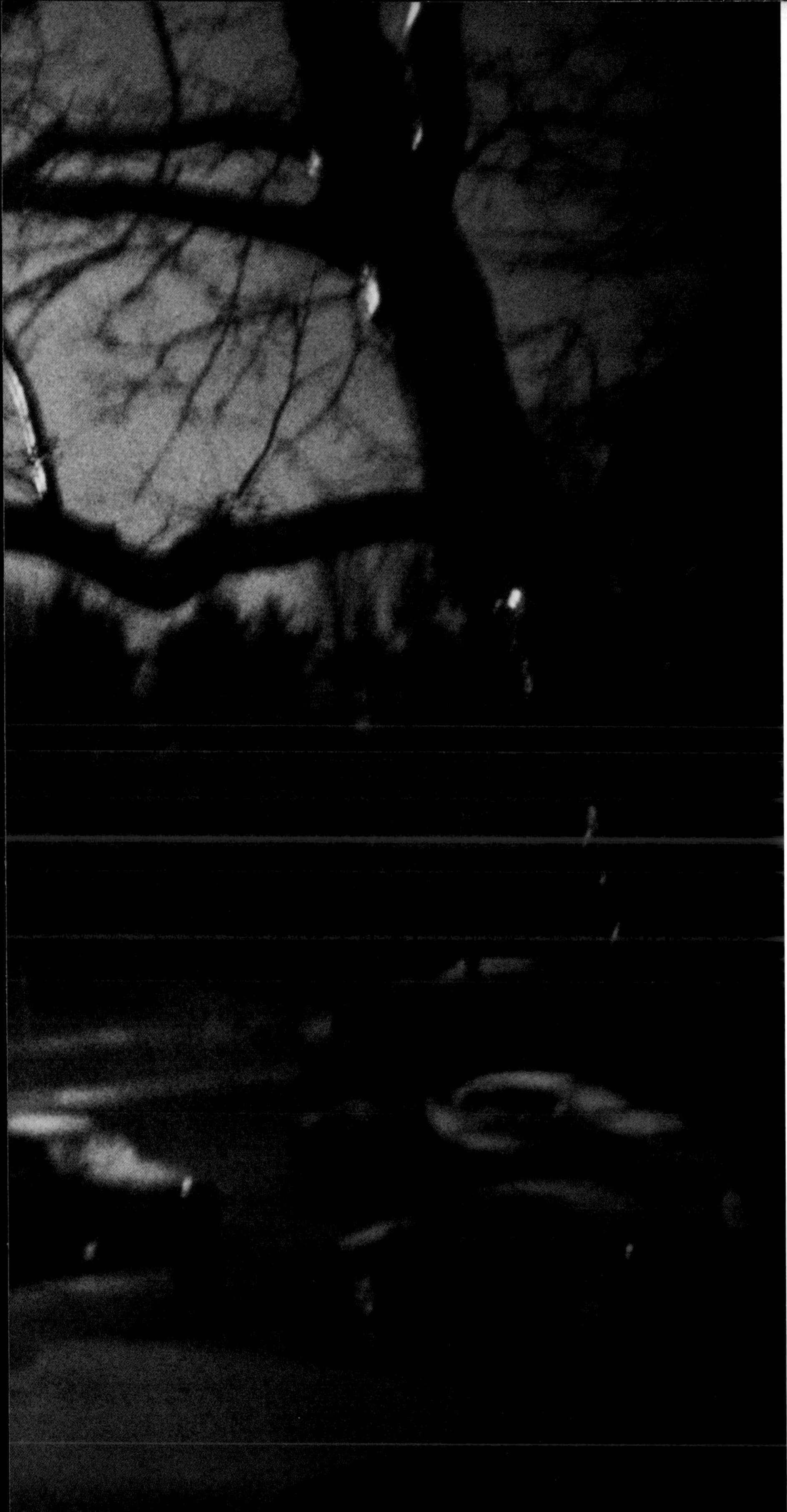

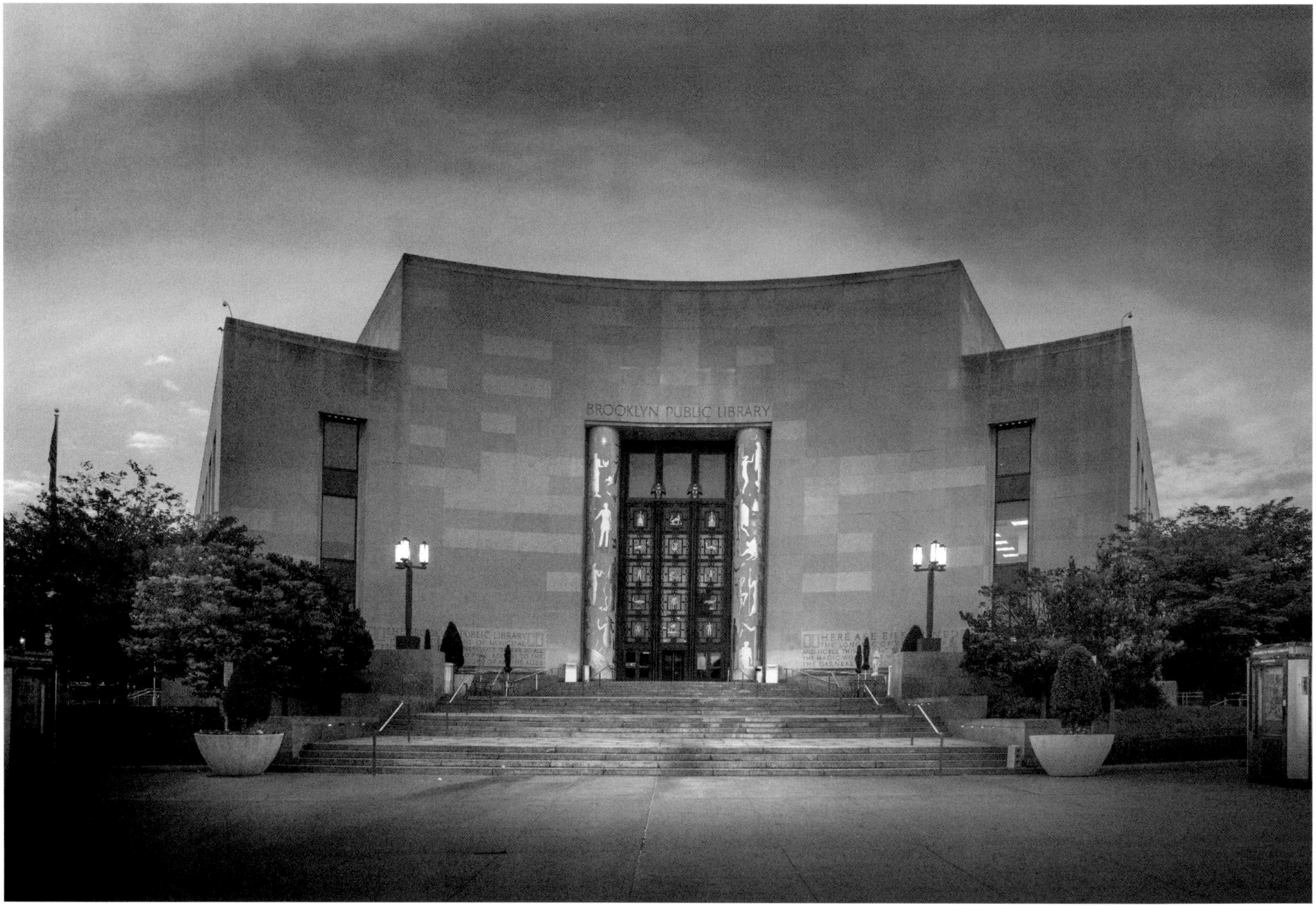
BROOKLYN PUBLIC LIBRARY

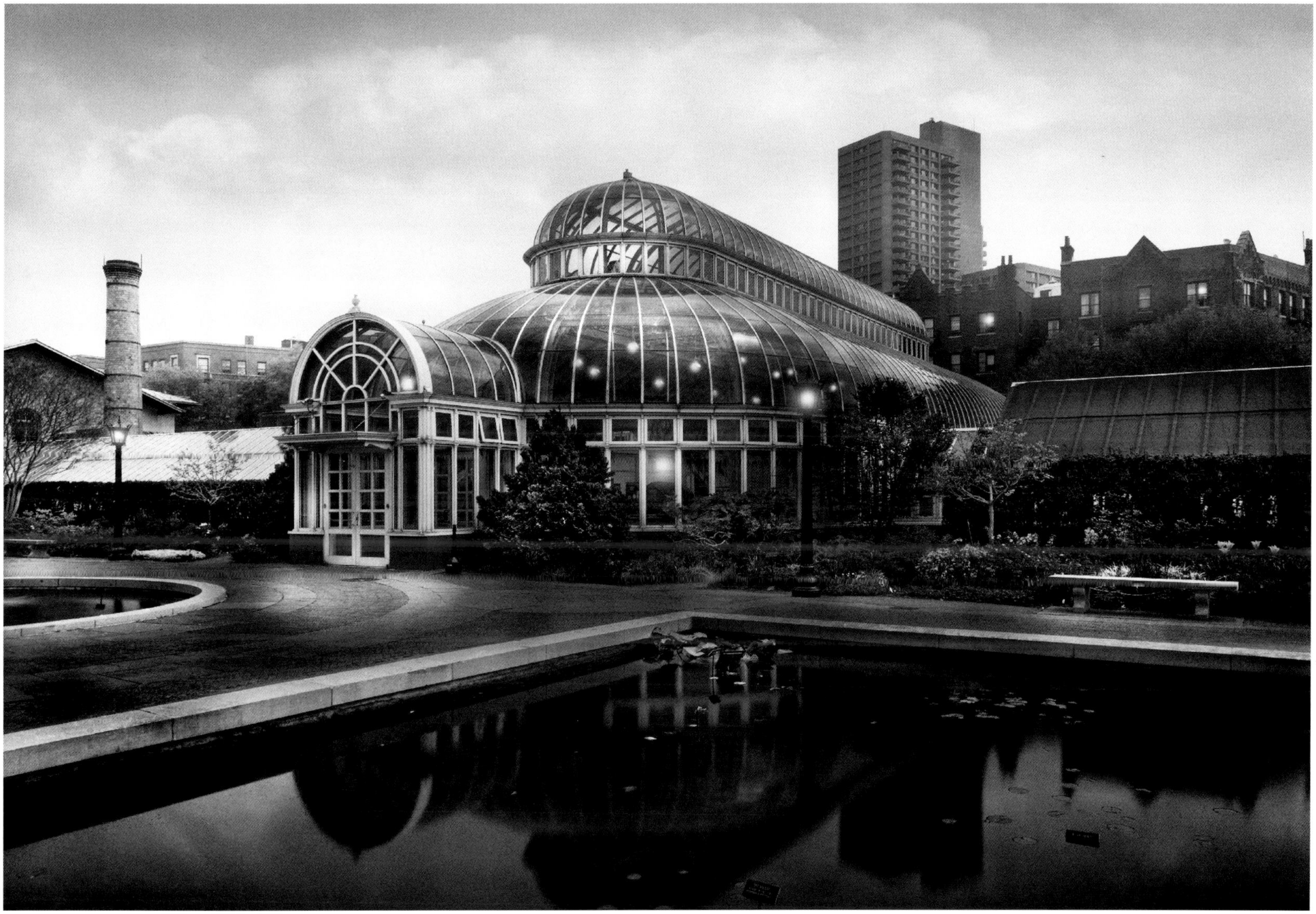

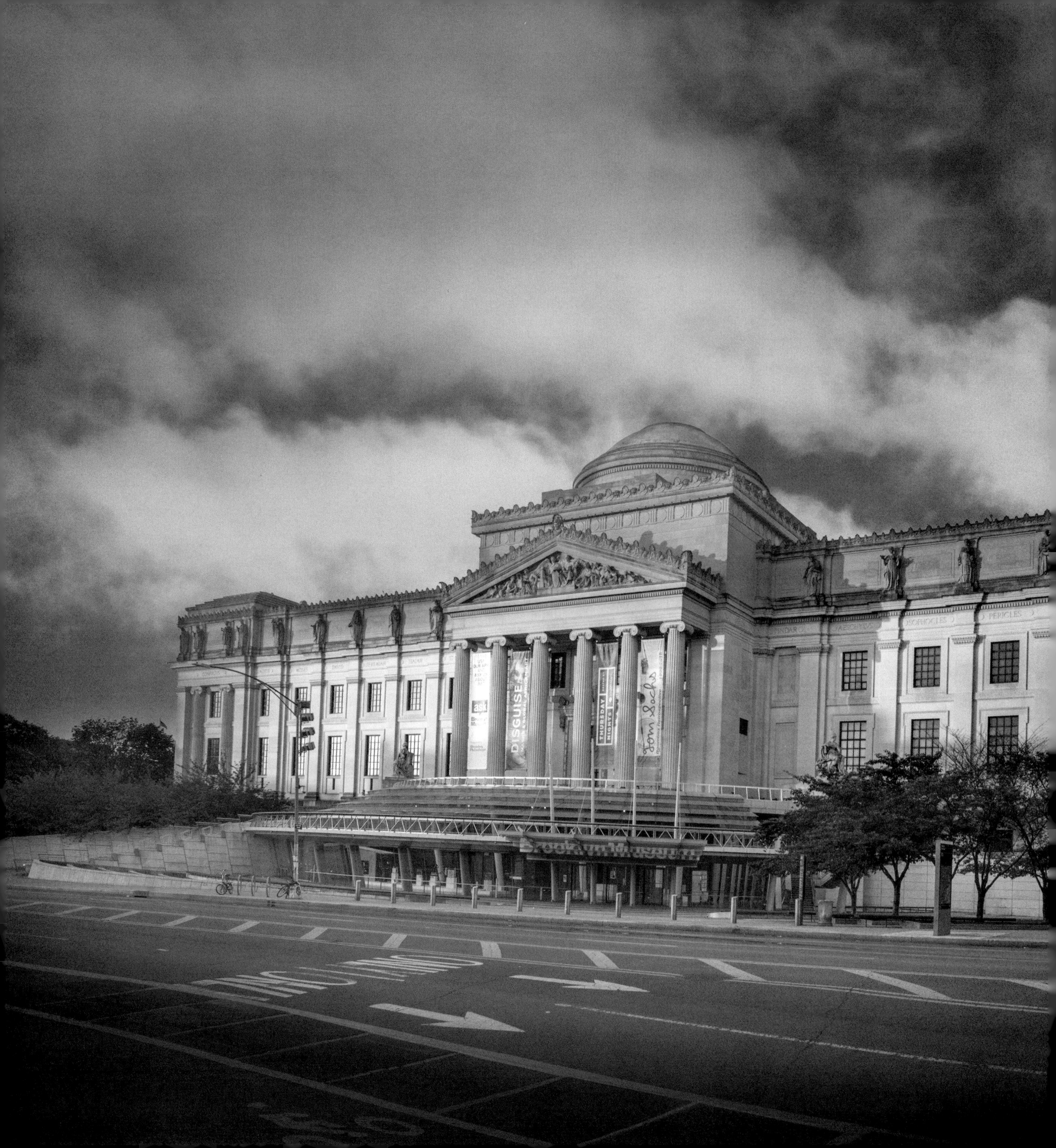
PERICLES
DISGUISE
THURSDAY
NIGHTS
ask

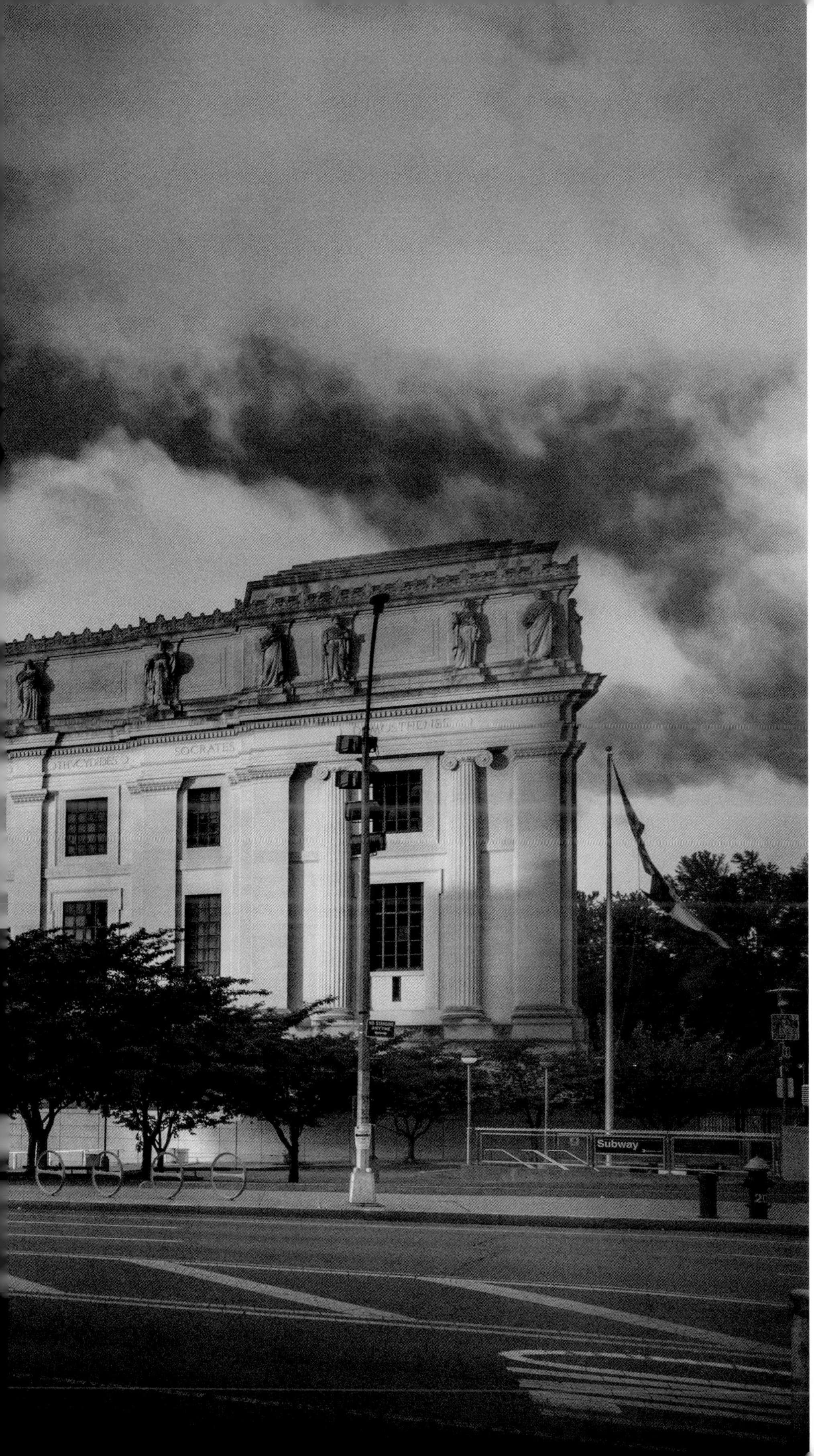
THVCYDIDES
SOCRATES
Subway

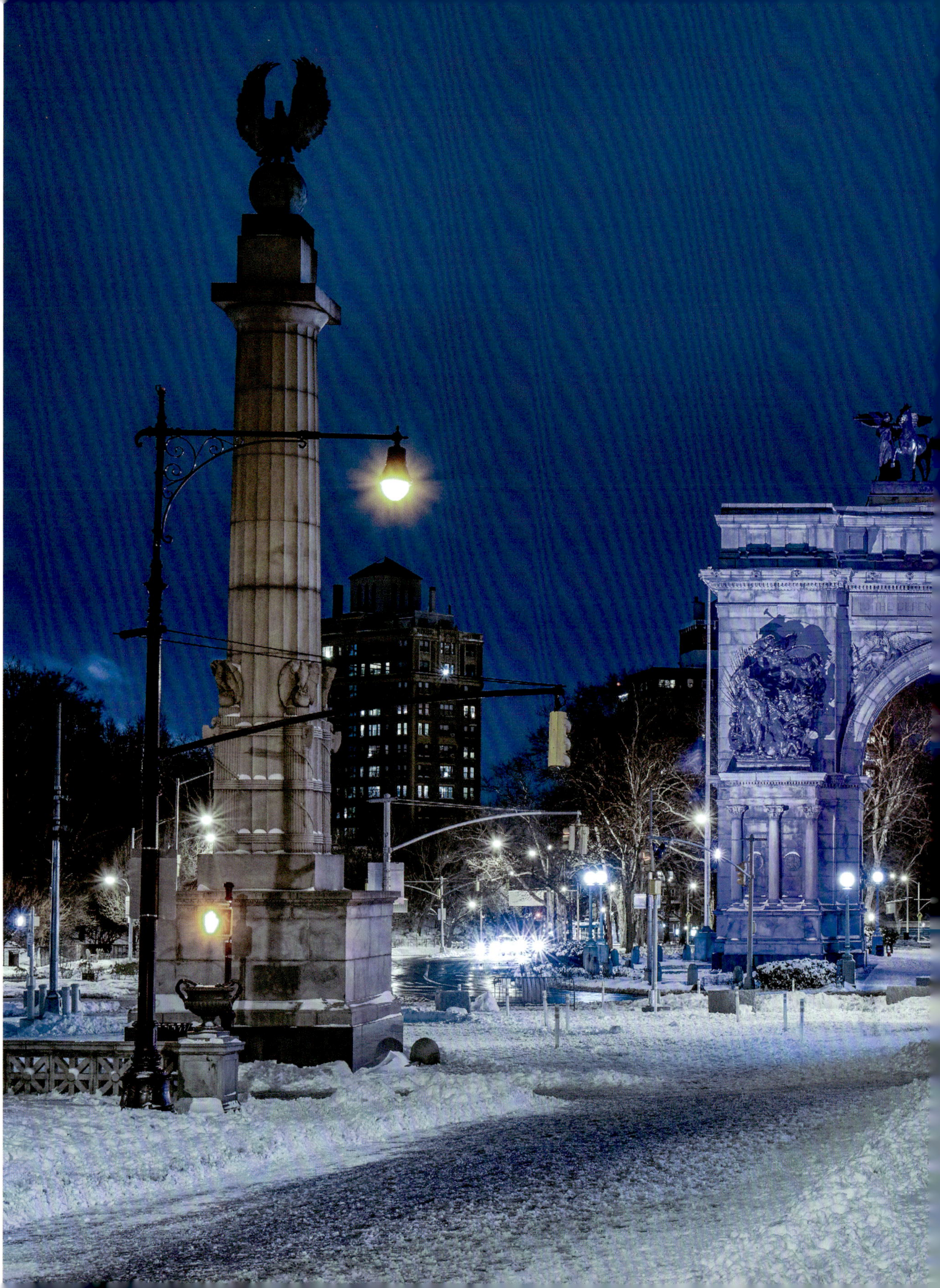

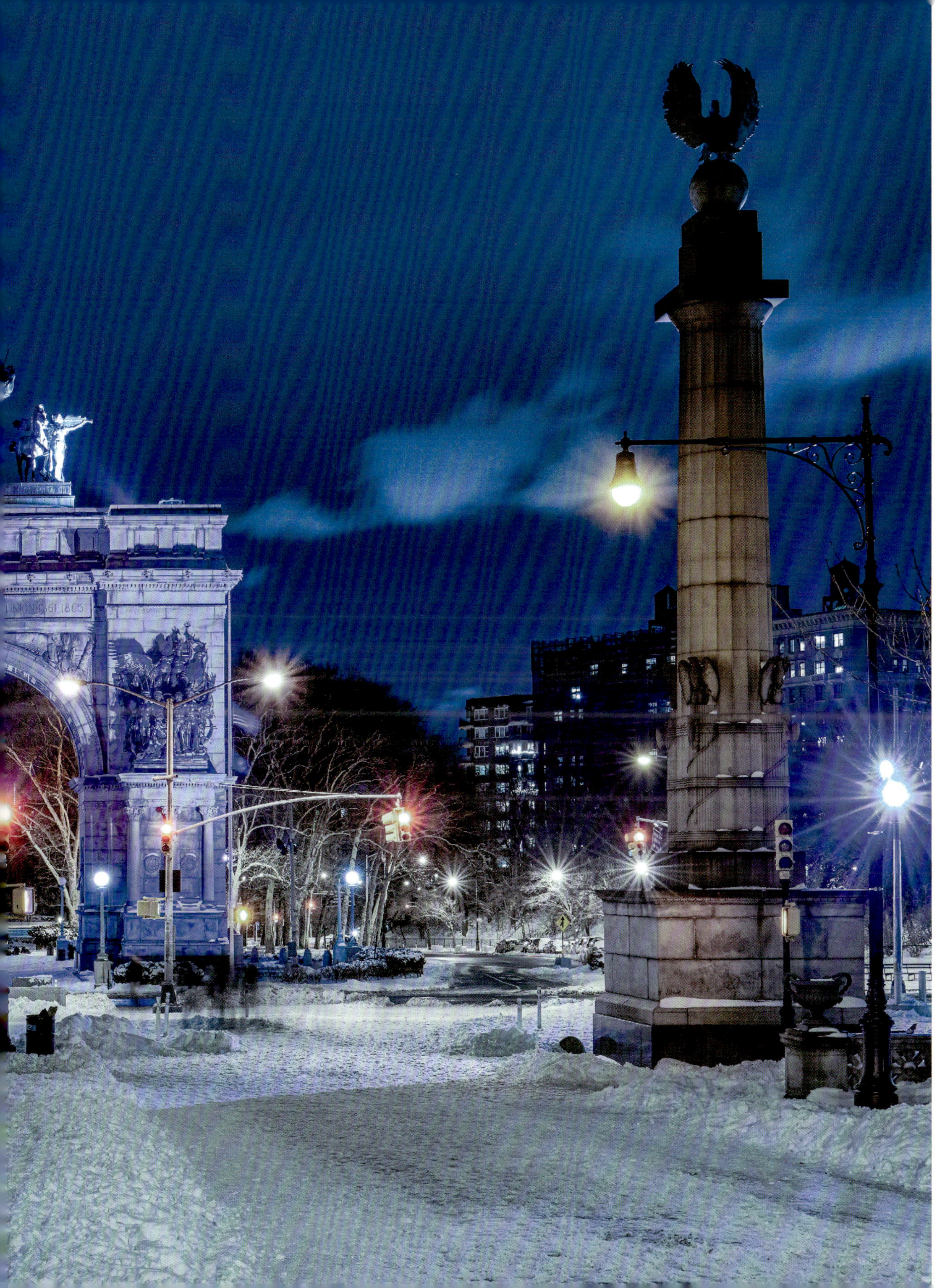

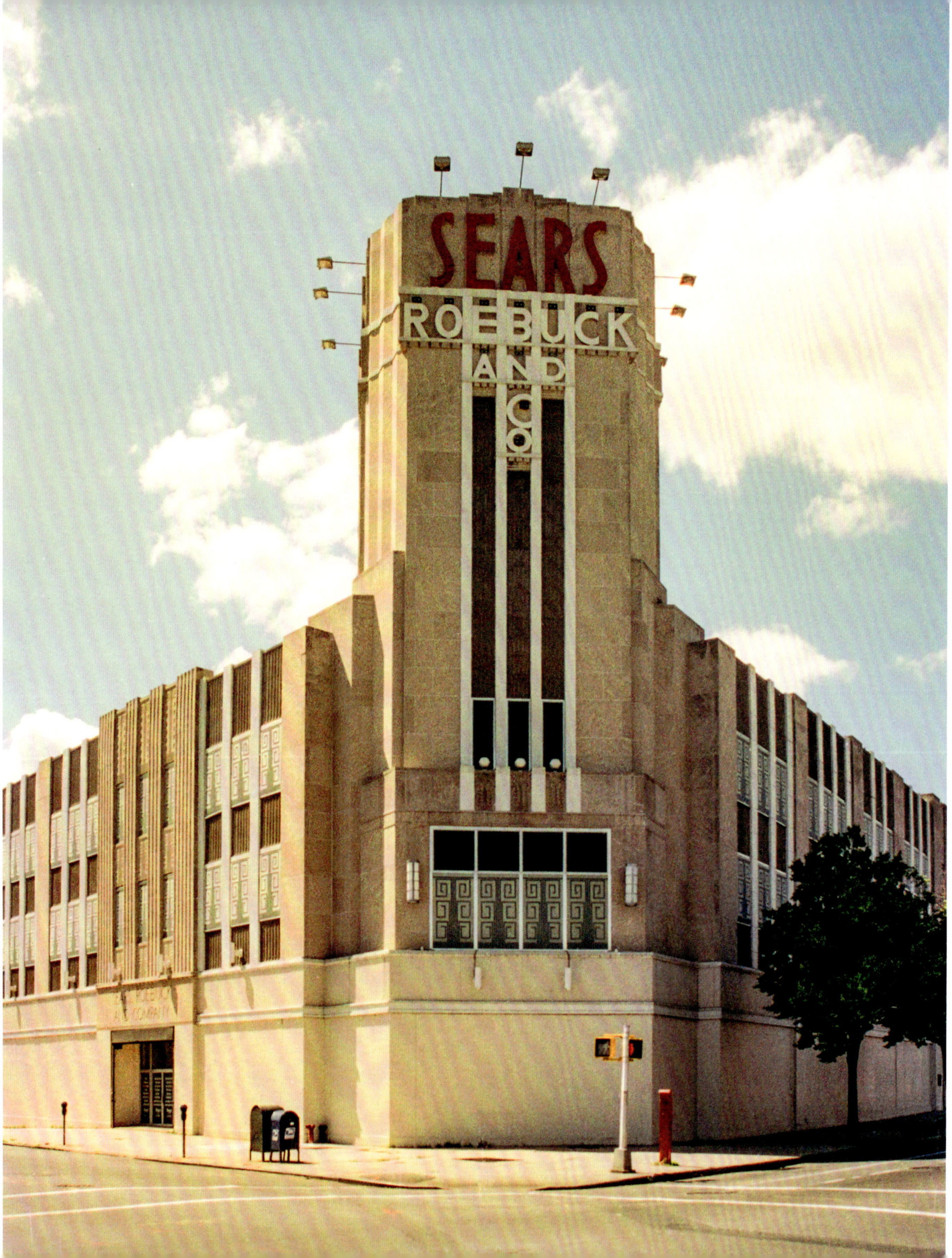
SEARS
ROEBUCK
AND
CO.

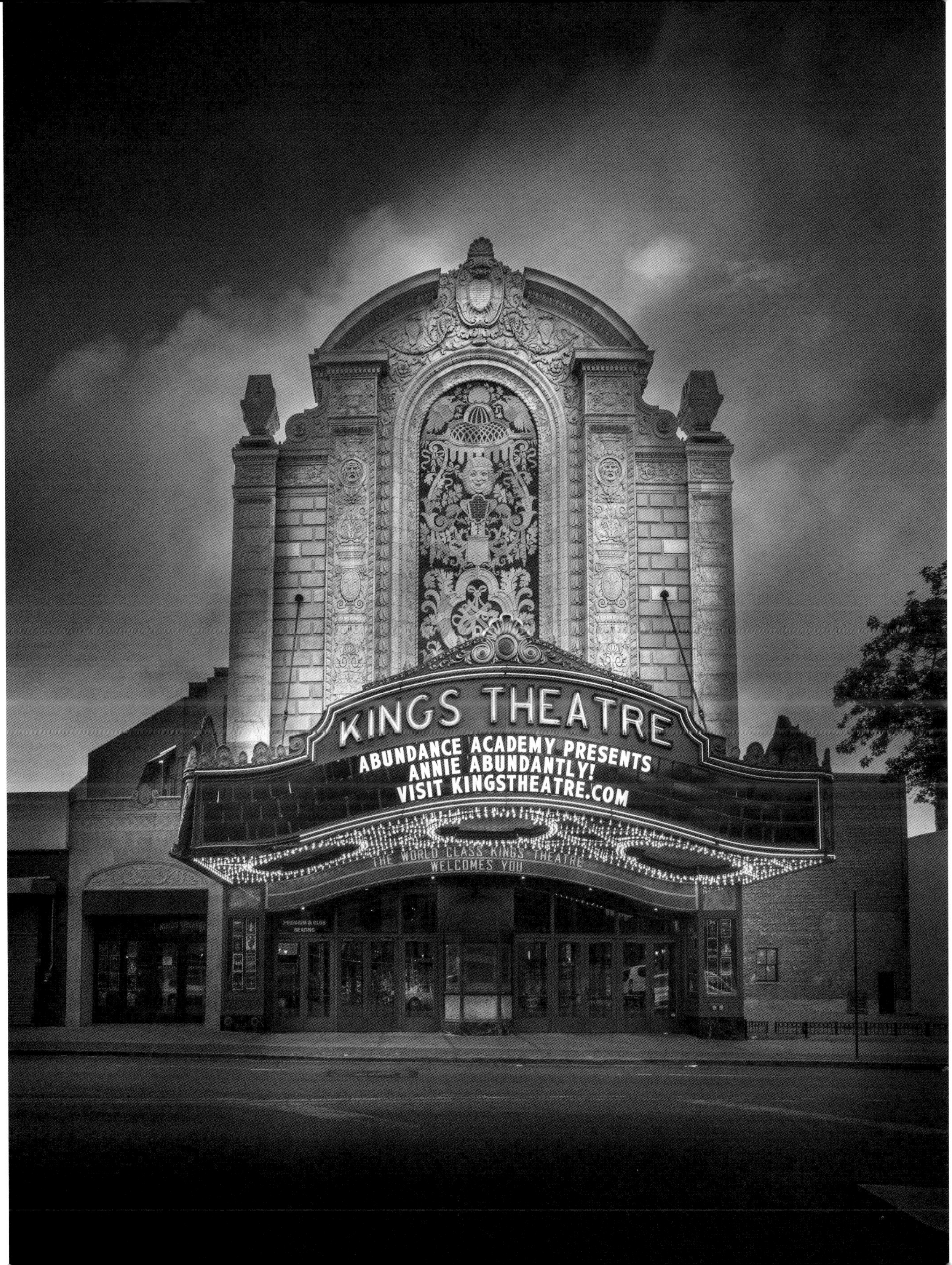
KINGS THEATRE
ABUNDANCE ACADEMY PRESENTS
ANNIE ABUNDANTLY!
VISIT KINGSTHEATRE.COM
THE WORLD CLASS KINGS THEATRE
WELCOMES YOU
PREMIUM & CLUB SEATING

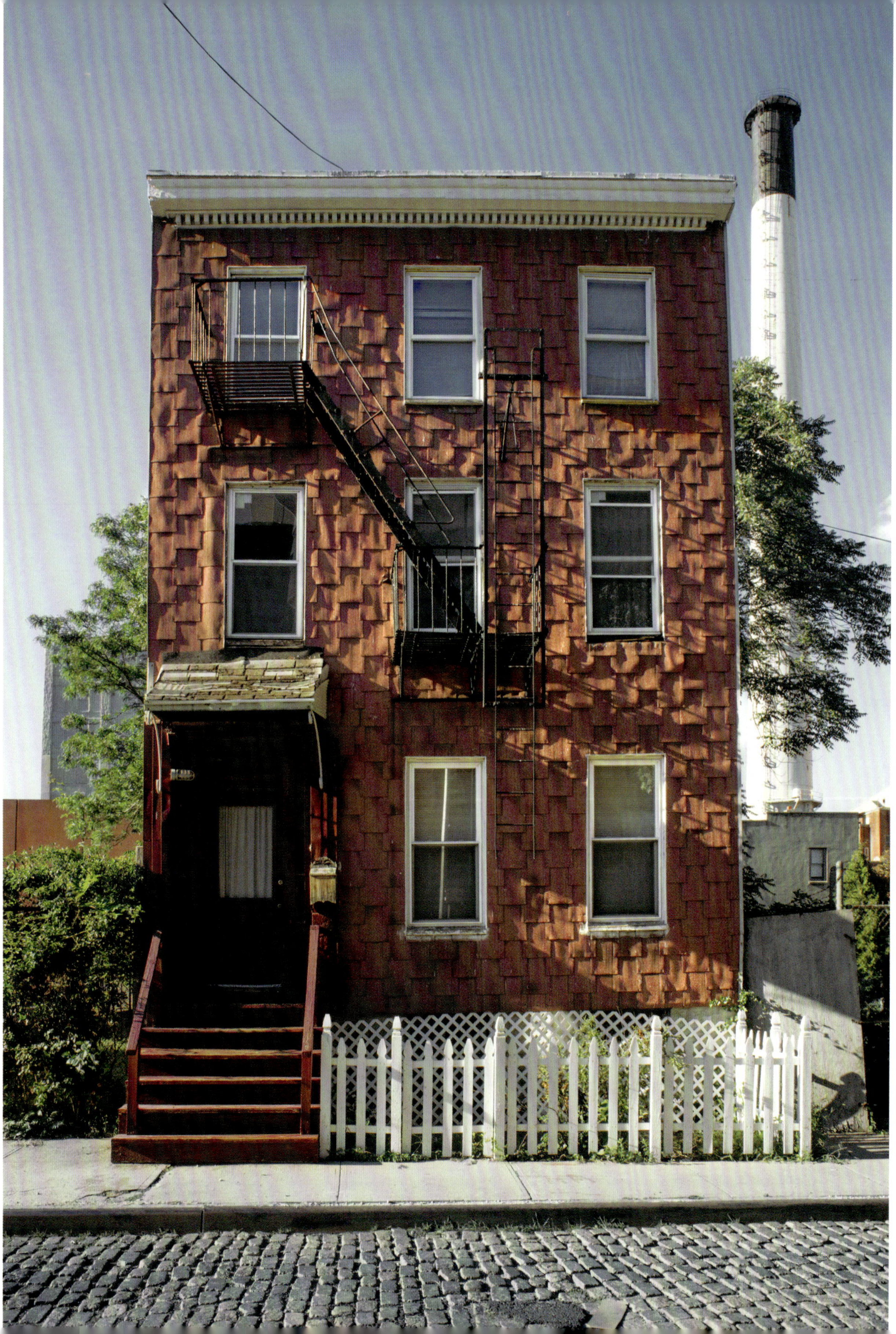

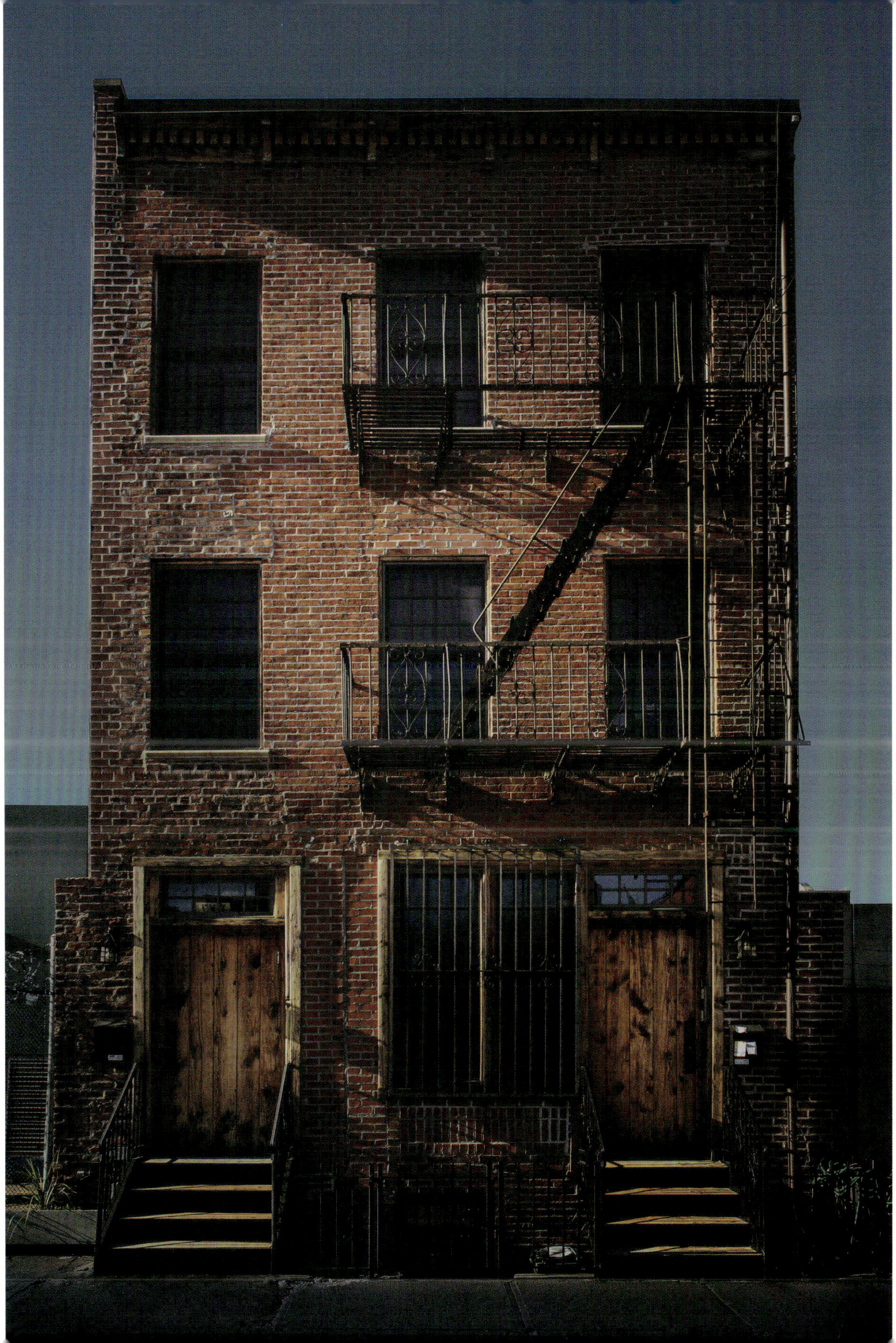

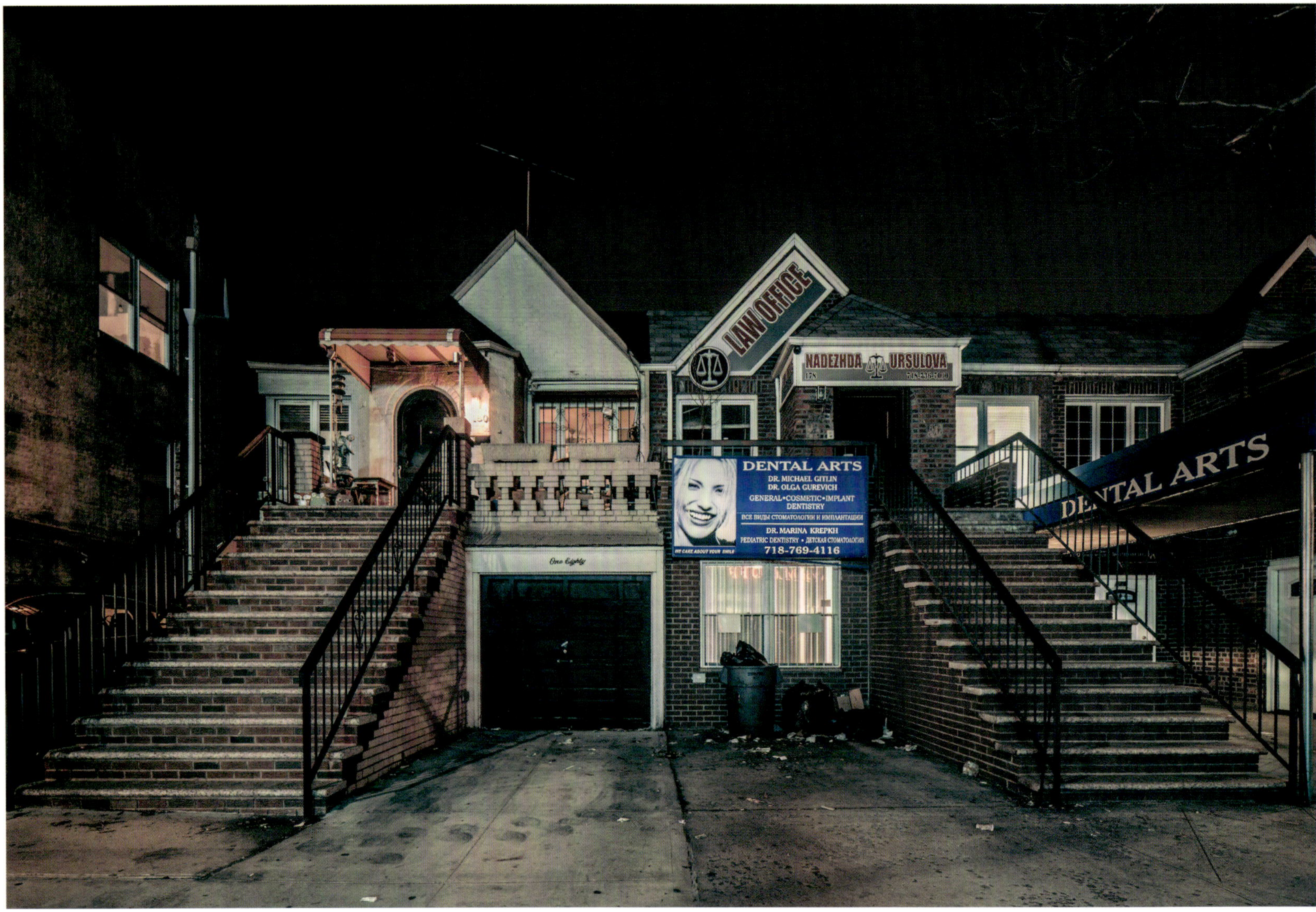
LAW OFFICE
NADEZHDA URSULOVA
DENTAL ARTS
DR. MICHAEL GITLIN
DR. OLGA GUREVICH
GENERAL•COSMETIC•IMPLANT
DENTISTRY
ВСЕ ВИДЫ СТОМАТОЛОГИИ И ИМПЛАНТАЦИИ
DR. MARINA KREPKH
PEDIATRIC DENTISTRY • ДЕТСКАЯ СТОМАТОЛОГИЯ
718-769-4116
WE CARE ABOUT YOUR SMILE
DENTAL ARTS

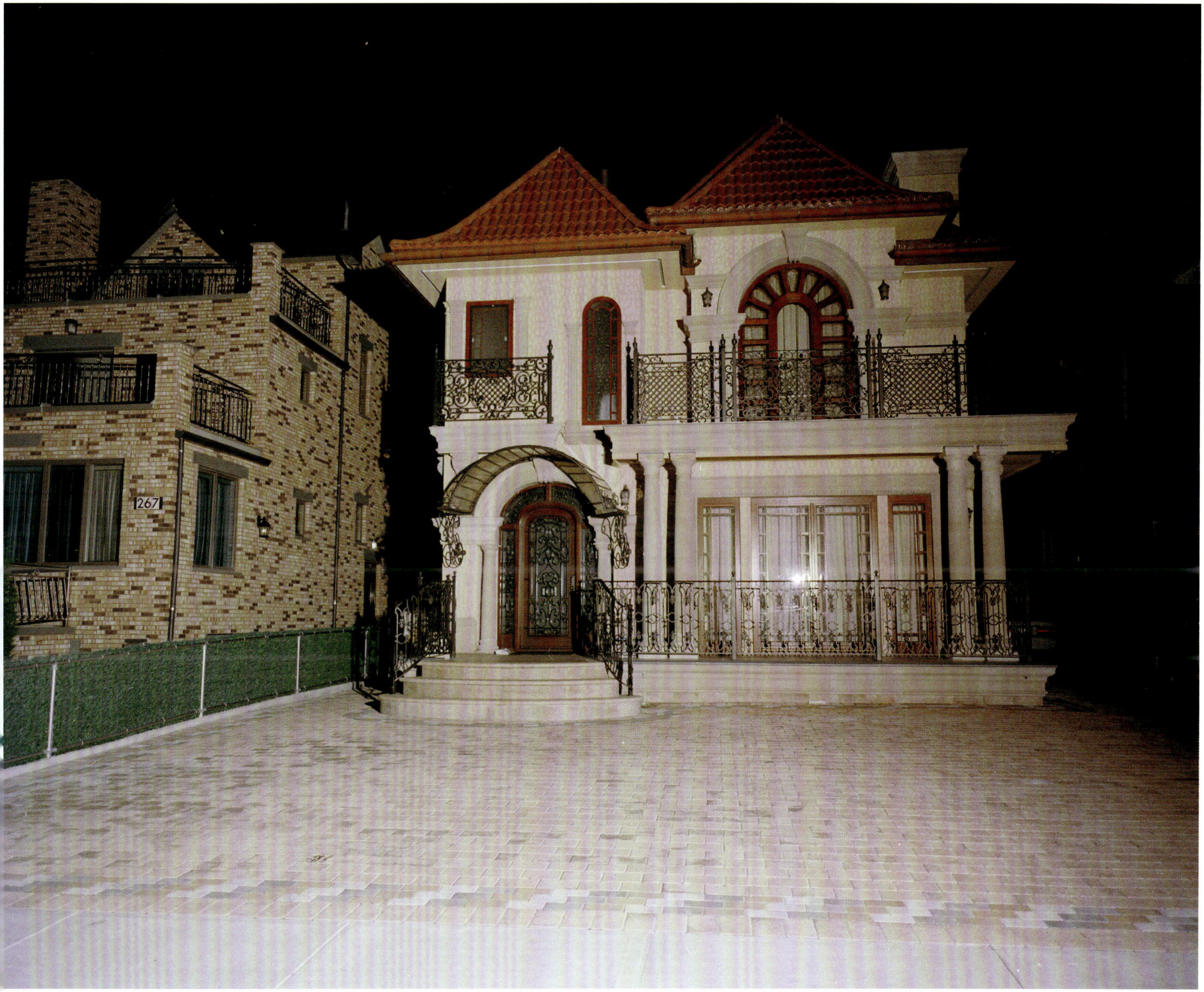
267

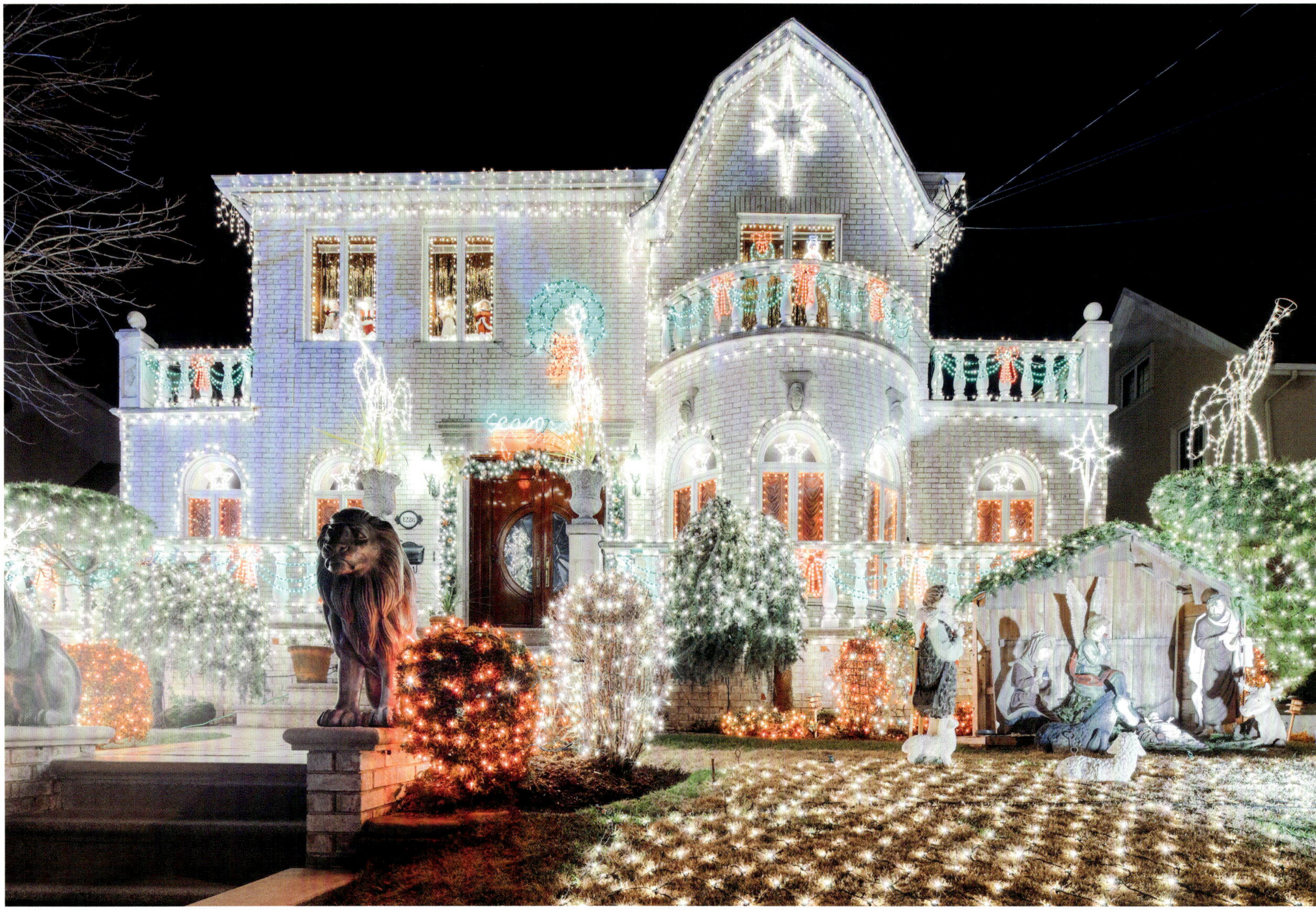

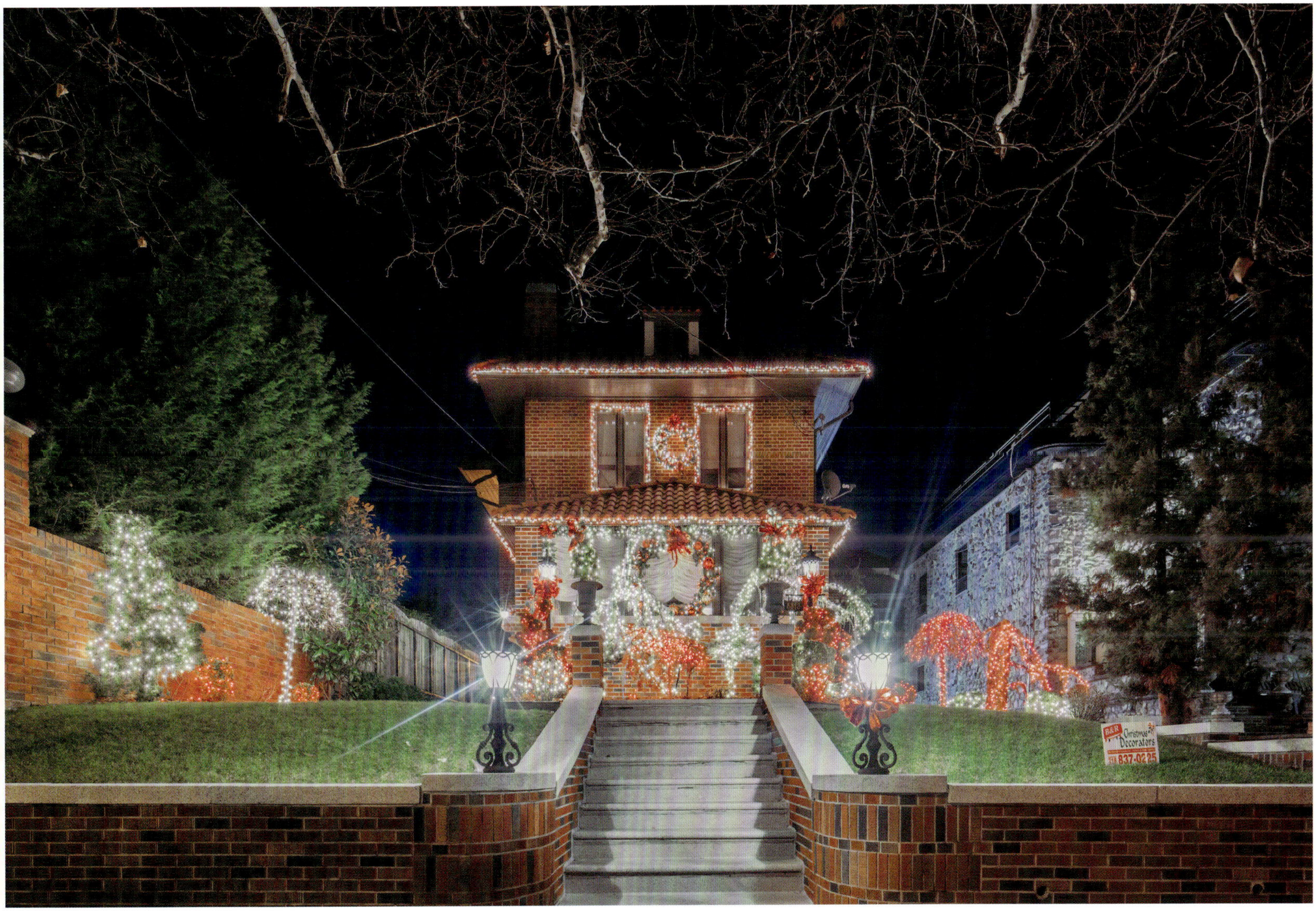
B&R
Christmas
Decorators
718 837-0225

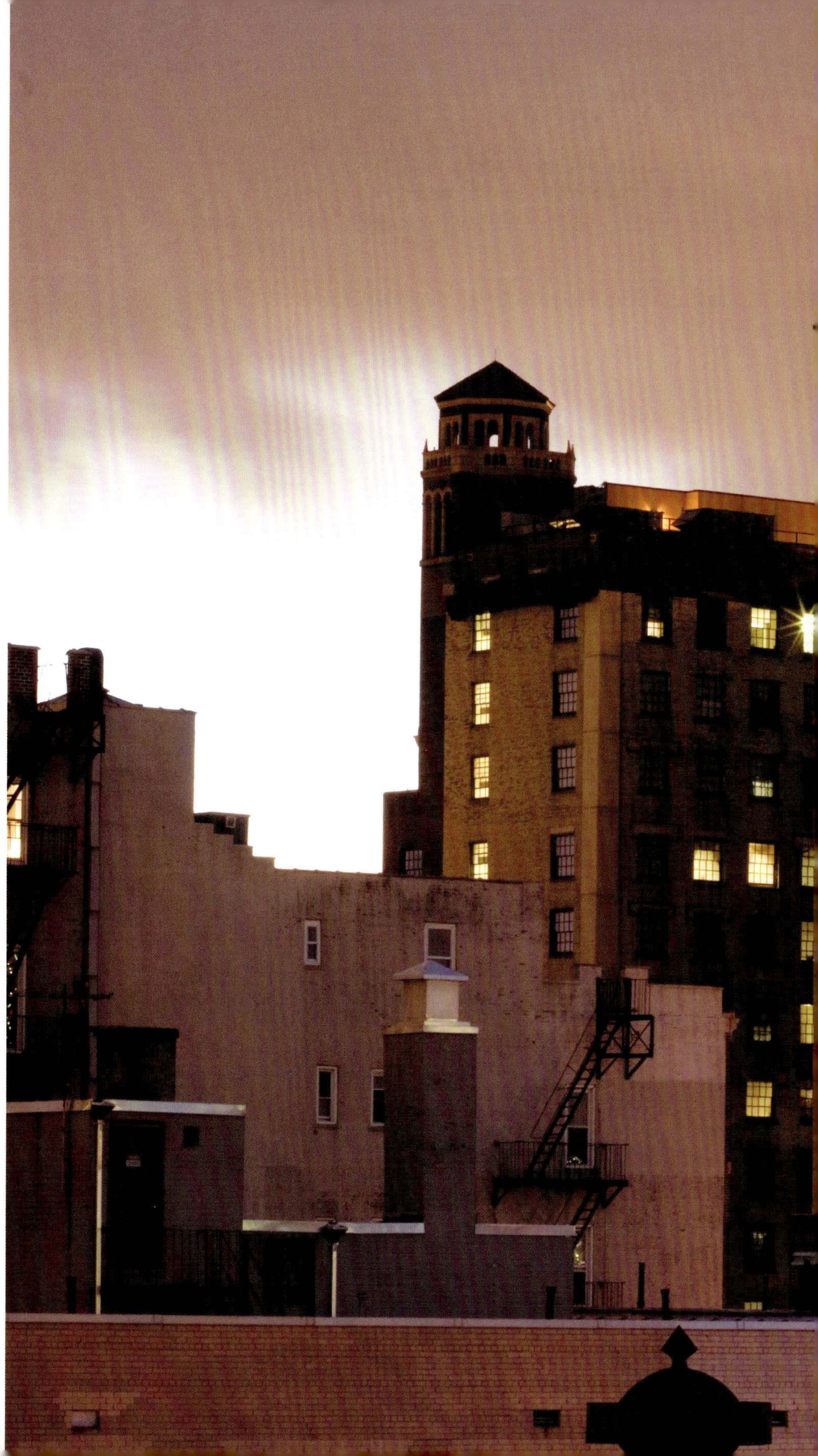

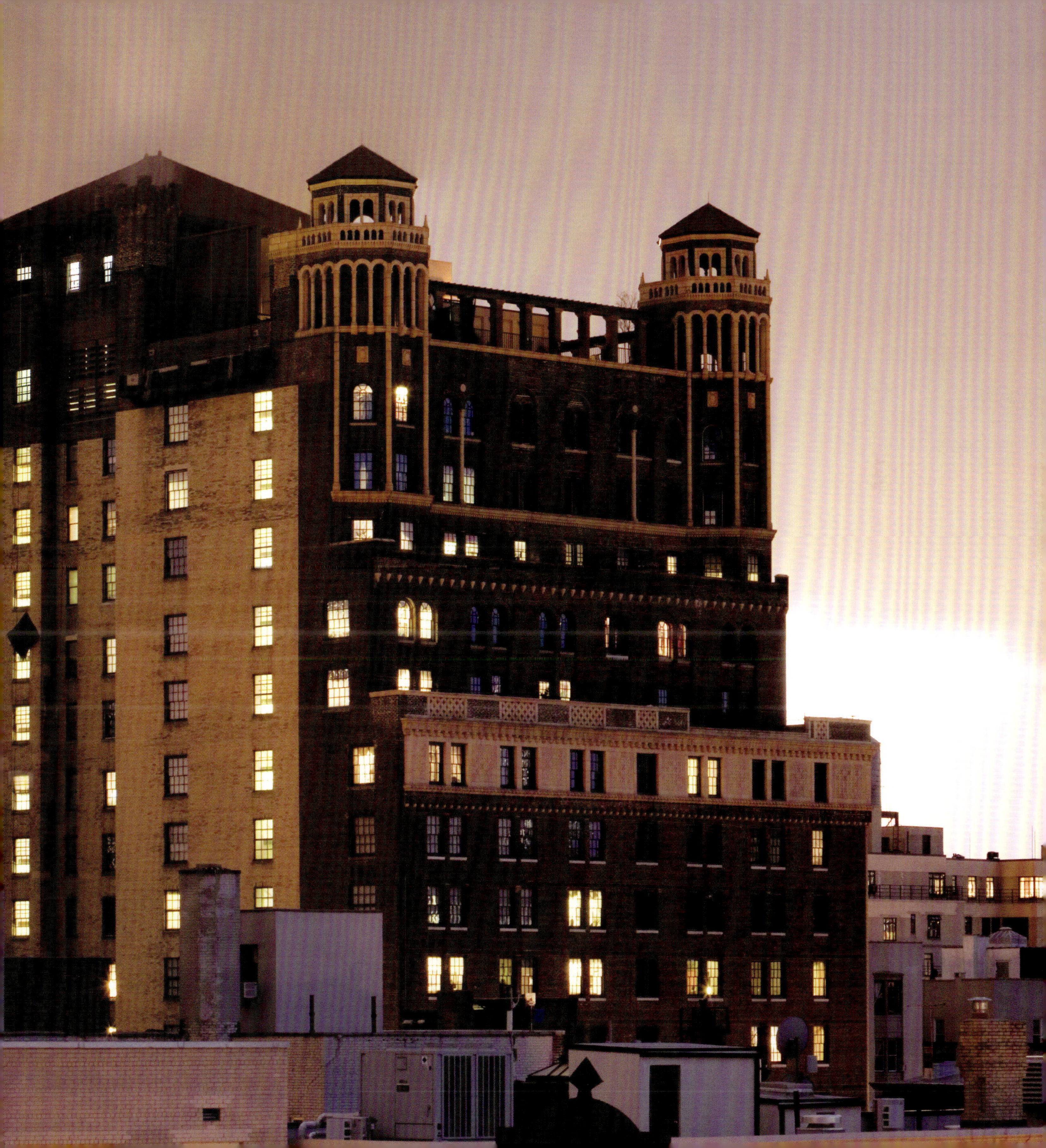

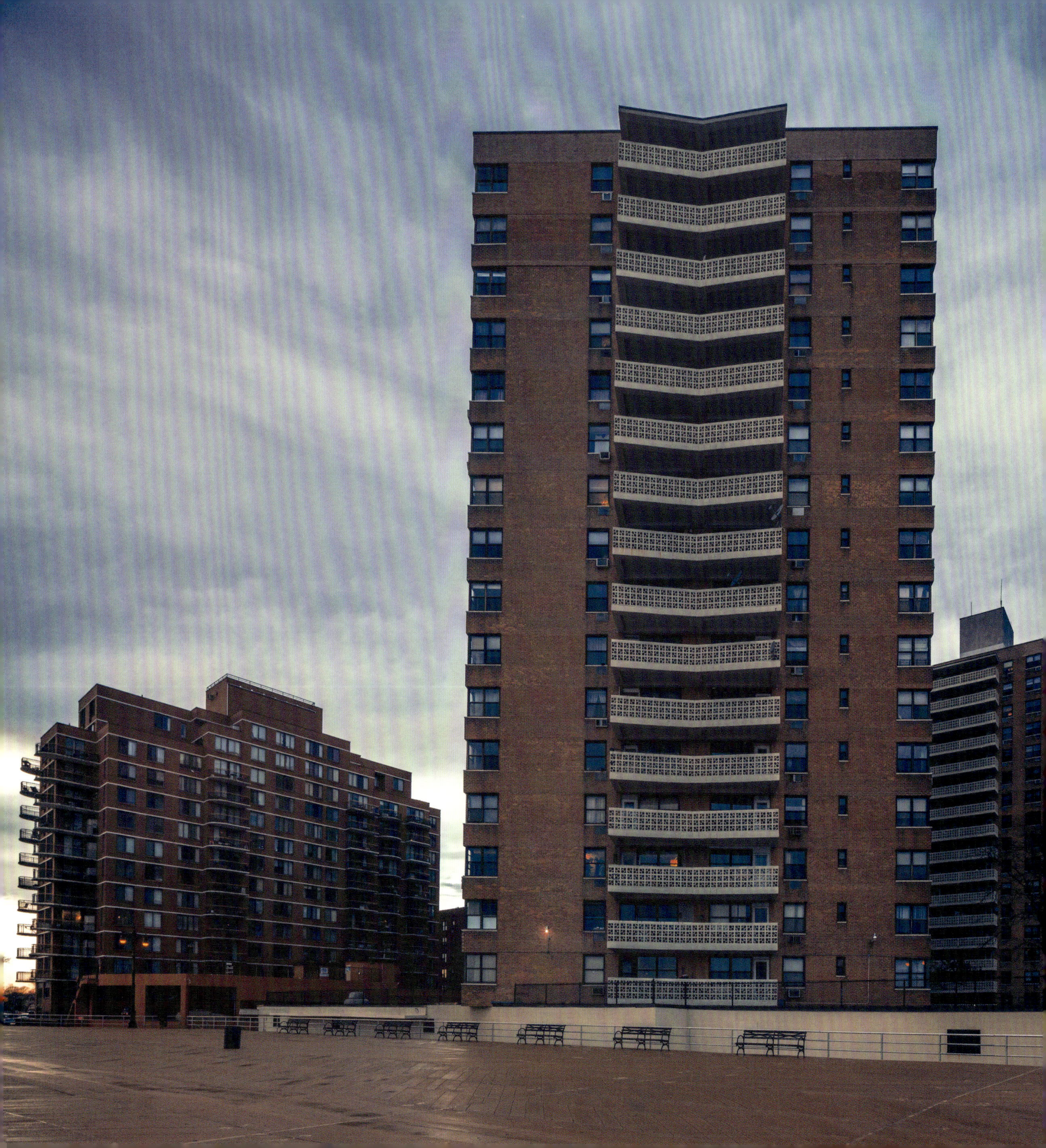

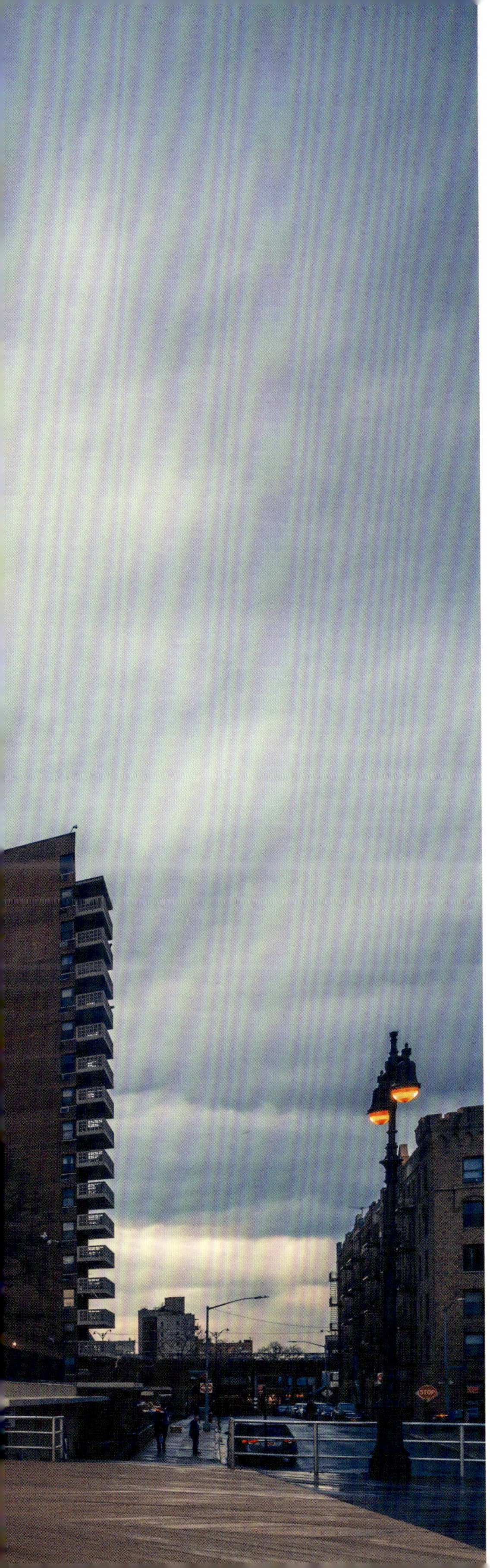

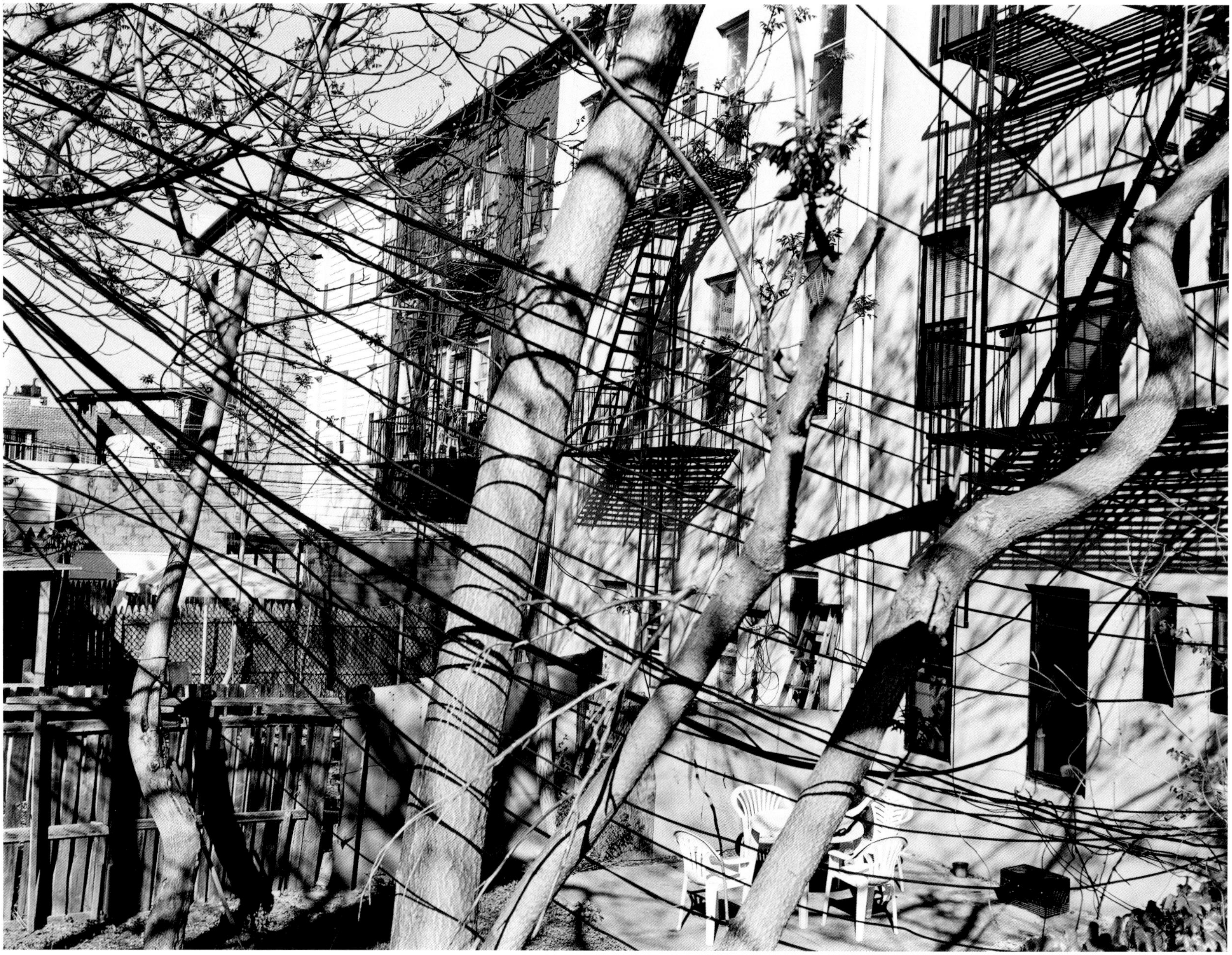

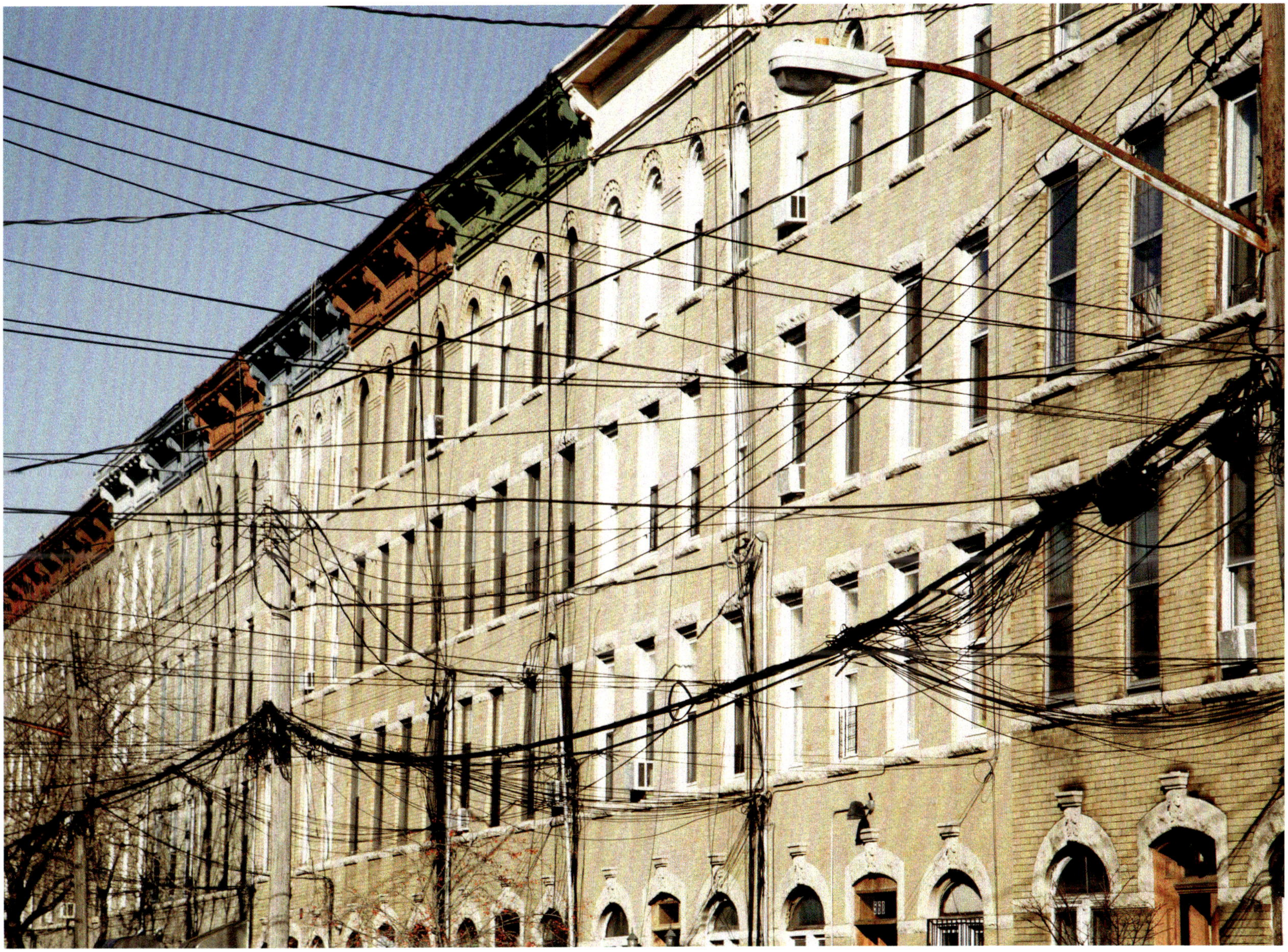

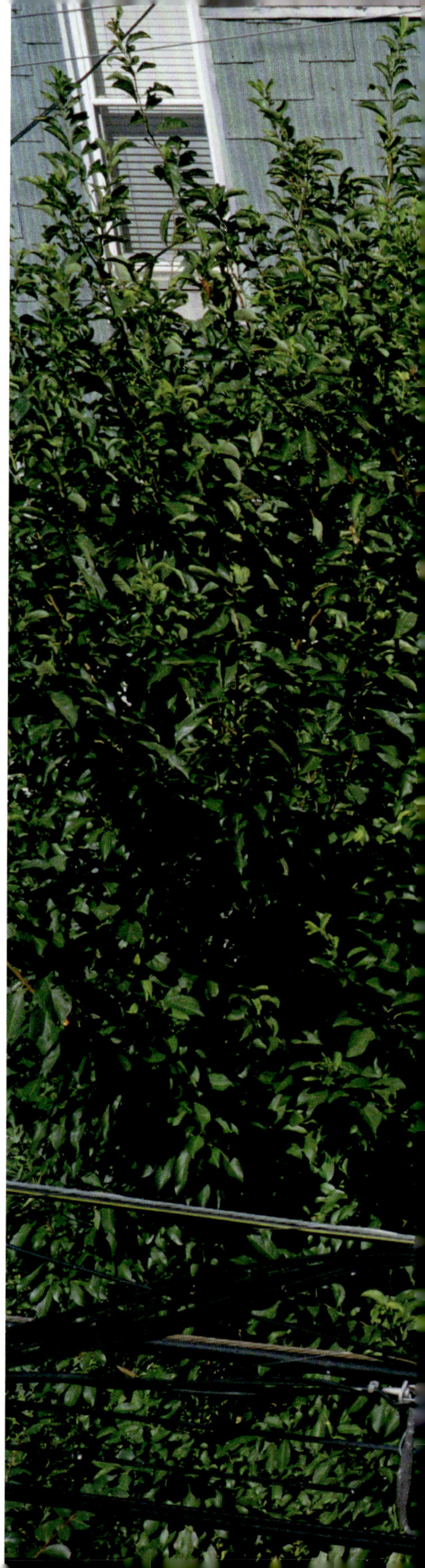

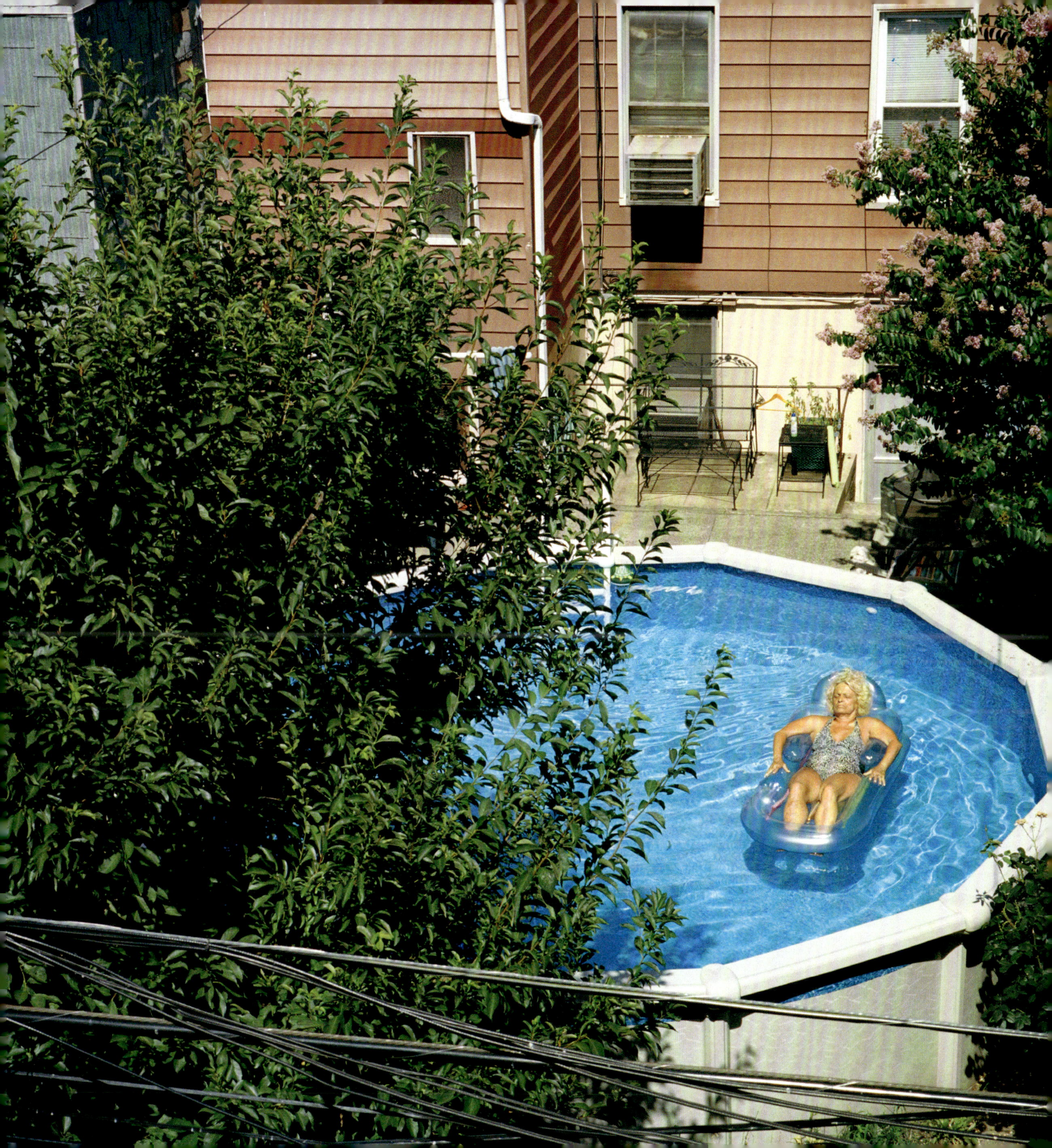

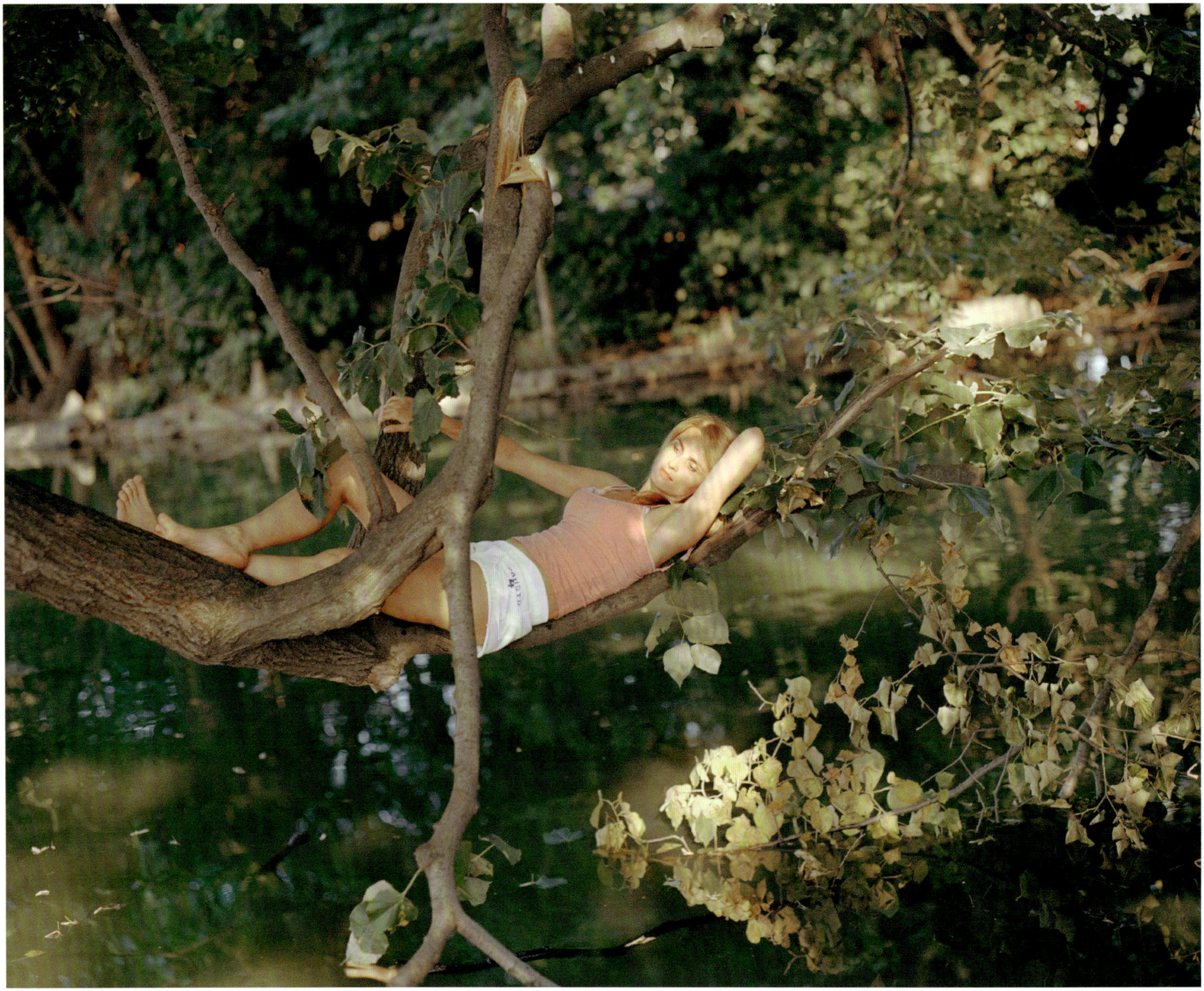

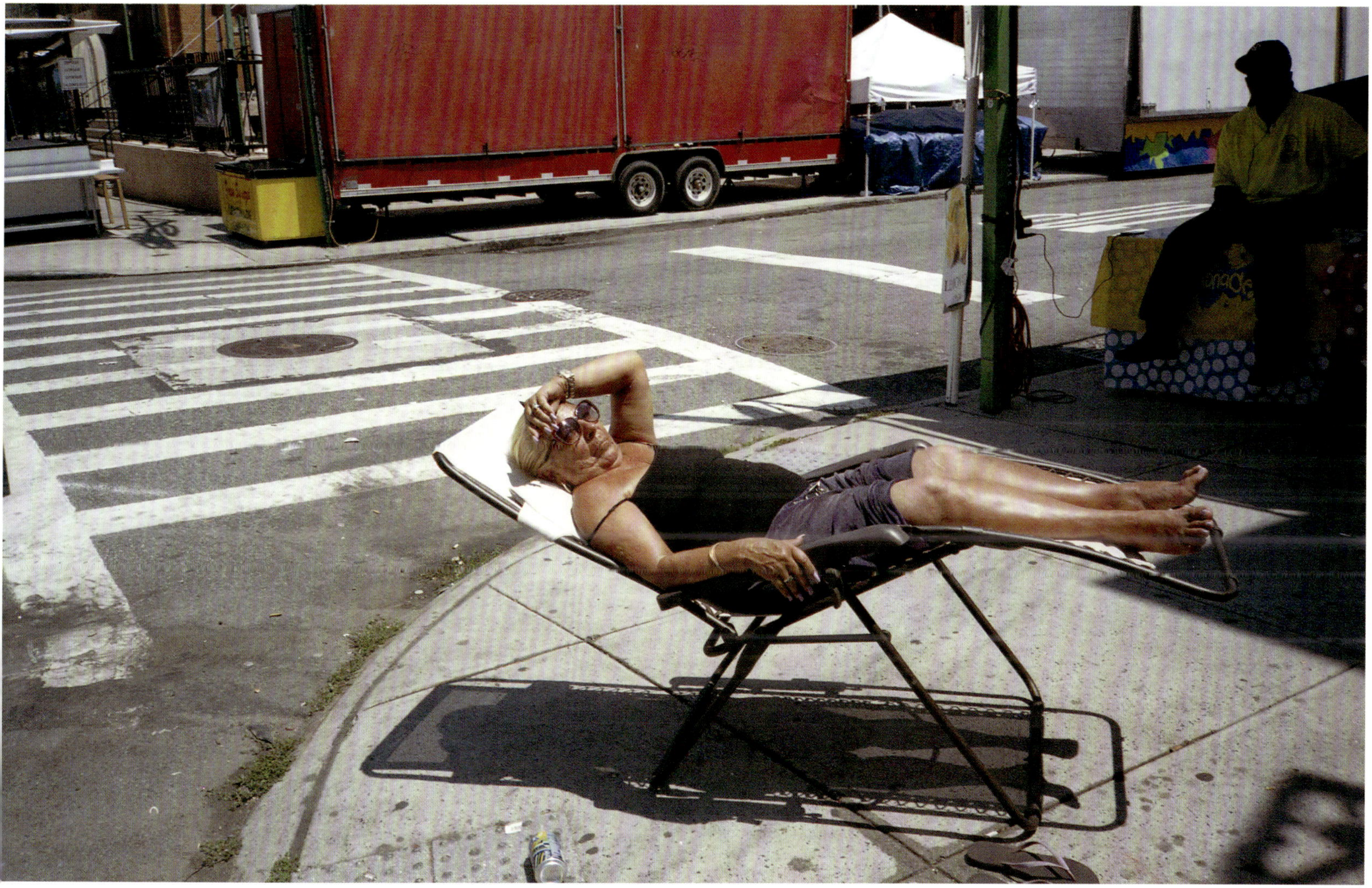

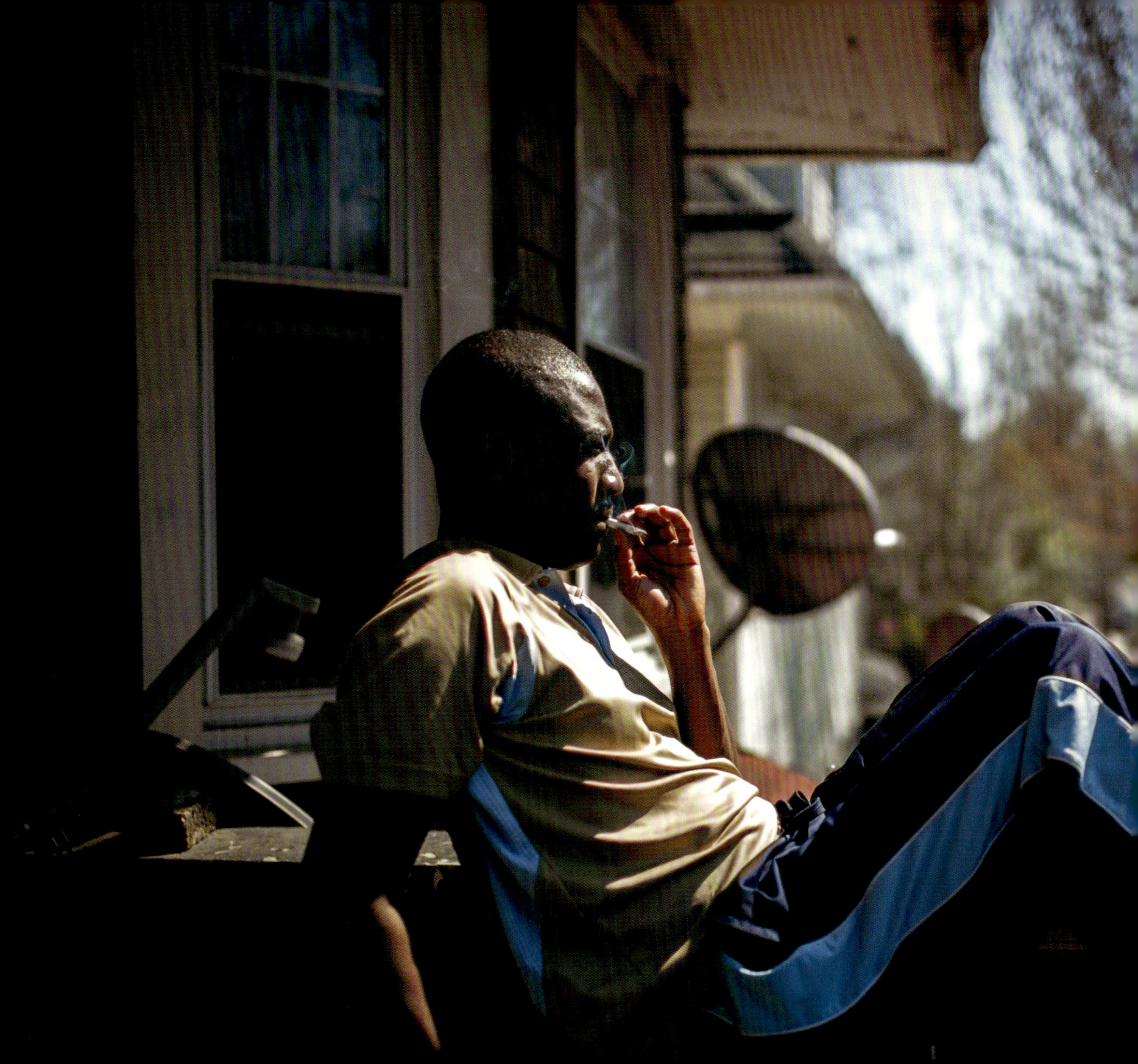

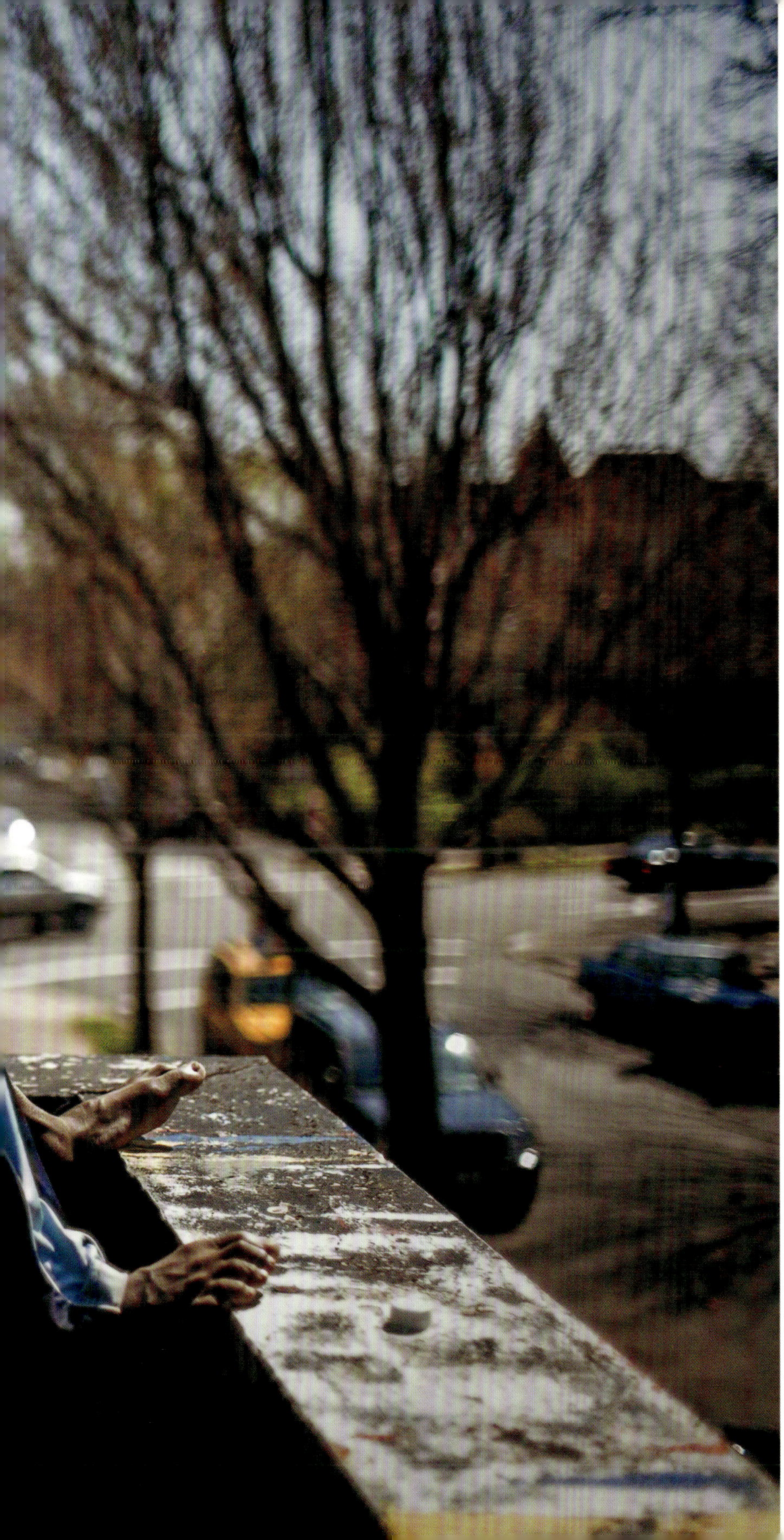

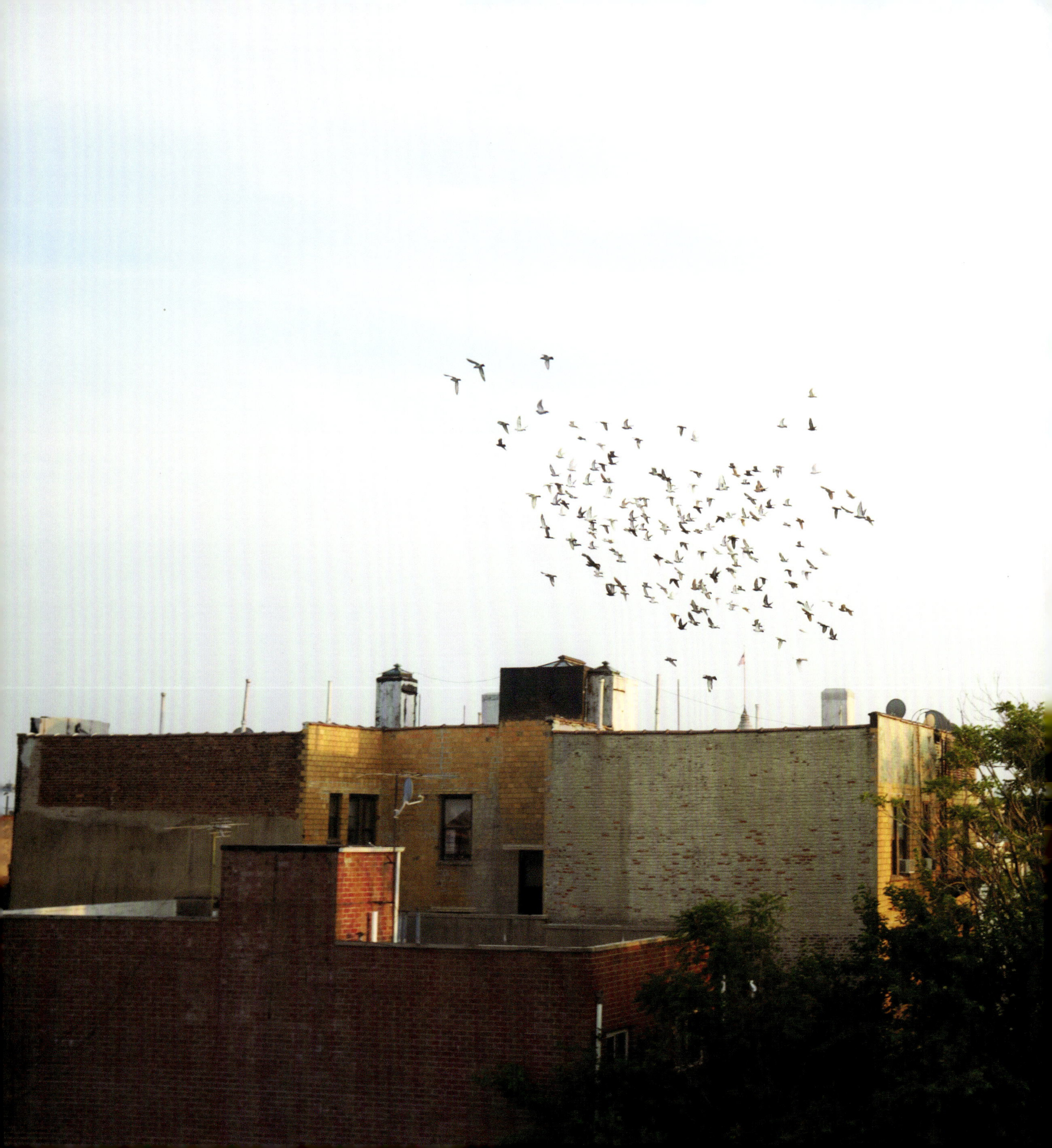

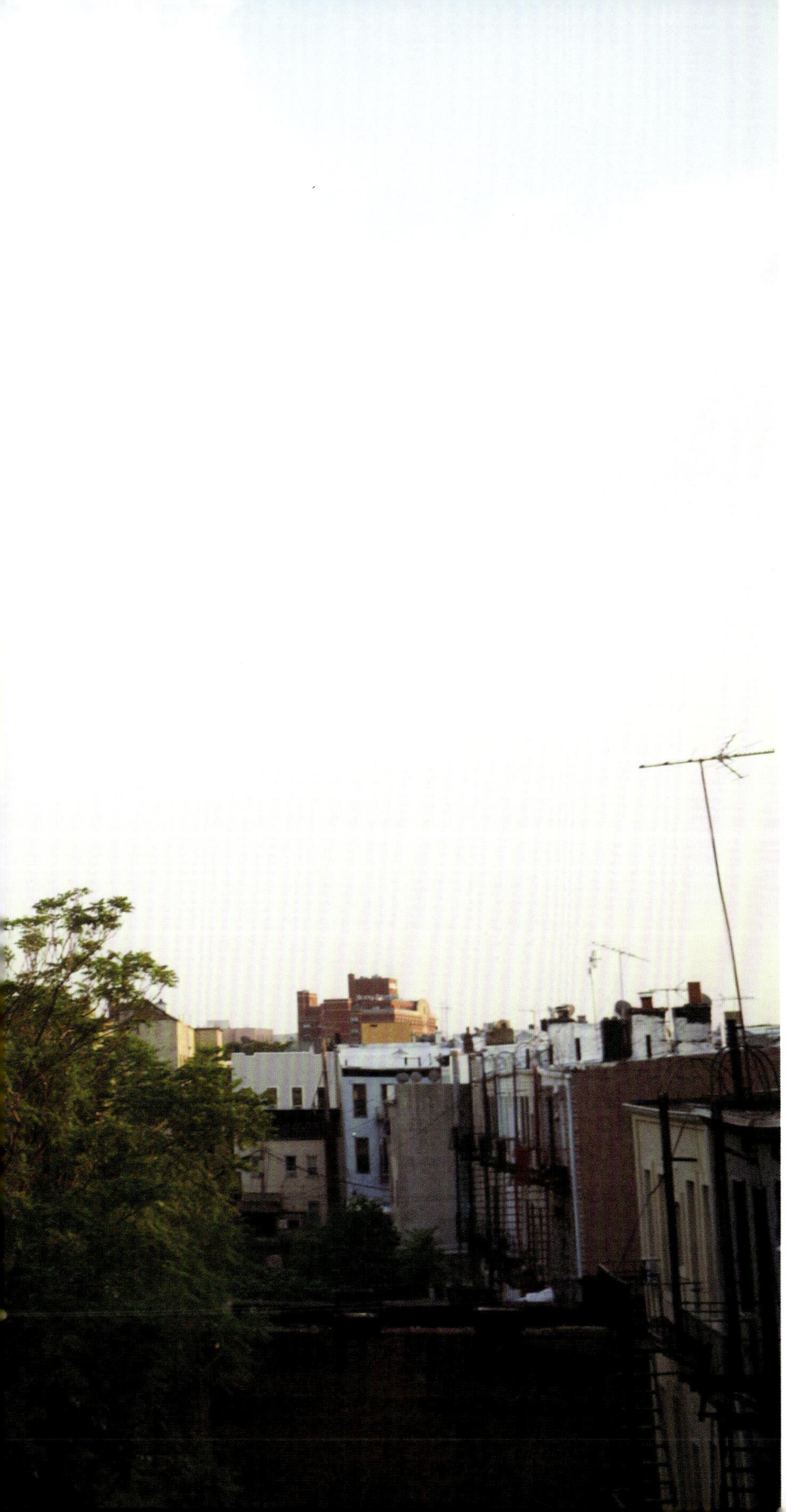

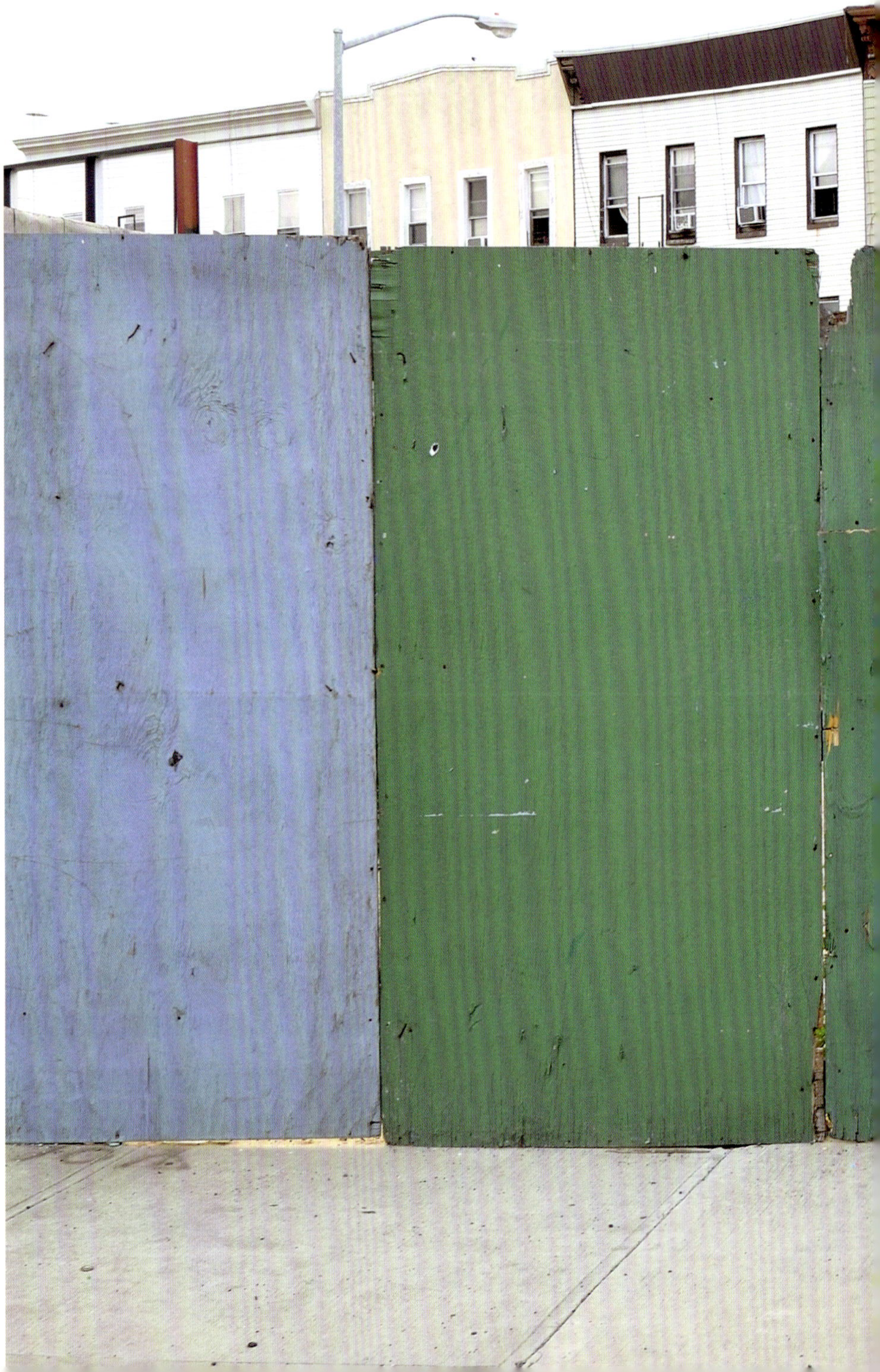

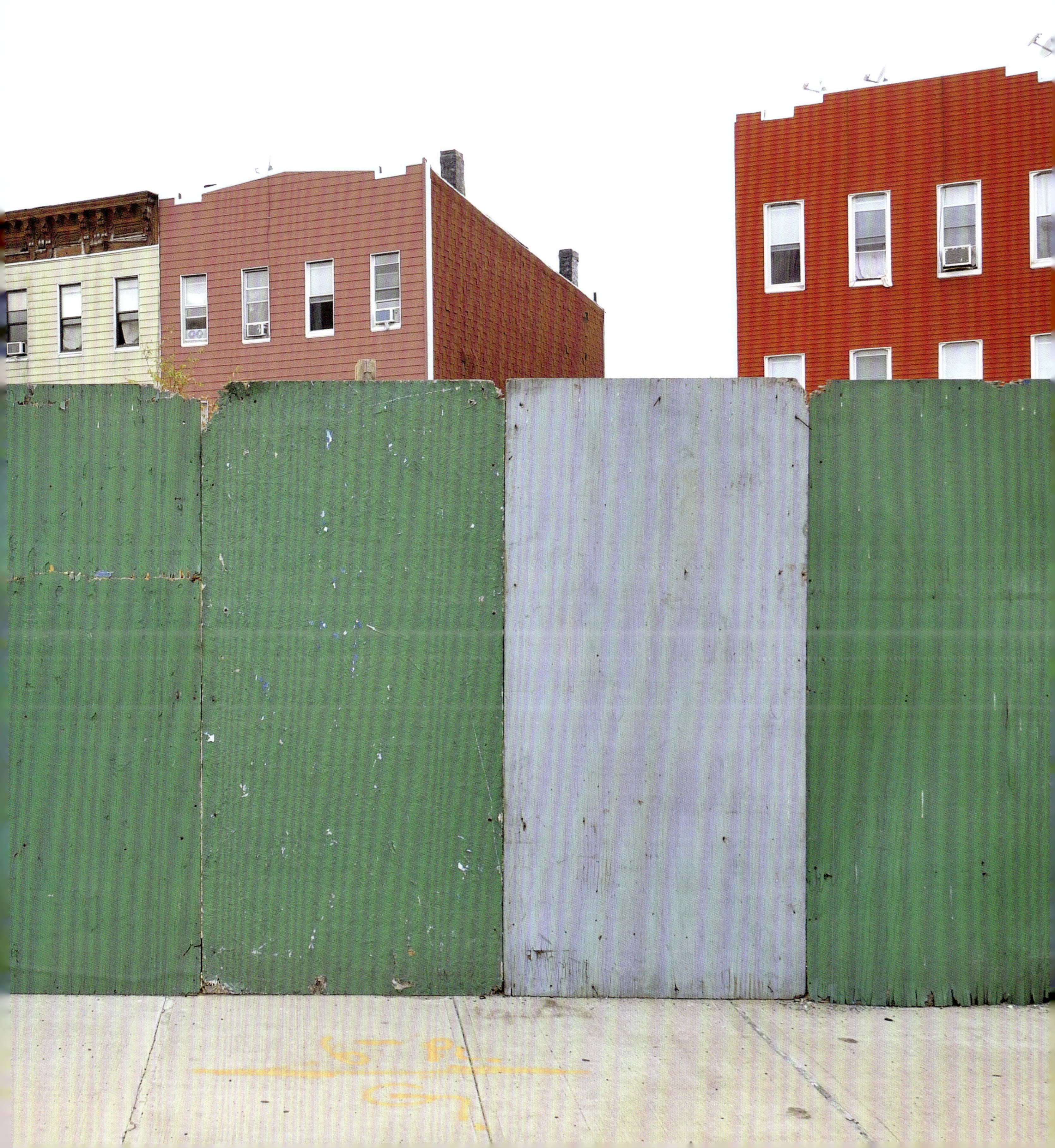

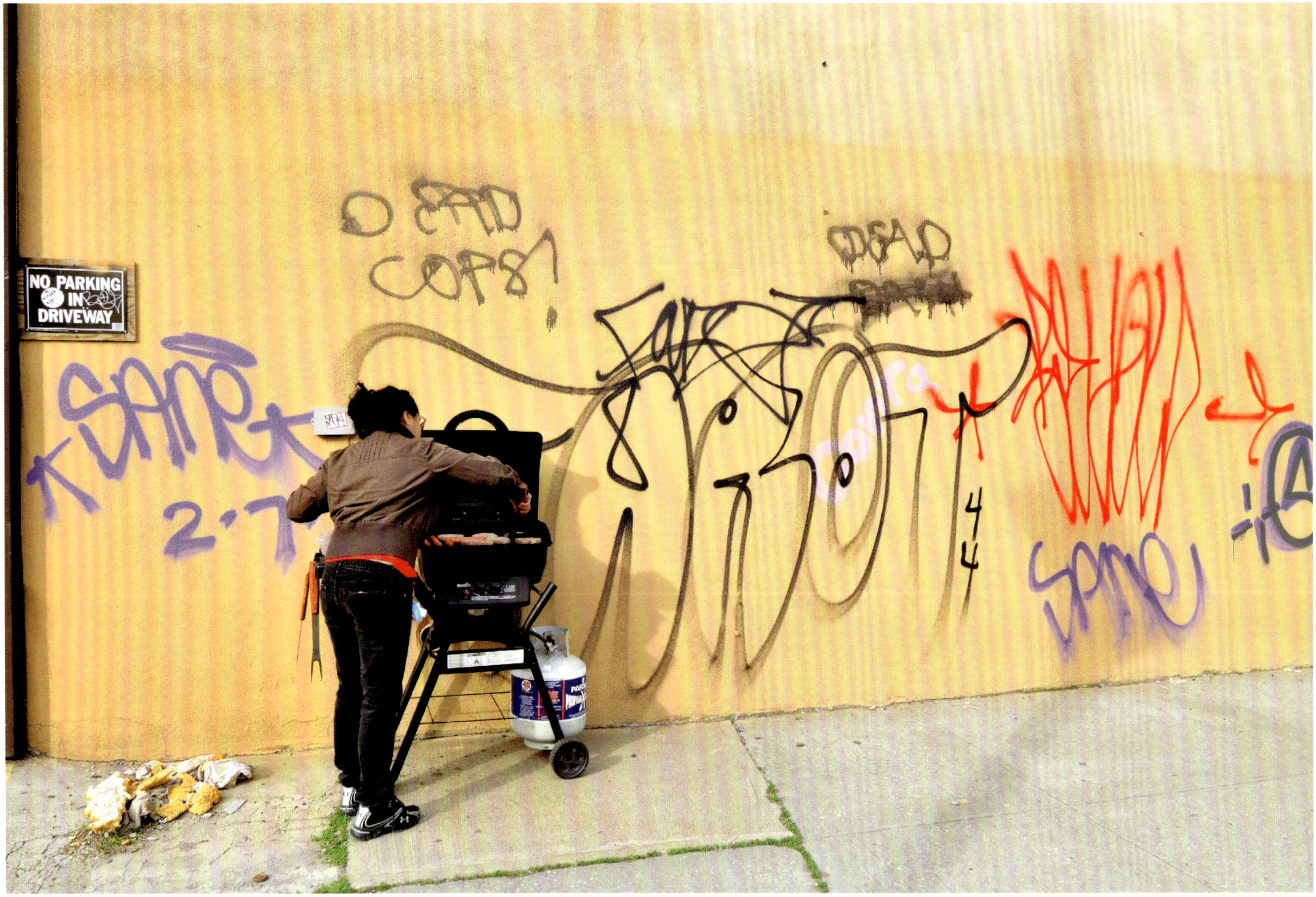
NO PARKING
IN
DRIVEWAY

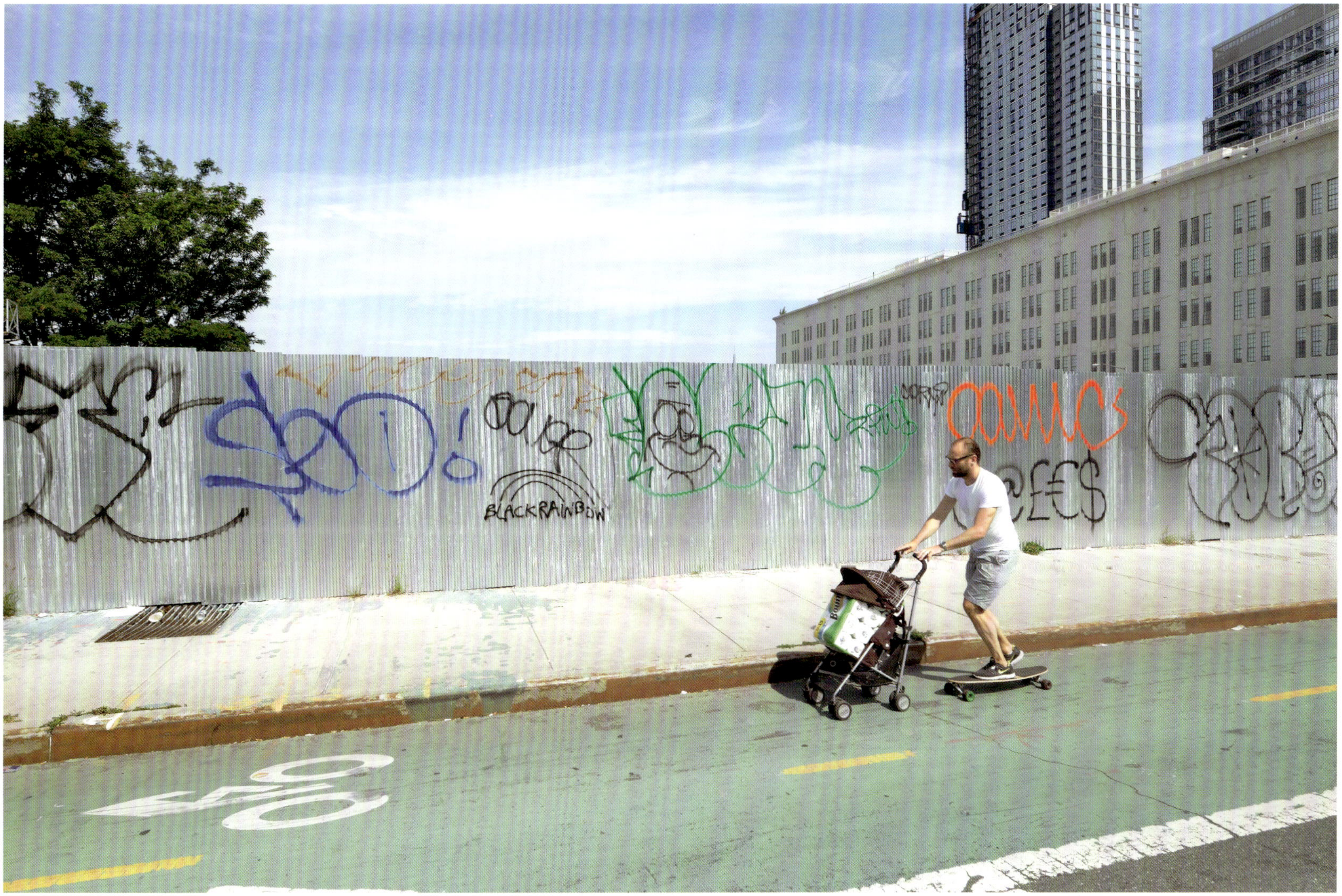
BLACKRAINBOW

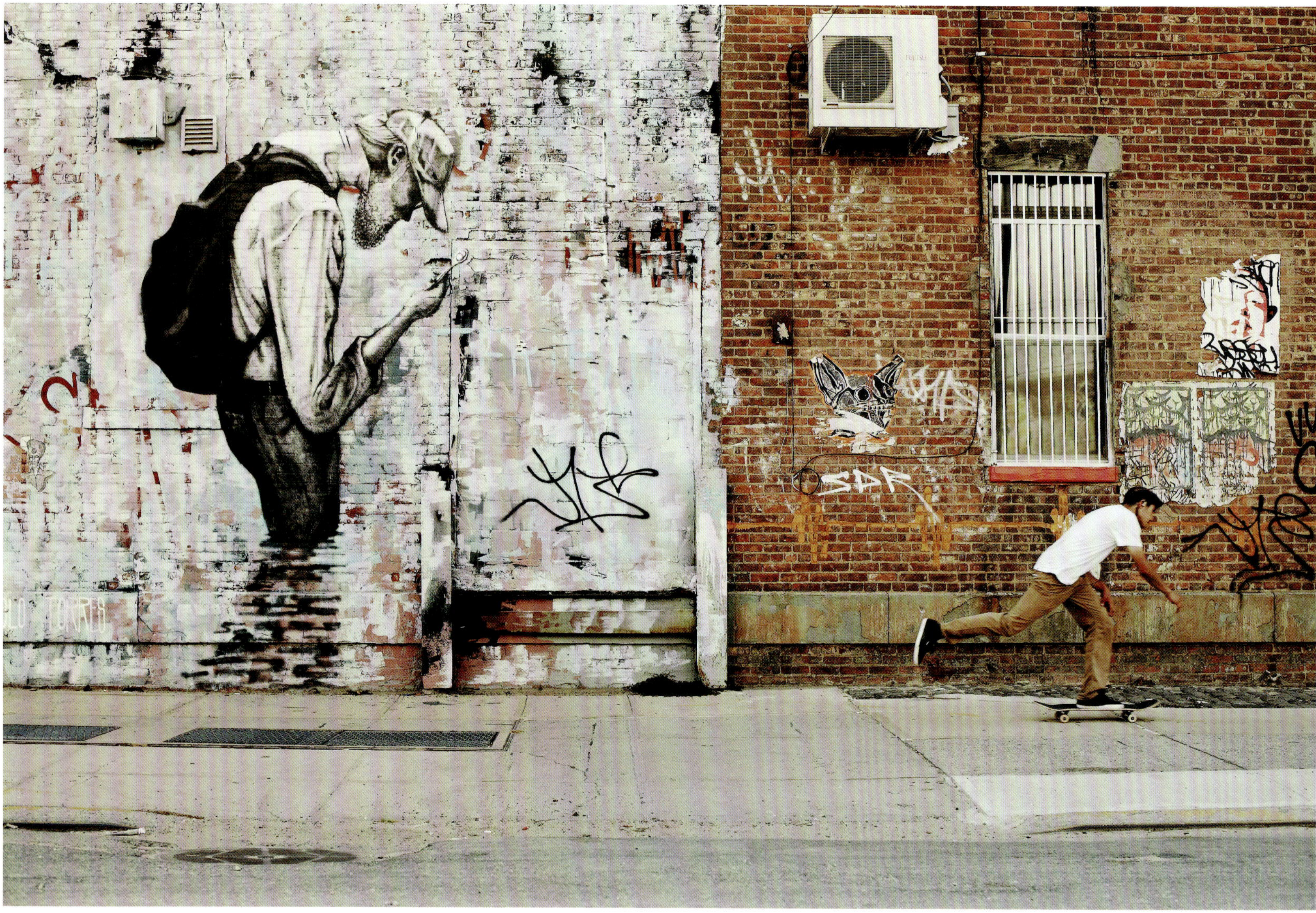
SDR

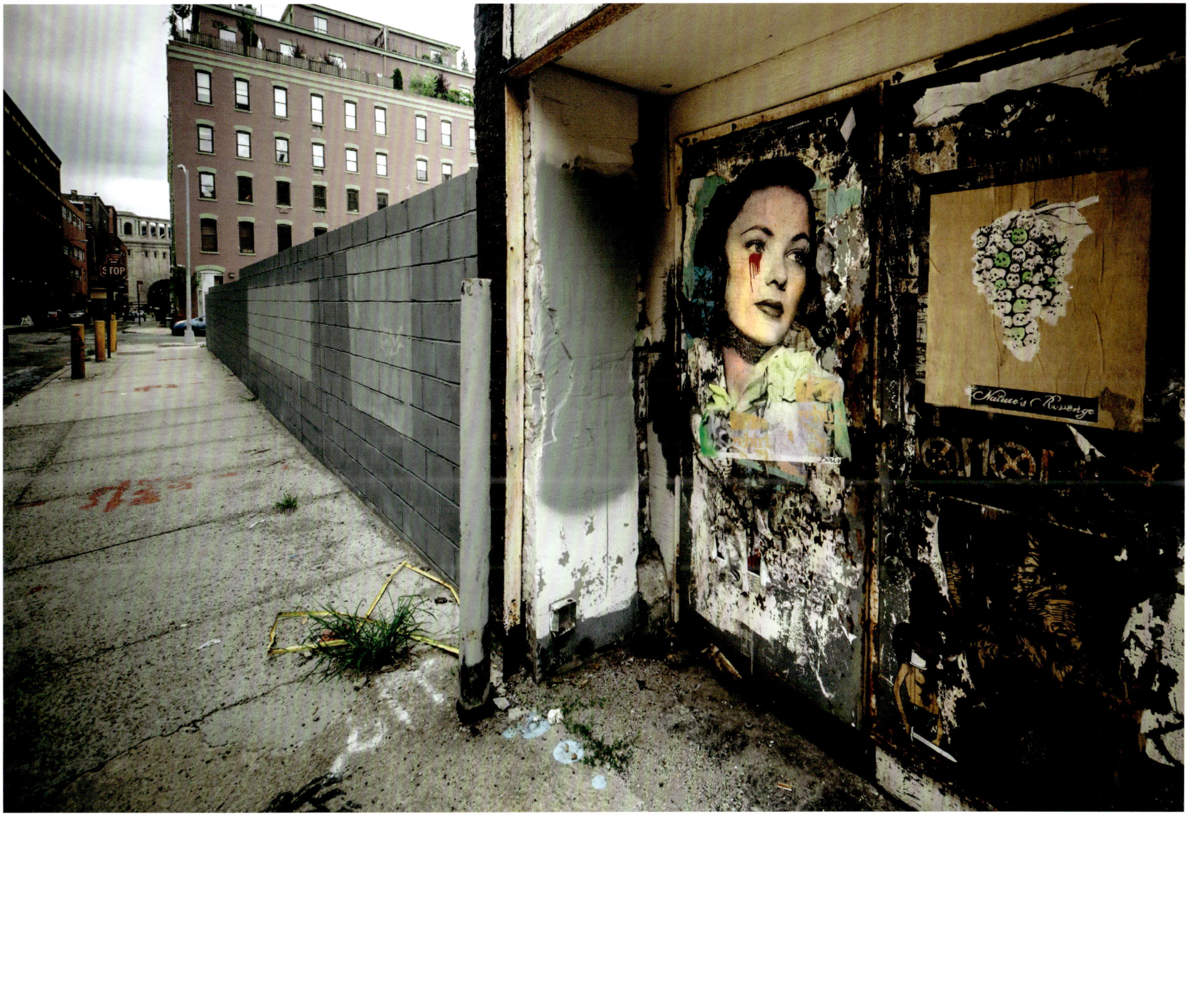
STOP
Nature's Revenge

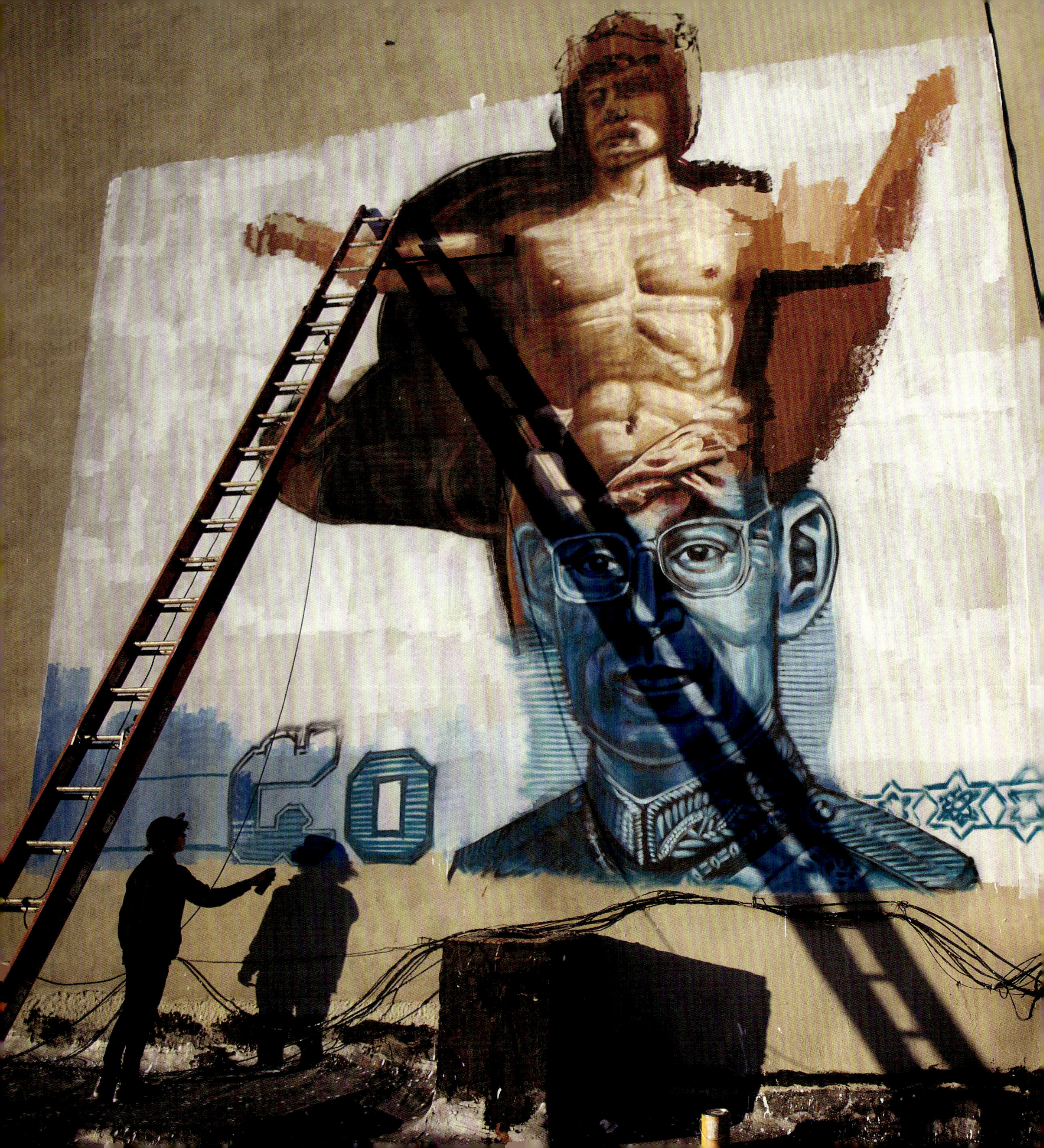

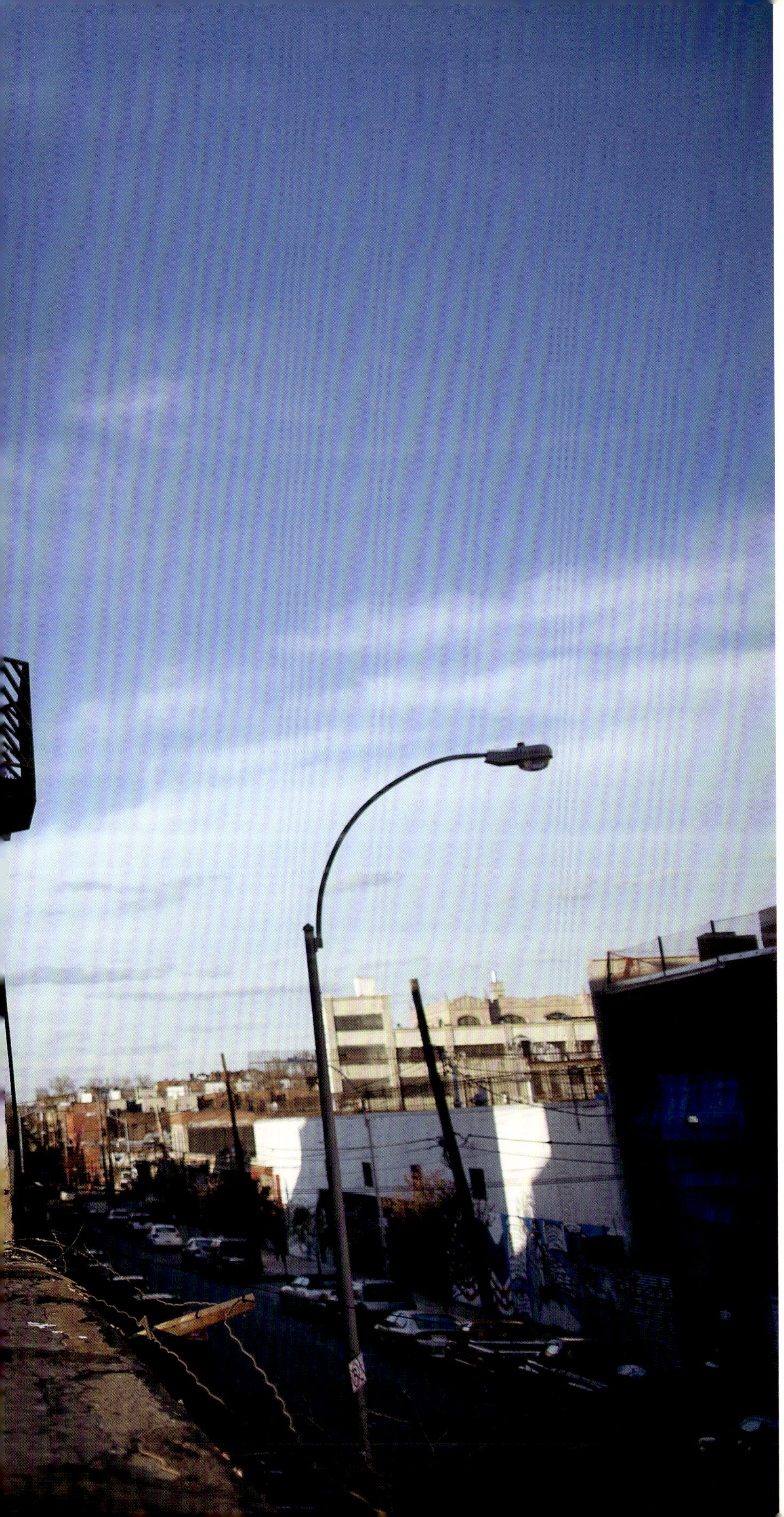

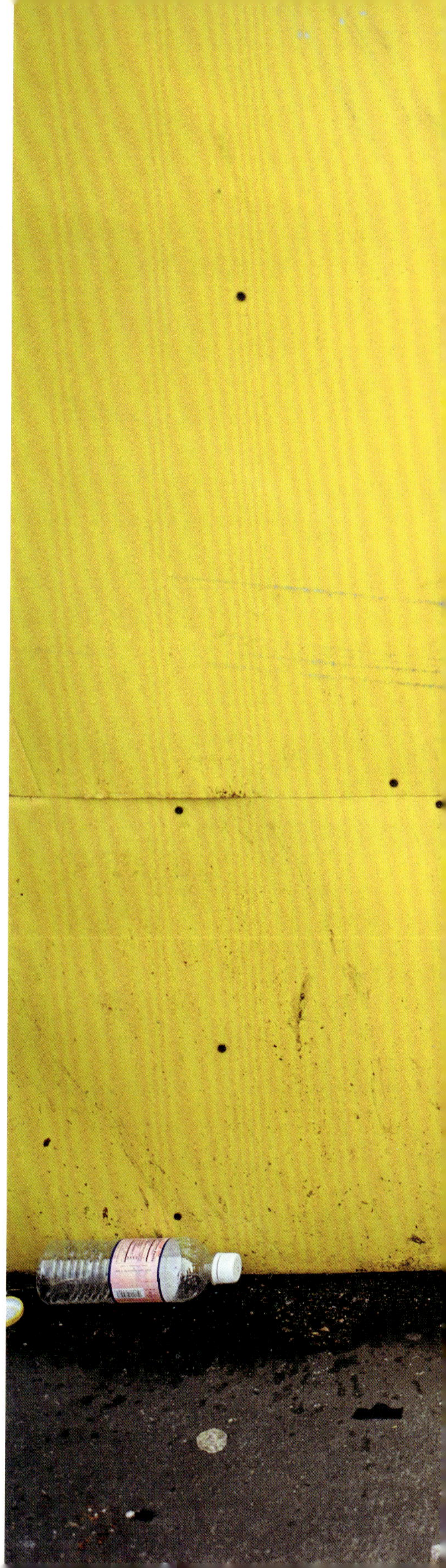

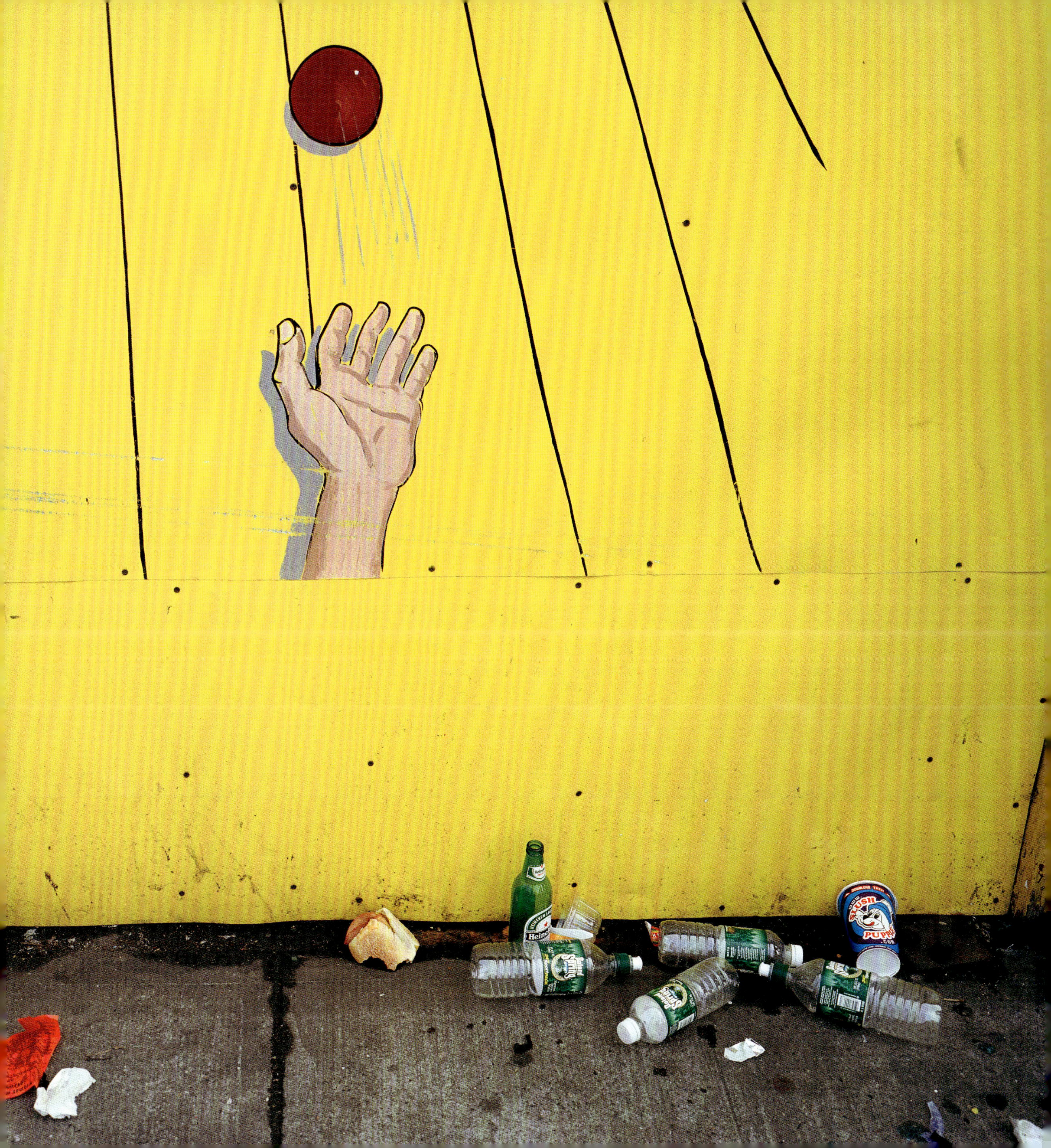
Poland Spring
SLUSH

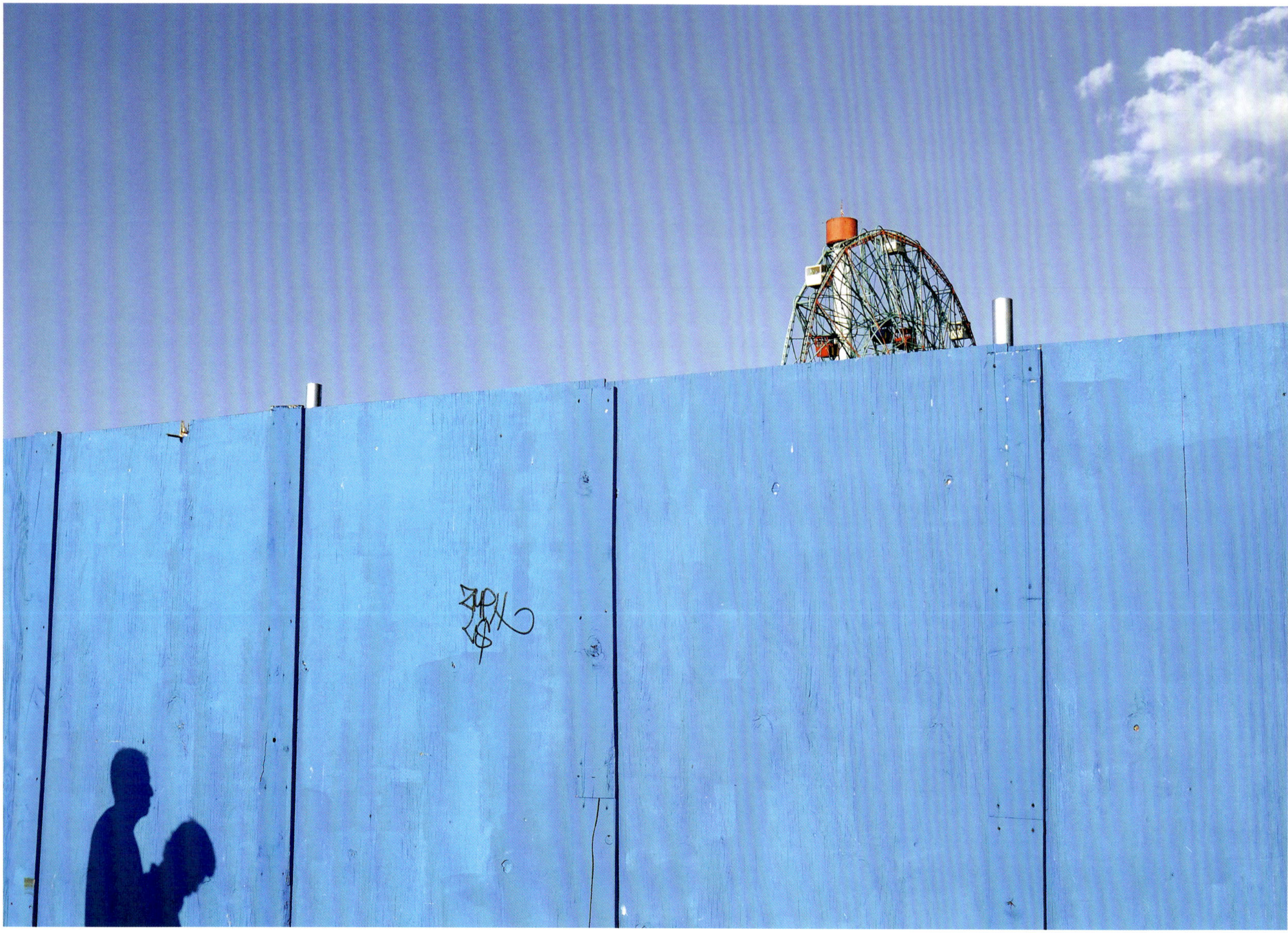

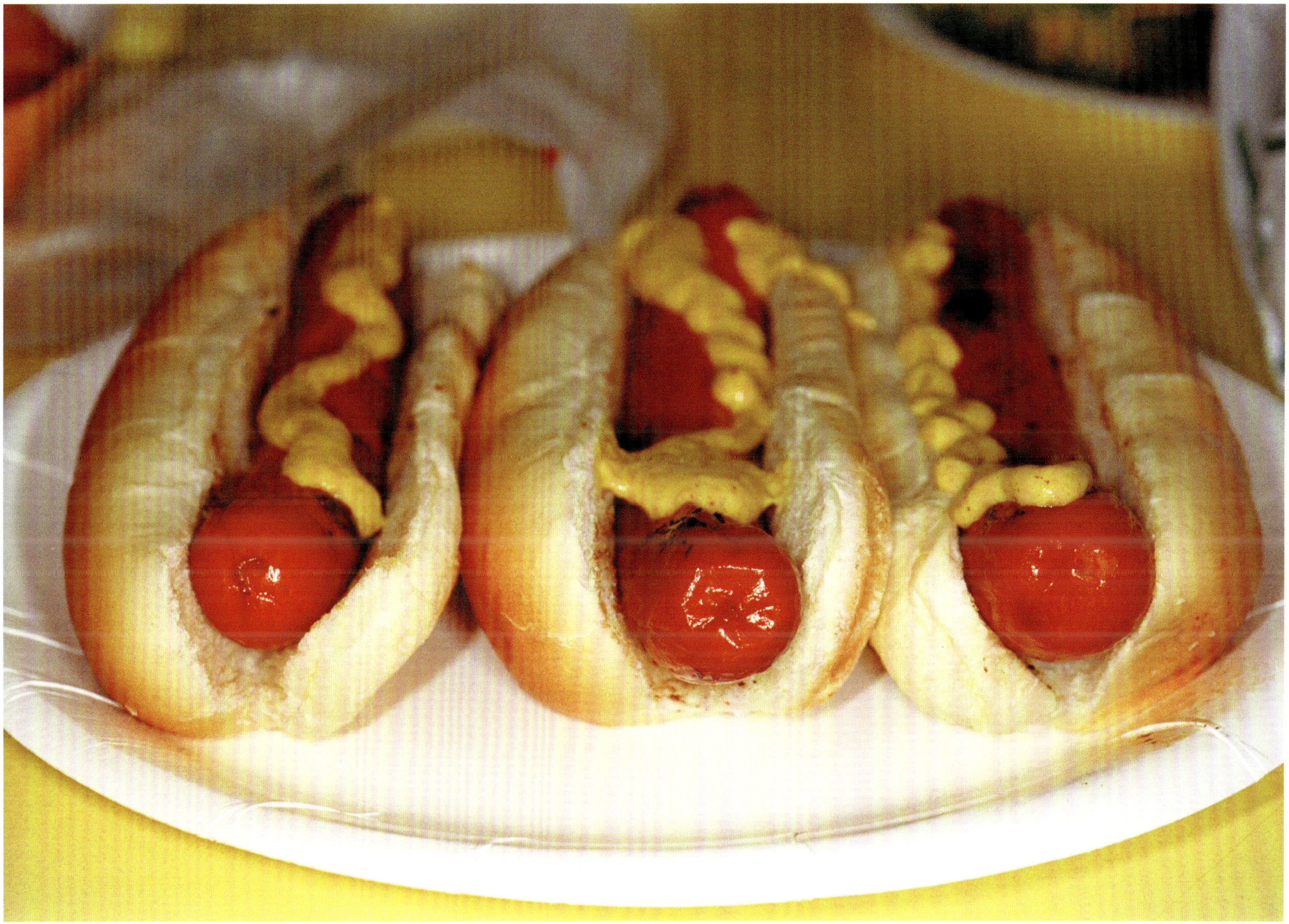

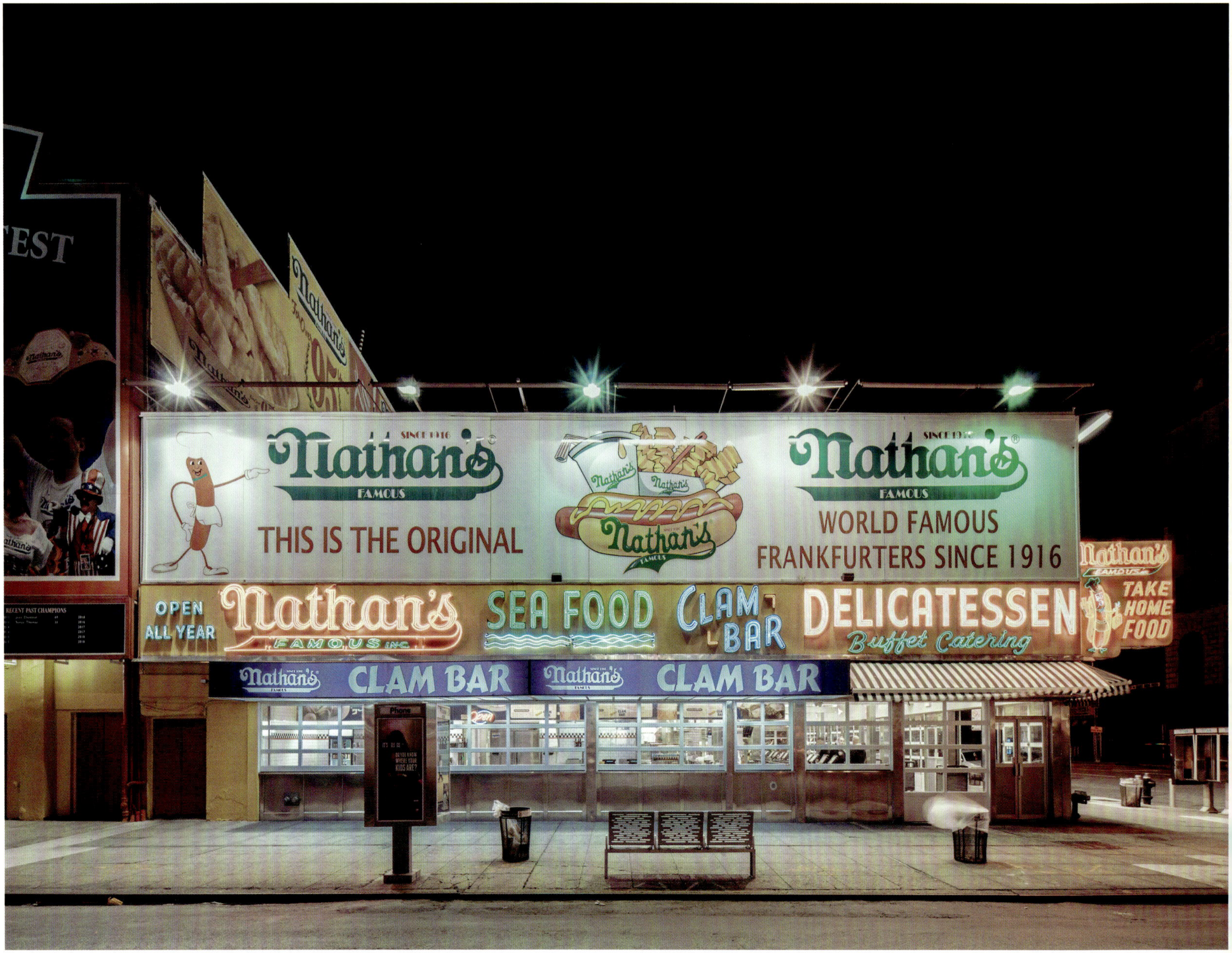
EST
Nathan's
SINCE 1916
FAMOUS
THIS IS THE ORIGINAL
Nathan's
SINCE 1916
FAMOUS
WORLD FAMOUS
FRANKFURTERS SINCE 1916
RECENT PAST CHAMPIONS
OPEN
ALL YEAR
Nathan's
FAMOUS INC.
SEA FOOD
CLAM
BAR
DELICATESSEN
Buffet Catering
Nathan's
TAKE
HOME
FOOD
Nathan's
CLAM BAR
Nathan's
CLAM BAR
Phone

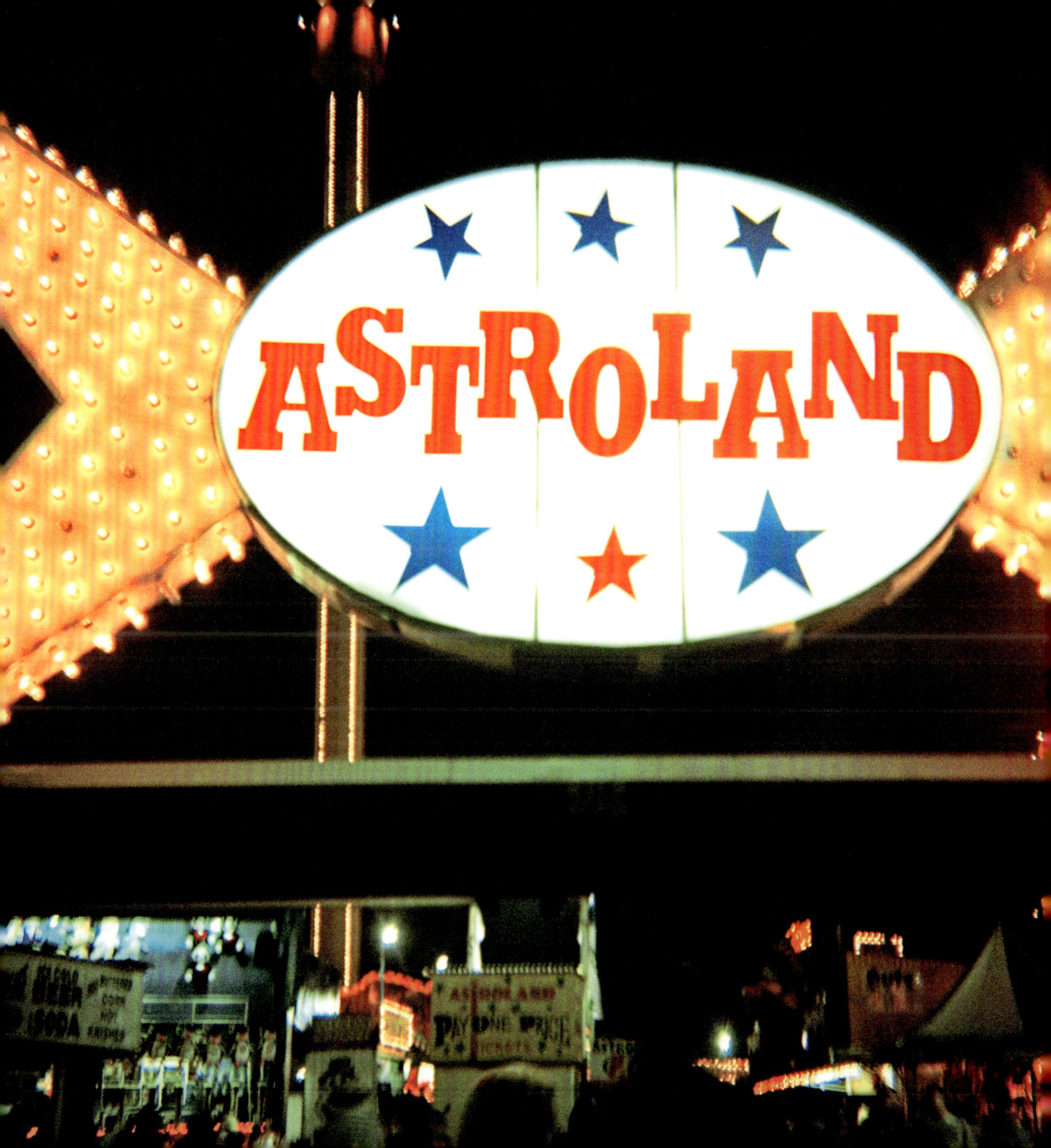
ASTROLAND

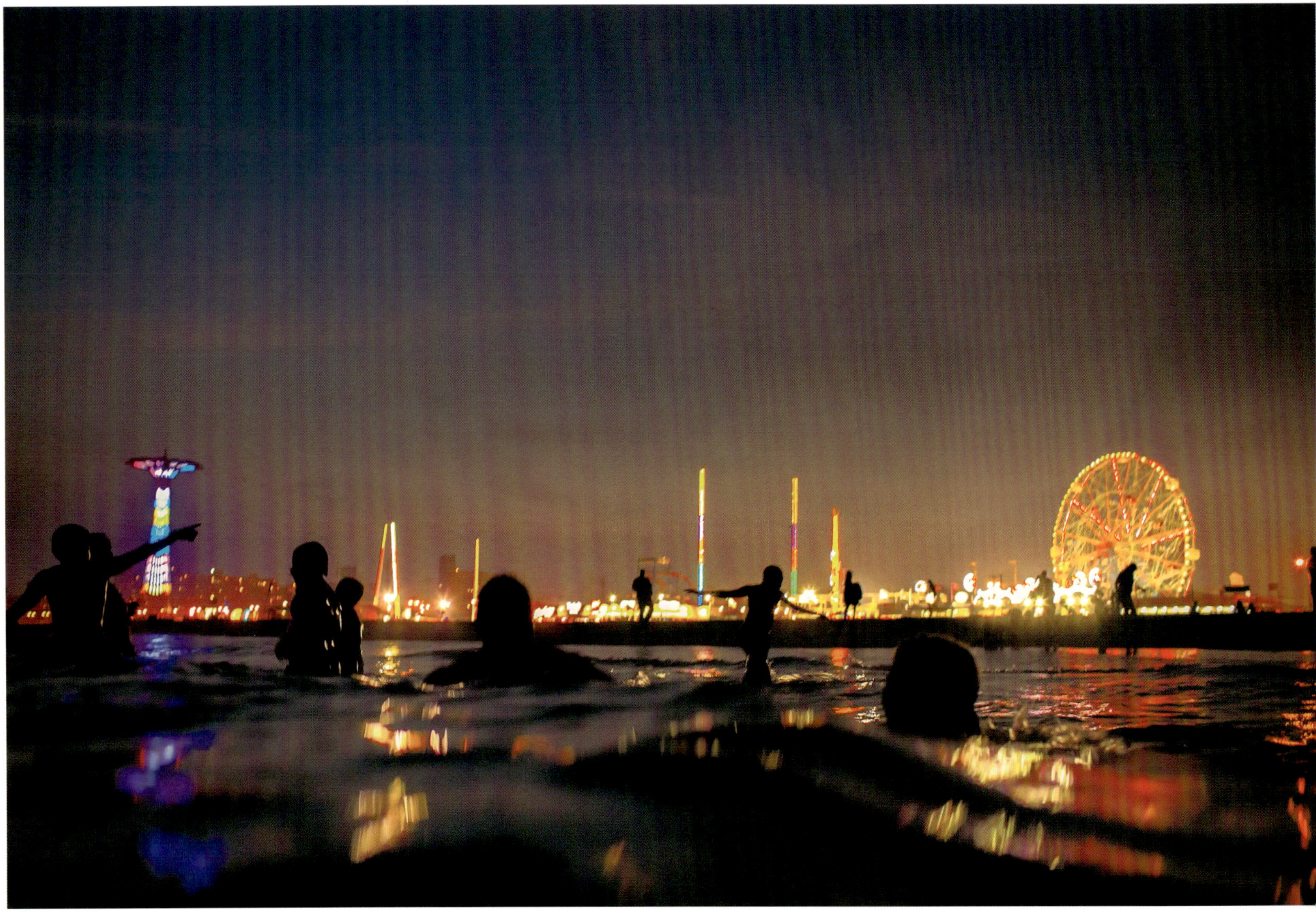

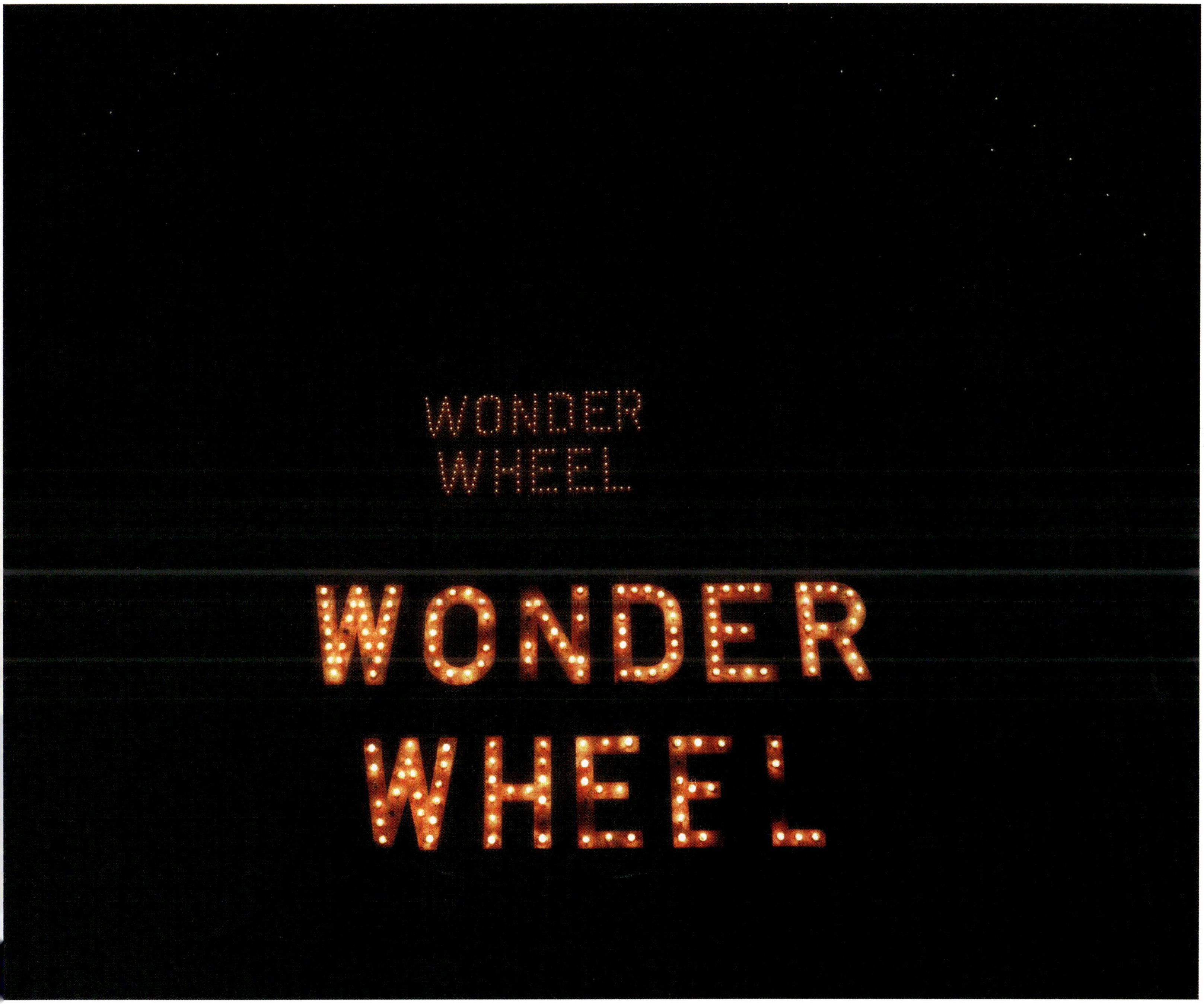
WONDER
WHEEL
WONDER
WHEEL

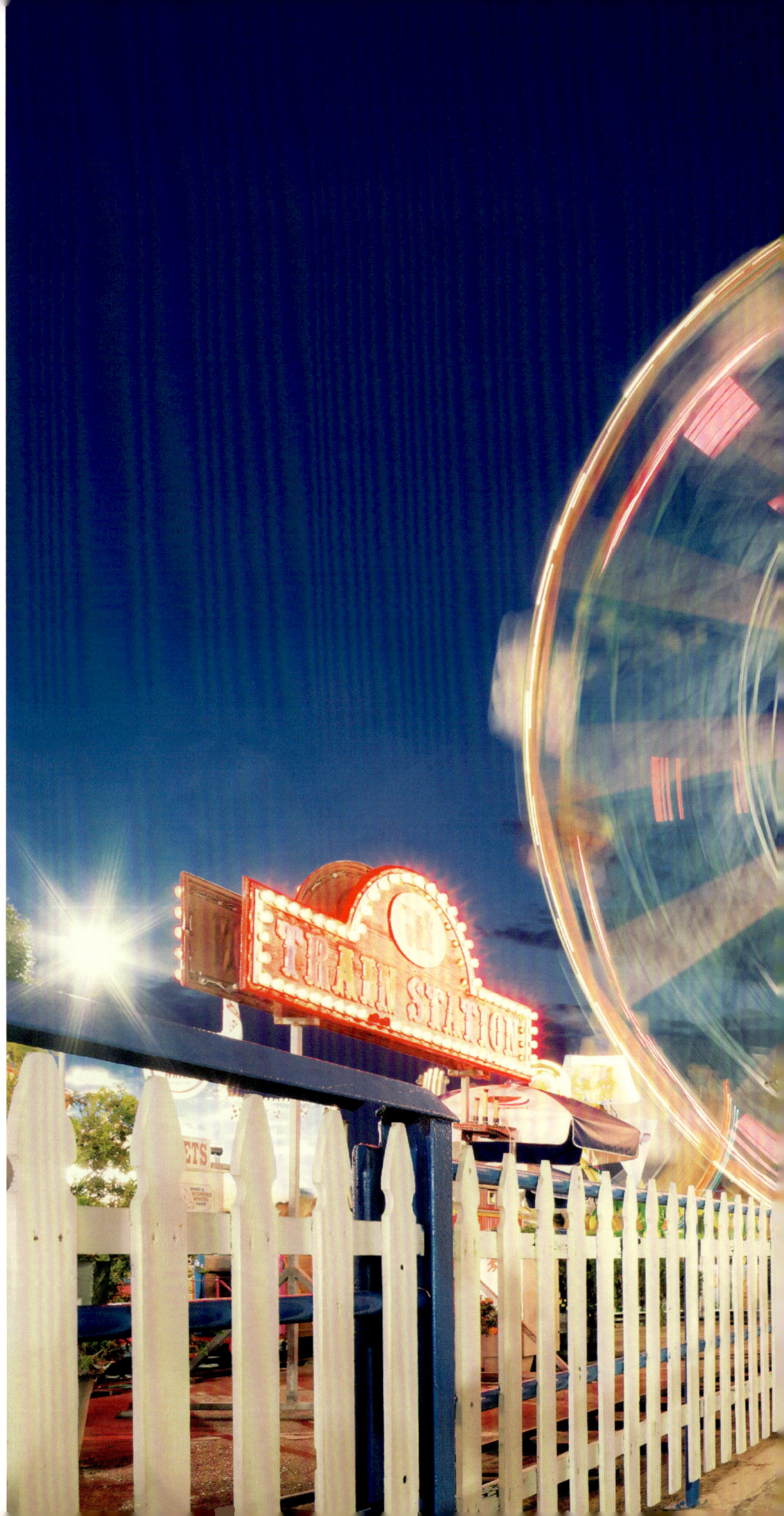
TRAIN STATION

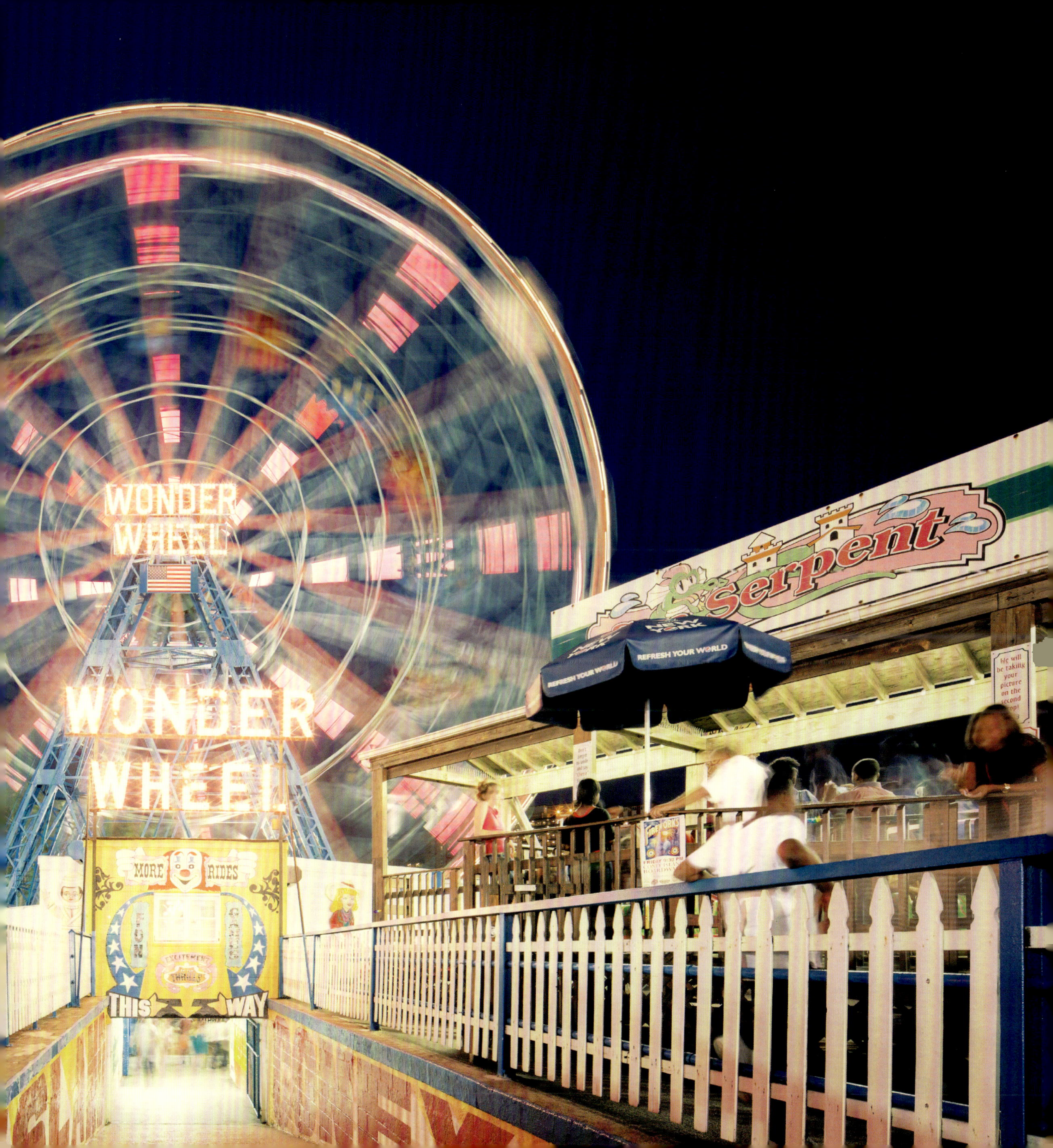
WONDER
WHEEL
WONDER
WHEEL
MORE
RIDES
THIS
WAY
Serpent
REFRESH YOUR WORLD

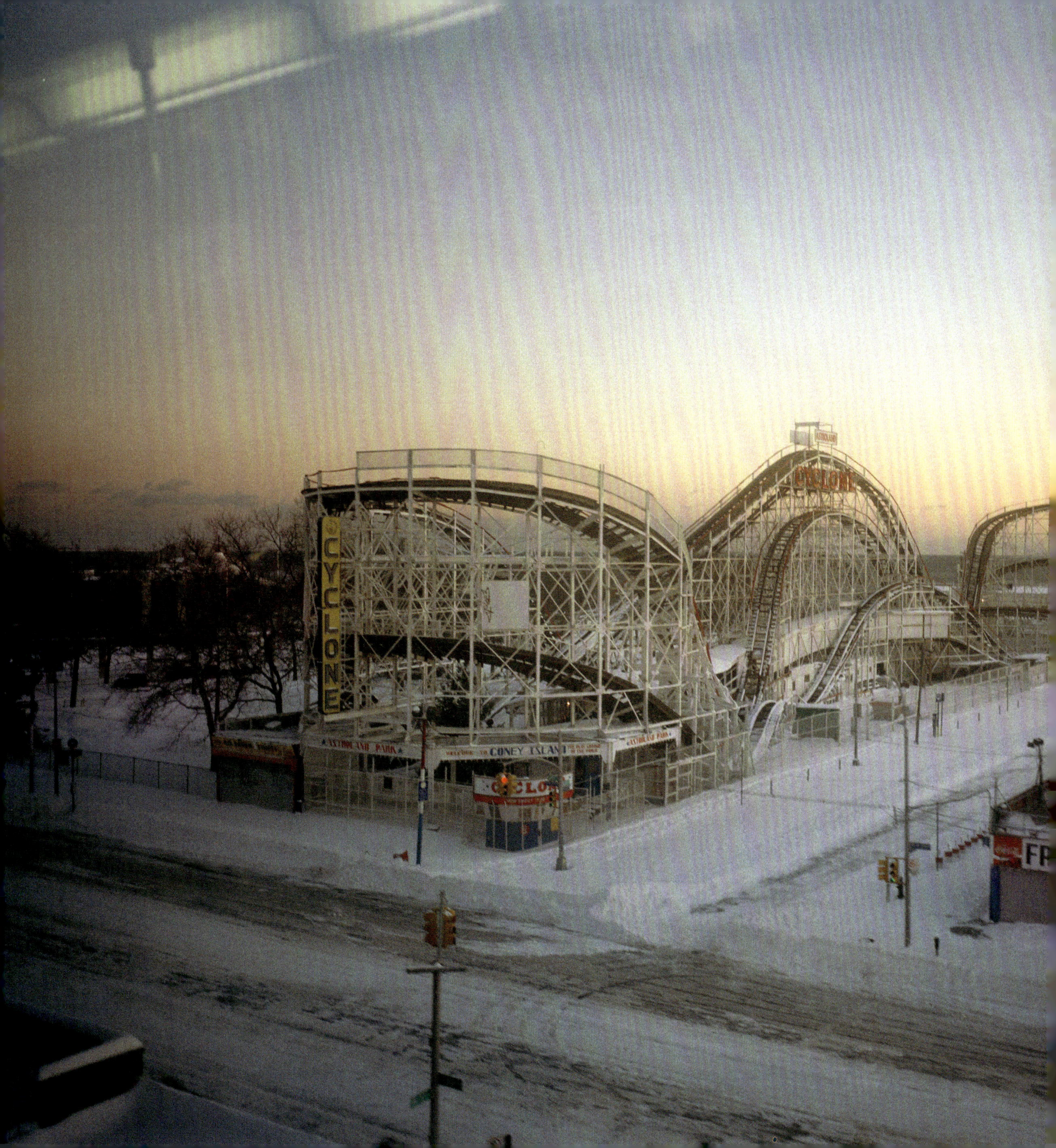
CYCLONE
CONEY ISLAND

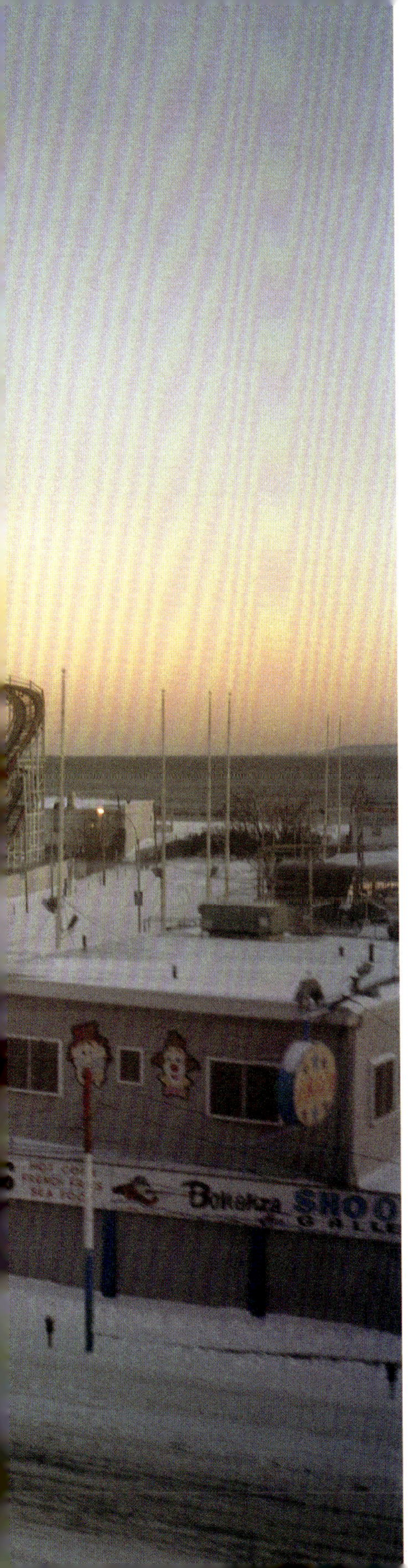
Bonanza

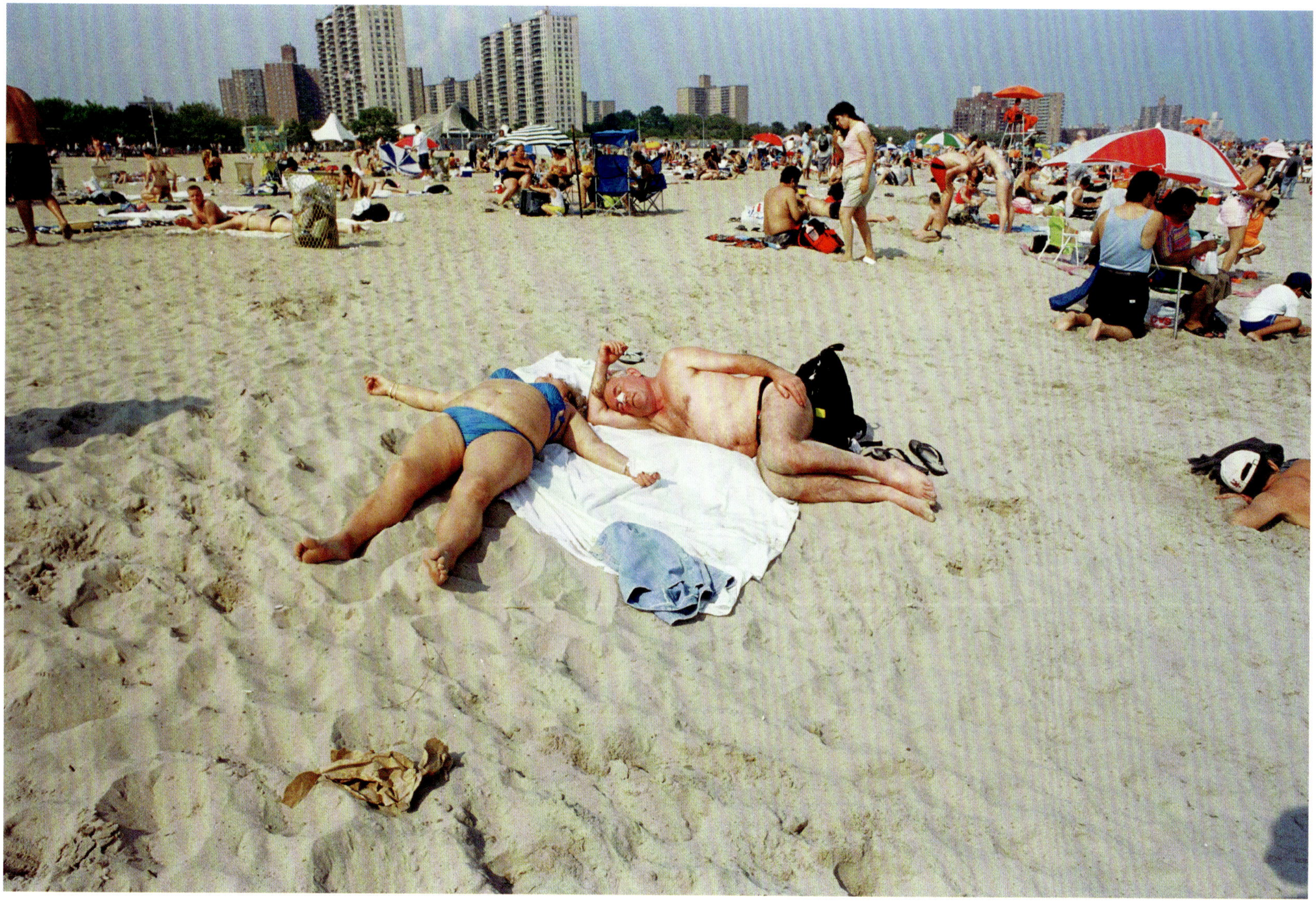

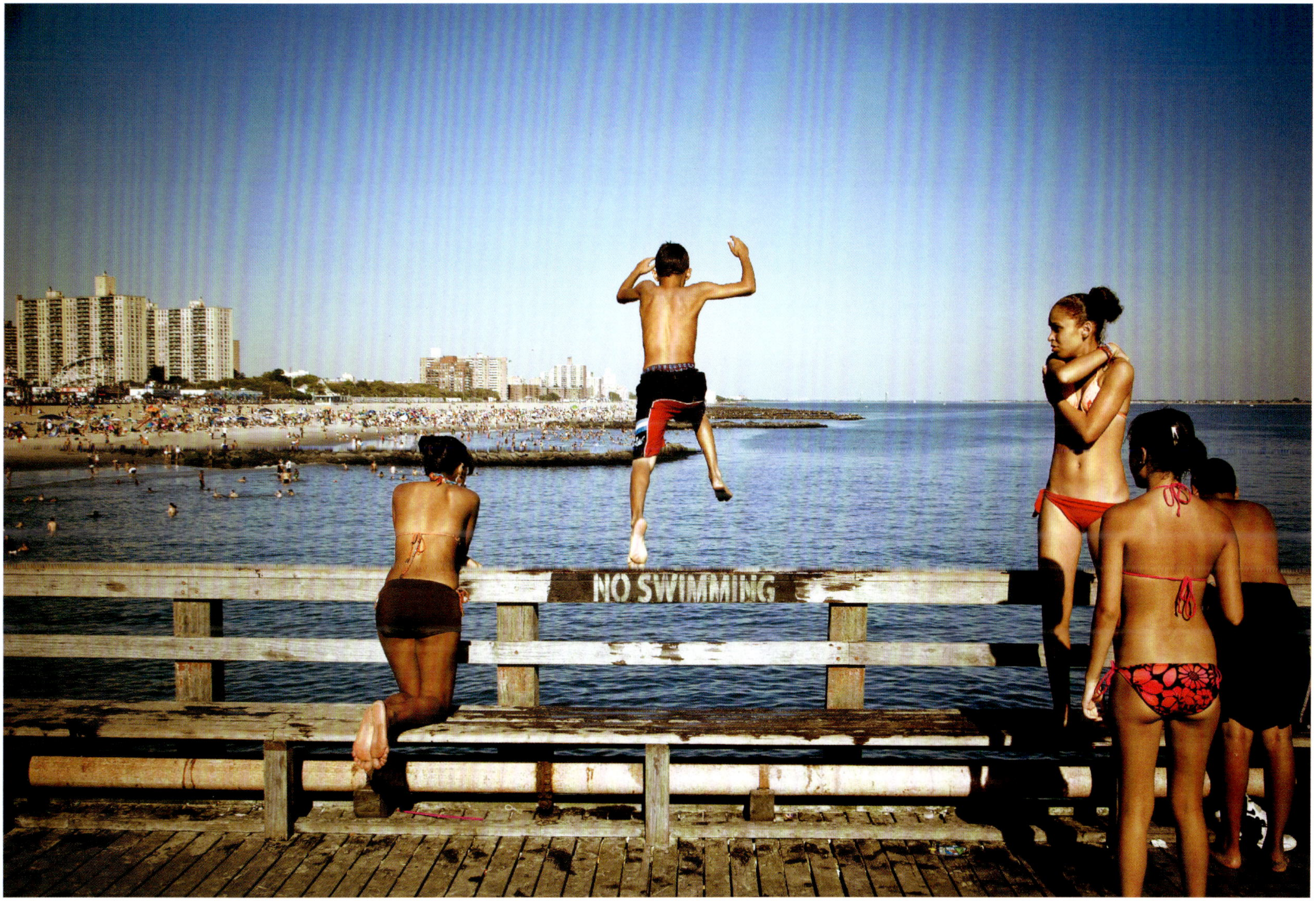
NO SWIMMING

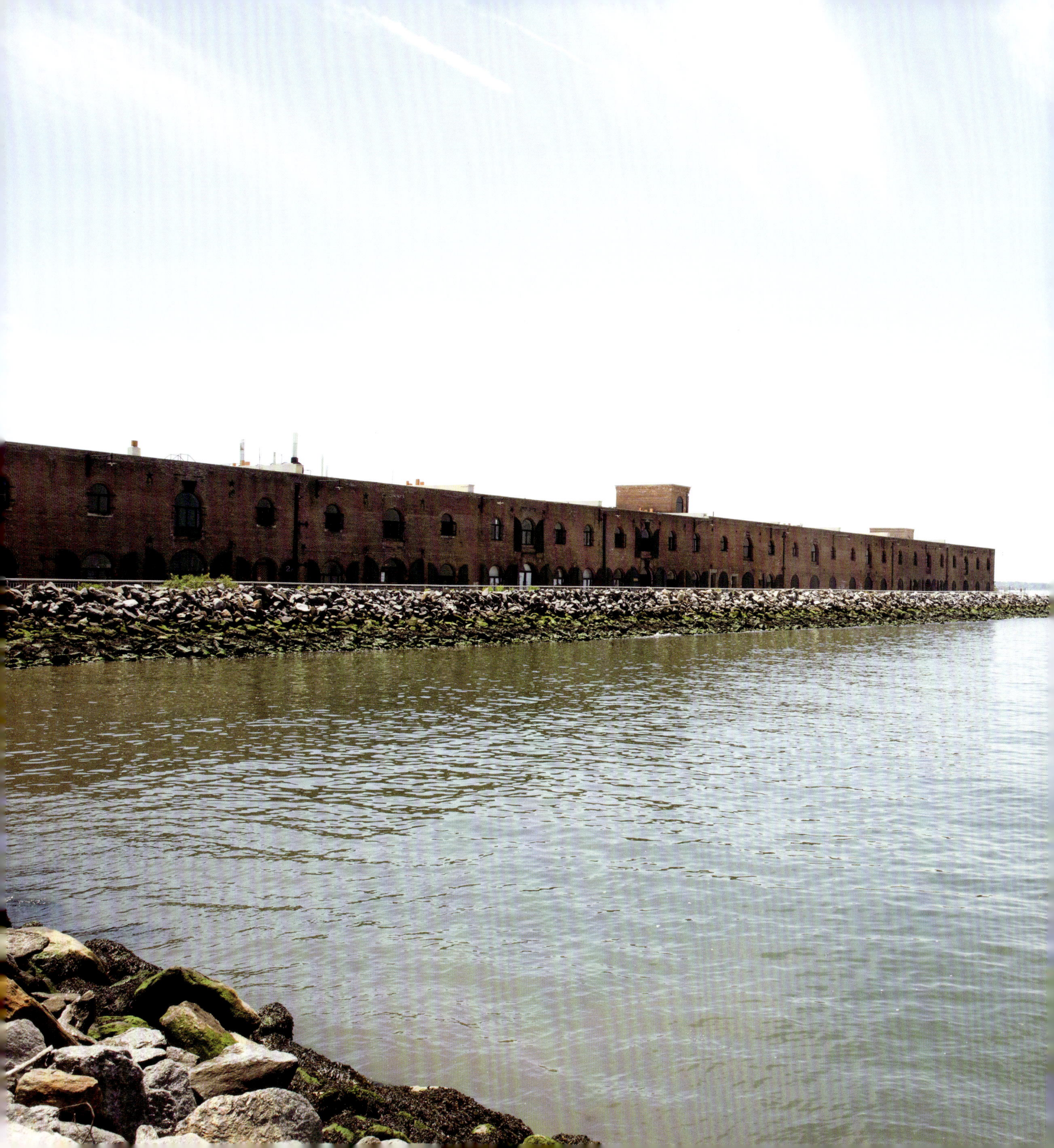

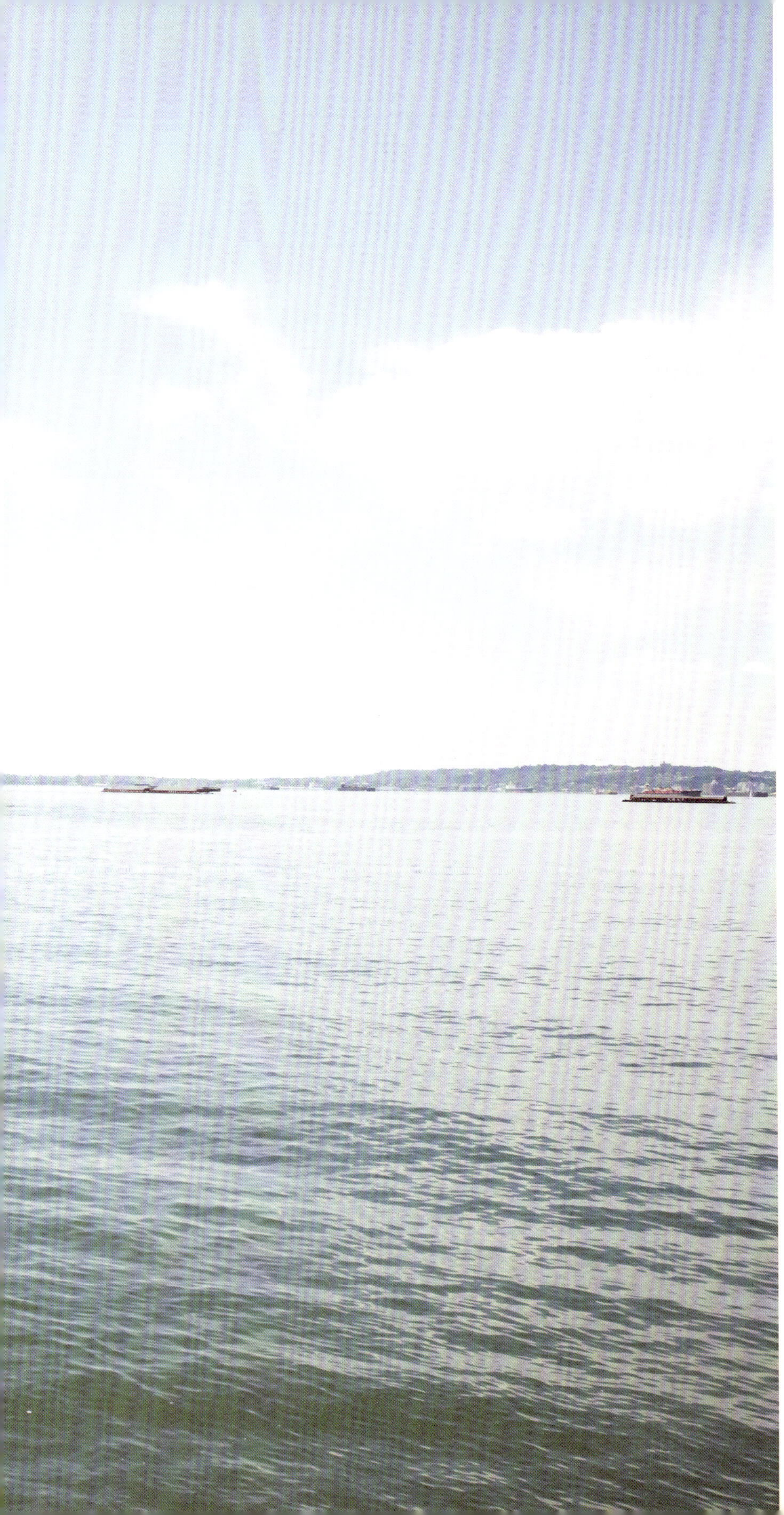

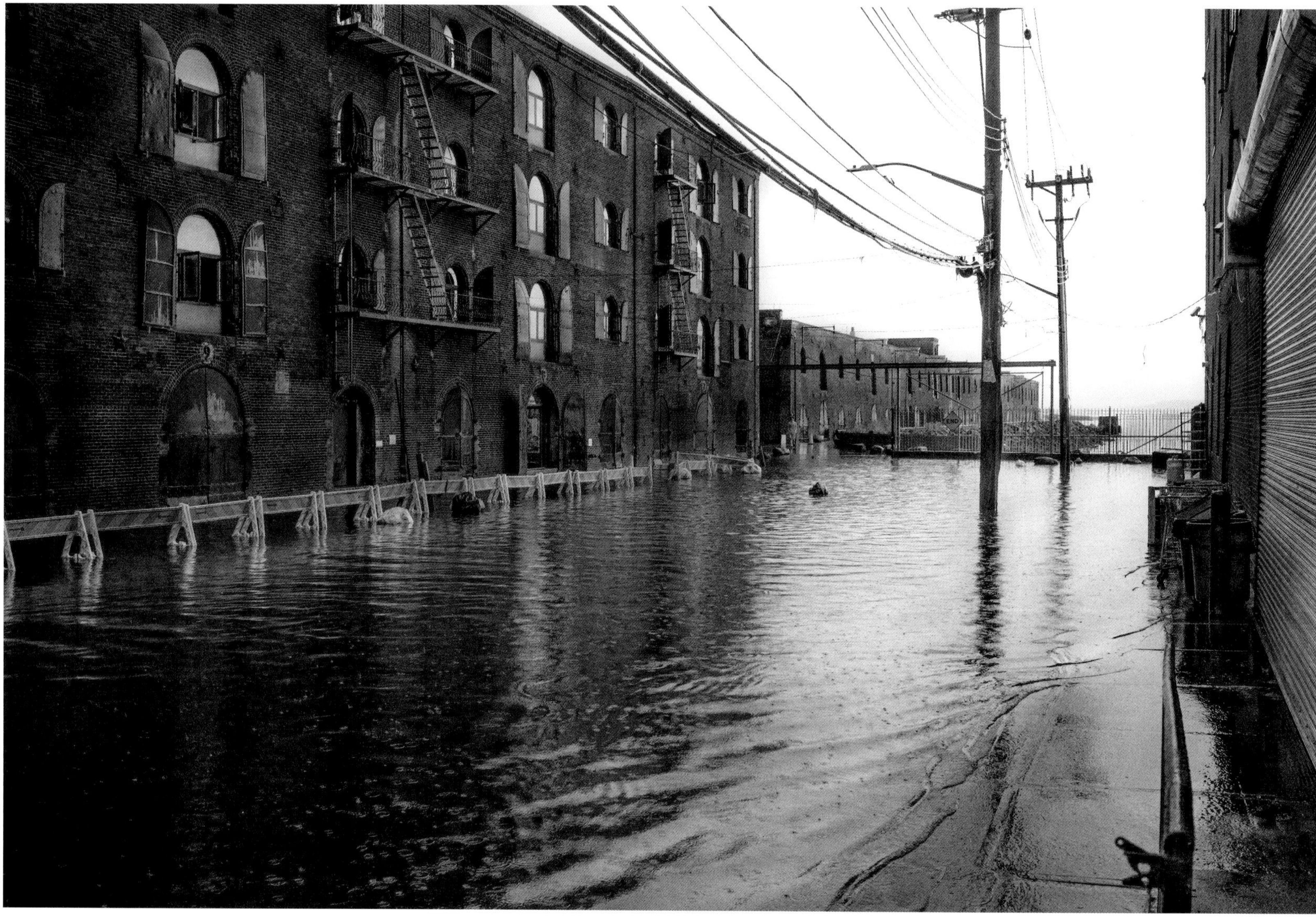

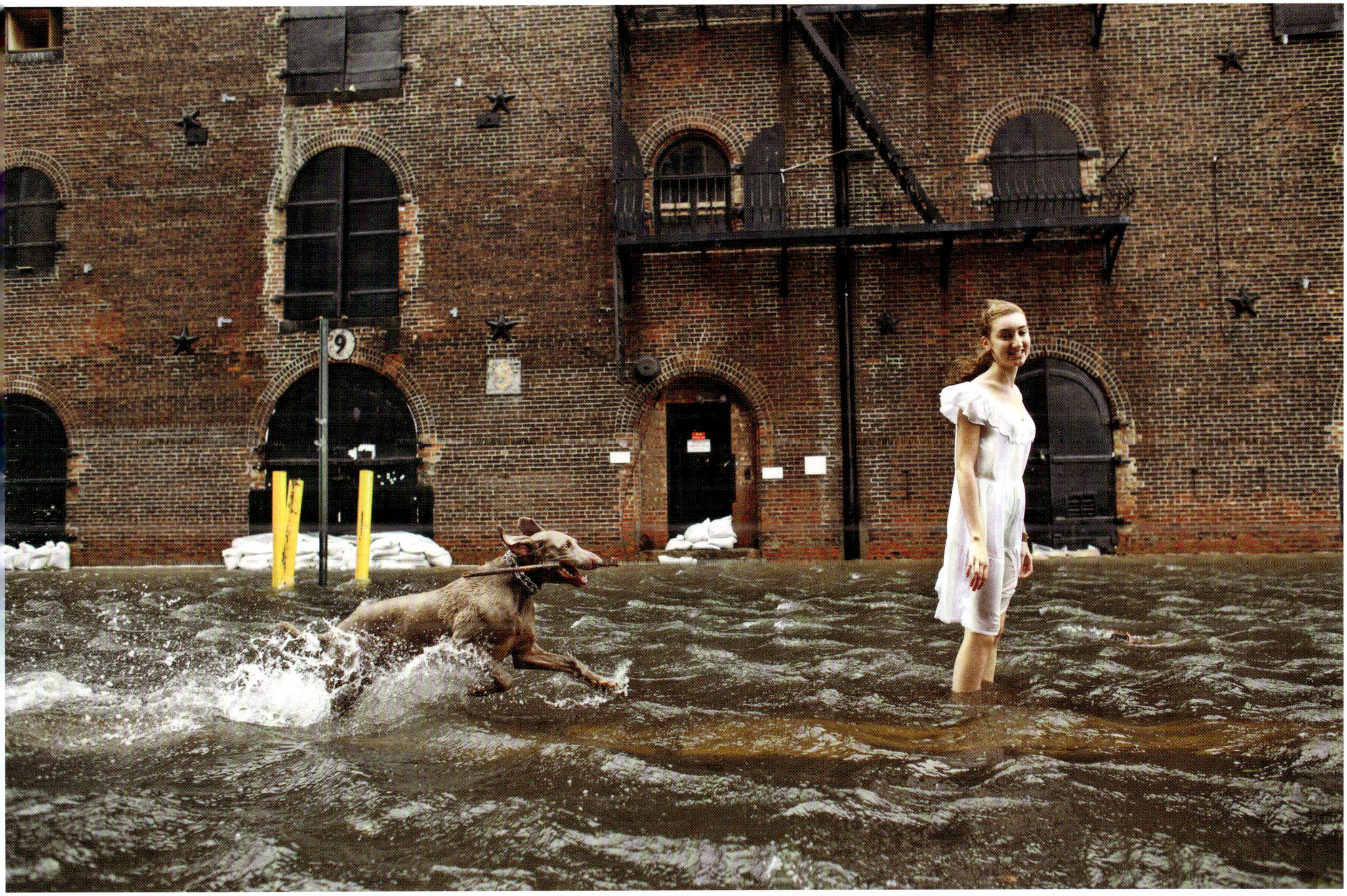
9

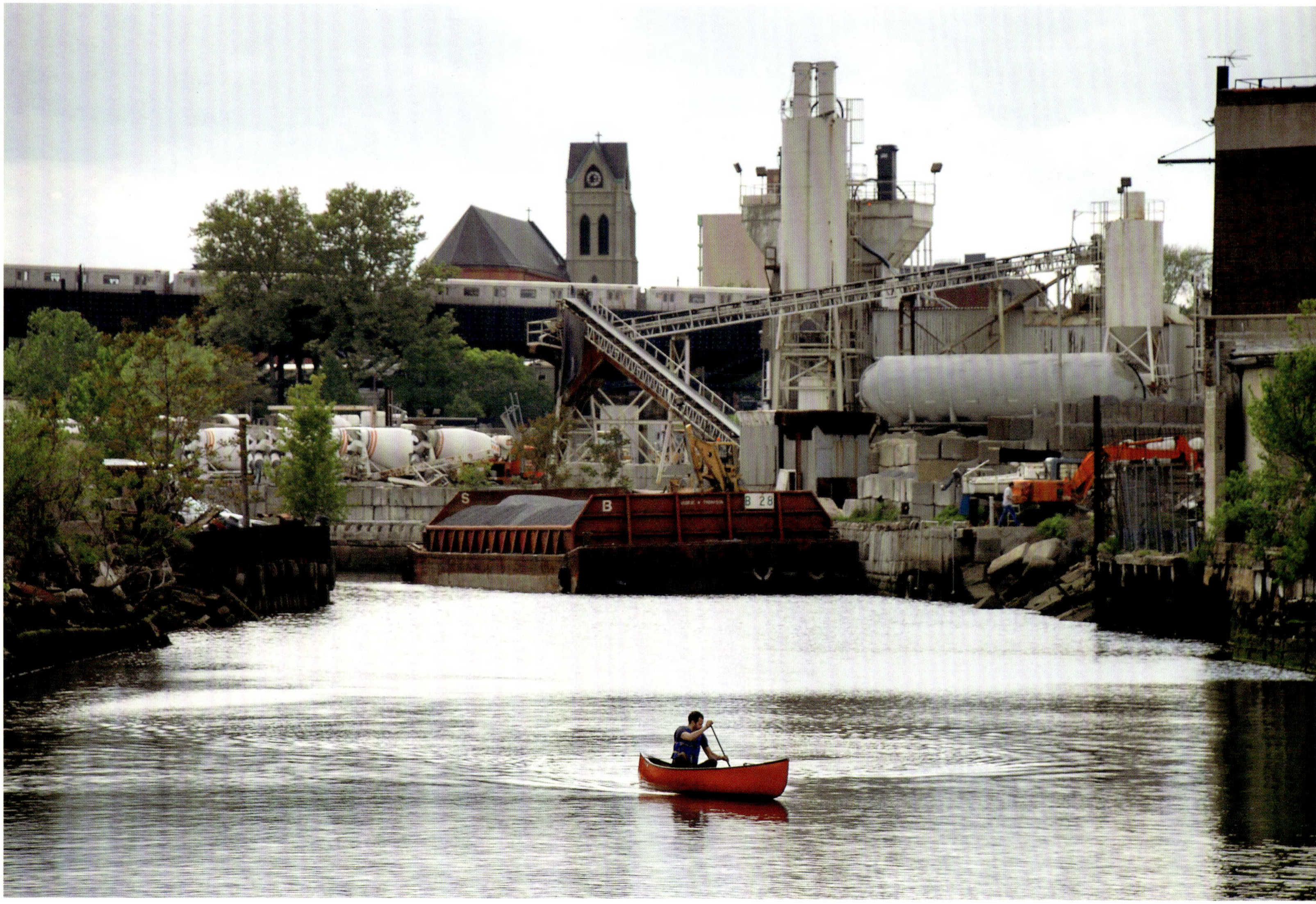
S
B
B 28

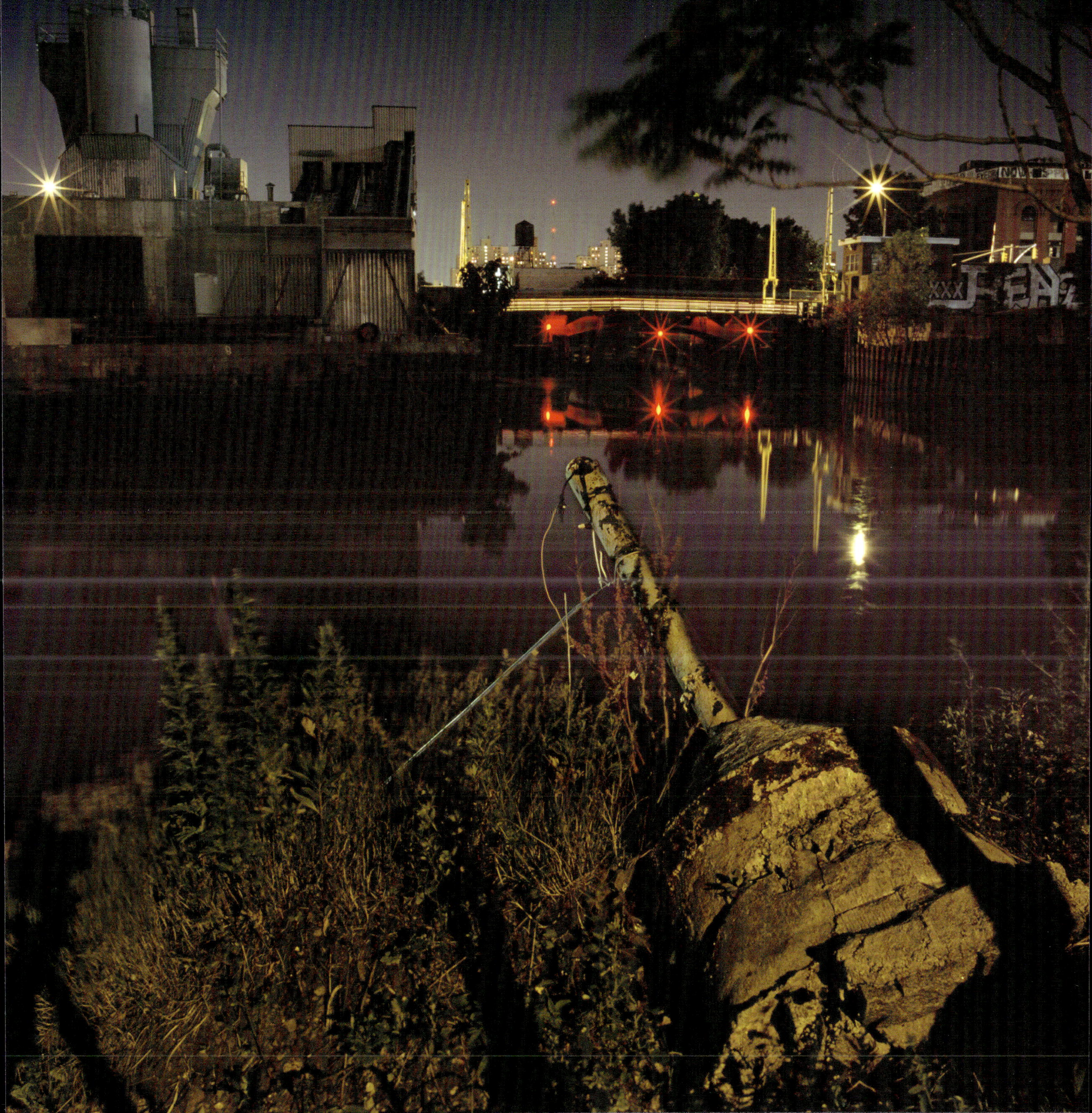

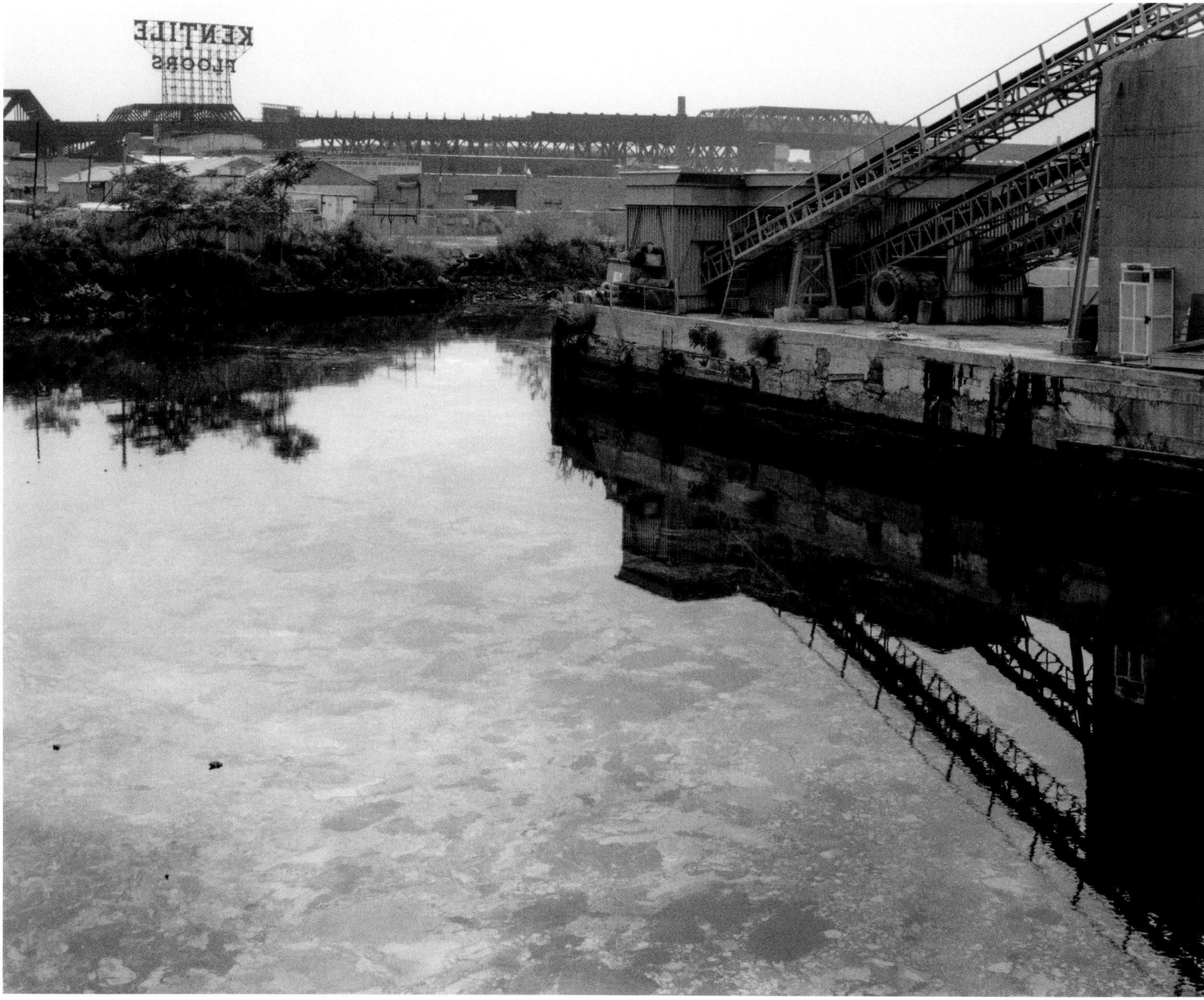
KENTILE
FLOORS

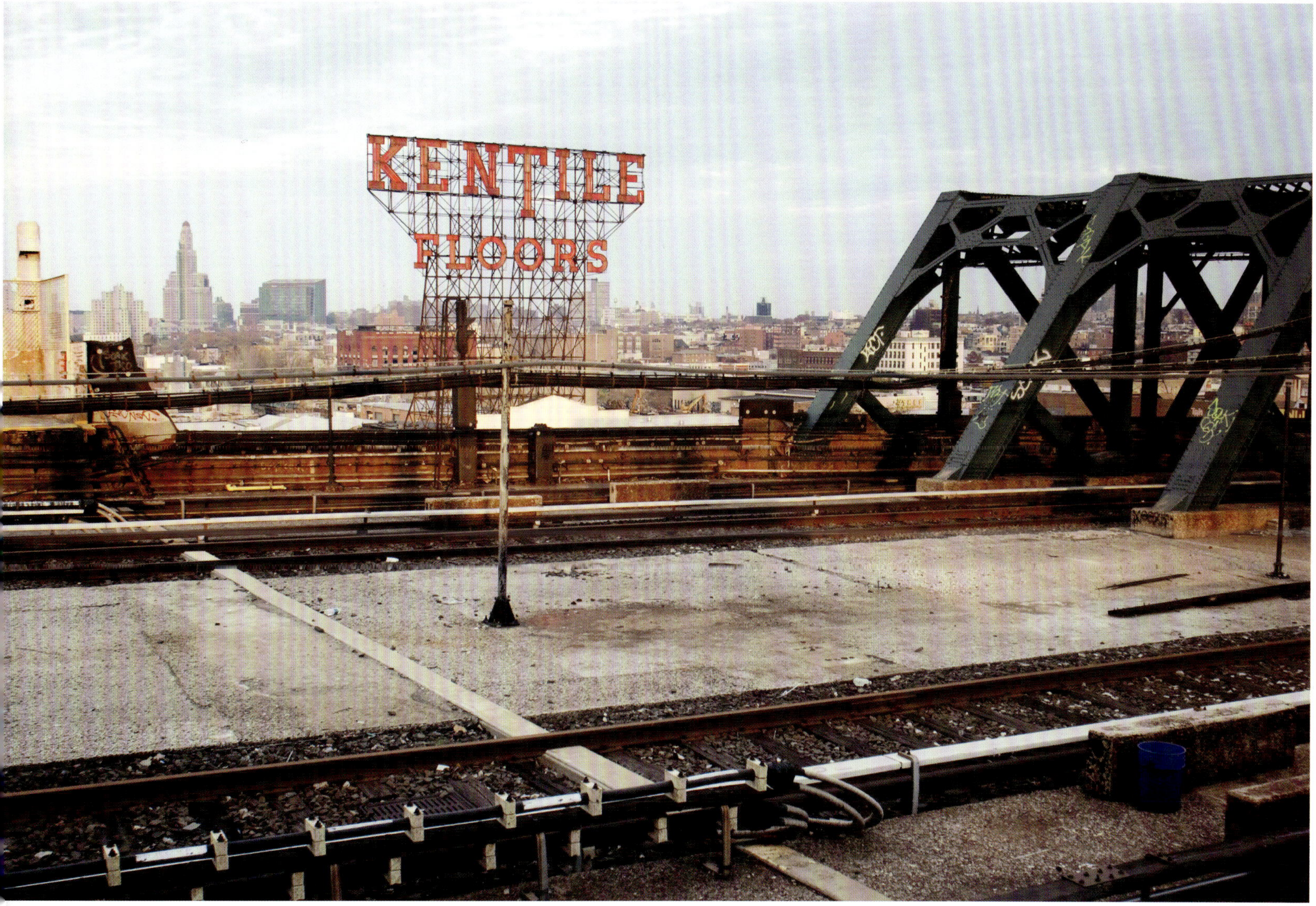
KENTILE
FLOORS

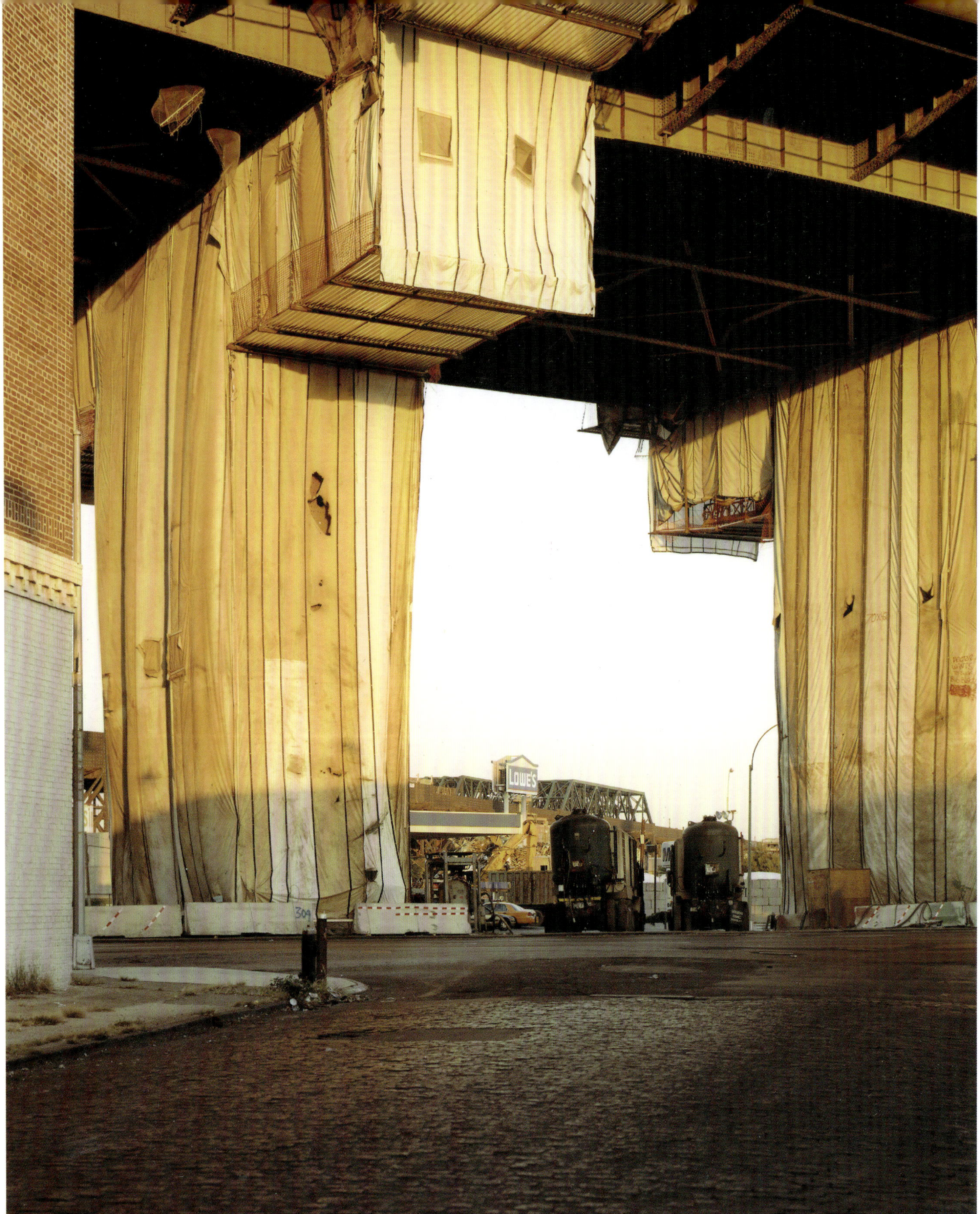
LOWE'S

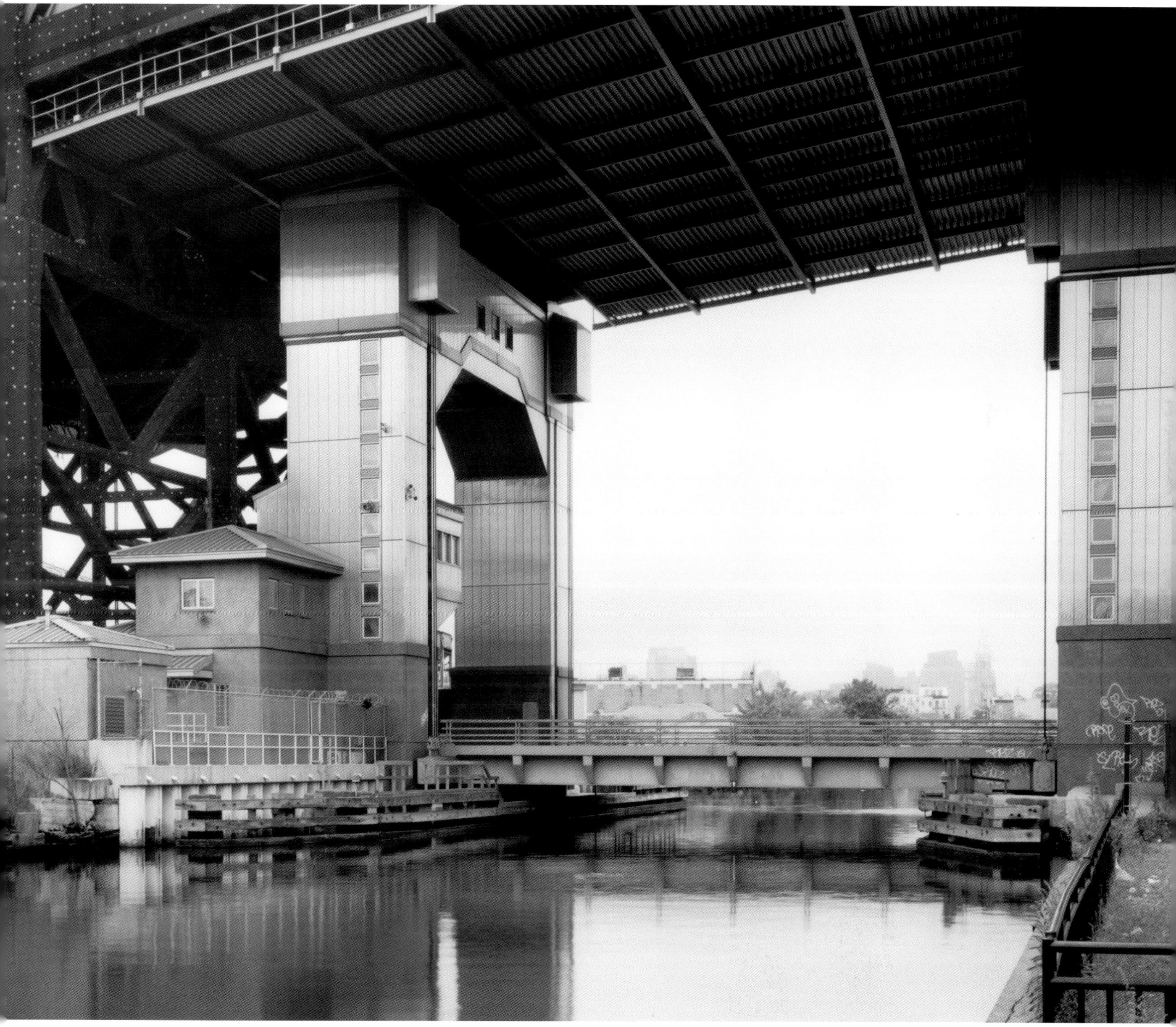

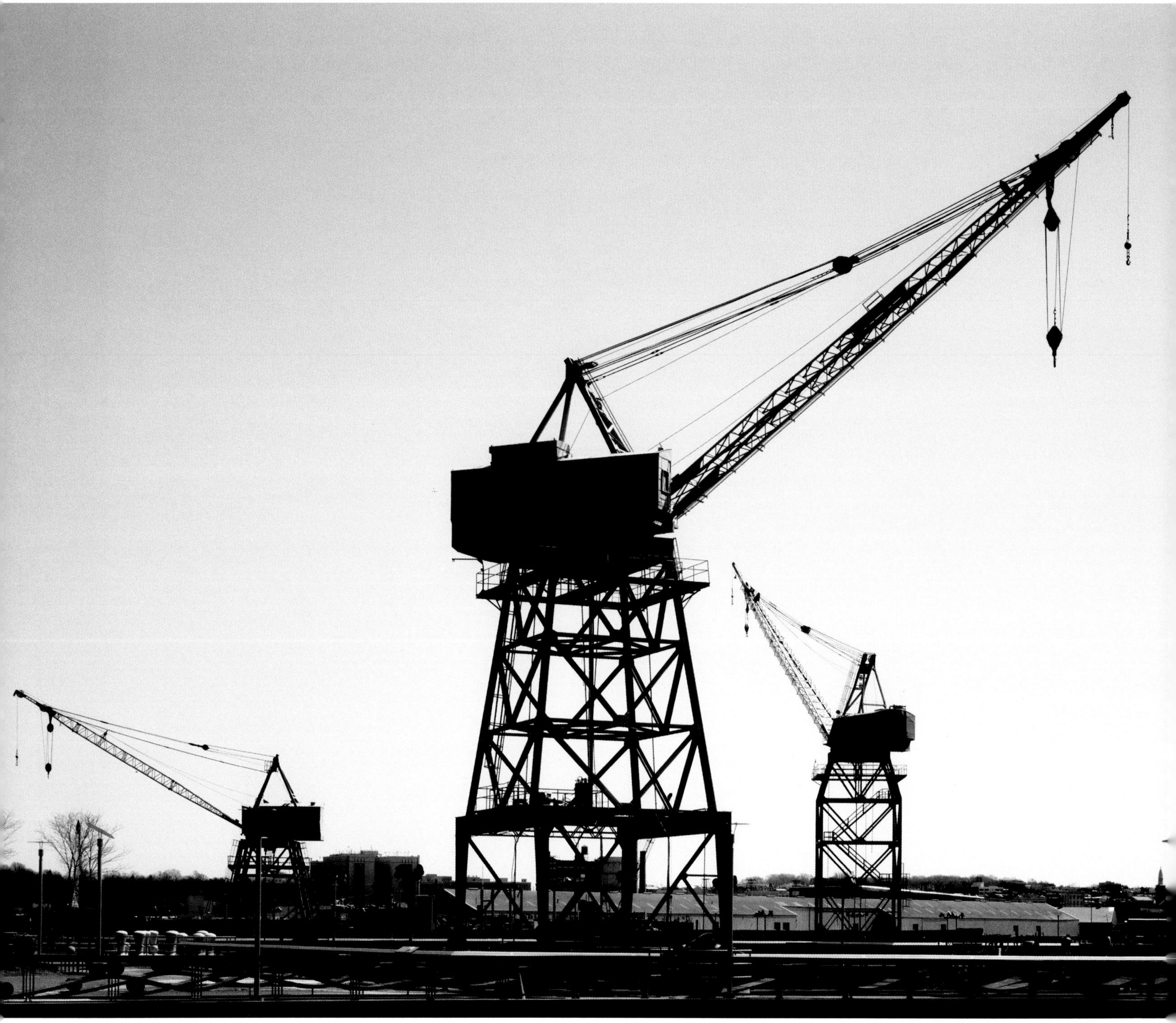

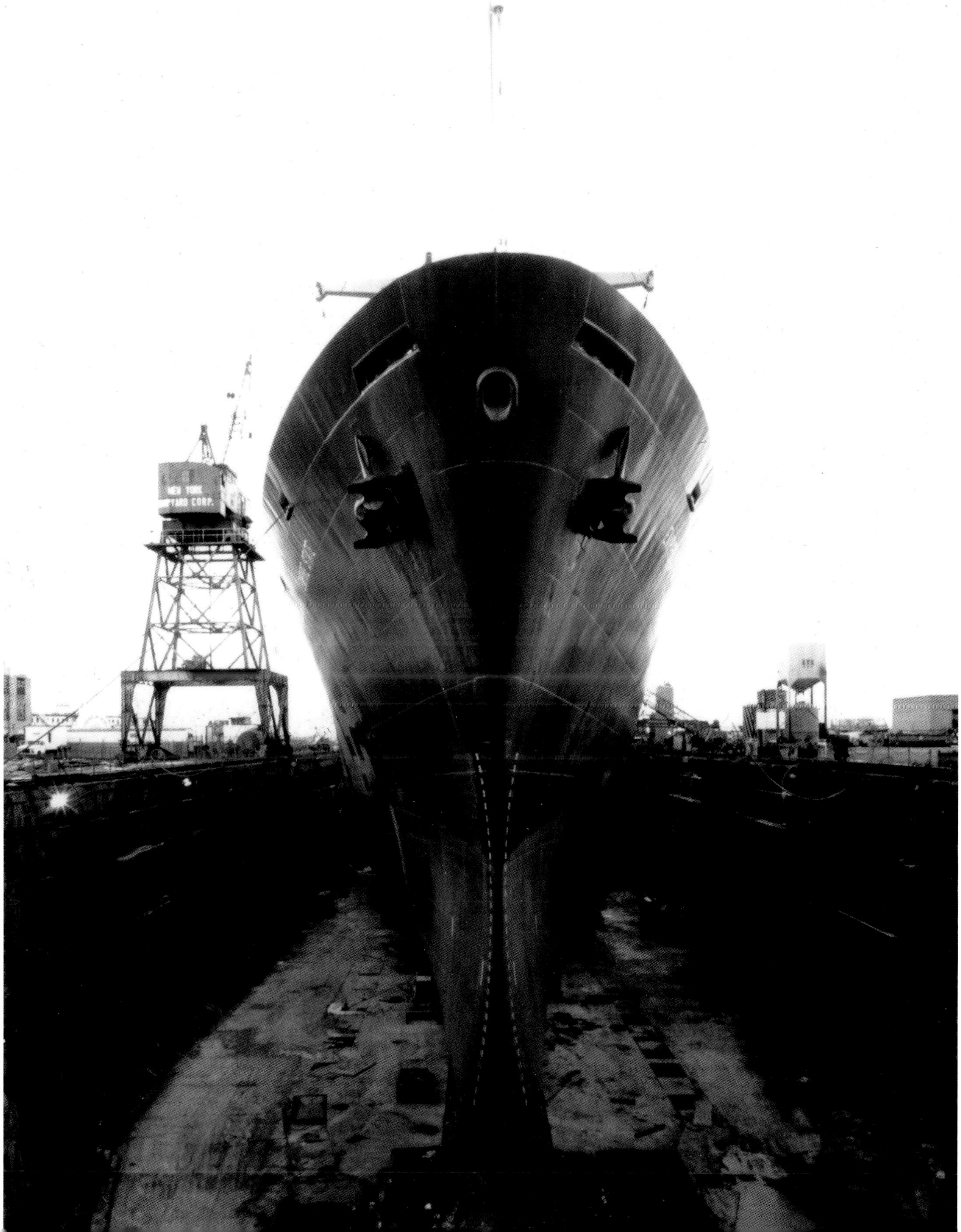
NEW YORK

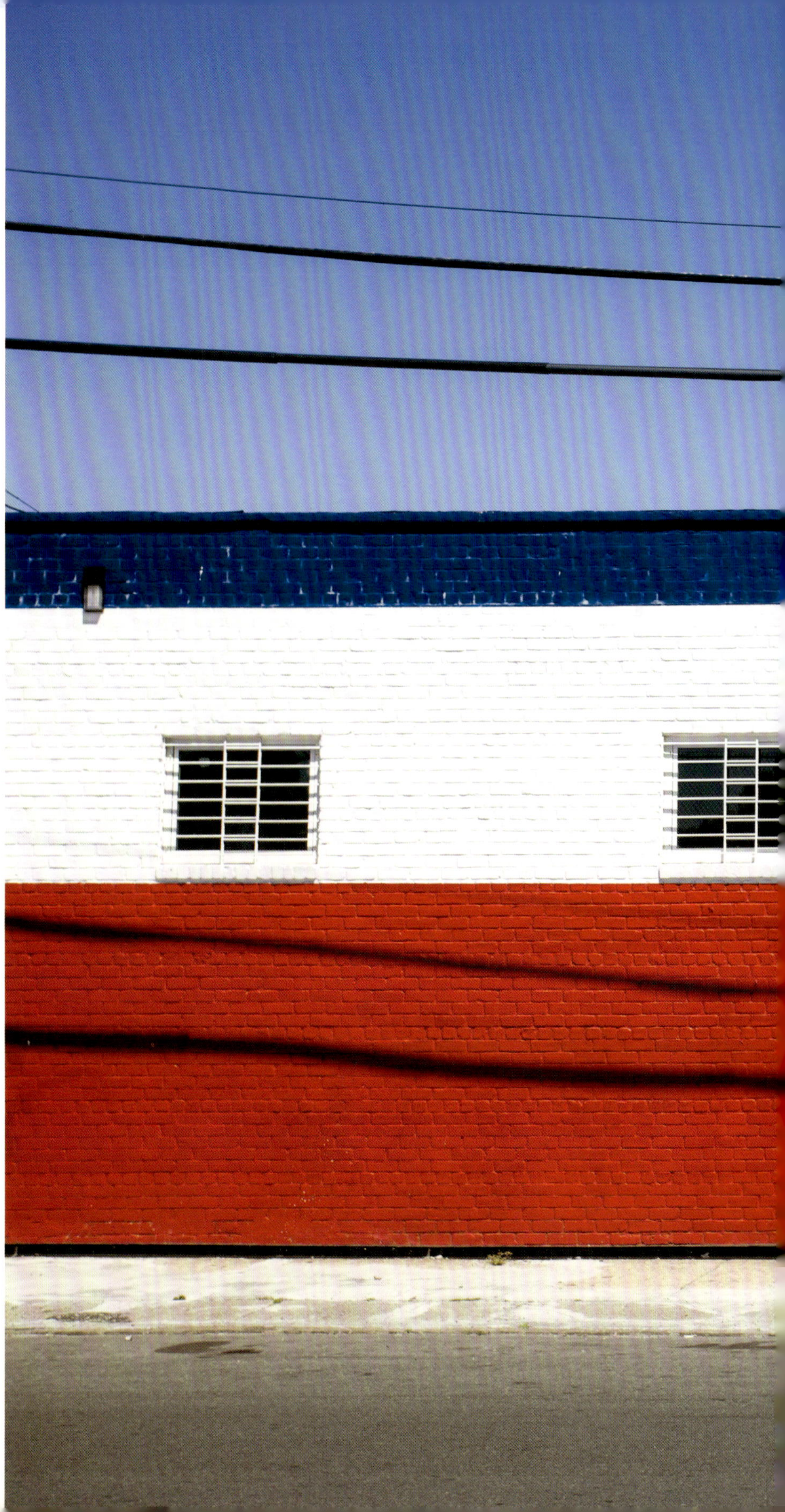

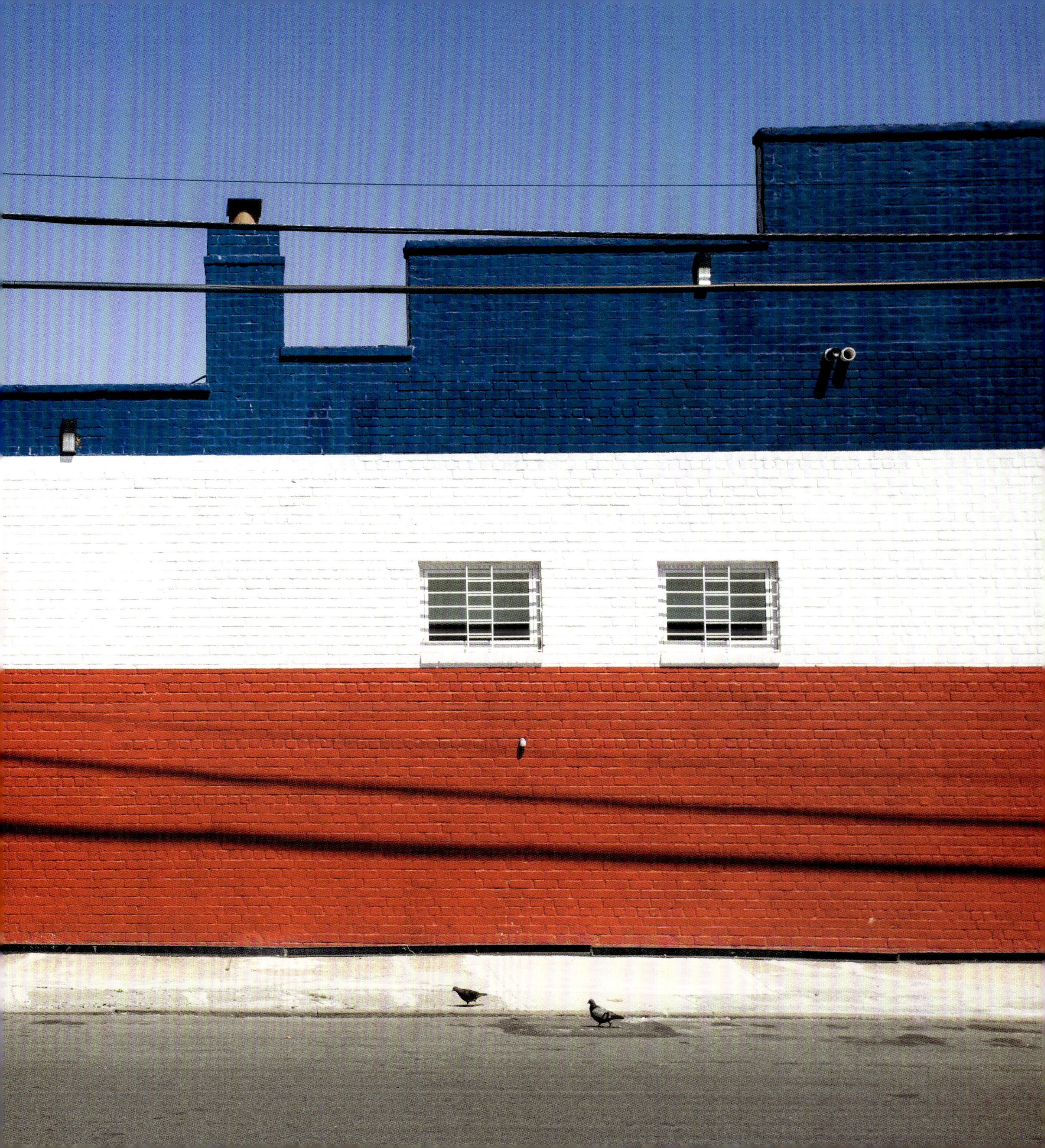

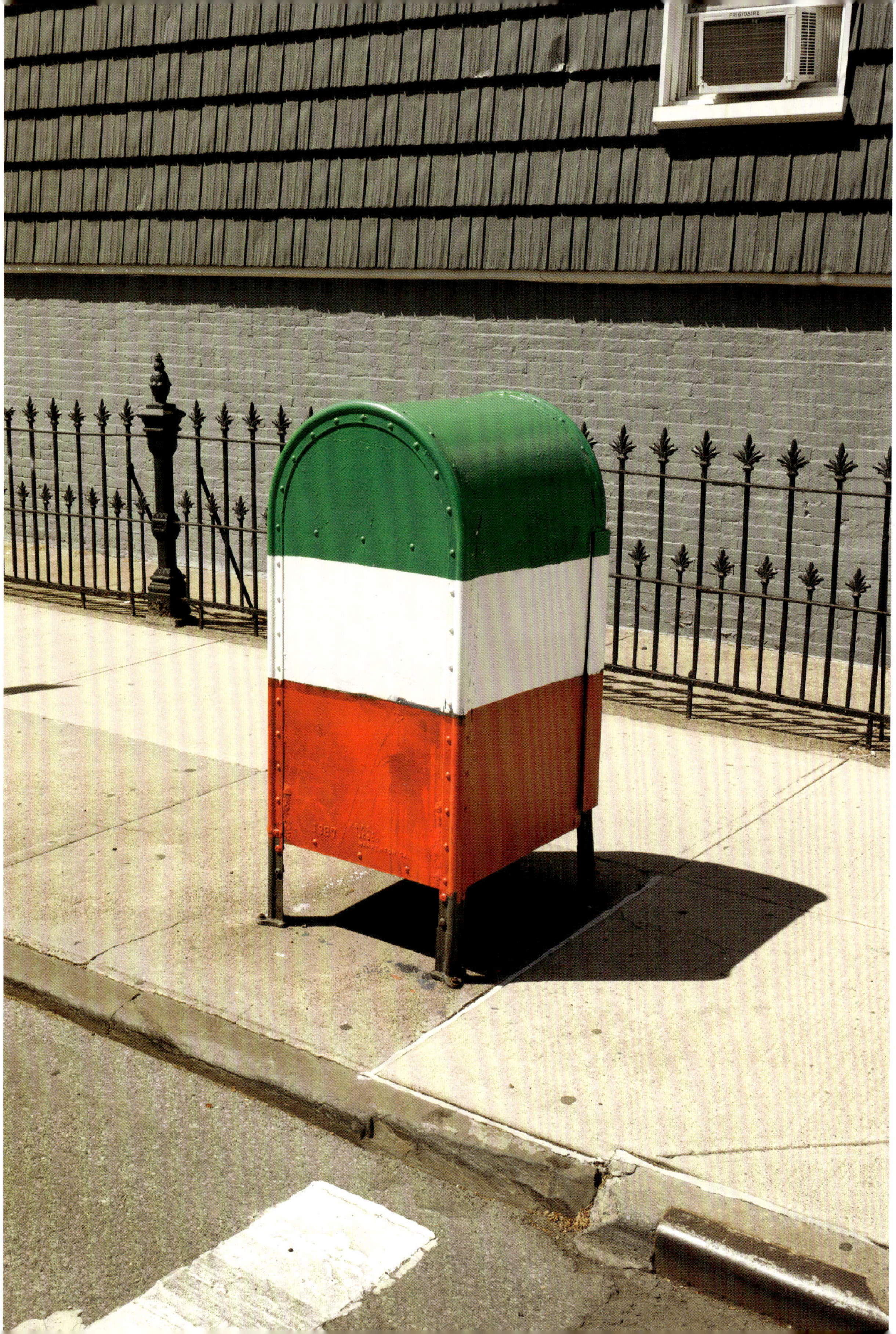

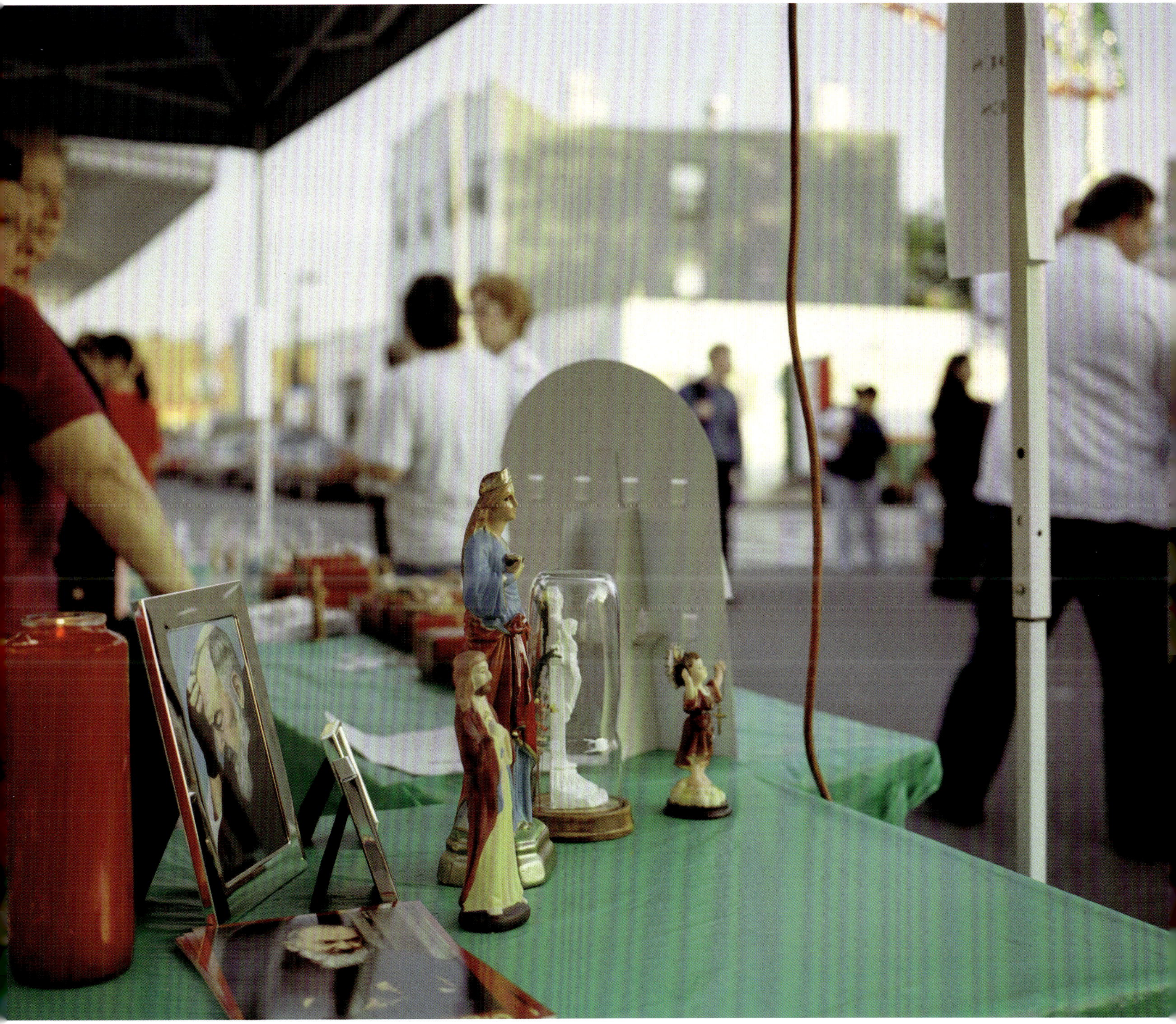

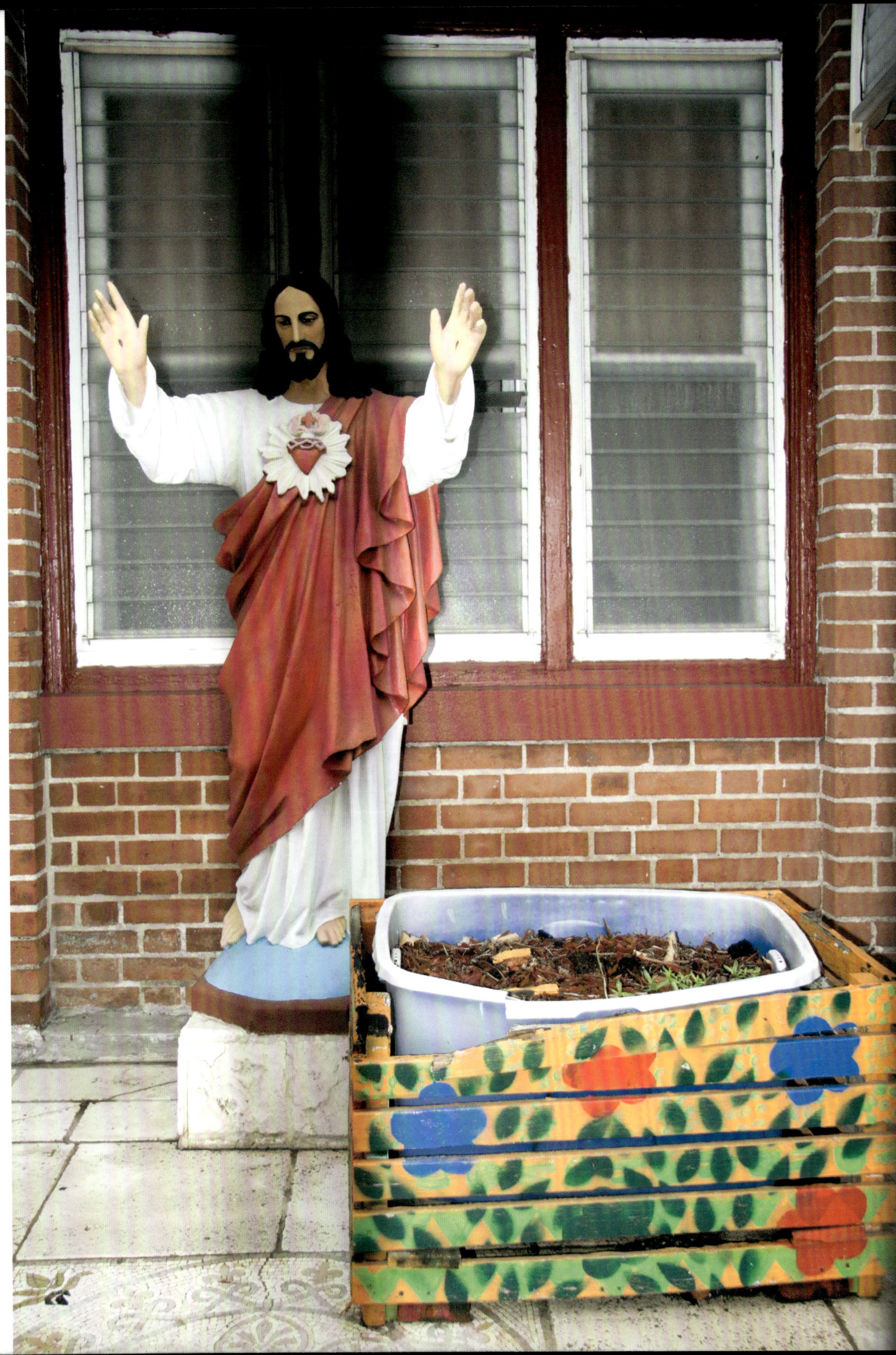

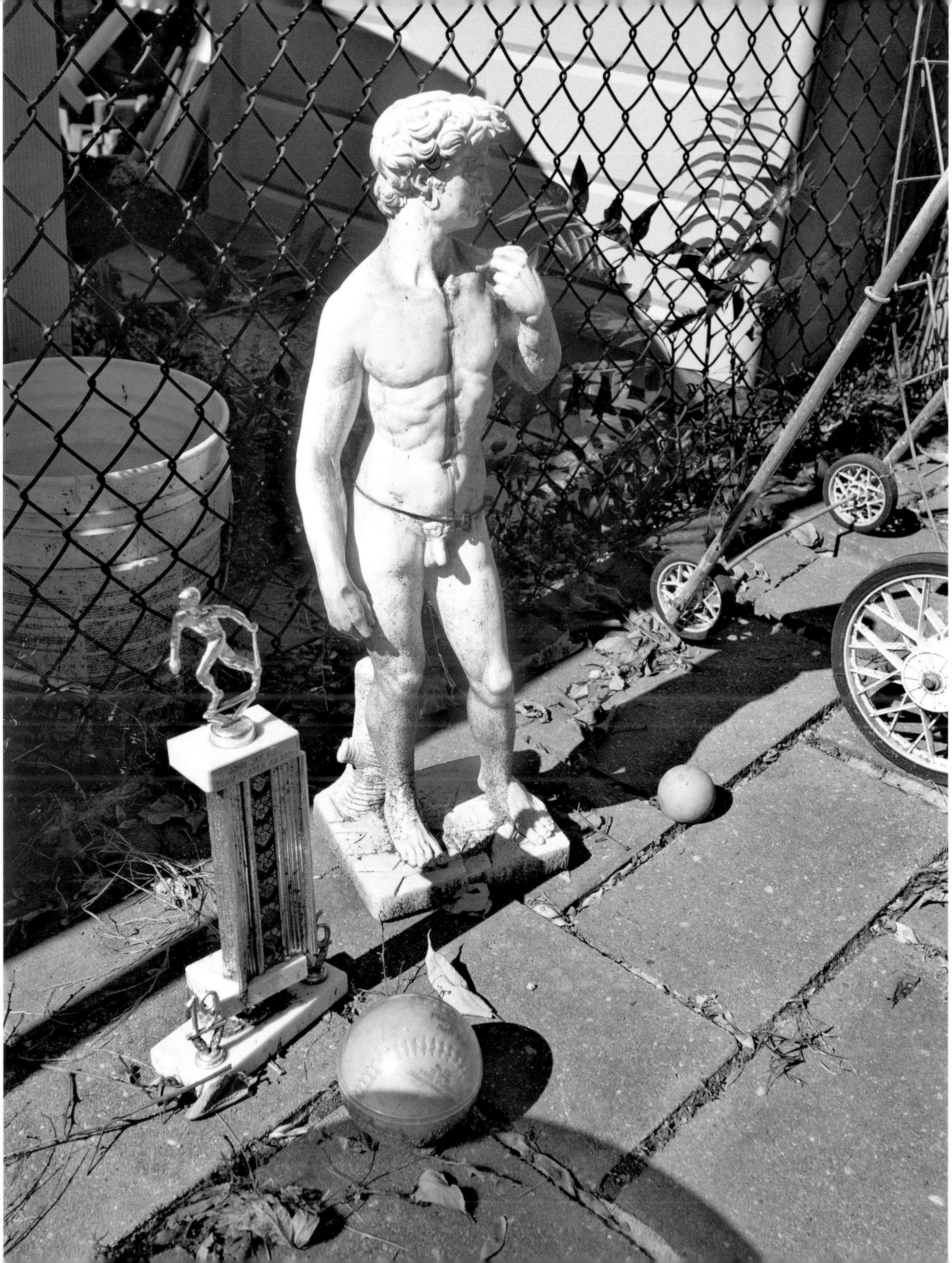

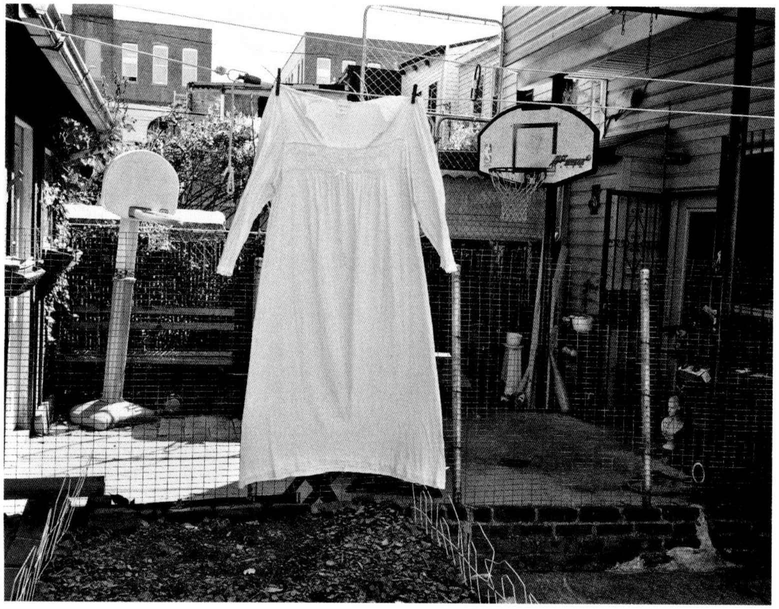

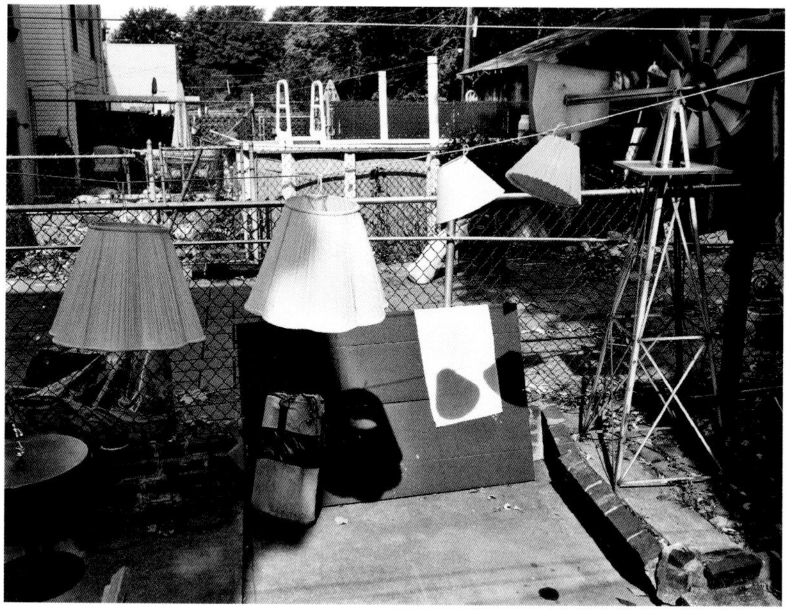

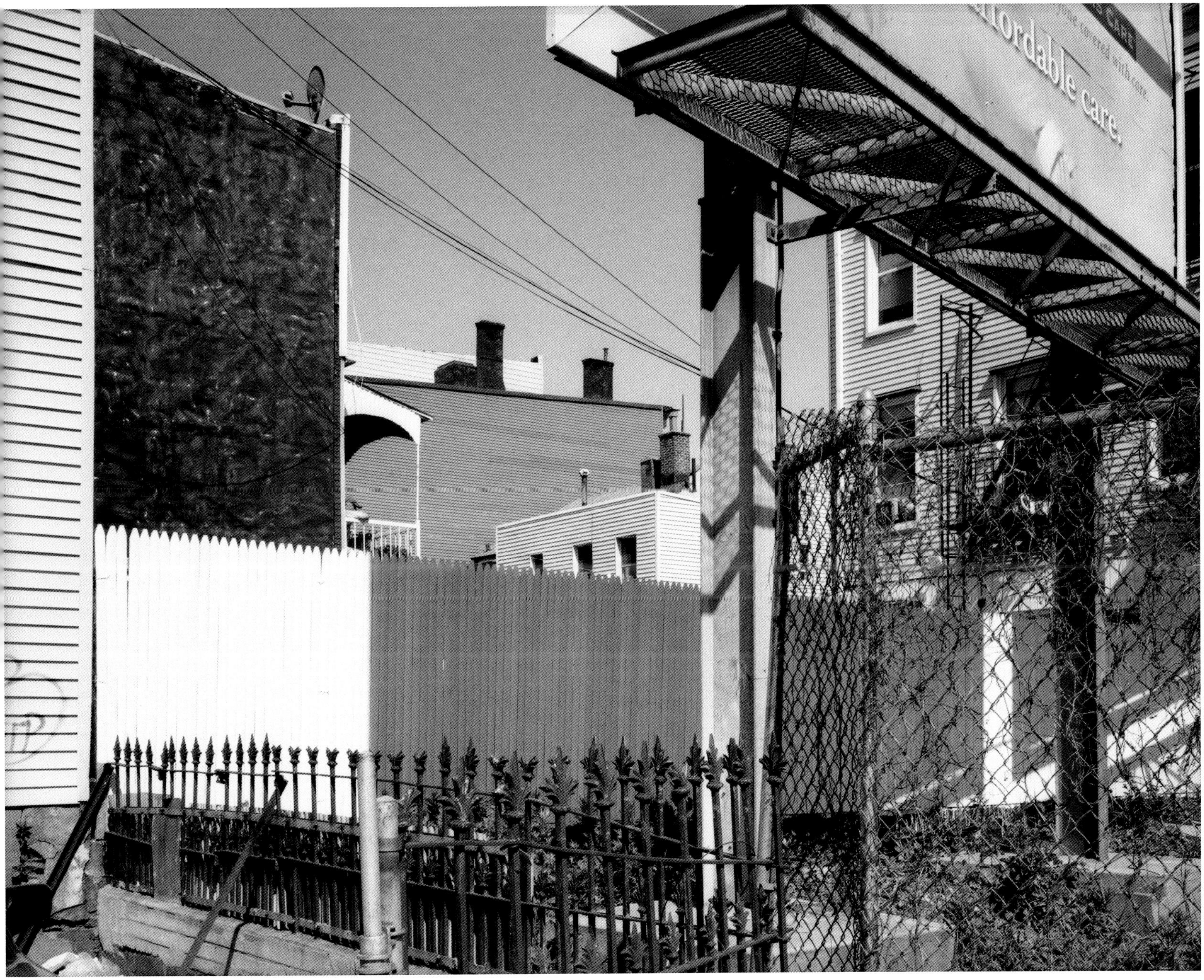
ffordable care.

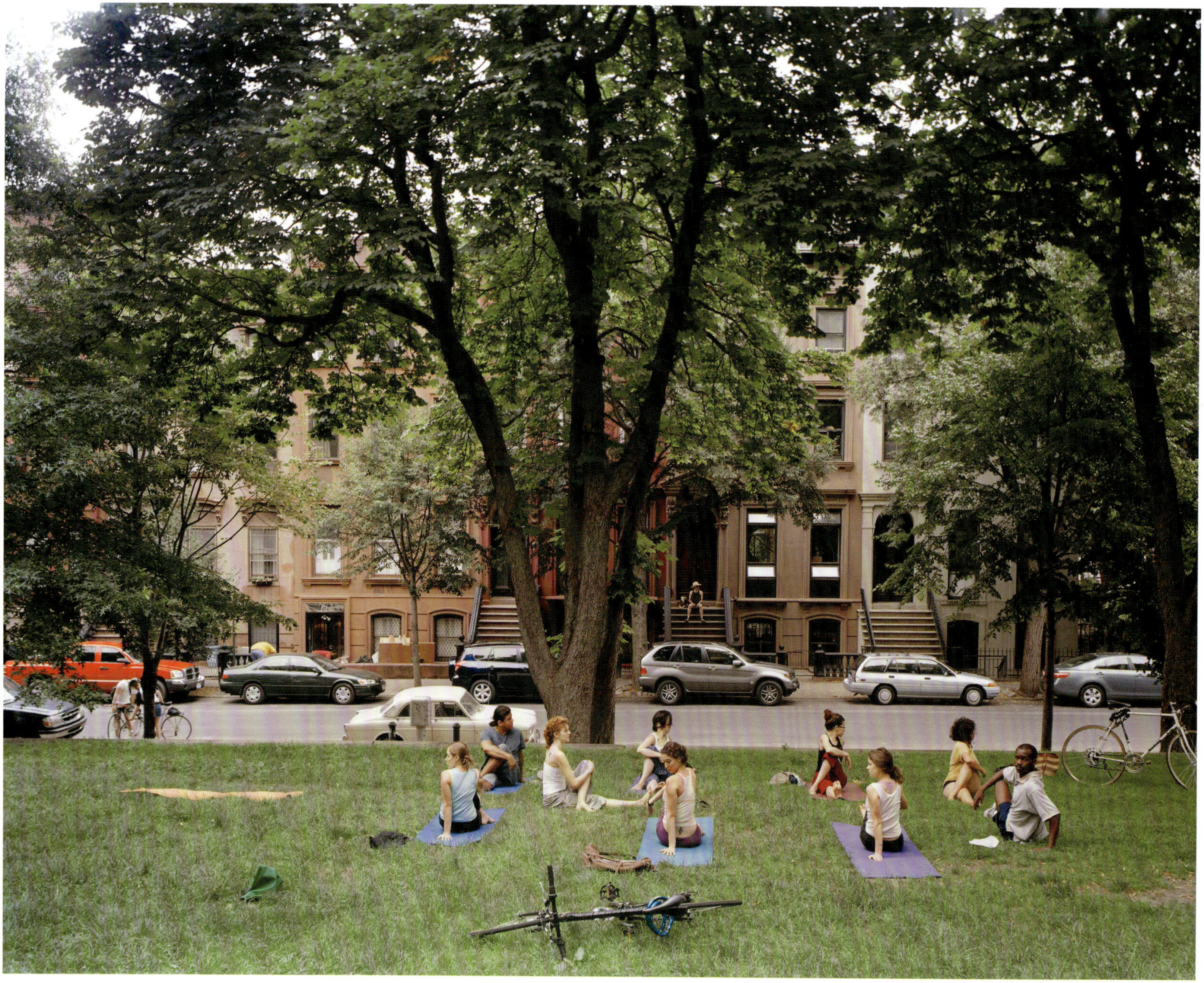

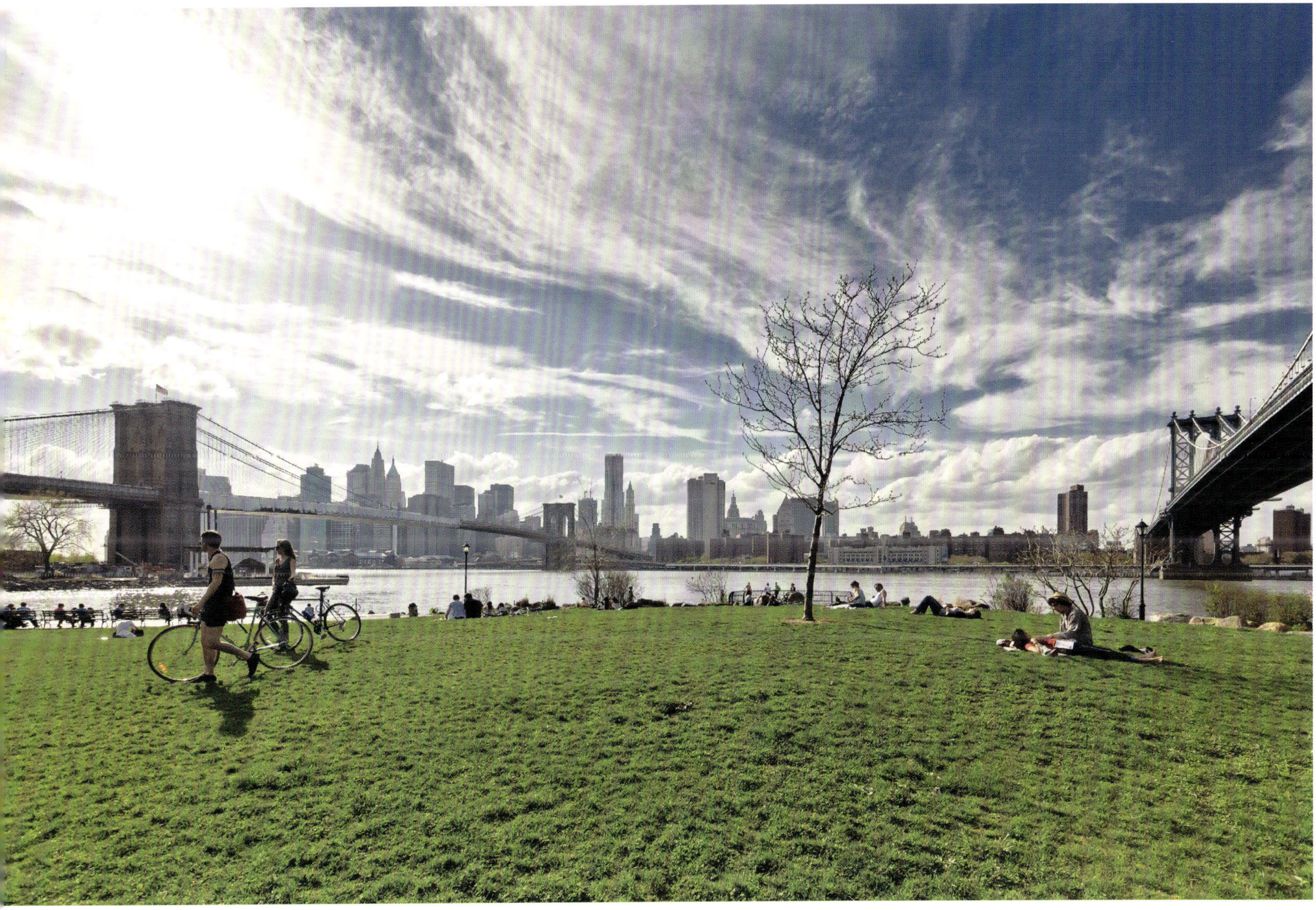

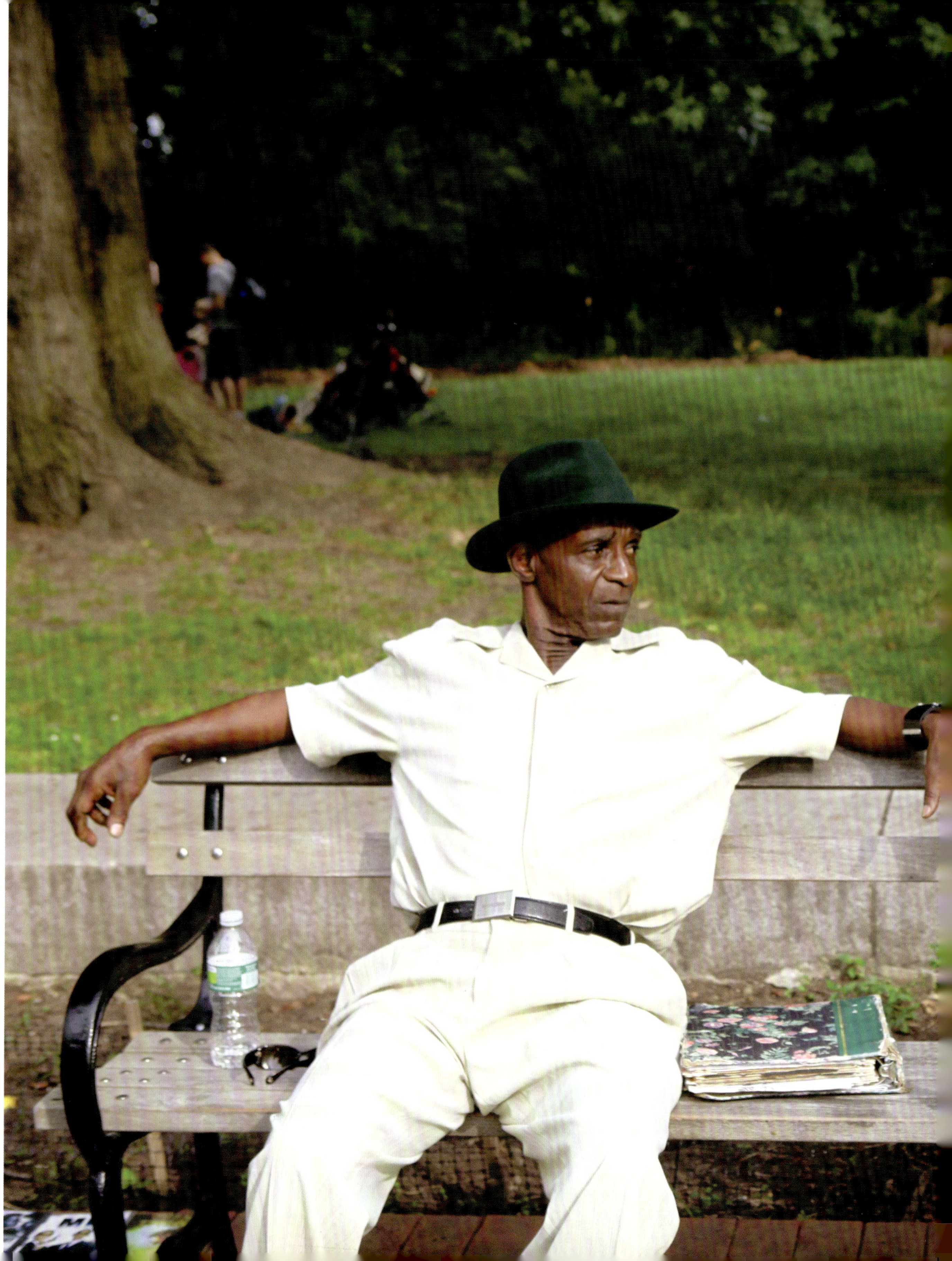

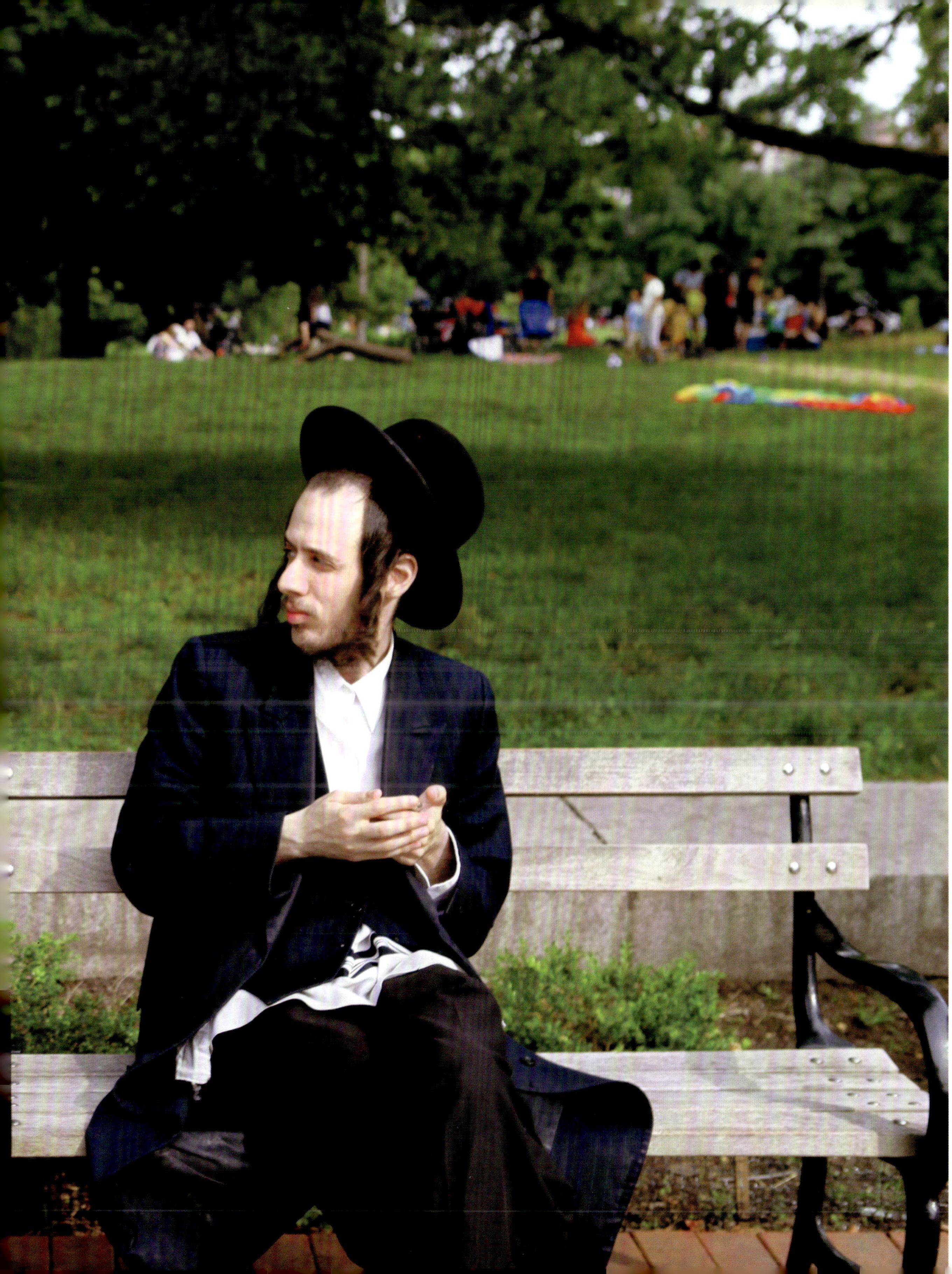

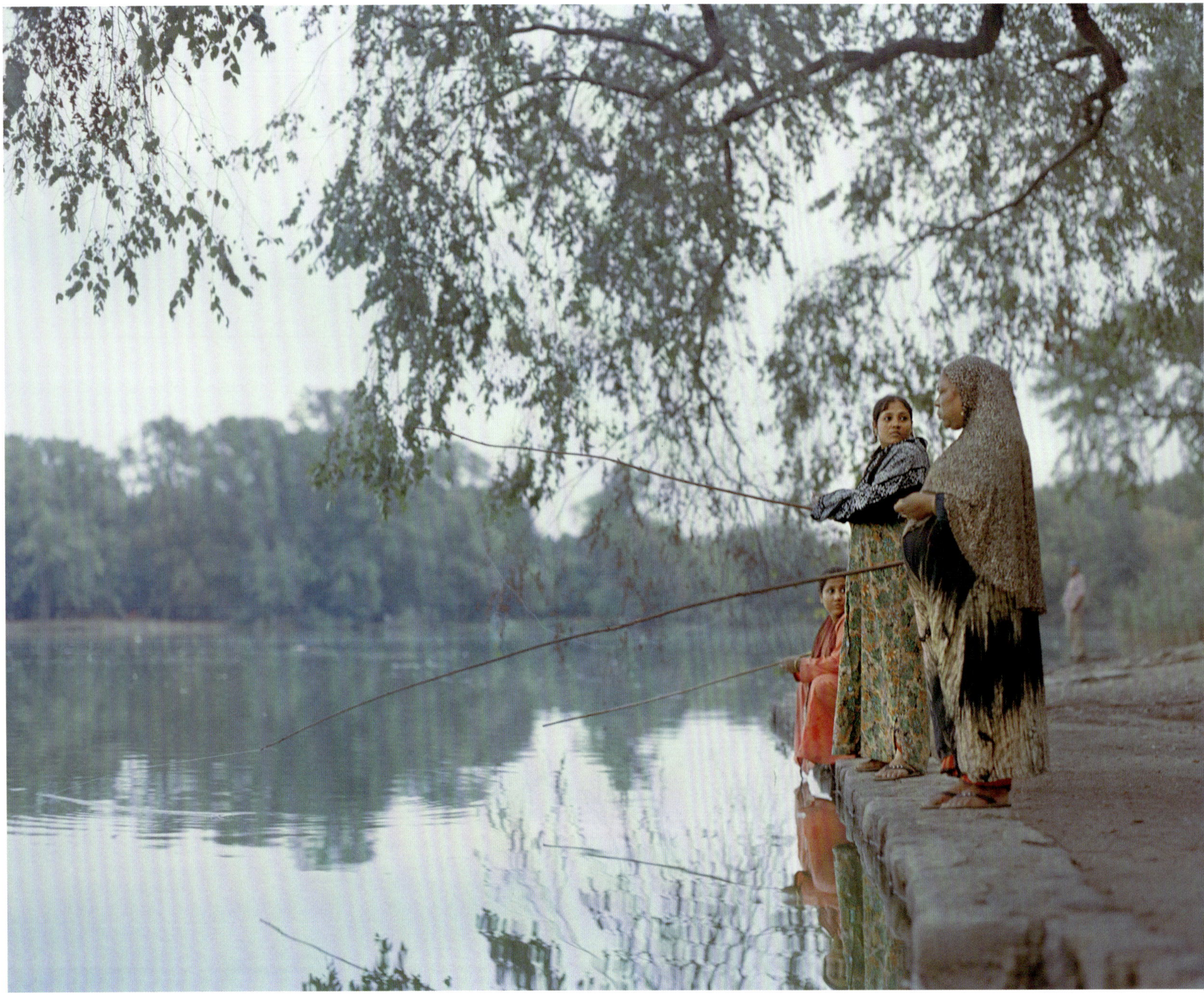

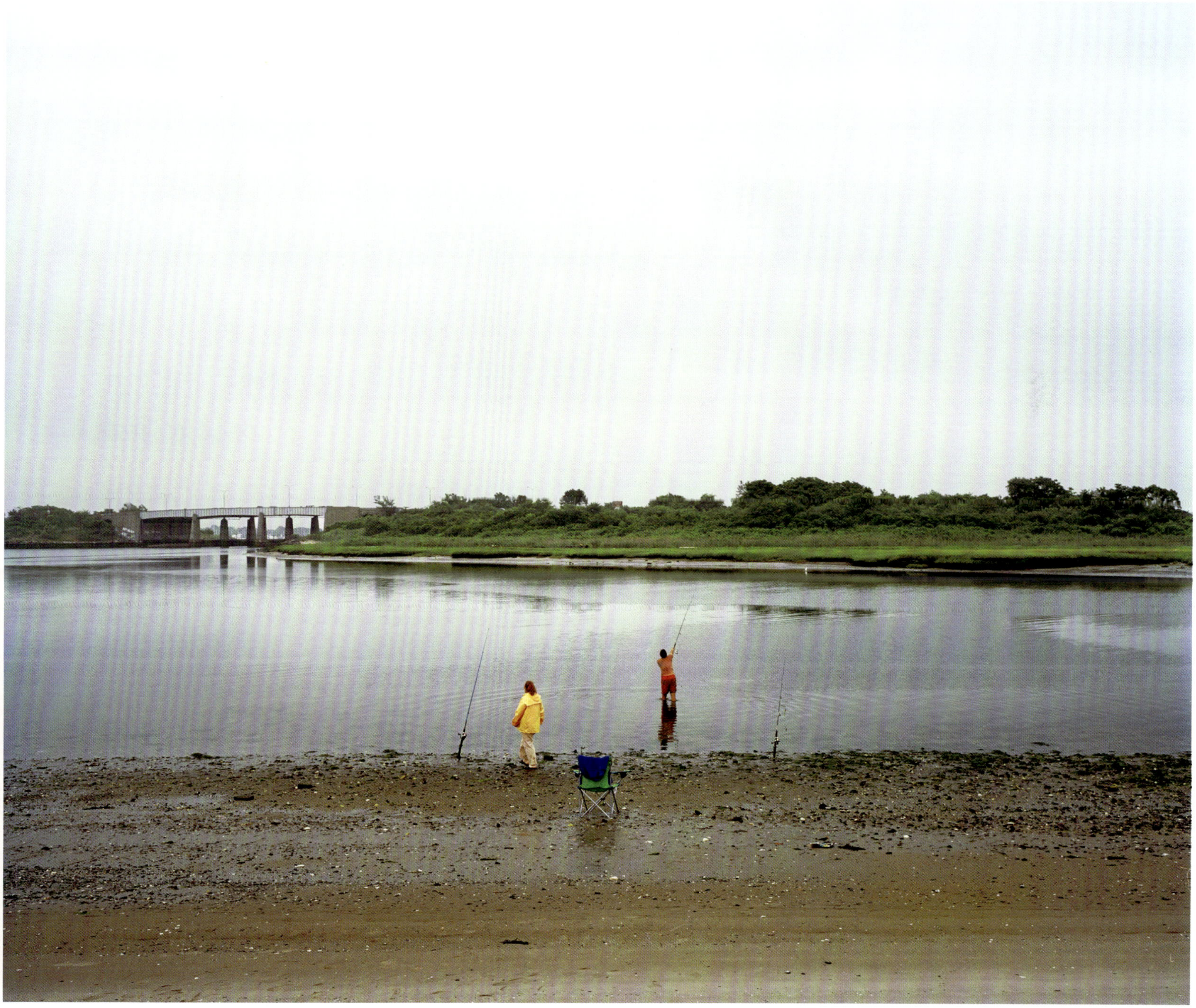

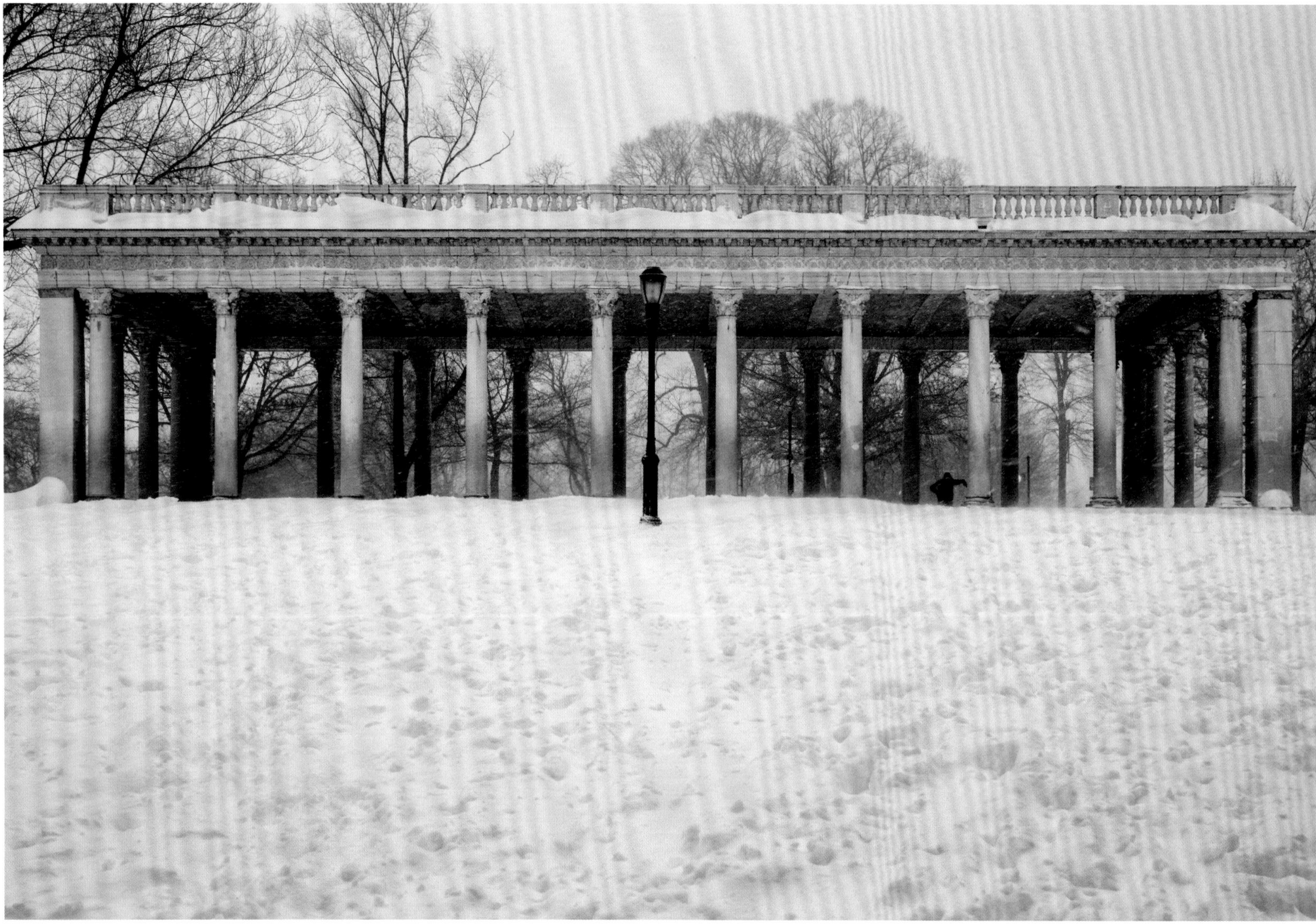

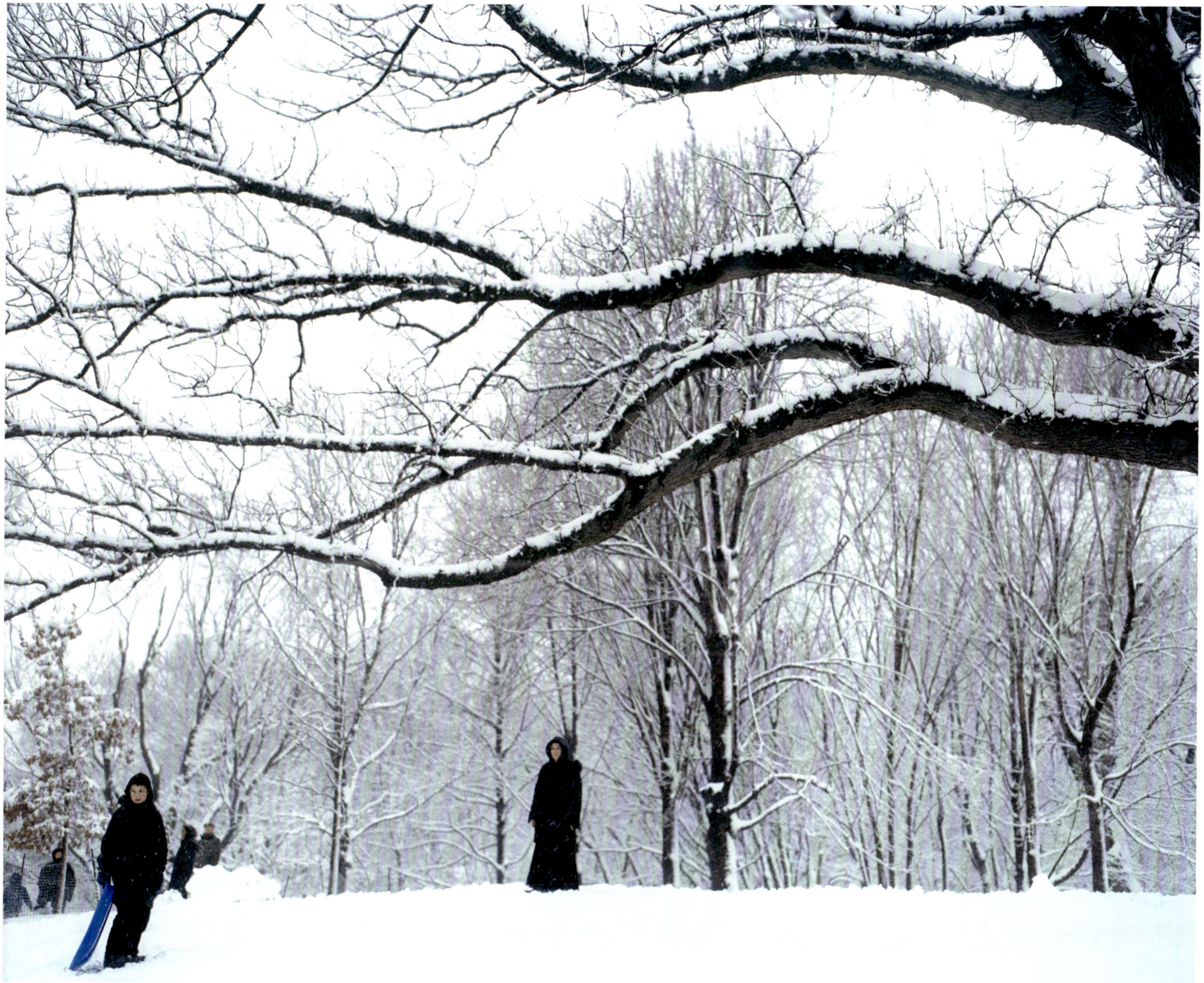

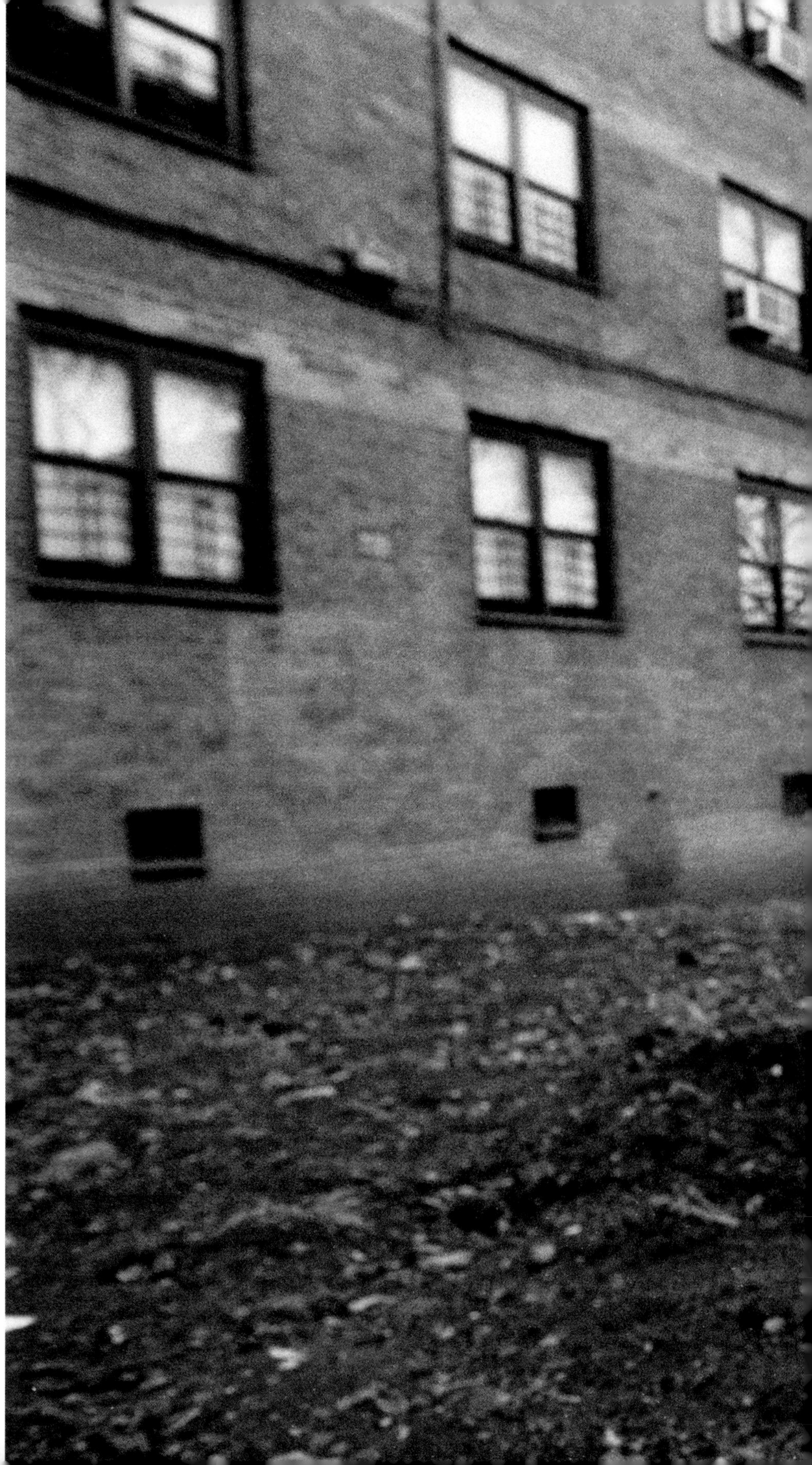

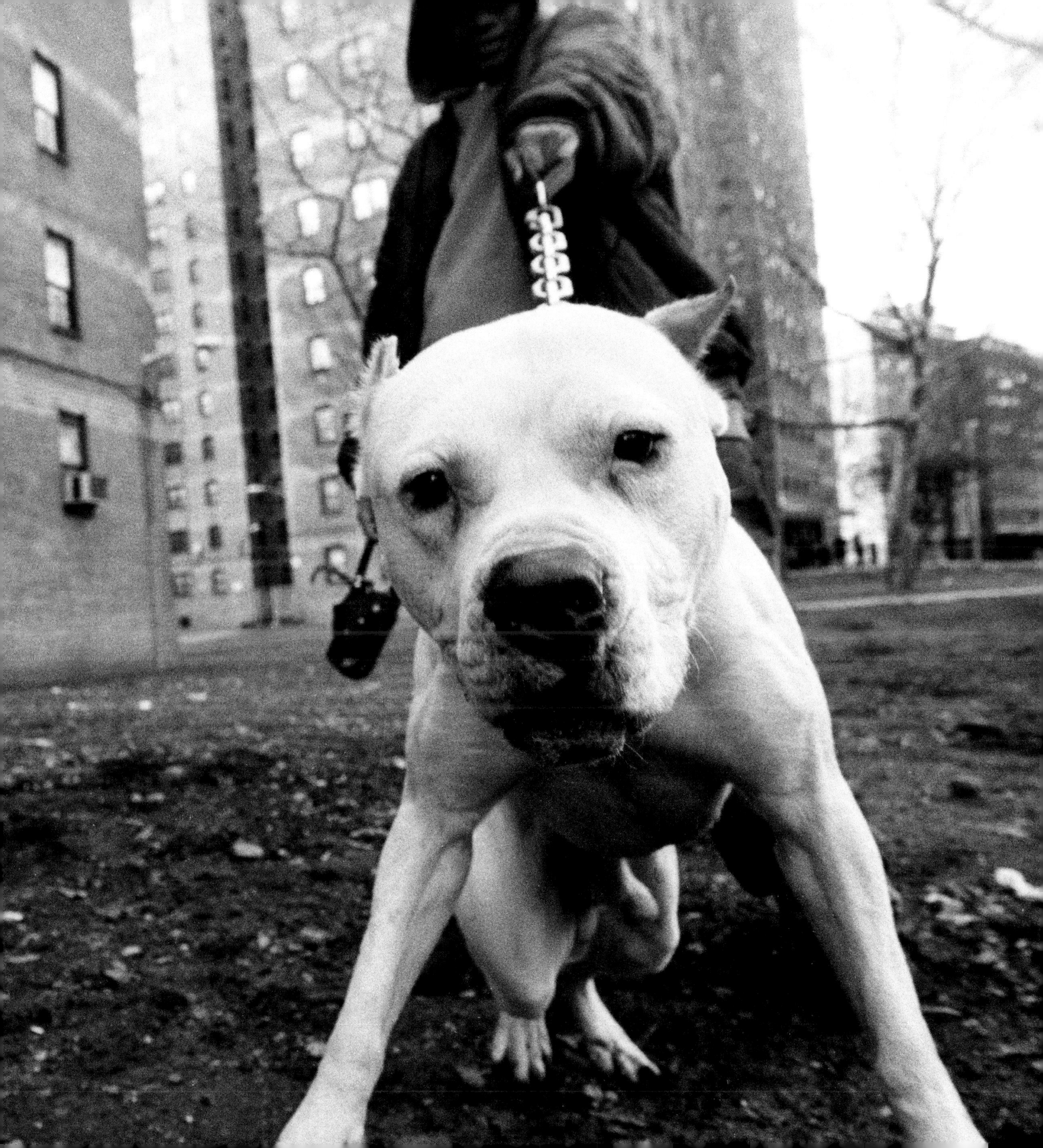

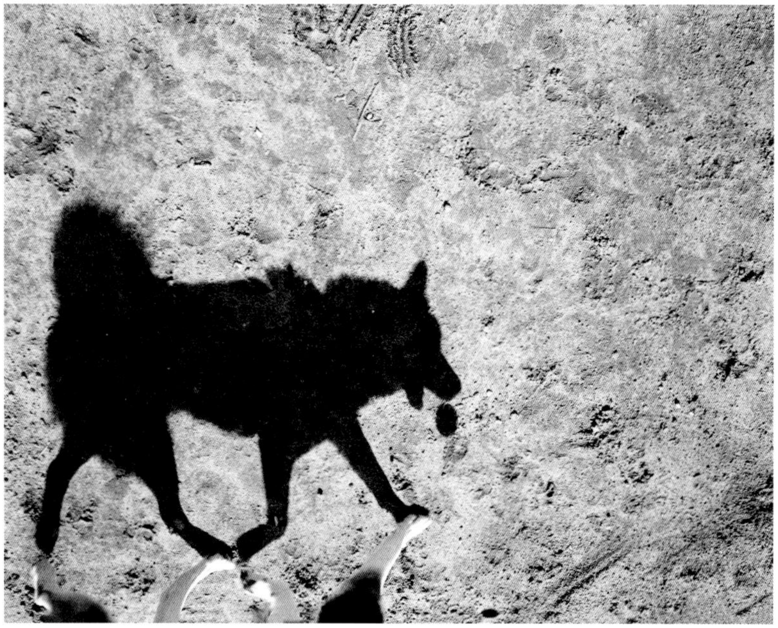

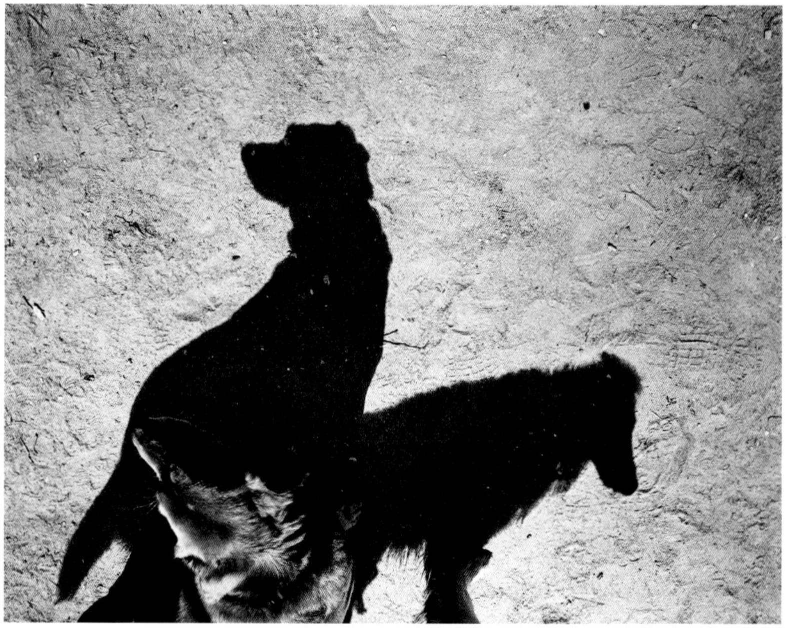

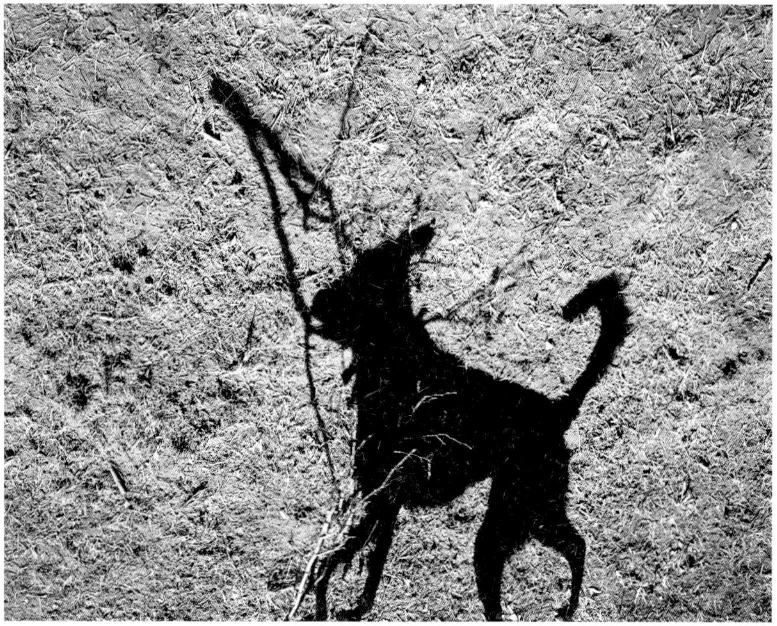

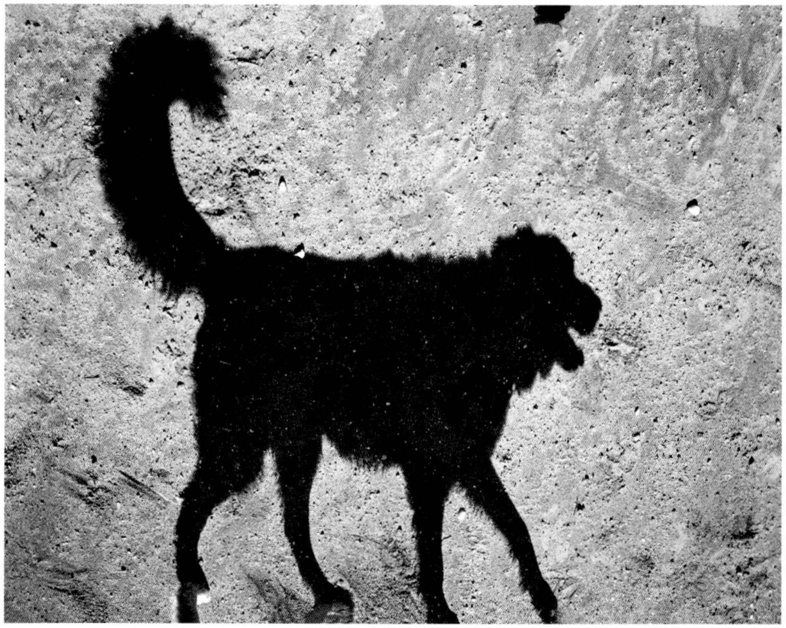

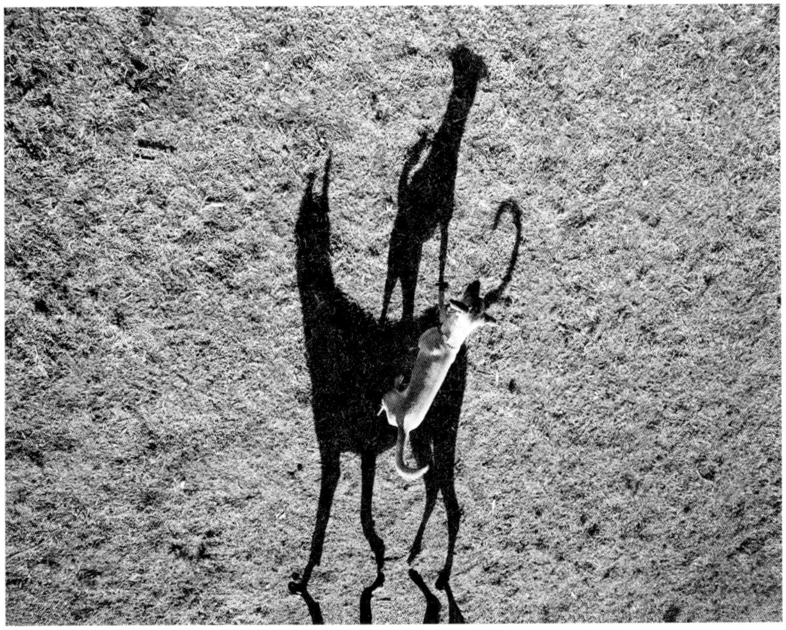

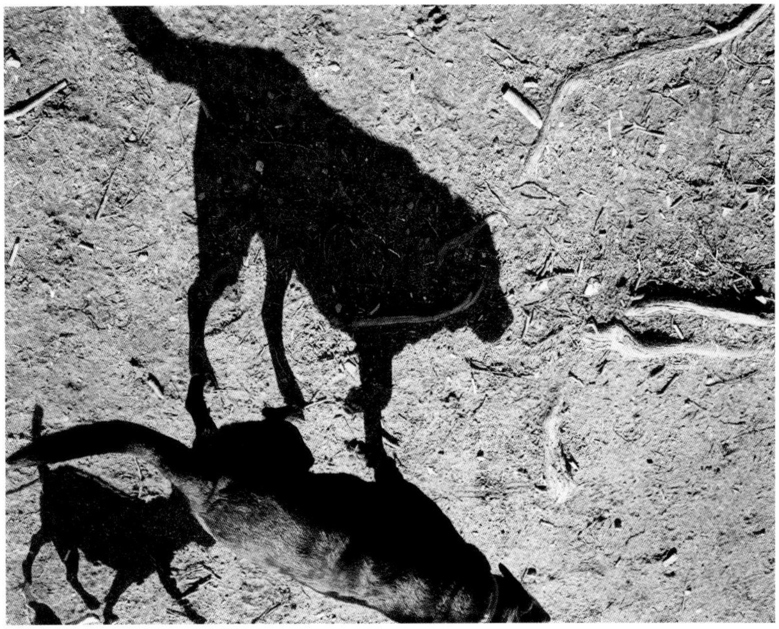

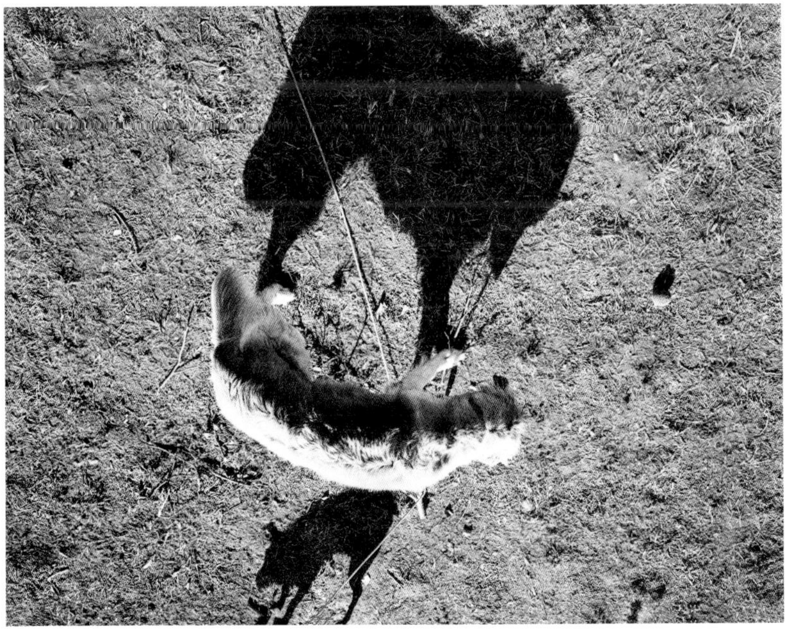

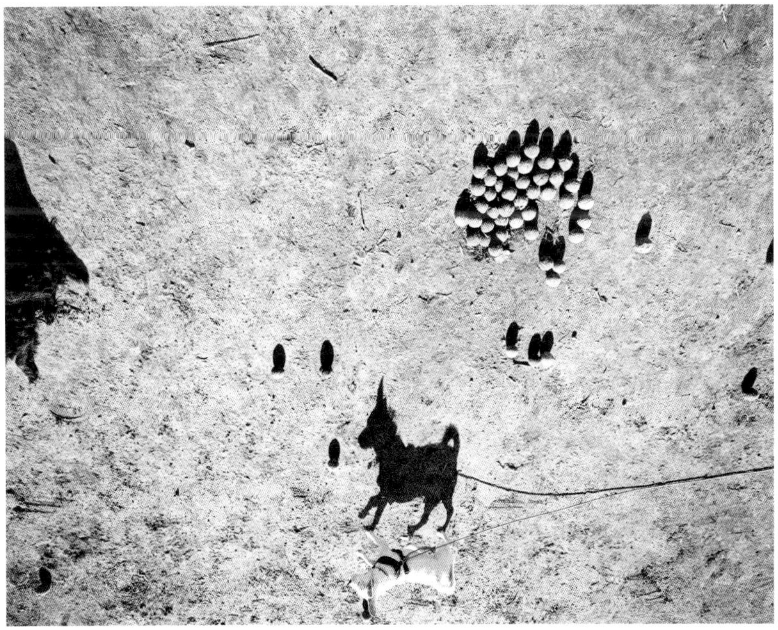

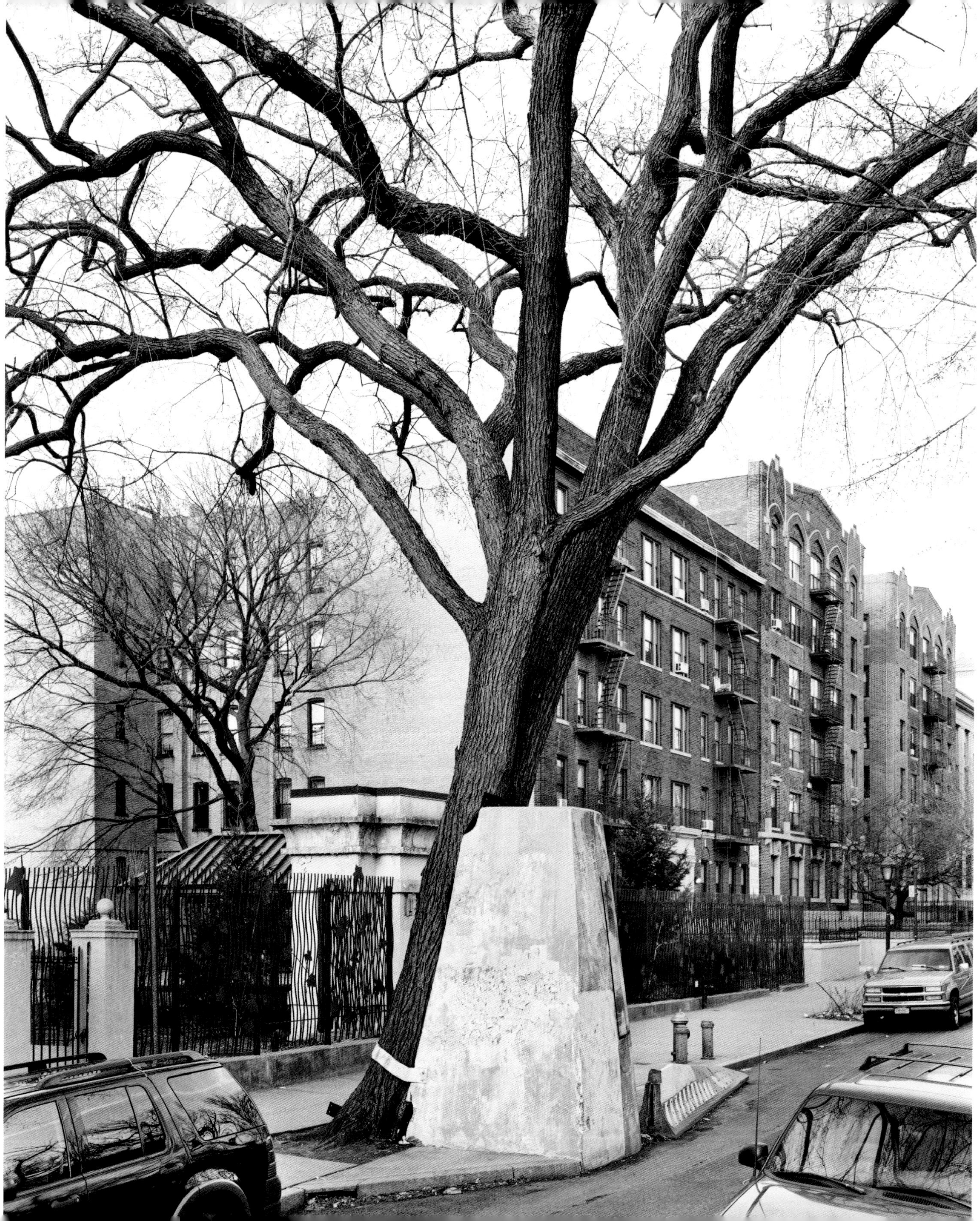

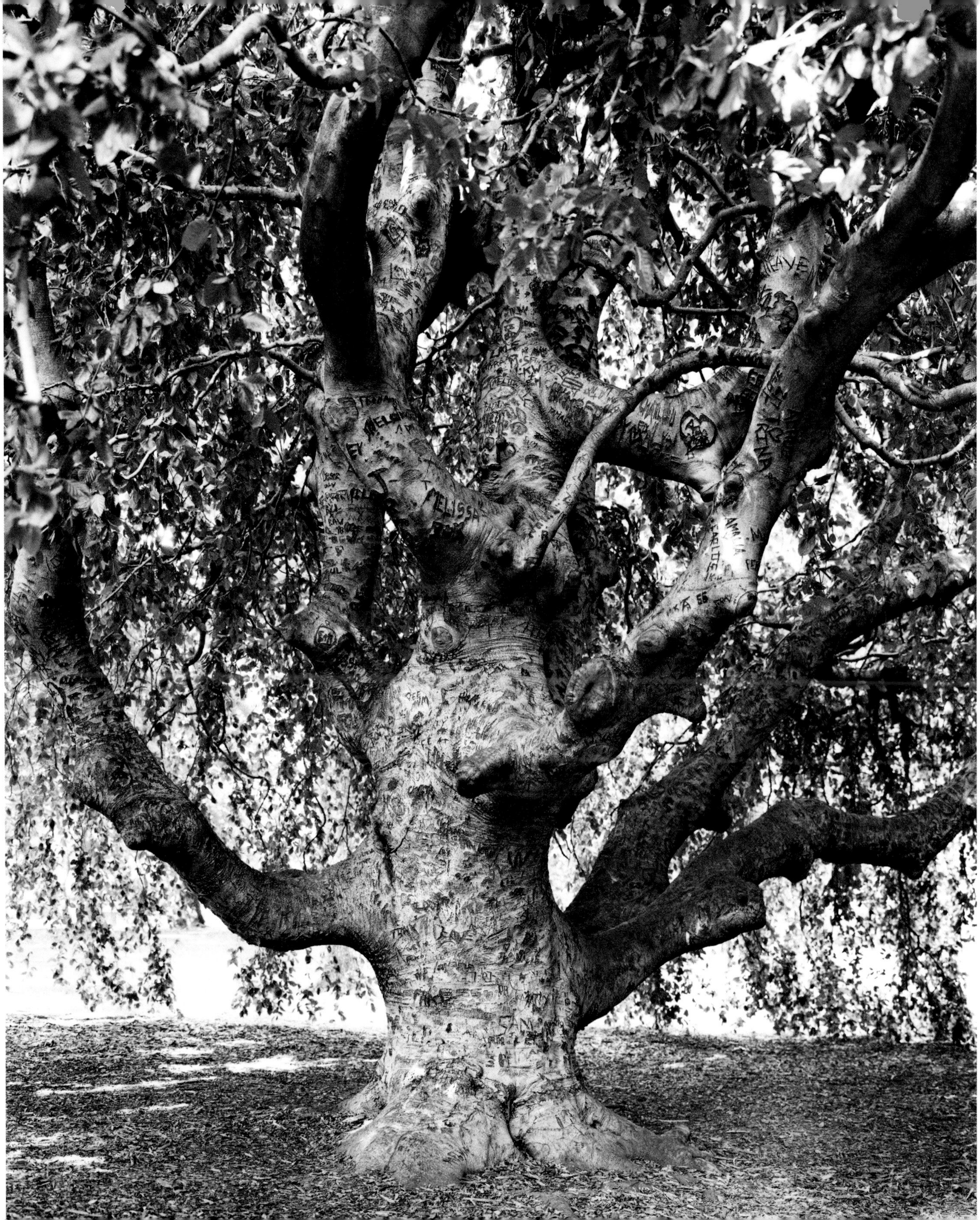
MELISSA

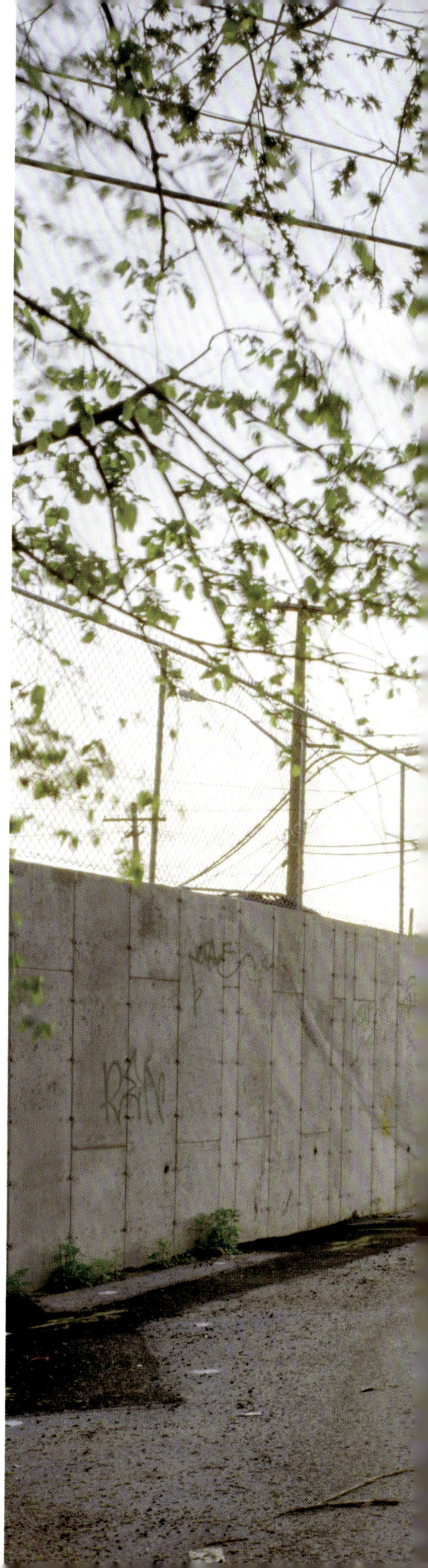

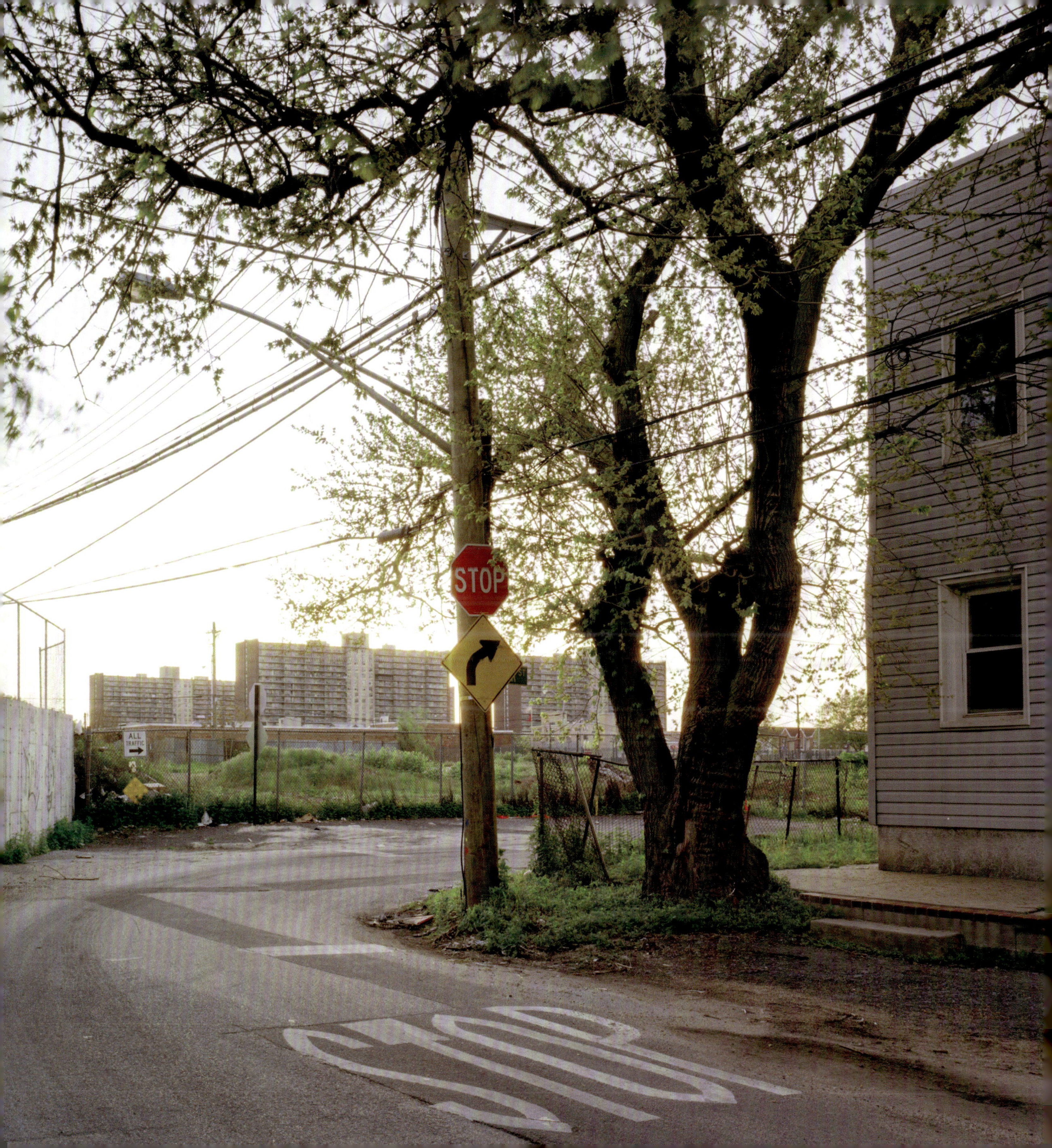
STOP
ALL TRAFFIC
STOP

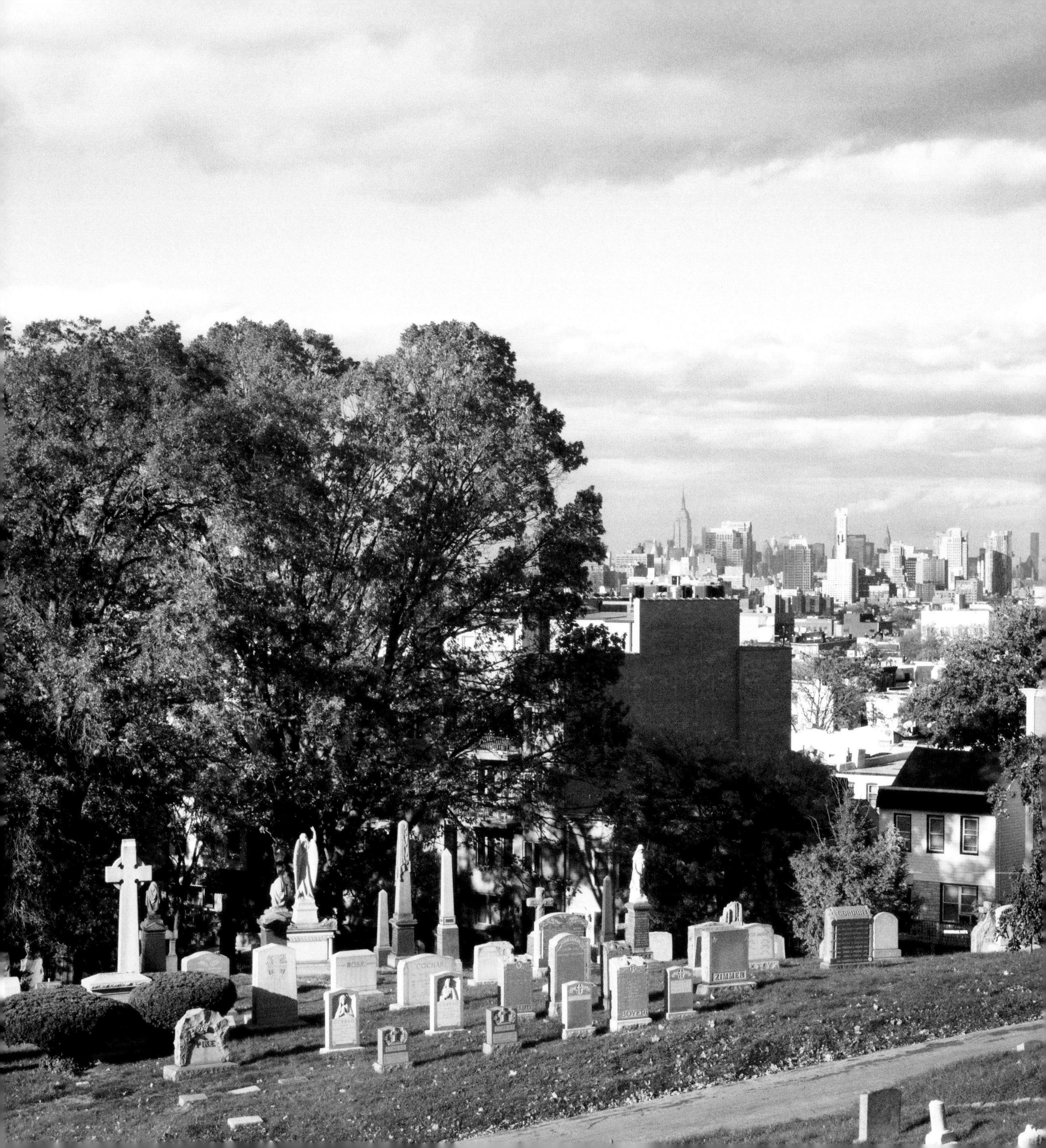
ZIMMER
BOYER

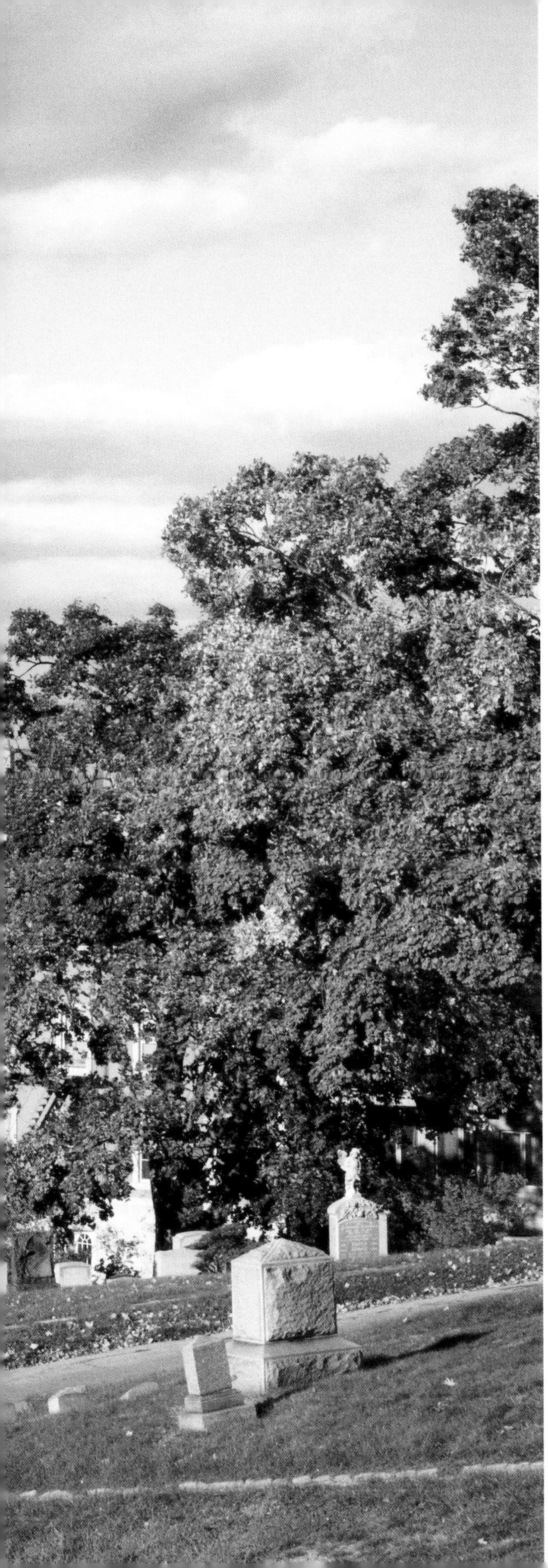

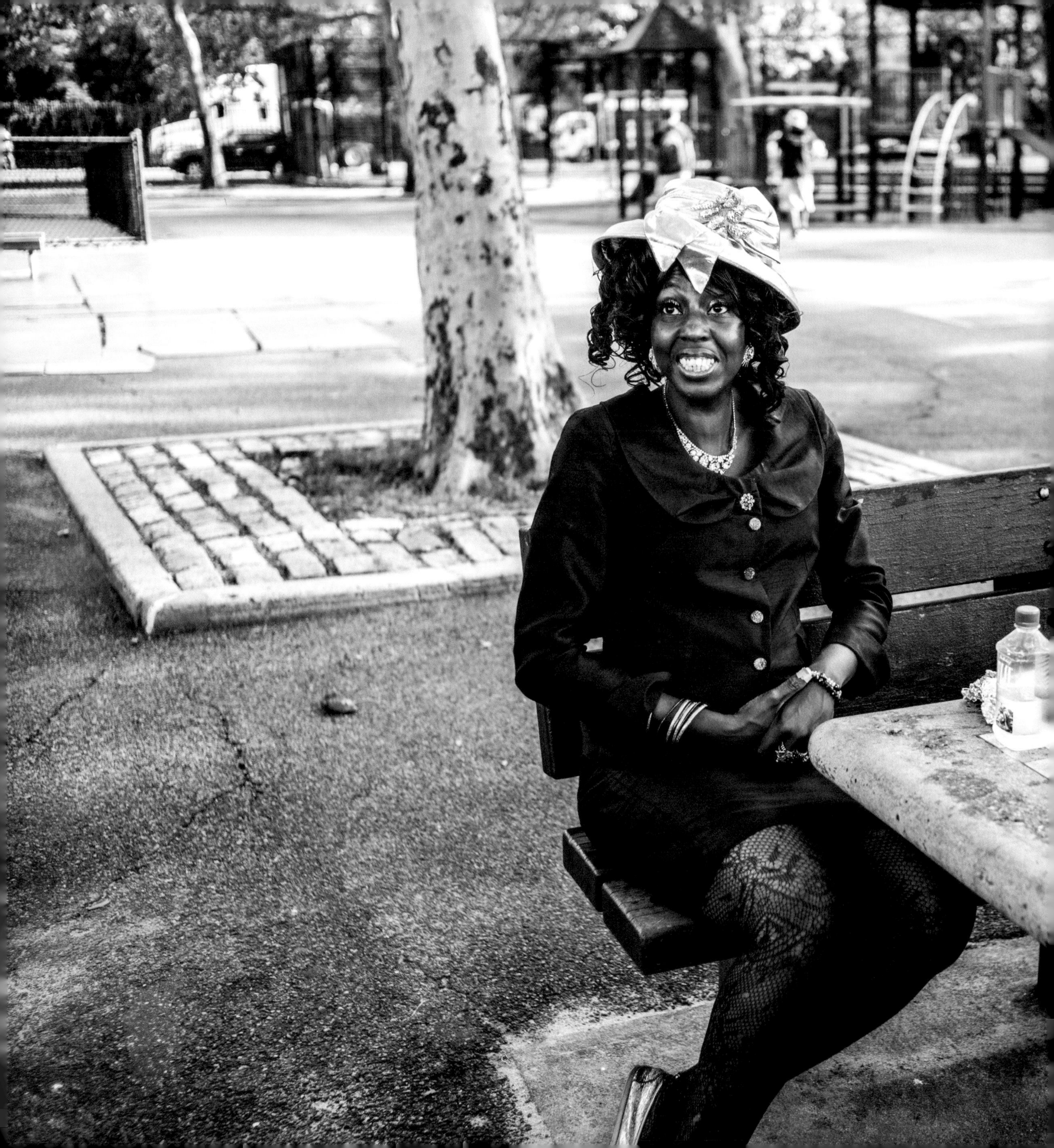

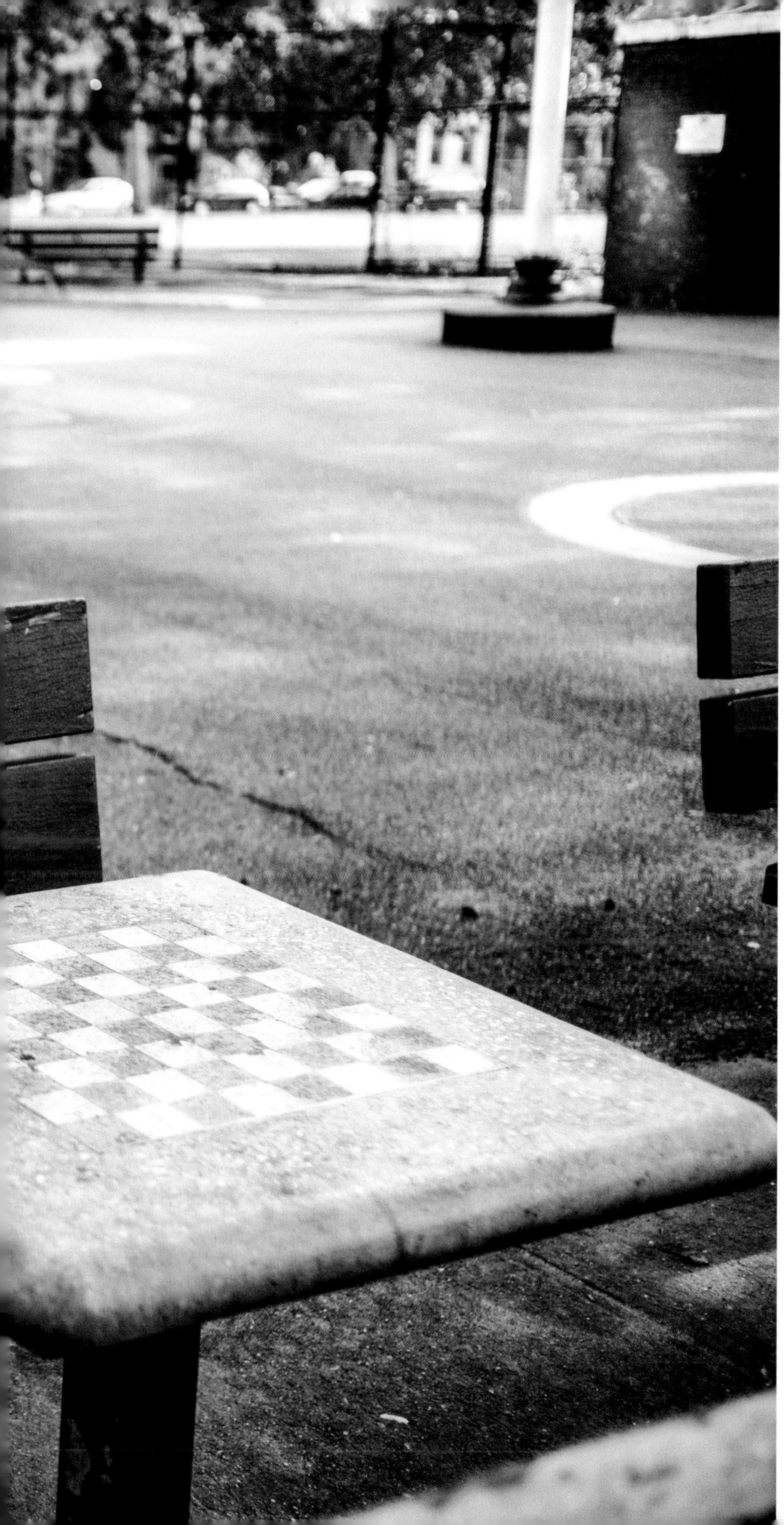

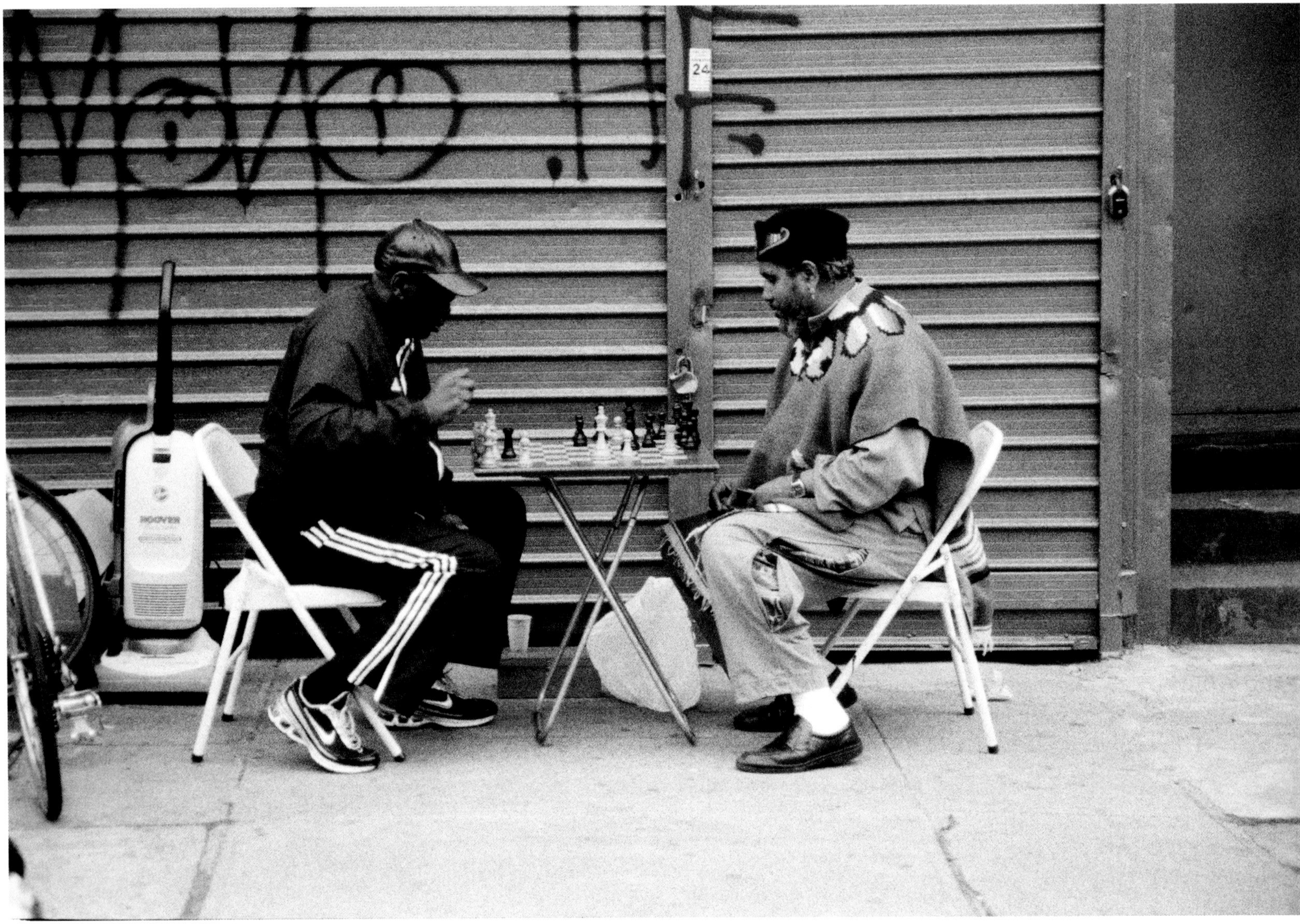
24
HOOVER

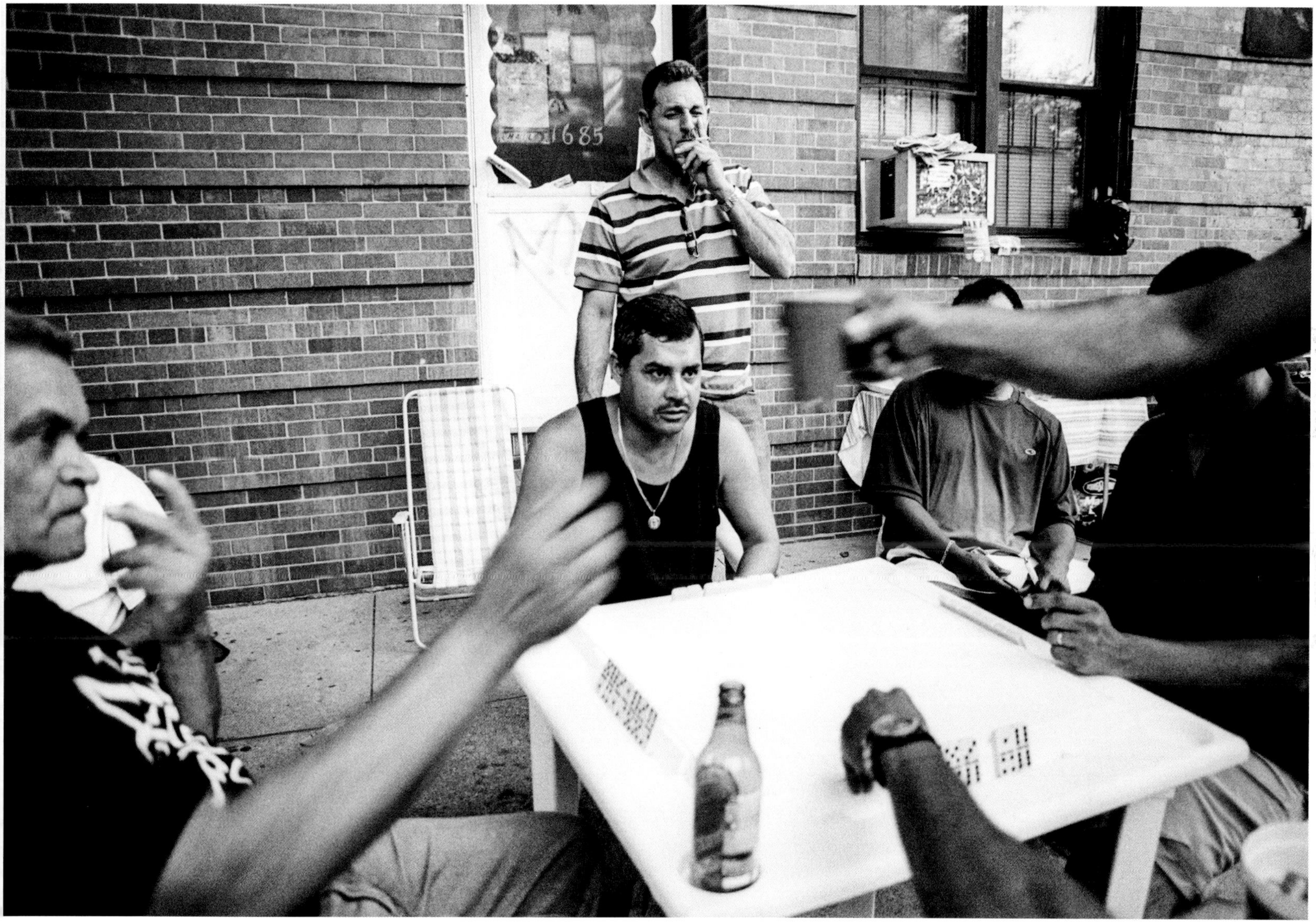
1685

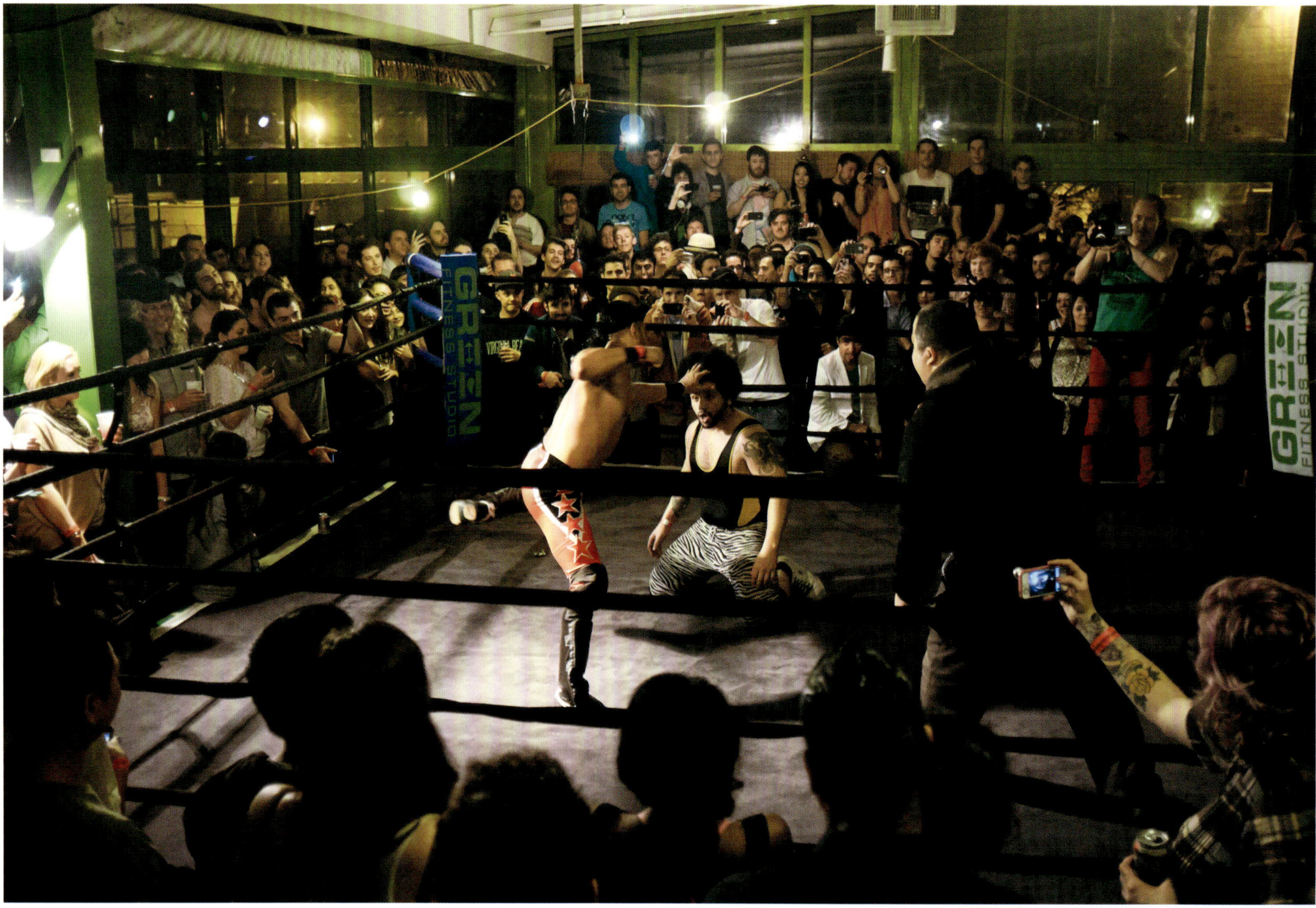
GREEN
FITNESS STUDIO
GREEN
FITNESS STUDIO

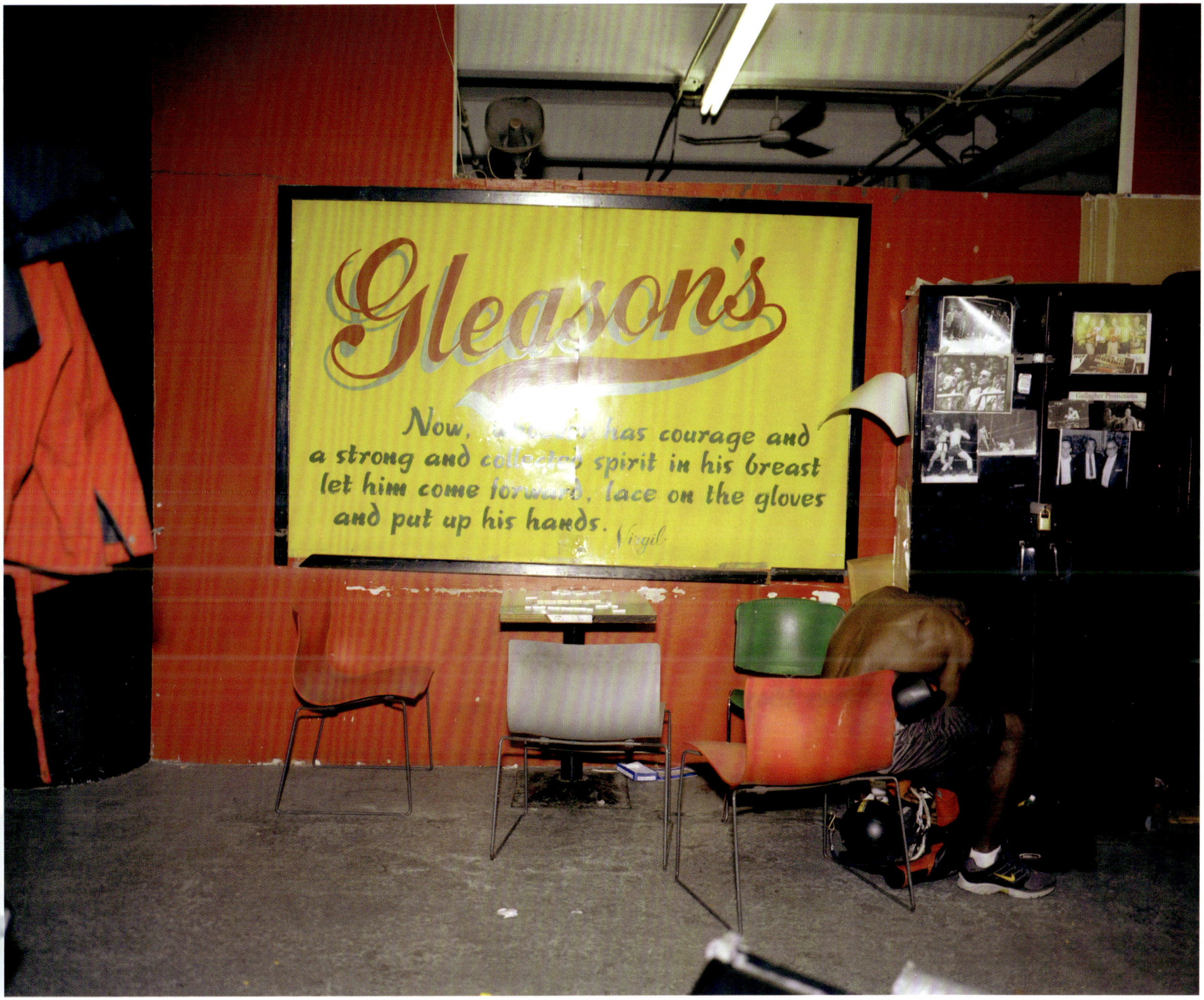
Gleason's
Now, has courage and
a strong and spirit in his breast
let him come forward, lace on the gloves
and put up his hands.
Virgil

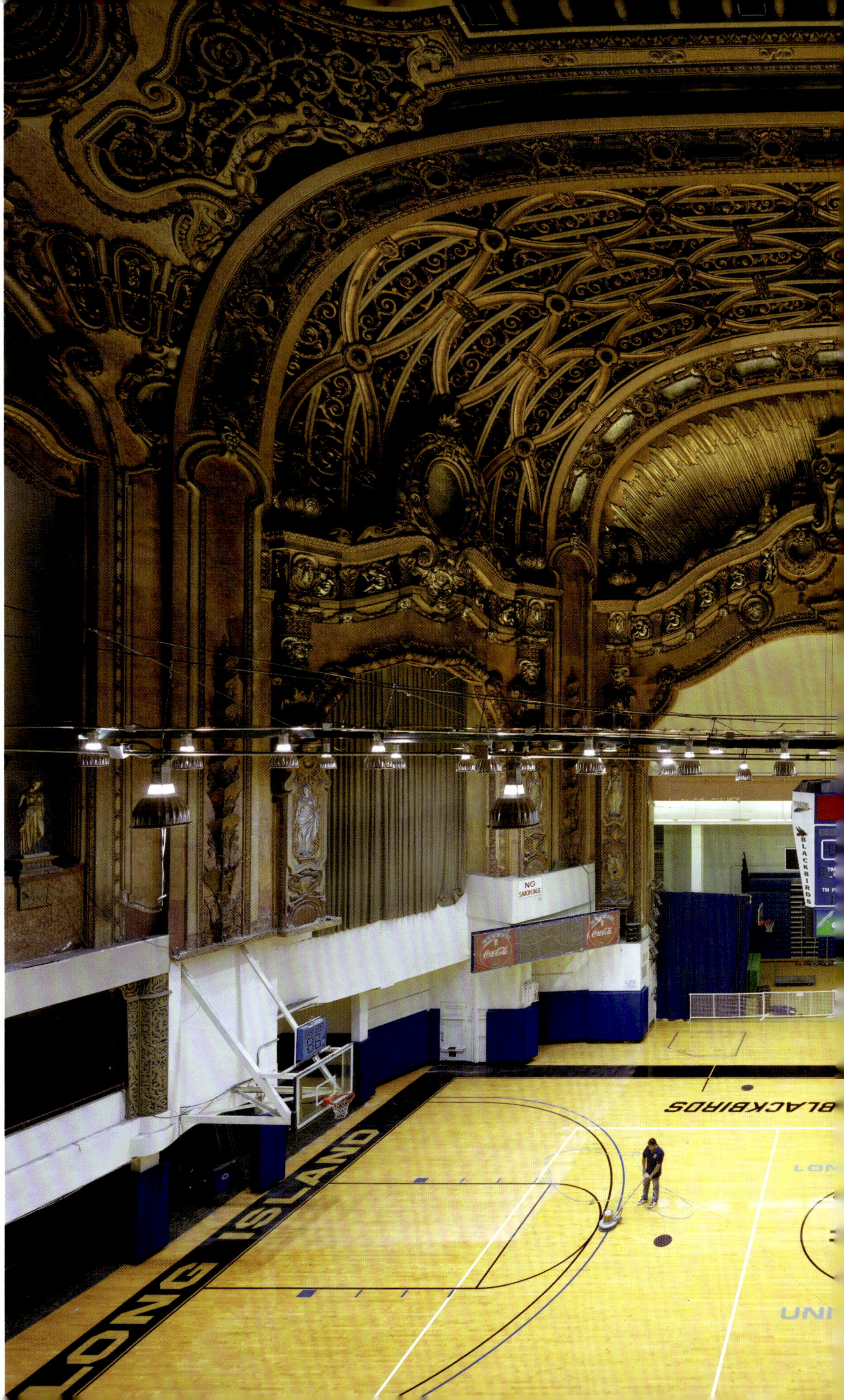
NO SMOKING
Coca-Cola
Coca-Cola
BLACKBIRDS
LONG ISLAND
BLACKBIRDS

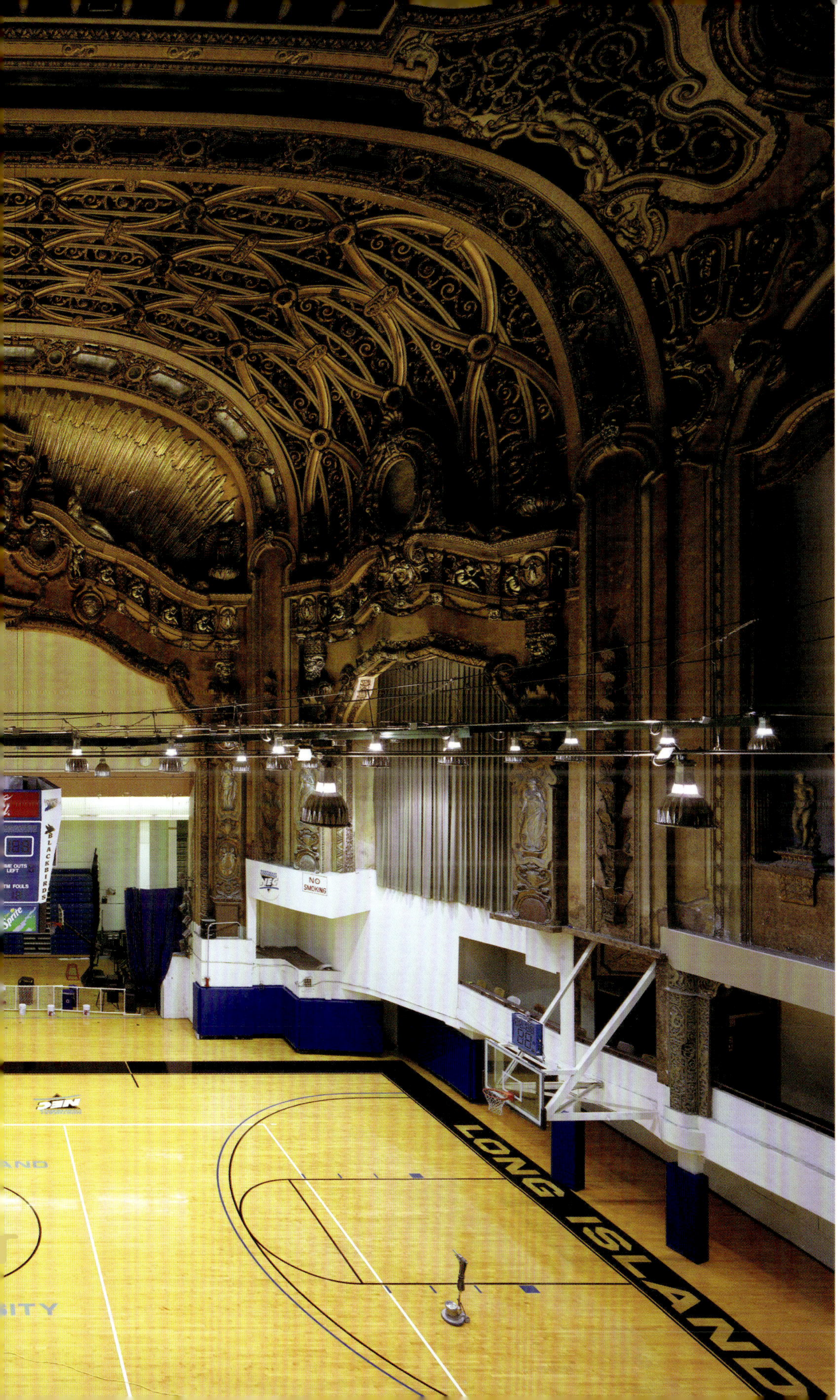
NO SMOKING
LONG ISLAND

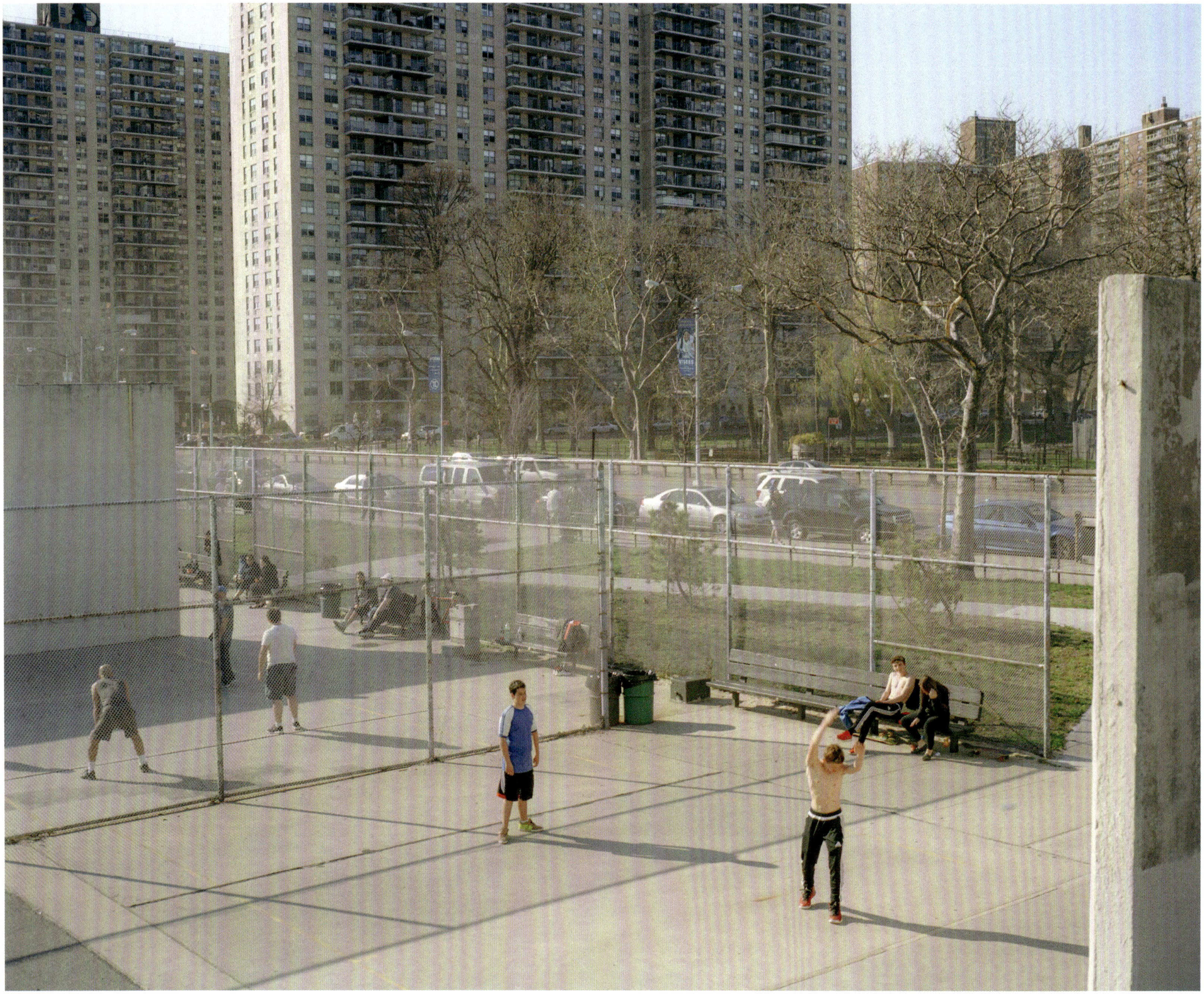

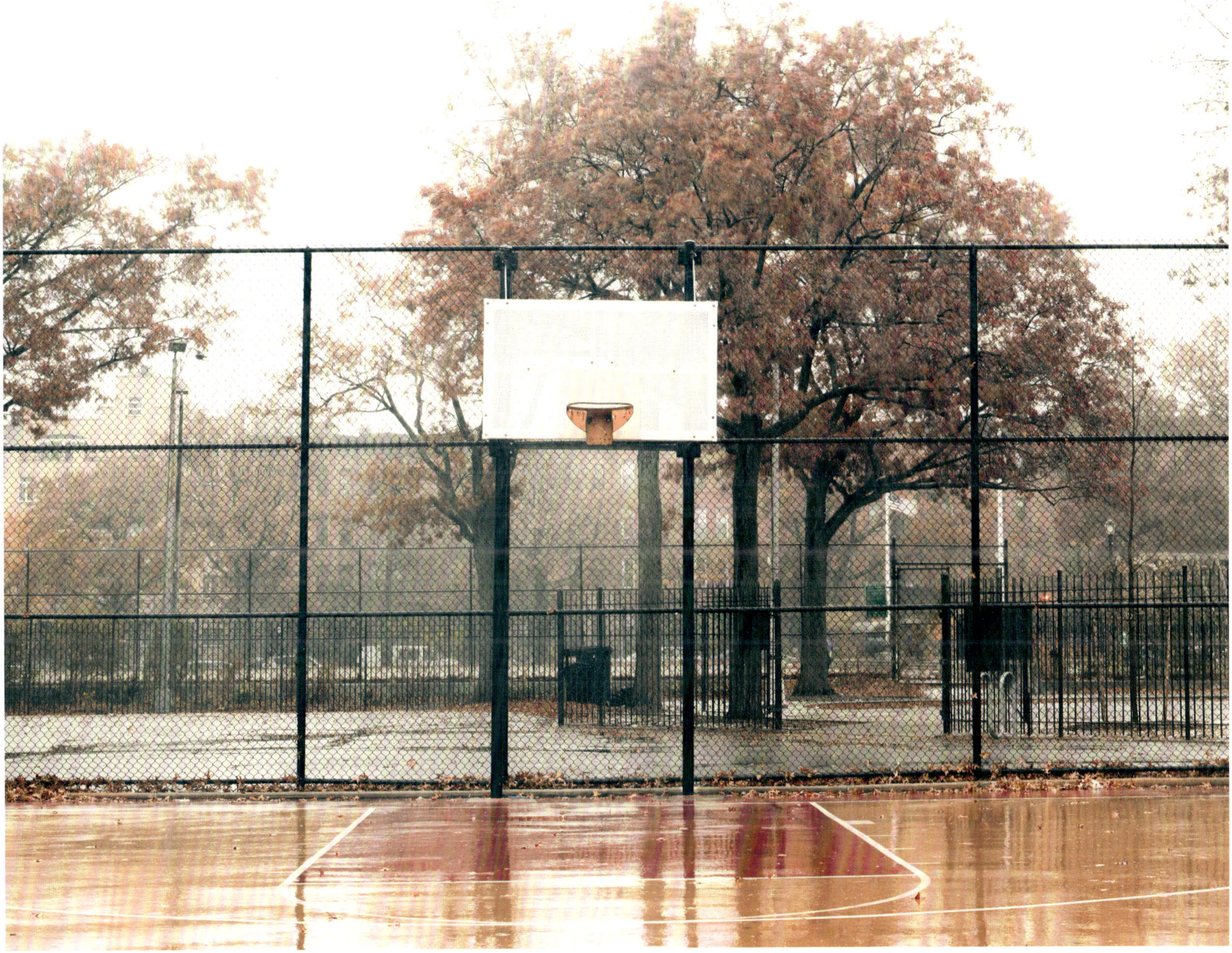

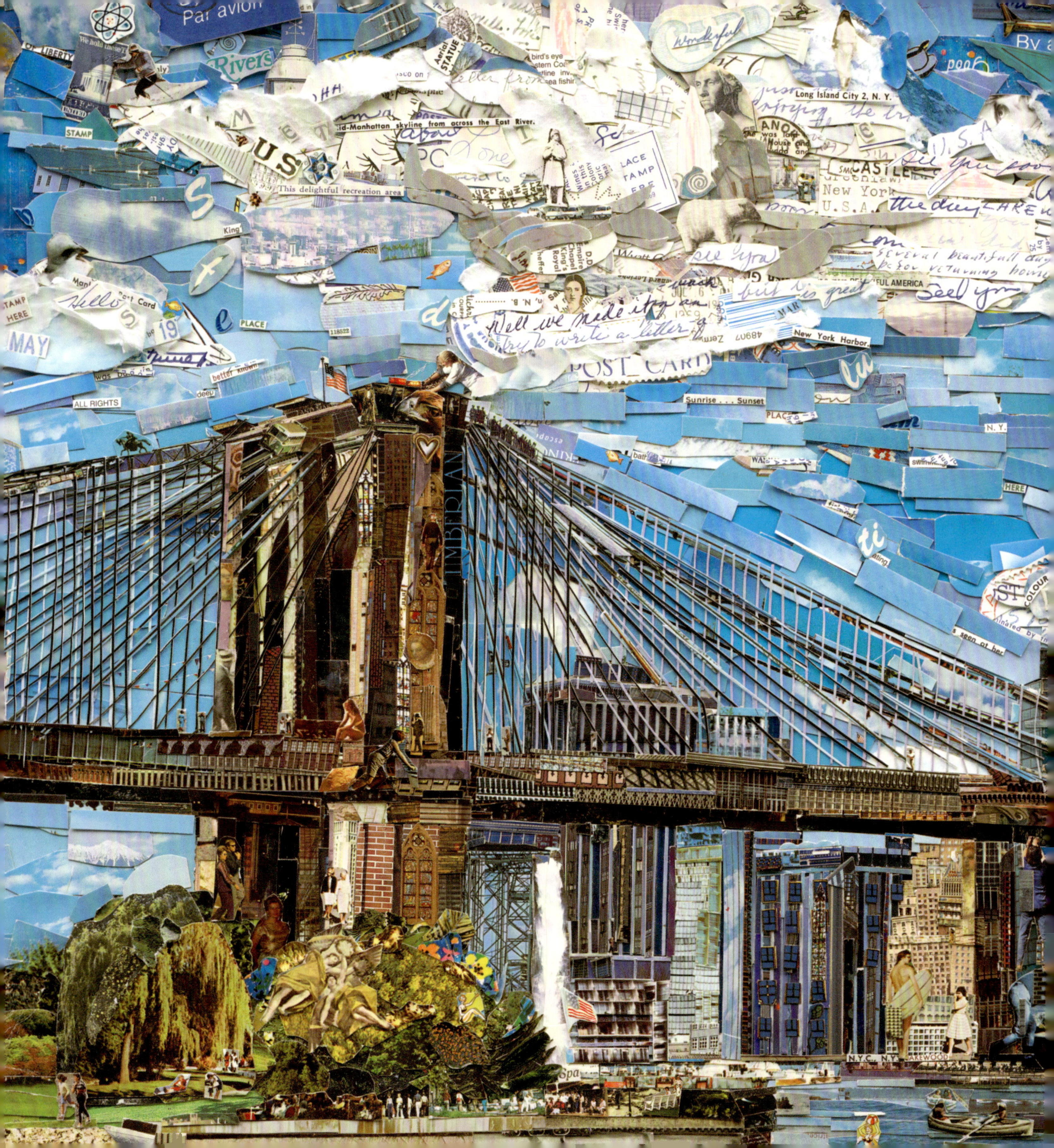

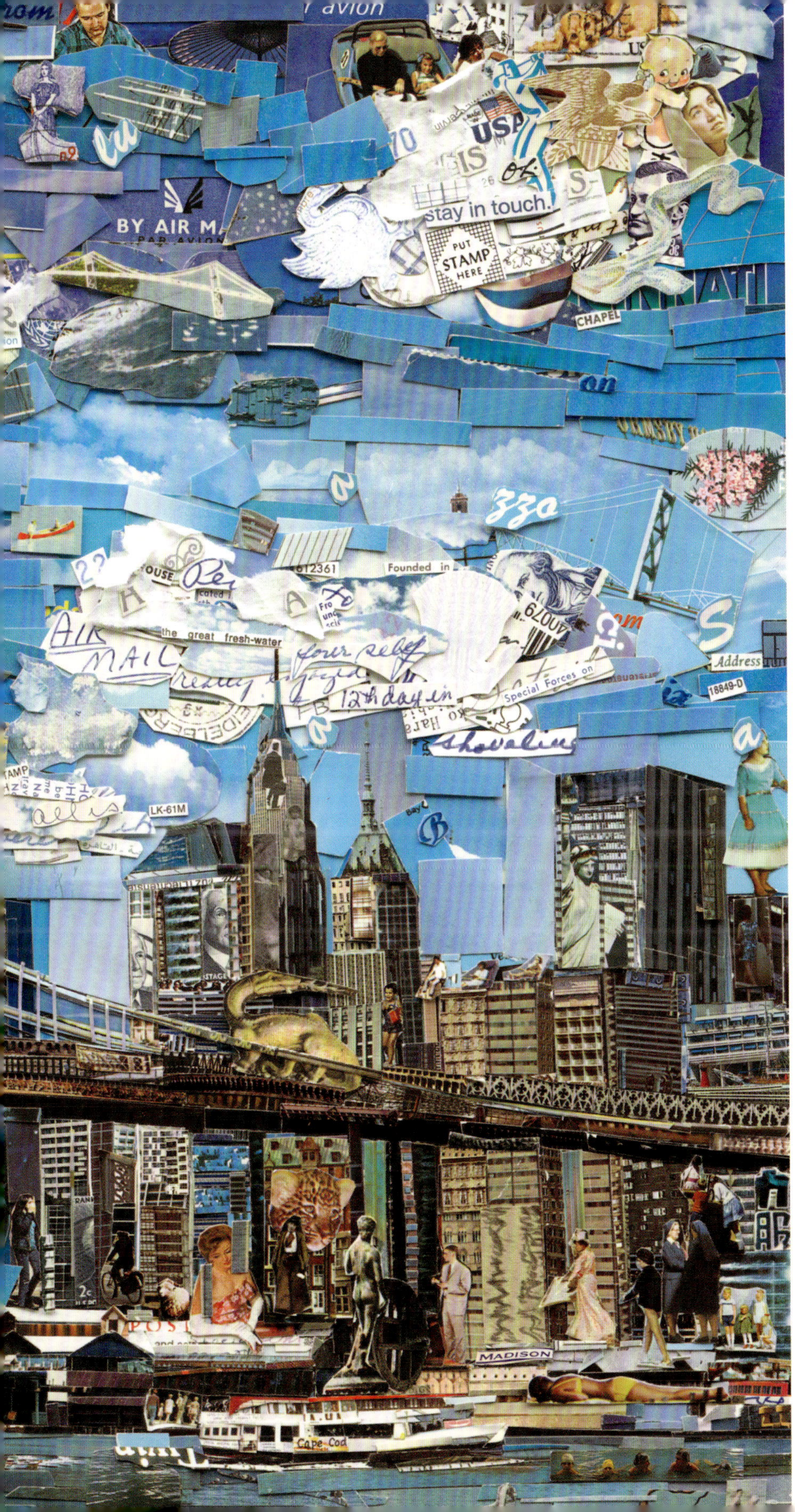
par avion
BY AIR MA
PAR AVION
USA
stay in touch.
PUT
STAMP
HERE
CHAPEL
612361
Founded in
the great fresh-water
AIR
MAIL
Address
18849-D
Special Forces on
12th day in
LK-61M
MADISON
Cape Cod

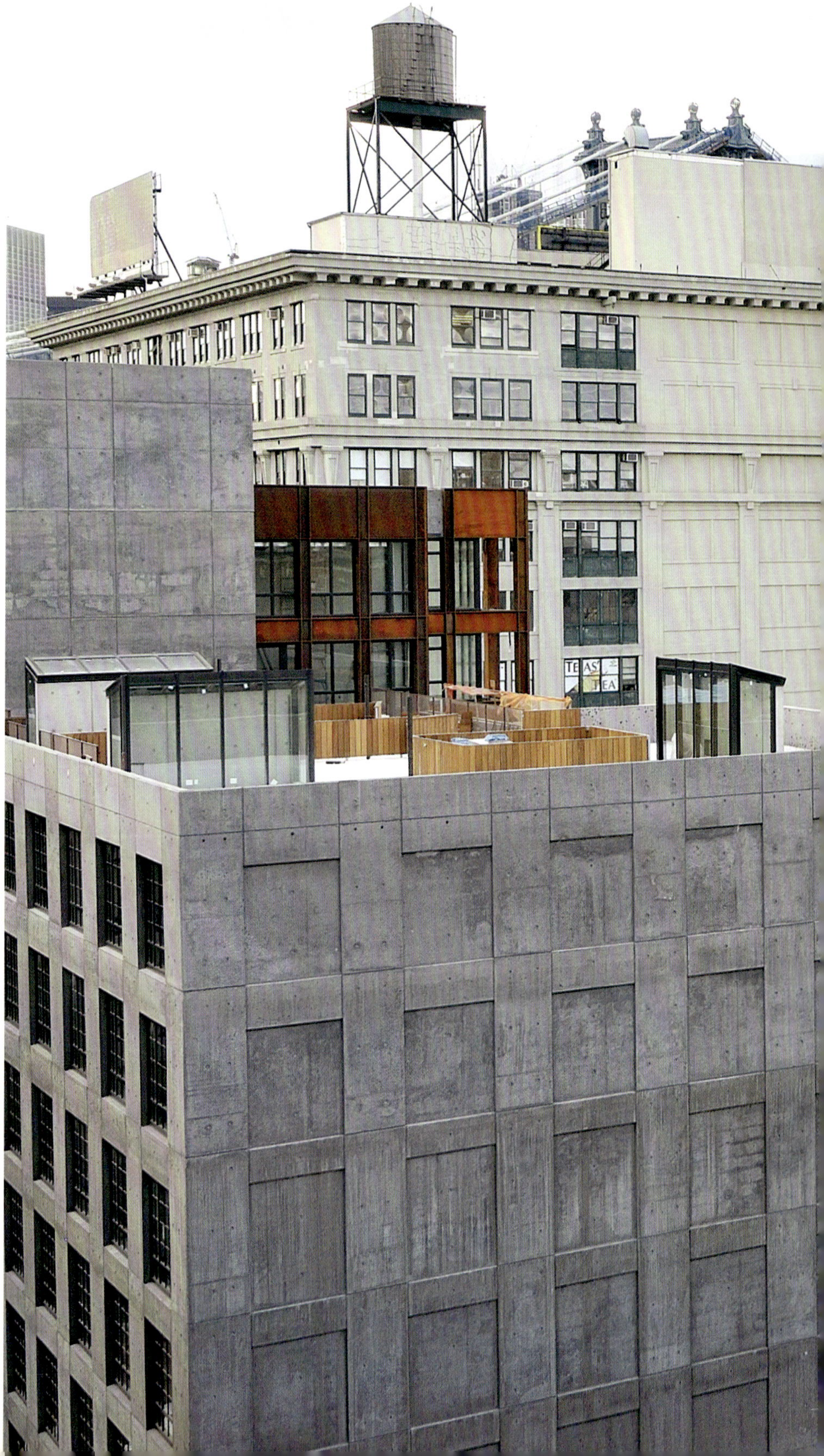

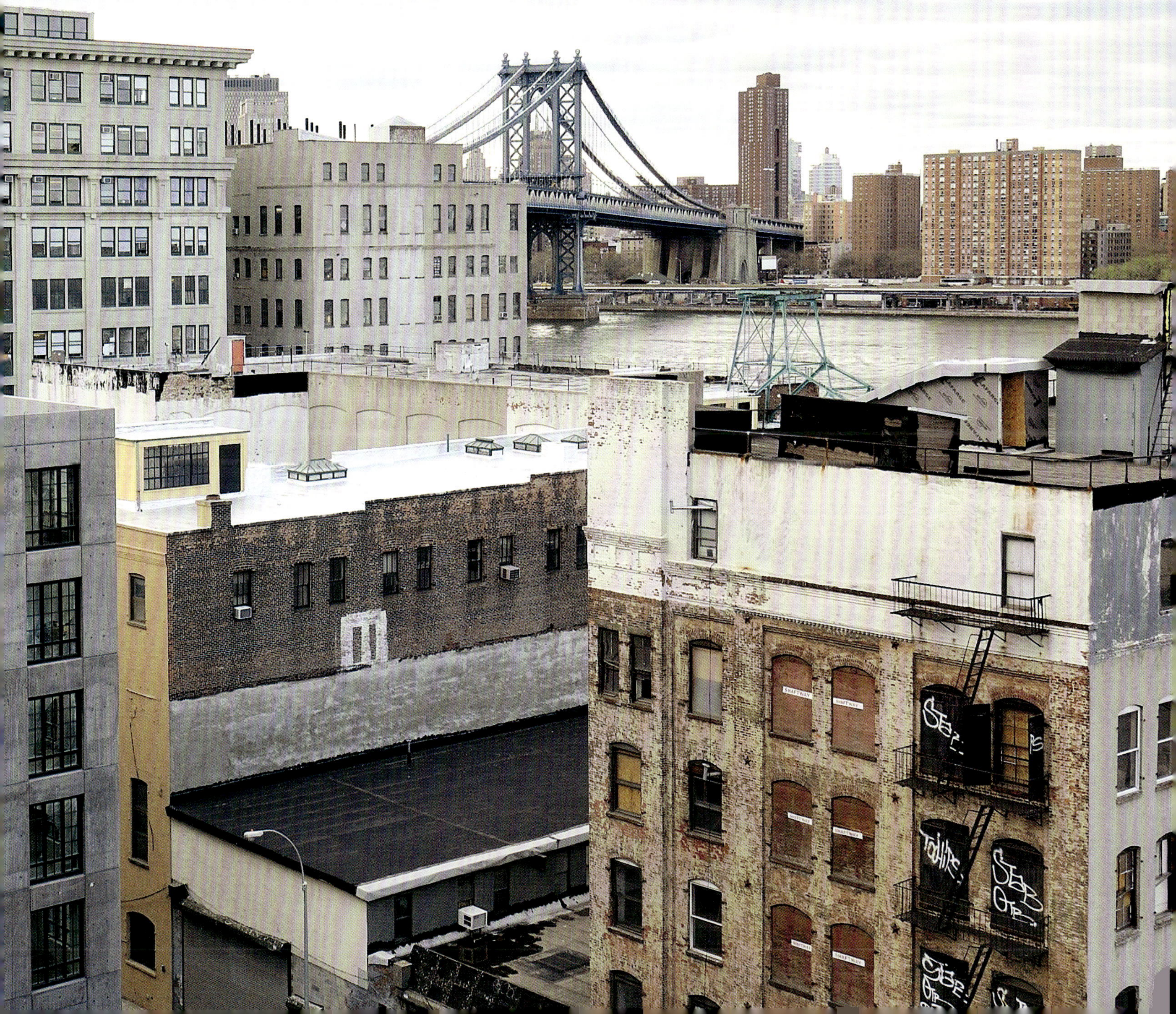

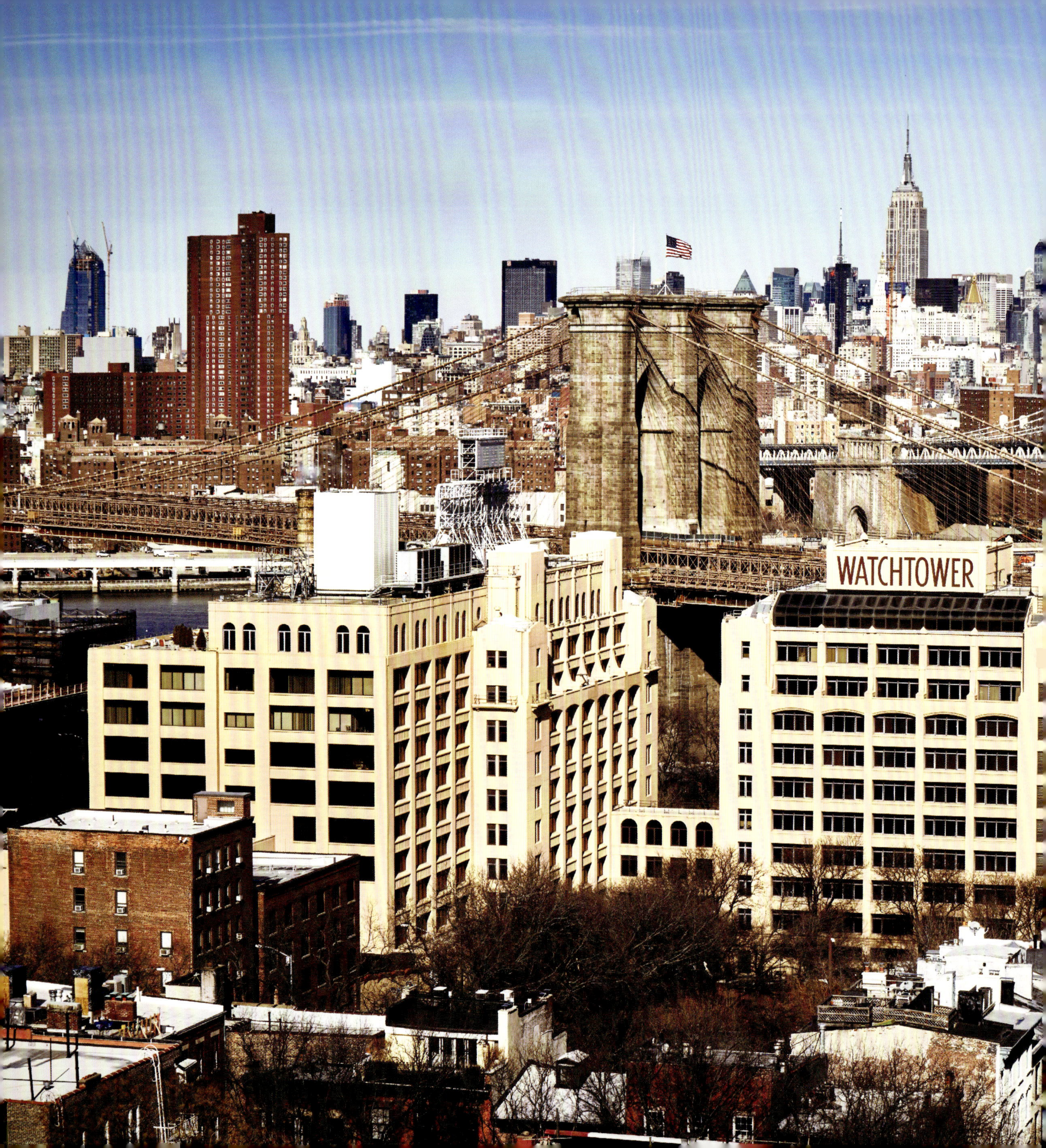
WATCHTOWER

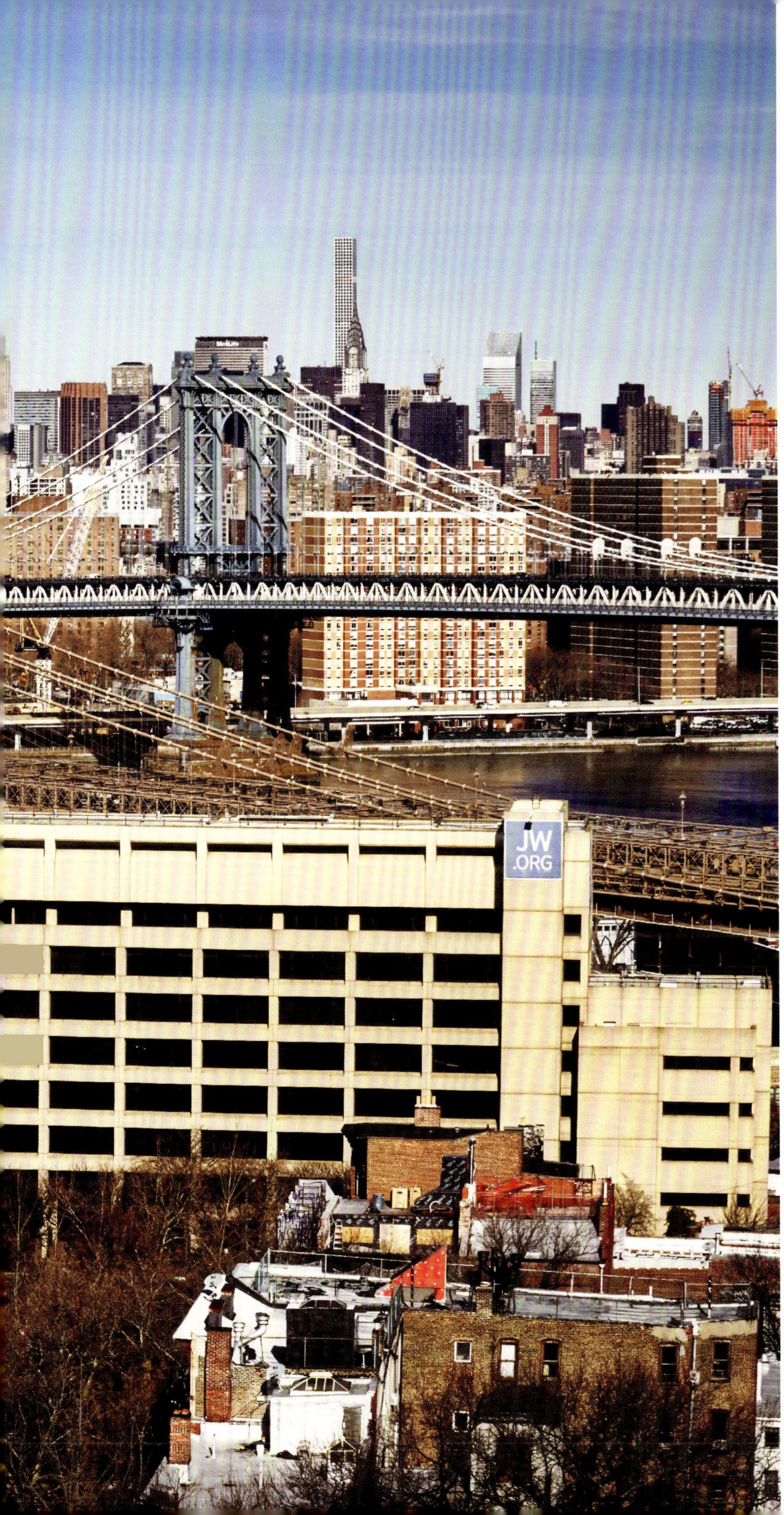
JW
.ORG

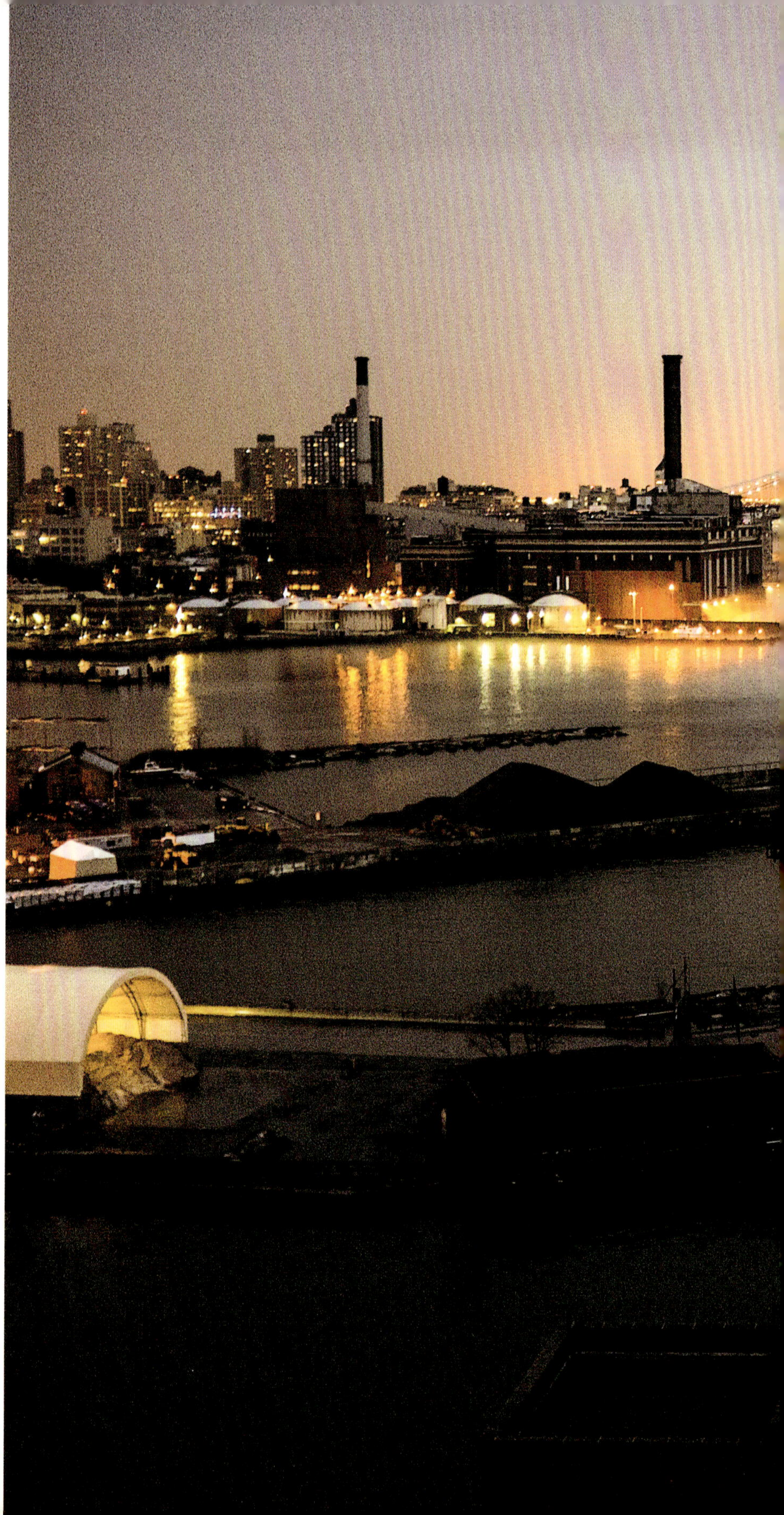

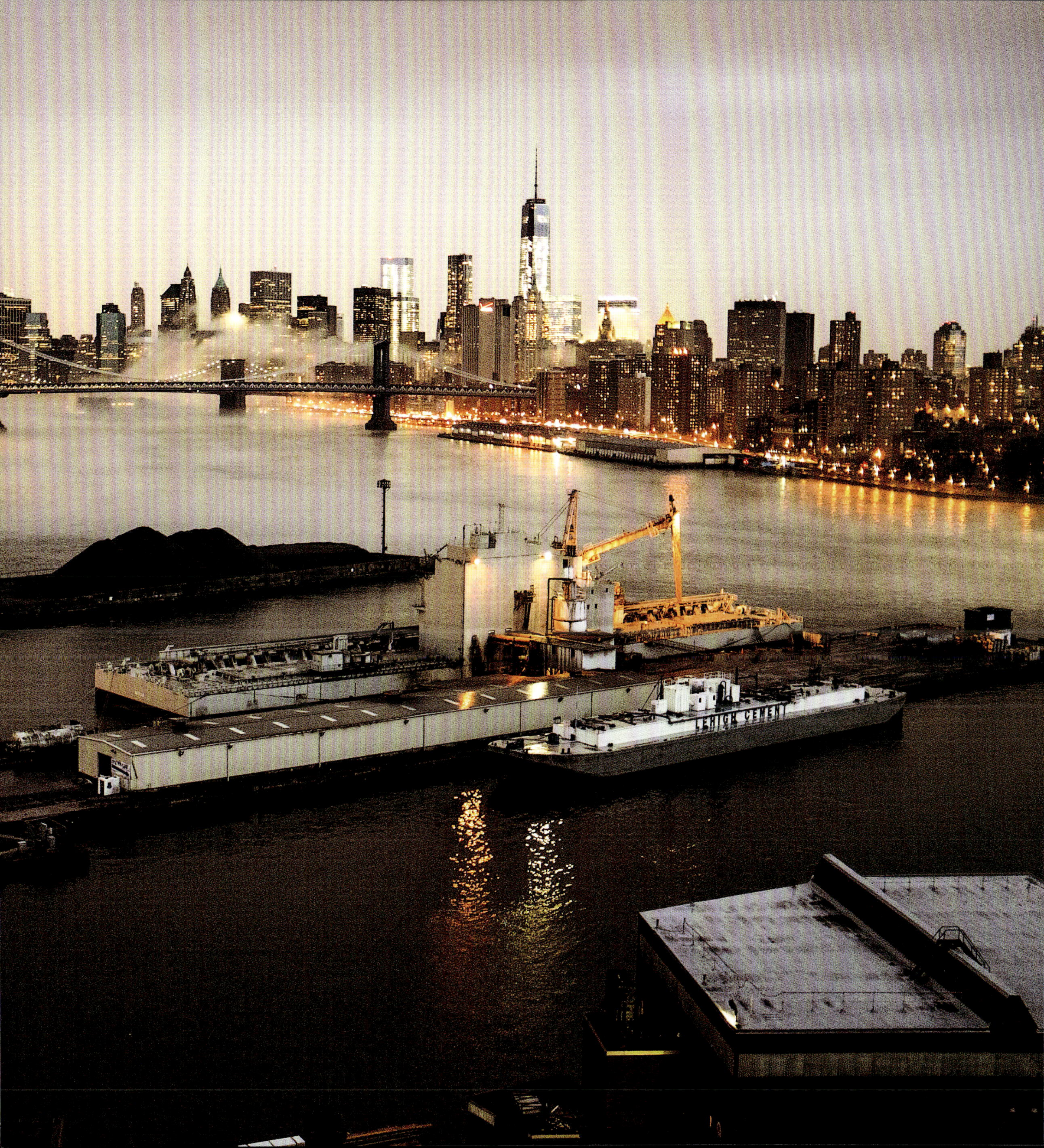
LEHIGH CEMENT

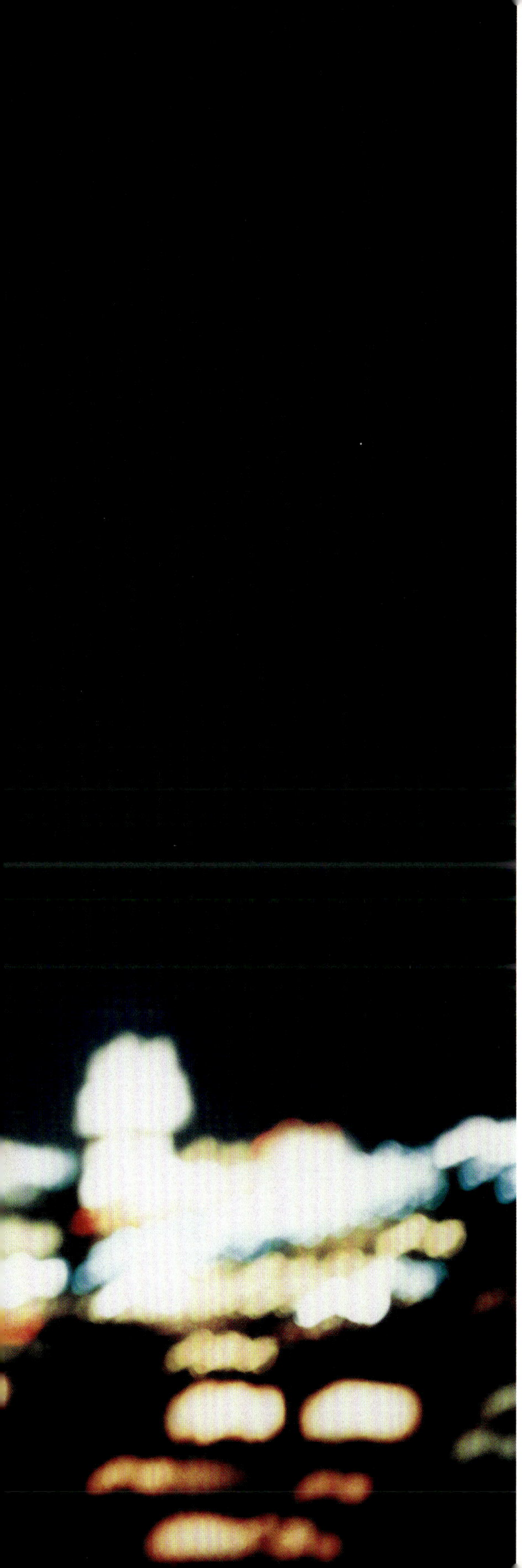

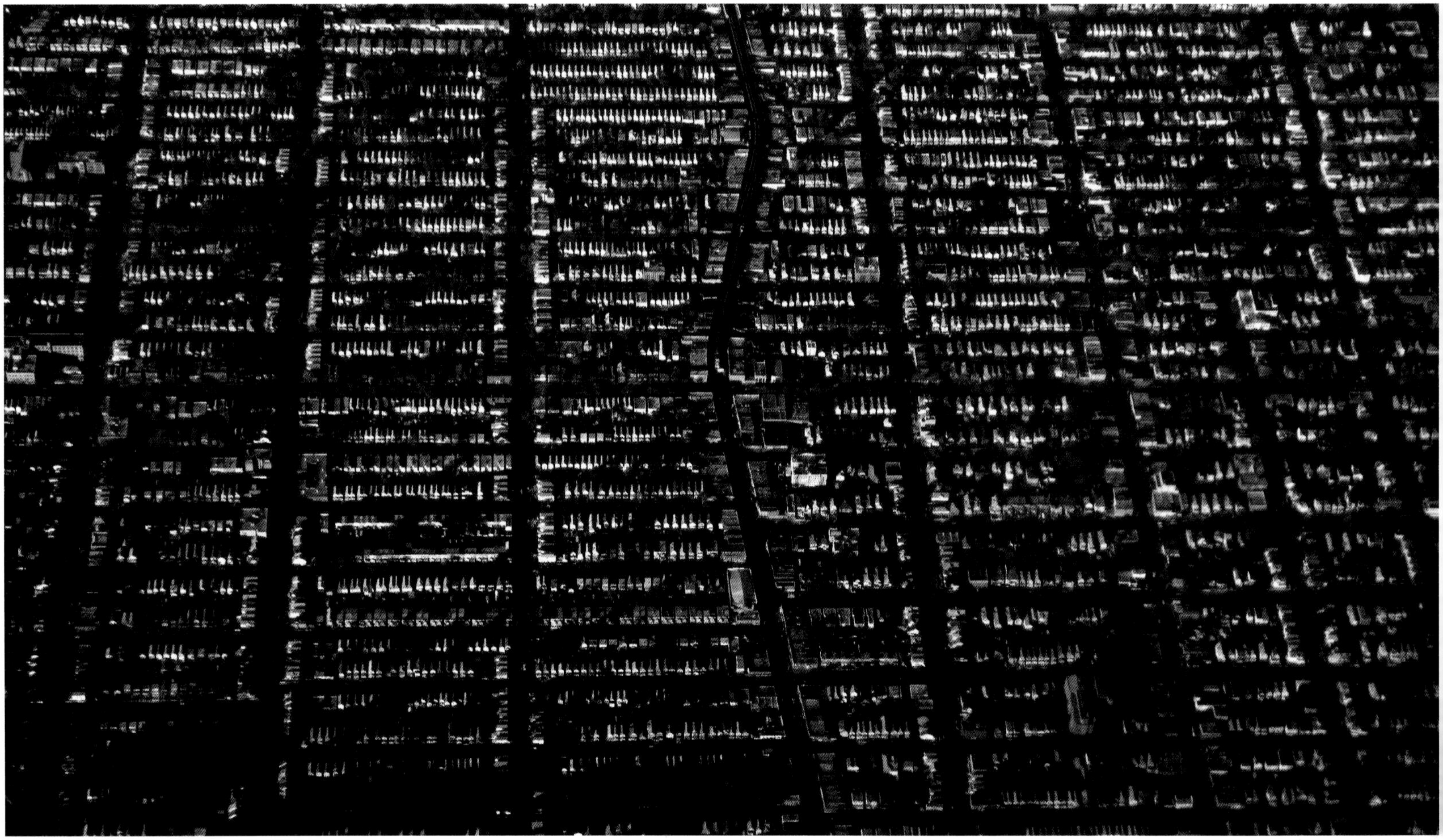

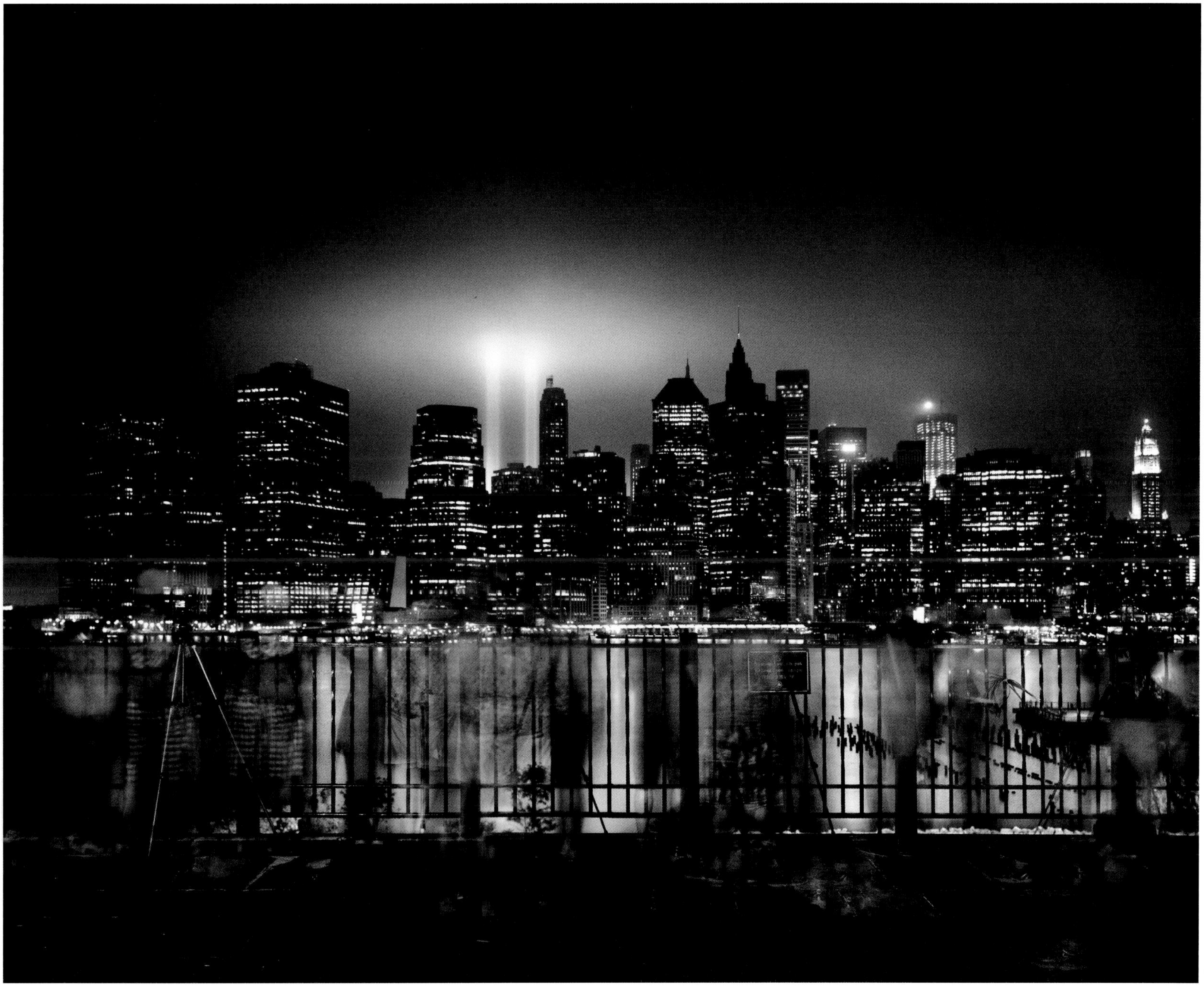

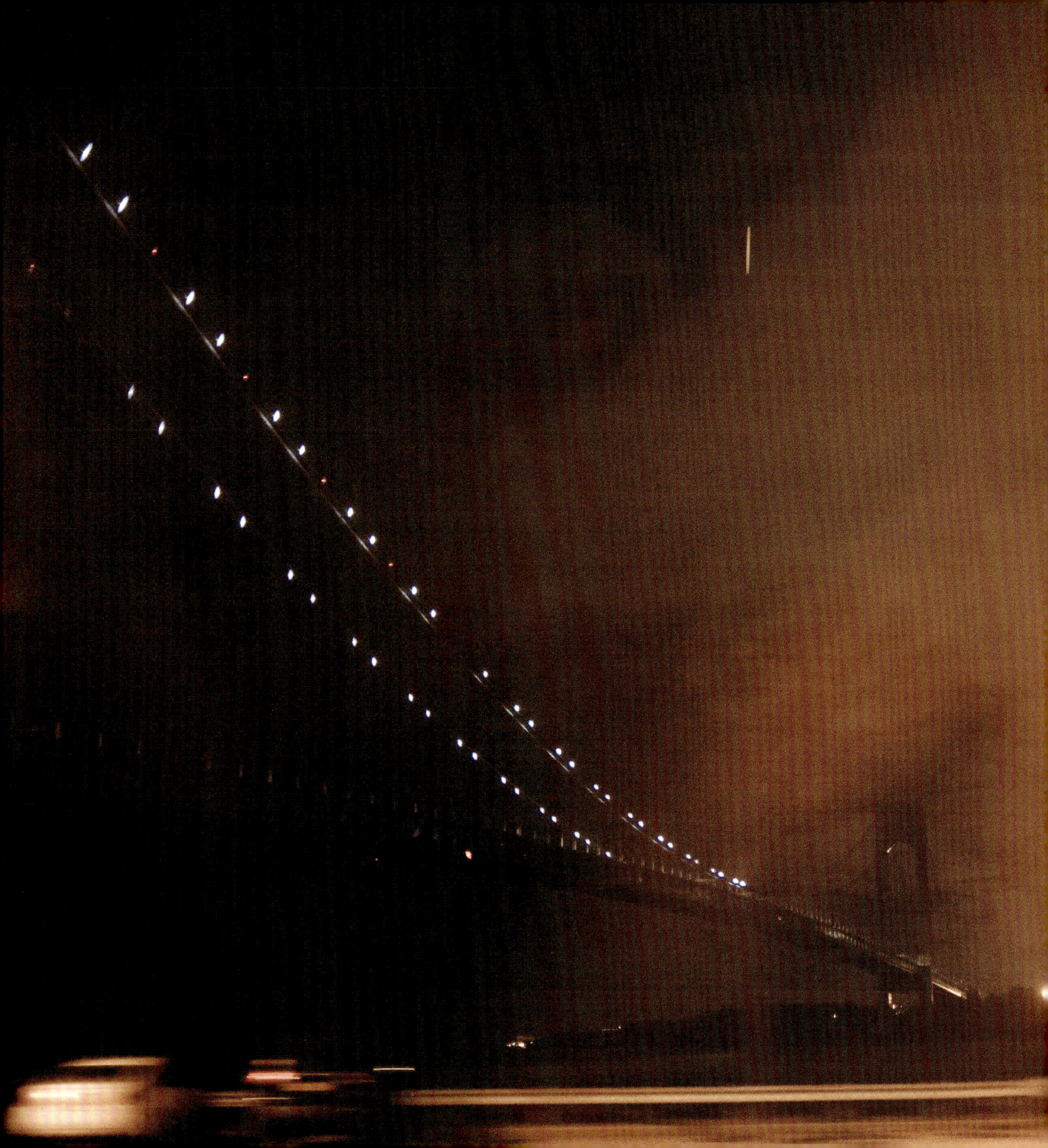

CAPTIONS

page 2
BOOGIE

pages 10–11
Antonio M. Rosario
Moonrise over Brooklyn, 2012

pages 12–13
Dan Dealy
Hello Brooklyn, 2009

pages 14–15
Guillaume Gaudet
Girls Chatting in Brooklyn Bridge Park, 2010

page 16
Barbara Mensch
Roebling's Folly (The New York Tower), 2008

page 17
Franck Bohbot
Light on Dumbo, Brooklyn, NY, 2016

pages 18–19
Julienne Schaer
Williamsburg, 2017

page 20
Julienne Schaer
Blizzard, 2016

page 21
Julienne Schaer
Sunny's Bar, 2014

pages 22–23
Franck Bohbot
The Brooklyn Love Building, Brooklyn NY, 2014

pages 24–25
Guillaume Gaudet
Bushwick Skateboarders, 2013

page 26
Jake Dobkin
Flushing Avenue, 2010

page 27
Anthony Lanzilote
Hurricane Sandy, 2012

pages 28–29
Michael Tessier
Untitled, 2015

pages 30–31
Michael Tessier
Untitled, 2015

pages 32–33
Anderson Zaca
Park Place and Saratoga Ave, Brooklyn, from the series *Block Party*, 2009

page 34
Andre D. Wagner
Bushwick, Brooklyn, 2015

page 35
Jason John Würm
Shoppers, 2014

pages 36–37
Anthony Lanzilote
Trash Bar, 2015

pages 38–39
Alexandra Batsford
Smith Street, 2004

pages 40–41
Douglas Ljungkvist
Untitled, October 2011

page 42
Amy Touchette / Clamp Art
Us No. 30, 2011

page 43
Amy Touchette / Clamp Art
Us No. 25, 2011

page 44
Robert J. Vizzini
Pink Locks, Coney Island, Brooklyn, NY, 2007

page 45
Anthony Lanzilote
Trash Bar, 2015

pages 46–47
Terrence Jennings
Walking on Stilts, 2017

pages 48–49
Andrew L. Moore
Betsy Head Pool, Brownsville, Brooklyn, 2005

pages 50–51
Dan Dealy
Franklin's Day Out, 2011

pages 52–53
James Petrozzello
Fete no. 37, 2014

pages 54–55
Mathieu Bitton
Afropunk, 2015

page 56
Andre D. Wagner
Tomorrows Leaders, Bed Stuy, Brooklyn, 2013

page 57
Evan Sklar
Ava Playing in Open Fire Hydrant at Block Party, Brooklyn, NY, 2014

pages 58–59
Camilo Fuentealba
Untitled, Purim, Brooklyn, NY, 2016

page 60
Pascal Perich
Brooklyn Summit, 2014

page 61
Douglas Ljungkvist
Untitled, September 2010

page 62
Douglas Ljungkvist
Untitled, June 2011

page 63
Douglas Ljungkvist
Untitled, November 2011

pages 64–65
Douglas Ljungkvist
Untitled, April 2010

page 66
David S. Allee
Room, 2013
Courtesy David S. Allee and Morgan Lehman Gallery

page 67
Hannah Frishberg
On Top of Brooklyn, March 2013

pages 68–69
David S. Allee
Panel Facade, Navy Yard, 2012
Courtesy David S. Allee and Morgan Lehman Gallery

page 71
Iannis Delatolas
Gowanus Fence, 2014

pages 72–73
Harlan Erskine
July on 2nd Avenue by My Studio in Sunset Park, Brooklyn, 2016

pages 74–75
Mathieu Bitton
Brooklyn Do or Die, 2015

page 76
Franck Bohbot
El Camino, Park Slope, Brooklyn, 2014

page 77
Douglas Ljungkvist
Untitled, May 2011

page 78
Josh Ethan Johnson
Magnification 02, 2017

page 79
Josh Ethan Johnson
Magnification 03, 2016

page 80
Daniel Arnold
Untitled, n.d.

page 81
Abelardo Morell
Camera Obscura: View of the Manhattan Bridge–April 30th / Afternoon, 2010
Courtesy Edwynn Houk Gallery

page 82
Mark Seliger
Brooklyn Bridge, 2007

page 83
Todd Boebel
Manhattan Bridge from Brooklyn, 2007

page 84
Rob Stephenson
Williamsburg Waterfront, 2016

page 85
Abelardo Morell
Tent-Camera Image on Ground: Rooftop View of the Brooklyn Bridge, 2010
Courtesy Edwynn Houk Gallery

pages 86–87
Matthew Schenning
Kosciuszko Bridge, 2017
Courtesy Matthew Schenning

pages 88–89
Dave Sanders
Bay Ridge, 2016

page 90
Jean Michel Berts
Fulton St., n.d.

page 91
Rob Stephenson
Downtown Brooklyn, 2015

page 92
Shai Kremer
Williamsburg Waterfront 2016 Merging Williamsburg Plaza of 1906, 2016

page 93
Matthew Pillsbury
Jane's Carousel, Brooklyn Bridge Park, 2011, 2011
Courtesy of Benrubi Gallery

pages 94–95
Nathan Kensinger
Brooklyn Army Terminal Tracks, 2007

pages 96–97
Guillaume Gaudet
Defonte's, 2011

page 98
Antonio M. Rosario
Red Hook, 2013

page 99
Antonio M. Rosario
Coney Island, 2014

page 100
Rob Stephenson
The Hottest Coffee Around, 2016

page 101
Rob Stephenson
Fulton Street, 2016

page 102
Charles Johnstone
New Church of Christ Holiness unto the Lord, 470 Ralph Ave. Brooklyn NY, 2010

page 103
Charles Johnstone
Grace Baptist Church, 1200 Bedford Street, Brooklyn NY, 2010

page 104
Camilo José Vergara
Iglesia Pentecostal La Sinagoga, 247 Snediker Ave., Brooklyn, 2004

page 105
Thomas Roma
From *On Three Pillars Brooklyn, NY*, 2002

page 106
Todd Boebel
Broadway & Lorimer, 2001

page 107
Todd Boebel
Brooklyn Tile, 2009

pages 108–109
Franck Bohbot
Gourmet Food, Brighton Beach, Brooklyn, NY, 2016

pages 110–111
Franck Bohbot
Stillwell Avenue, Brooklyn, NY, 2016

page 112
Alexey Titarenko
J Train Arriving at Marcy Ave Subway Station, 2009
Courtesy Nailya Alexander Gallery

page 113
Kate Glicksberg
East New York Farm, Brooklyn, NY, 2010

pages 114–115
Christopher Anderson / Magnum Photos
Poster Boy, Brooklyn, NY, 2008

pages 116–117
BOOGIE

pages 118–119
Philippe Dollo
Brooklyn Museum, 2005

page 120
Jean Michel Berts
Brooklyn Public Library, 2016

page 121
Jean Michel Berts
Brooklyn Botanic Garden, 2016

pages 122–123
Jean Michel Berts
Brooklyn Museum, 2016

pages 124–125
Harlan Erskine
Winter Night at Grand Army Plaza, 2014

page 126
Todd Boebel
Sears Roebuck & Co., Beverly Road, 2007

page 127
Jean Michel Berts
Kings Theater, n.d.

page 128
Jean Michel Berts
Water St., n.d.

page 129
Jean Michel Berts
Water St., n.d.

page 130
Franck Bohbot
Law Office & Dental Arts, Brighton Beach, Brooklyn, NY, 2016

page 131
Martin Hyers and William Mebane
BROOKLYN–155305, 2012

page 132
Franck Bohbot
American Fantasy #17, Dyker Heights, Brooklyn, NY, 2014

page 133
Franck Bohbot
American Fantasy #7, Dyker Heights, Brooklyn, NY, 2014

pages 134–135
Jake Dobkin
Brooklyn Heights, 2011

pages 136–137
Franck Bohbot
The Building, Brighton Beach, Brooklyn, NY, 2016

page 138
Thomas Roma
From *The Waters of Our Time, Brooklyn NY*, 2002

page 139
Andrew Smith
Greenpoint, 2013

pages 140–141
Matthew Schenning
Swimming Pool, 2014
Courtesy Matthew Schenning

page 142
Irina Rozovsky
Untitled from *In Plain Air*, 2011

page 143
Martin Cartegena
Woman Sunbathing, 2013

pages 144–145
Dave Sanders
Marlborough Road, April 04, 2010

pages 146–147
Dan Dealy
Clement's Birthday, 2011

pages 148–149
Douglas Ljungkvist
Untitled, August 2010

page 150
Douglas Ljungkvist
Untitled, May 2011

page 151
Douglas Ljungkvist
Untitled, August 2014

page 152
Ryan Zimmerman
Push, Hiroki Muraoka, 2013

page 153
Guillaume Gaudet
The Girl of Water Street, DUMBO, 2010

pages 154–155
Victor J. Blue
Bushwick Mural, 2013

pages 156–157
Lisa Kereszi
Ball Toss, Coney Island, 2001
Courtesy Lisa Kereszi / Yancey Richardson Gallery

page 158
Douglas Ljungkvist
Untitled, August 2007

page 159
Martin Parr / Magnum Photos
Nathan's Famous, Coney Island, NY, 1998

page 160
Franck Bohbot
Nathan's Famous, Coney Island, Brooklyn, NY, 2014

page 161
Robert J. Vizzini
Astroland Entrance, Coney Island, Brooklyn, NY, 2007

page 162
Dave Sanders
Night Swimming, August 30, 2013

page 163
Lisa Kereszi
Wonder Wheel at Night, Coney Island, 2003
Courtesy Lisa Kereszi / Yancy Richardson Gallery

pages 164–165
Franck Bohbot
Wonder Wheel, Coney Island, Brooklyn, NY, 2013

pages 166–167
David Leventi
Coney Island Cyclone, Brooklyn, NYC, 2005
Courtesy Rick Wester Fine Art, New York

page 168
Alexandra Batsford
Coney Island, 2005

page 169
Guillaume Gaudet
No Swimming, Coney Island, 2010

pages 170–171
Sara Wight
Red Hook, 2016

page 172
Christian Witkin
Dead-end at Van Brunt Street, Red Hook, Brooklyn, from the series *Notorious Spaces*, 2016

page 173
Ramin Talaie
Hurricane Irene in Red Hook August 28, 2011, 2011

page 174
Nathan Kensinger
Gowanus Canal Canoeist, 2009

page 175
Robert J. Vizzini
Third Street Bridge-1, Gowanus Canal, Gowanus Brooklyn, NY, 2011

page 176
John Cyr
View from Third Street Bridge, 2008

page 177
Jake Dobkin
Smith and 9th Street Station, 2010

page 178
Joel Sternfeld
Looking Towards Gowanus from Red Hook, Late September, Circa 2003, 2003

page 179
John Cyr
9th Street Bridge, 2008

page 180
John Cyr
Red Hook, 2013

page 181
Todd Boebel
Empire State, Red Hook, 2005

pages 182–183
Jake Dobkin
Bushwick, 2012

page 184
William Mebane
Untitled, 130501, 2013

page 185
Lisa Kereszi
Booth at Italian Festival, East Williamsburg, 2004
Courtesy Lisa Kereszi / Yancey Richardson Gallery

page 186
Meryl Meisler
Jesus Statue, Painted Planter and Red Brick Building, Bushwick, Brooklyn, 2012

page 187
Thomas Roma
From *The Waters of Our Time Brooklyn, NY*, 2002

page 188 (left)
Thomas Roma
From *The Waters of Our Time Brooklyn, NY*, 2000

page 188 (right)
Thomas Roma
From *The Waters of Our Time Brooklyn, NY*, 2004

page 189
Peter Holzhauer
Fence and Shadows 2002

page 190
Joel Meyerowitz
Fort Greene Park, 2006

page 191
Guillaume Gaudet
Brooklyn Bridge Park, 2011

pages 192–193
Jamel Shabazz
When Two Worlds Cross, 2013

page 194
Irina Rozovsky
Untitled, from the series *In Plain Air*, 2011

page 195
Joel Meyerowitz
Marine Park, 2006

page 196
Harlan Erskine
The Peristyle after the Blizzard, 2016

page 197
Irina Rozovsky
Untitled, from the series *In Plain Air*, 2014

pages 198–199
BOOGIE

page 200 (top left)
Thomas Roma
From *Plato's Dogs, Brooklyn, NY*, 2011

page 200 (top right)
Thomas Roma
From *Plato's Dogs, Brooklyn, NY*, 2012

page 200 (bottom left)
Thomas Roma
From *Plato's Dogs, Brooklyn, NY*, 2011

page 200 (bottom right)
Thomas Roma
From *Plato's Dogs, Brooklyn, NY*, 2013

page 201 (top left)
Thomas Roma
From *Plato's Dogs, Brooklyn, NY*, 2012

page 201 (top right)
Thomas Roma
From *Plato's Dogs, Brooklyn, NY*, 2011

page 201 (bottom left)
Thomas Roma
From *Plato's Dogs, Brooklyn, NY*, 2012

page 201 (bottom right)
Thomas Roma
From *Plato's Dogs, Brooklyn, NY*, 2013

page 202
Mitch Epstein
American Elm, Eastern Parkway, Brooklyn, 2012
Courtesy Yancey Richardson Gallery, New York / Sikkema Jenkins & Co., New York

page 203
Mitch Epstein
Weeping Beech, Brooklyn Botanic Garden, 2011
Courtesy Yancey Richardson Gallery, New York / Sikkema Jenkins & Co., New York

pages 204–205
Rob Stephenson
City Line, 2008

pages 206–207
Evan Sklar
Manhattan Seen from atop Green-Wood Cemetery, Brooklyn, NY, 2014

pages 208–209
Mathieu Bitton
The Queen of Bedford Stuyvesant, August 22, 2015, 2015

page 210
Todd Boebel
Kingston Avenue, 2009

page 211
Anderson Zaca
Norman Street and Wyckoff Ave, Brooklyn, from the series *Block Party*, 2009

page 212
Dan Dealy
Cinco de Drinko, 2012

page 213
Lisa Kereszi
Gleason's Gym, 2005
Courtesy Lisa Kereszi / Yancey Richardson Gallery

pages 214–215
Yves Marchand & Romain Meffre
Paramount Theater, Brooklyn, NY, 2008

page 216
Franck Bohbot
Handball Game, Brighton Beach, Brooklyn, NY, 2015

page 217
Franck Bohbot
PS 443, Park Slope, Brooklyn, NY, 2013

pages 218–219
Vik Muniz
Brooklyn Bridge, from the series *Postcards from Nowhere*, 2015
Art © Vik Muniz / Licensed by VAGA, New York, NY

pages 220–221
Douglas Ljungkvist
Untitled, March 2012

pages 222–223
Edward Caruso
The Watchtower Building, 2016

pages 224–225
Alexander Haessner
The Temptation, 2014

pages 226–227
Jack Pierson
Bridge, 1998
Courtesy Cheim & Read, New York

page 228
Pascal Perich
Miscalculation, 2008

page 229
Matthew Pillsbury
Tribute of Light, Sunday, September 11, 2011, 2011
Courtesy Benrubi Gallery

pages 230–231
Peter van Agtmael / Magnum Photos
The Verrazano Bridge, Brooklyn, NY, October 31, 2012, 2012

AUTHOR BIOGRAPHIES

Marla Hamburg Kennedy is a renowned art and photography curator and dealer. The founder of HK Photographs, HK Art Advisory, and Picture This Publications, she has been the publisher, editor, and author of over fifteen critically acclaimed photography books, including books on New York and Los Angeles, her two favorite cities. A graduate from Barnard College, she has lived in New York City since 1976, including a stint as a Dumbo pioneer in a loft on Jay Street on the East River from 1985 to 1989, and her current residence in an Upper West Side brownstone with her husband, dogs, and cats.

Since 2015, **Anne Pasternak** has served as the Shelby White and Leon Levy Director of the Brooklyn Museum. For more than thirty years, she has devoted her career to engaging broad audiences with the limitless power of art to move, motivate, and inspire. A staunch advocate for the civic and democratic roles our cultural and educational institutions can play, Anne is committed to projects that demonstrate the crucial links between art and social justice. During her time there, Anne has focused on strengthening the Museum as a global center for the visual arts that is courageous, pioneering, and inclusive. Through her leadership, Anne has expanded exhibitions, educational offerings and public programs. Previously, Anne served as the President and Artistic Director of Creative Time. She collaborated with hundreds of artists commissioning and presenting works as well as *Tribute in Light*, the twin beacons of light that illuminate the former World Trade Center site, on the anniversary of 9/11.

Phillip Lopate is the author of over fifteen fiction, nonfiction and poetry books, including *Being with Children*, *Bachelorhood*, *Against Joie de Vivre*, *Art of the Personal Essay*, *Waterfront*, *Portrait Inside My Head* and *To Show and To Tell*. He has also written extensively about photography, with critical appreciations of Rudy Burckhardt, Joel Meyerowitz, Barbara Mensch, Sally Gall, and Thomas Roma. He is a professor at Columbia University, and lives in Brooklyn with his wife, Cheryl, and daughter Lily.

ACKNOWLEDGMENTS

This book, over three years in the making, would not have been possible without the tireless efforts of the staff at HK Art Advisory and the many interns who assisted me on this project. I especially thank my co-editor, John Patrick Fitzgerald, whose genius eye and good humor have made creating this book a most memorable experience. To Phillip Lopate and Anne Pasternak, a special thank-you: your brilliant contributions could not have more succinctly put words to this visual homage to contemporary Brooklyn. To my dear Charles Miers, publisher of Rizzoli, and to the brilliant Jessica Fuller and Elizabeth Smith at Rizzoli, my heartfelt thanks. And finally, my thanks to Amy Wilkins and Robin Brunelle at Matsumoto Incorporated for their mastery in creating such a beautiful object.

Published by
Rizzoli International Publications, Inc.
300 Park Avenue South
New York, NY 10010
www.rizzoliusa.com

Front cover: Ryan Zimmerman. Detail of *Push, Hiroki Muraoka*, 2013
Front endpapers: Jack Pierson. Detail of *Bridge*, 1998. Courtesy Cheim & Read, New York
Back endpapers: Pascal Perich. Detail of *Miscalculation*, 2008
Back cover: Abelardo Morell. *Tent-Camera Image on Ground: Rooftop View of the Brooklyn Bridge*, 2010

2018 2019 2020 2021 2022 / 10 9 8 7 6 5 4 3 2 1
Printed in China

Creative direction by Takaaki Matsumoto/Matsumoto Incorporated, New York
Design by Robin Brunelle/Matsumoto Incorporated, New York
Design supervision by Amy Wilkins/Matsumoto Incorporated, New York

ISBN-13: 978-0-8478-6238-2
Library of Congress Catalog Control Number: 2017947376

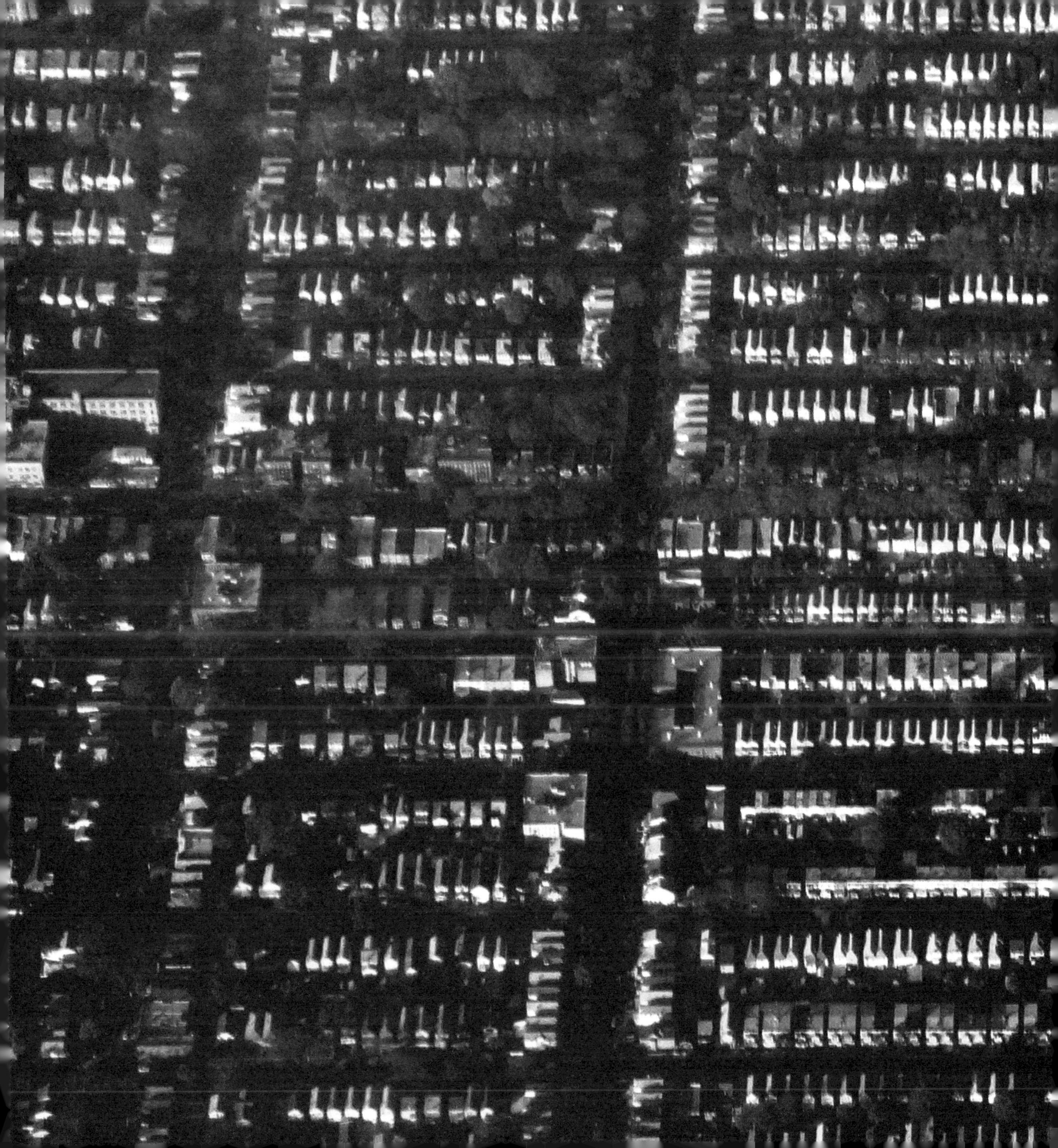

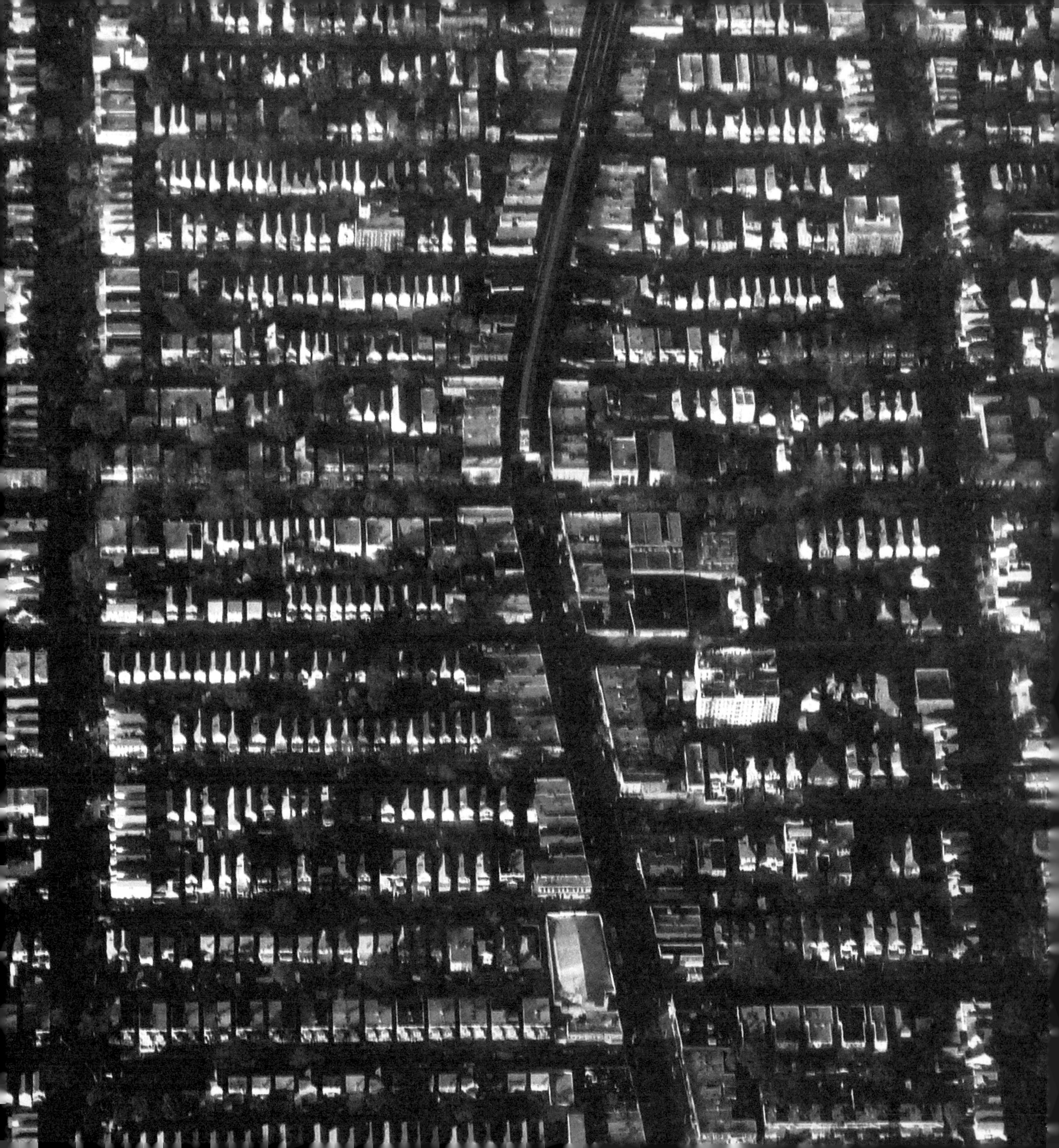